REFERENCE GUIDES IN LITERATURE
NUMBER 13
Ronald Gottesman, *Editor*
Joseph Katz, *Consulting Editor*

Ernest Hemingway:
A Reference Guide

Linda Welshimer Wagner

G. K. HALL & CO., 70 LINCOLN STREET, BOSTON, MASS.

Copyright © 1977 by Linda W. Wagner

Library of Congress Cataloging in Publication Data

Wagner, Linda Welshimer.
    Ernest Hemingway : a reference guide.

    (Reference guides in literature ; no. 13)
    Includes index.
    1. Hemingway, Ernest, 1899-1961--Bibliography.
Z8396.3.W33 [PS3515.E37]   016.813'5'2   76-21821
ISBN 0-8161-7976-X

This publication is printed on permanent/durable acid-free paper
MANUFACTURED IN THE UNITED STATES OF AMERICA

Contents

Introduction

From 1924, when Edmund Wilson and other critics responded favorably to Hemingway's in our time and Three Stories & Ten Poems, criticism of Hemingway's writing has never diminished. In fact, more than three times as much criticism was published in 1971 than in 1940, the year of the then politically-controversial novel, For Whom the Bell Tolls. Despite the present critical cliché that Hemingway's reputation is in decline,[1] few modern authors are mentioned so frequently in literary criticism the world over. Hemingway is more than a modern American writer; he is a touchstone, a reference point for literature in the twentieth century.

As this bibliography demonstrates, there has been no scarcity of explication, criticism, reminiscence, and casual reference; if anything, such items have increased in the last half dozen years. Notice, as example, major critical essays on Hemingway's work appearing in the 1974 numbers of such quarterlies as The American Scholar, College Literature, Contemporary Literature, Journal of American Studies, The Lost Generation Journal, Modern Fiction Studies, Studies in American Fiction, Studies in Short Fiction, and more than half of the Fitzgerald-Hemingway Annual. Notice too the expert use Walter J. Ong makes of Hemingway's style--as a least-common-denominator for every reader--in his 1975 PMLA essay. Simultaneous with this appeared a Detroit Free Press feature on "Hemingway's Michigan"; a piece titled "The Hunts of Papa Hemingway" in Argosy; a column in American Poetry Review by Clarence Major which opened "Dear Ernest" and closed with "Keep your nose clean, Yours truly, Sherwood"; and a survey by John Raeburn of Hemingway as public writer in Journal of Popular Culture.[2] From PMLA to APR and the Free Press: one can perhaps conclude that Hemingway-watching appeals to more than just an elite--or perhaps to many kinds of elites.

HEMINGWAY. No one ever bothers to describe who Hemingway was. Few people use his first name, at least not in conjunction with his last, because it is understood. There is only one Hemingway, and he has become everyone's property. As Raeburn suggests in his essay, Hemingway has become the "celebrity,"[3] the writer whose personality was in some ways more important than his writing, at least to his contemporaries; a man who won the Nobel Prize for Literature alongside a berth in Look magazine's "Photoquiz."

vii

More important, Hemingway has become a reference point. Whether the discussion is of modern philosophy or modern aesthetics, Hemingway must be accounted for. He is an early existentialist: Camus and Sartre knew him thirty years ago. And as for craft, well, Hemingway said it first in <u>Death in the Afternoon</u>: "the great artist goes beyond what has been done or known and makes something of his own."[4] Later, near the end of his life, he reminisced,

> From my very first novel . . . I never for a moment doubted that I was the pioneer of a new era.

No other writer doubted it either. In fiction workshops the world over, people are still "coping" with Papa--they change styles, not wanting to be any more reminiscent of Hemingway than Hemingway wanted to be of Anderson; they avoid dialogue, sometimes at great loss; they run from the deft scene that implies it all as they create their own fictional methods. They do not, however, these young writers, deny him. Scratch a writer, and you'll find a Hemingway aficionado every time.

Scratching critics, however, sometimes brings different results. One fairly common one is suspicion, because Hemingway's writing does remain popular, and some academics find popularity reprehensible. Yet ordinary readers continue to like poems and books that move them, accessible books, books about things they can understand and relate to, things that carry a vivid emotional weight. Perhaps it is this quality that readers respond to in Hemingway's writing, his clear statement of attitude, his consistent moral vision. As he lamented late in his writing life, "Too many modern novels teach no lesson and serve no purpose, except to chill the blood by mere revolting physical horror."

Hemingway's initial reputation, however, in the 1920's, was hardly that of moralist. It was rather that of precocious infant. "Strikingly original," Edmund Wilson barked. "Among the first men writing today," claimed Ernest Walsh; "he has a touch of genius," praised Gerald Gould. Paul Rosenfeld thought that <u>In Our Time</u> possessed "a new, tough, severe and satisfying beauty." "Brilliant," decided Conrad Aiken; "magnificent writing," claimed the <u>New York Times</u>. "Incorruptible," F. Scott Fitzgerald said of his prose style, and Louis Kronenberger added, "suggestive and illuminating." Allen Tate praised even the parody, <u>The Torrents of Spring</u>, as being "a small masterpiece of American fiction."[7]

It is almost anticlimactic to say that criticism of Hemingway's writing began near its zenith. In the 1920's, thanks partly to backing by Ezra Pound, Sherwood Anderson, Ford Madox Ford, Gertrude Stein, and F. Scott Fitzgerald, most literary critics were "for" Hemingway. Even a poet like Louise Bogan felt that she had "discovered him" and some fellow writers worked very hard to give him rave reviews. But besides the tide of personal friendship, criticism of the early writing is accurate: it centers on the innovation, the craft, and the effect of unquestionable reality which Hemingway achieved through that craft. There was very little negative reaction to even The Torrents of Spring, perhaps because The Sun Also Rises followed so closely on its heels, perhaps because other readers had also been disappointed in Sherwood Anderson's Dark Laughter.

Although there were the few "morally outraged" critics after the sensational banning of the Scribner's Magazine carrying an installment of A Farewell to Arms (in Boston), praise continued through that 1929 novel. Arnold Bennett called A Farewell to Arms "a superb performance"; Fanny Butcher opted for its being "technically and stylistically the most interesting novel of the year"; John Dos Passos praised its great management of literary technique. Critics generally, however, were more enthusiastic about the scope and themes of the novel than they were over Hemingway's expert craft; they had come to expect technical proficiency. Bernard De Voto claimed for the book "passion," "sublimity," and "the dignity of a tragic emotion." Most other critics agreed.[8]

The zenith, however, was short-lived. As early as 1931, attacks on what people viewed as Hemingway's "place" in modern letters had begun. Arthur Dewing was among the first to suggest that Hemingway's "vision" was so limited that he needed to create an intellectually perceptive narrator, someone like Conrad's Marlowe. Earlier that year, Isidor Schneider had criticized the so-called "writers of the Hemingway school" on grounds both stylistic and thematic.[9]

To compound the problem of maintaining his enviable position as innovative man of modern letters, Hemingway in 1932 published Death in the Afternoon. Remarkable labor of enthusiasm that the book was, it was no novel, and some reviewers were bewildered. Most of them did not fault the book for being a treatise on bullfighting so much as for the ultra-personal commentary it contained (H. L. Mencken termed these sections "gross and irritating cheapness"; to Curtis Patterson, they were "smut"; to Max Eastman, the whole book was an indication of Hemingway's psychic ill-health[10]).

The snowball of negativism was rolling. Abetted by the appearance of the unclassifiable Green Hills of Africa, Hemingway's reputation during the 1930's also suffered from the primacy of Marxist criticism. Until the Spanish Civil War, Hemingway's writing was far too little concerned with social and political injustices to suit these critics. In 1937, To Have and Have Not (although highly praised by the previously disappointed social critics) bewildered some readers further because it was an aesthetically unsatisfying book. Only For Whom the Bell Tolls, coming in 1940, saved Hemingway's reputation. Political interest aside, the novel today remains moving, memorable, and, as J. Donald Adams claimed, "one of the major novels in American literature."[11]

So Hemingway was again on top, only to be torpedoed—this time unequivocally—after Across the River and into the Trees. By 1950,

some personal vendettas were evident as a few critics took every op-
portunity to slur Hemingway the man as well as the writer. So vitu-
perative were some of the reviews of this novel, in fact, (set against
an equal number of enthusiastic comments) that several critics were
tempted to assess the reason for the evident vindictiveness. Evelyn
Waugh, for one, claimed that many professional reviewers were "anti-
Hemingway" because in his novels they found "decent feeling," respect
for women, pity for the weak, and love of honor.[12] Waugh's implica-
tion was that the reviewers were incapable of recognizing the merits
of Across the River and into the Trees because of their private
jealousies and public tastelessness. Not all such assessment was so
positive, and when, in 1952, The Old Man and the Sea appeared, it was
to a chorus of relief. Although detractors eventually appeared, the
immediate reaction to Hemingway's novella was positive. "Mr. Hemingway is once again 'the champ,'" British critic Arthur Calder-Marshall
reported; and Cyril Connolly echoed:

> I believe this is the best story Hemingway has ever
> written. Get it at once, read it, wait a few days, read
> it again, and you will find . . . that no page of this
> beautiful master-work could have been done better or dif-
> ferently.[13]

Praise in the United States was also consistently high, and renewed
honor peaked with the Nobel Prize for Literature in 1954.

Before the Nobel Prize, serious study of Hemingway's work had been
limited. In 1952, however, the now "classic" books by Carlos Baker
and Philip Young appeared--the former stressing Hemingway's skill as
craftsman; the latter using what, viewed retrospectively, was a mod-
erate psychological approach. These books changed the nature of the
critical response appreciably: serious, well-founded scholarly essays
began to appear, in quantity, and they have continued.

Until the late 1960's, however, some of this scholarly writing
existed only to devalue the Hemingway stock. Had The Old Man and the
Sea been followed by a major novel or two in the decade that remained
before Hemingway's suicide, criticism would probably have been less
severe. A tone of disappointment flavors much of the unfavorable comment. When both Falkner and Hemingway died within a year, critical
issues were complicated by the "play-off" stance some people adopted.
In the process of evaluating either writer--or both--many critics
were guilty of belittling one or the other. Thankfully, most serious
students of literature have now come to recognize the fact that America
has produced (at least) two great modern novelists.

In 1975, what Hemingway had called in 1924 "this terrible personal
stuff"[14] has given way, for the most part, to relatively objective
stylistic or linguistic studies, comparative treatments, or fresh
assessments of wide themes or techniques. Critics seem more willing
to follow the leads Hemingway himself gave us, about the need for con-
tinuous movement, the iceberg principle, or the "suggestive" quality

of his prose. There is also a healthy tendency to view the novels and stories as a unified whole. Especially important with a lyric writer like Hemingway, this wholistic approach lets the reader recognize thematic strains (as Scott Donaldson does in his essay "The Morality of Compensation"), or follow Daniel Fuchs' lead in his essay on Hemingway as literary critic[15] in paying more attention to the origins of Hemingway's aesthetic ideas. Considering that Wallace Stevens had called Hemingway "the poet of EXTRAORDINARY ACTUALITY" and Ezra Pound had said that "Hem never disappoints,"[16] perhaps such tardy interest in the bases of his writing principles will be well rewarded.

In the past twenty years, many excellent book-length studies in addition to those by Baker and Young have been published, both in this country and abroad. No modern American writer, except perhaps T. S. Eliot, has received such full and generally competent treatment. In 1967, Audre Hanneman's important bibliography of both primary and secondary materials appeared; in 1969 Carlos Baker's biography, Ernest Hemingway, A Life Story. Some idea of unpublished materials remaining can be gained from The Hemingway Manuscripts, An Inventory, compiled in 1969 by Philip Young and Charles W. Mann. Although Hemingway's letters are supposedly never to be published, Matthew J. Bruccoli and C. E. Frazer Clark, Jr., have included the many interesting excerpts previously used in auction catalogs in their 1973 Hemingway at Auction, 1930-1973.

Bibliographically, in addition to Hanneman and the projected supplement to the bibliography, see also the Modern Fiction Studies, Hemingway issue, Autumn, 1968; Frederick J. Hoffman's survey of criticism in 16 Modern American Authors, ed. Jackson Bryer; the Fitzgerald-Hemingway Annual since 1969; the Hemingway chapters in American Literary Scholarship (annually since 1963); the bibliographies of both PMLA and the Journal of Modern Literature; and David Pownall, Articles on Twentieth Century Literature: An Annotated Bibliography, 1954 to 1970. Also helpful is the extended checklist in Jackson J. Benson's The Short Stories of Ernest Hemingway: Critical Essays (1975).

Drawing from all of these sources, with thanks, I have attempted in this Reference Guide to present a comprehensive listing of criticism since 1924. Omitted have been items relating only to Hemingway's personal life; items written in a language other than English (unless published in readily available sources); or items so fragmentary that they seemed unimportant when compared with the great quantity of material that should be included in such a book. I have tried also to list many peripheral sources in which mention of Hemingway is not indicated by chapter or book title. Although this compilation is much indebted to the 1967 bibliography by Audre Hanneman, it differs from that book by including summary annotations rather than descriptive, and by arranging materials chronologically instead of alphabetically. It also includes materials published through 1974 and into 1975, presenting a half-century history of Hemingway criticism.

The Reference Guide lists materials in the year during which they first appeared as either "A. Books" (materials included under "A" are alphabetized essay collections following books by single authors) or "B. Shorter Writings" ("Shorter Writings" should be understood to include also parts of books not exclusively about Hemingway). Arrangement within each year is alphabetical, by author. All entries are annotated with a brief abstract of the content; an asterisk (*) indicates that since the material mentioned was not available for actual reading, the source of its listing is given instead of an annotation.

My thanks to Melody Zajdel and Tom and Carol Thompson for their various kinds of assistance. With thanks also to the Arts and Letters College of Michigan State University, and to the Radcliffe Institute.

1. The contention is made by Jay B. Hubbell in his fascinating Who Are the Major American Writers? (Durham, N. C.: Duke University Press, 1972), 284.

2. Walter J. Ong, S.J., "The Writer's Audience Is Always a Fiction," PMLA, XC, No. 1 (January 1975), 9-21; Dennis Moore, "Hemingway's Michigan, Michigan's Hemingway," Detroit (magazine), Detroit Free Press, November 24, 1974, 14-15, 17-18, 20-21; Steve Ferber, "The Hunts of Papa Hemingway," Argosy, CCLXXX, No. 5 (November 1974), 70-71; Clarence Major, "Open Letter," American Poetry Review, III, No. 5 (1974), 57; John Raeburn, "Ernest Hemingway: The Public Writer as Popular Culture," Journal of Popular Culture, VIII, No. 1 (Summer 1974), 91-98.

3. Despite some accurate designations, Raeburn persists in appearing to believe that Hemingway sought the role of "celebrity." R. F. Lucid, however, writing in "Three Public Performances: Fitzgerald, Hemingway, Mailer" (American Scholar, XLIII, Summer, 1974, 447-66) finds Hemingway the least public of the three. Unlike Fitzgerald and Mailer, Hemingway (Lucid believes) avoided the kind of personal publicizing Raeburn suggests.

4. Death in the Afternoon (New York: Charles Scribner's Sons, 1932), 100.

5. "A Man's Credo," Playboy, X, No. 1 (January 1963), 120.

6. Ibid., 124. Hemingway also wrote, "I have never deserved the enormous success and fame that have been bestowed upon me . . . . I have had many enthusiastic admirers who never read a single book of mine. But the public has always tended to exaggerate my importance--and underestimate my significance."

7. Edmund Wilson, "Mr. Hemingway's Dry-Points," The Dial, LXXVII, No. 4 (October, 1924), 340-41; E. W. [Ernest Walsh], "Review of In Our Time," This Quarter, I (Autumn-Winter, 1925-26), 319-21; Gerald Gould, "Review of In Our Time," Observer (November 7, 1926), 8; Paul Rosenfeld, "Review of In Our Time," New Republic,

XLV (November 25, 1925), 22–23; Conrad Aiken, "Review of The Sun Also Rises," New York Herald Tribune Books (October 31, 1926), 4; Anon., "Review of The Sun Also Rises," New York Times Book Review (October 31, 1926), 7; F. Scott Fitzgerald, "How to Waste Material: A Note on My Generation," Bookman, LXIII (May, 1926), 262–65; Louis Kronenberger, "Review of In Our Time," Saturday Review of Literature, II (February 13, 1926), 555; and Allen Tate, "Review of The Torrents of Spring," Nation, CXXIII (July 28, 1926), 89–90.

8. Arnold Bennett, "Review of A Farewell to Arms," Evening Standard, London (November 14, 1929); Fanny Butcher, "Review of A Farewell to Arms," Chicago Daily Tribune (September 28, 1929), 11; John Dos Passos, "Review of A Farewell to Arms," New Masses, V (December 1, 1929), 16; Bernard De Voto, "Review of A Farewell to Arms," Bookwise, I (November, 1929), 5–9.

9. Arthur Dewing, "The Mistake about Hemingway," North American Review, CCXXXII (1931), 364–71 and Isidor Schneider, "The Fetish of Simplicity," Nation, CXXXII (February 18, 1931), 184–86, answered by Josephine Herbst's "Counterblast," Nation, CXXXII (March 11, 1931), 275–76.

10. H. L. Mencken, "Review of Death in the Afternoon," American Mercury, XXVII (December, 1932), 506–07; Curtis Patterson, "Review of Death in the Afternoon," Town & Country, LXXXVII (October 15, 1932), 50; Max Eastman, "Bull in the Afternoon," New Republic, LXXV (June 7, 1933), 94–97.

11. J. Donald Adams, "Review of For Whom the Bell Tolls," New York Times Book Review (October 20, 1940), 1.

12. Evelyn Waugh, "The Case of Mr. Hemingway," Commonweal, LIII (November 3, 1950), 97–98. William Faulkner also went on record supporting Hemingway (and Waugh) in Time, LVI (November 13, 1950), 6.

13. Arthur Calder-Marshall, "Review of The Old Man and the Sea," Listener, XLVIII (September 18, 1952), 477; Cyril Connolly, "Review of The Old Man and the Sea," Sunday Times, London (September 7, 1952), 5.

14. Letter from Hemingway dated October 18, 1924, as quoted in Edmund Wilson, The Shores of Light (New York: Farrar, Straus and Young, Inc., 1952), pp. 122–23.

15. Scott Donaldson, "Hemingway's Morality of Compensation," American Literature, XLIII, No. 3 (November, 1971), 399–420 and Daniel Fuchs, "Ernest Hemingway, Literary Critic," American Literature, XXXVI (January, 1965), 431–51.

16. Wallace Stevens to Henry Church, July 2, 1942. In fact Stevens
    champions Hemingway more fully: "Most people don't think of Hem-
    ingway as a poet, but obviously he is a poet and I should say,
    offhand, the most significant of living poets . . . ." Stevens
    gives Faulkner as his second choice but continues, "I don't think
    nearly so well of him as a poet as I do of Hemingway." (Letters
    of Wallace Stevens, ed. Holly Stevens. New York: Alfred A. Knopf,
    1966, 411-412.) Alan Levy, "Ezra Pound's Voice of Silence," The
    New York Times Magazine (January 9, 1972), 14-15, 59-68.

Hemingway's Major Works

<u>Three Stories & Ten Poems</u>. Paris and Dijon: Contact Publishing
Company, 1923.

<u>in our time</u>. Paris: Three Mountains Press, 1924.

<u>In Our Time</u>. New York: Boni and Liveright, 1925.

<u>The Torrents of Spring</u>. New York: Scribner's, 1926.

<u>The Sun Also Rises</u>. New York: Scribner's, 1926.

<u>Men Without Women</u>. New York: Scribner's, 1927.

<u>A Farewell to Arms</u>. New York: Scribner's, 1929.

<u>Death in the Afternoon</u>. New York: Scribner's, 1932.

<u>Winner Take Nothing</u>. New York: Scribner's, 1933.

<u>Green Hills of Africa</u>. New York: Scribner's, 1935.

<u>To Have and Have Not</u>. New York: Scribner's, 1937.

<u>The Fifth Column and the First Forty-Nine Stories</u>. New York:
Scribner's, 1938.

<u>For Whom the Bell Tolls</u>. New York: Scribner's, 1940.

<u>Across the River and Into the Trees</u>. New York: Scribner's, 1950.

<u>The Old Man and the Sea</u>. New York: Scribner's, 1952.

<u>A Moveable Feast</u>. New York: Scribner's, 1964.

<u>Islands in the Stream</u>. New York: Scribner's, 1970.

Essay Collections
Abbreviated in Text Proper

Asselineau (1965.A3)
Asselineau, Roger, ed. The Literary Reputation of Hemingway in Europe. Paris: Minard, Lettres Modernes Series, 1965.

Baker anthology (1961.A5)
Baker, Carlos, ed. Hemingway and His Critics: An International Anthology. New York: Hill and Wang, 1961.

Baker critiques (1962.A5)
Baker, Carlos, ed. Ernest Hemingway: Critiques of Four Major Novels. New York: Scribner's, 1962. (A Scribner Research Anthology.)

Benson (1975.A3)
Benson, Jackson J. The Short Stories of Ernest Hemingway: Critical Essays. Durham, N. C.: Duke University Press, 1975.

Gellens (1970.A2)
Gellens, Jay, ed. Twentieth Century Interpretations of "A Farewell to Arms": A Collection of Critical Essays. Englewood Cliffs, N. J.: Prentice Hall, 1970.

Graham (1971.A7)
Graham, John, ed. The Merrill Studies in "A Farewell to Arms." Columbus, Ohio: Charles E. Merrill Publishing Co., 1971.

Grebstein (1971.A8)
Grebstein, Sheldon Norman, ed. The Merrill Studies in "For Whom the Bell Tolls." Columbus, Ohio: Charles E. Merrill Publishing Co., 1971.

Howell (1969.A9)
Howell, John M., ed. Hemingway's African Stories: The Stories, Their Sources, Their Critics. New York: Charles Scribner's Sons, 1969.

Jobes (1968.A9)
Jobes, Katharine T., ed. Twentieth Century Interpretations of "The Old Man and The Sea": A Collection of Critical Essays. Englewood Cliffs, N. J.: Prentice-Hall, 1968.

McCaffery   McCaffery, John K. M., ed. Ernest Hemingway: The Man
(1950.A1;   and His Work. Cleveland: World, 1950. Reissued 1969,
1969.A10)   New York: Cooper Square Publishers.

Sarason   Sarason, Bertram D., ed. Hemingway and The Sun Set.
(1972.A8)   Washington, D. C.: Microcard Editions, 1972.

Wagner   Wagner, Linda Welshimer, ed. Ernest Hemingway: Five
(1974.A3)   Decades of Criticism. East Lansing: Michigan State
                   University Press, 1974.

Waldhorn   Waldhorn, Arthur. Ernest Hemingway: A Collection of
(1973.A7)   Criticism. New York: McGraw-Hill Book Company, 1973.

Weeks   Weeks, Robert P., ed. Hemingway: A Collection of Criti-
(1962.A6)   cal Essays. Englewood Cliffs, N. J.: Prentice-Hall,
                   1962 (Twentieth Century Views Series).

White   White, William, ed. The Merrill Studies in "The Sun
(1969.A11)   Also Rises." Columbus, Ohio: Charles E. Merrill Pub-
                   lishers, 1969.

Journal Abbreviations

ABC	American Book Collector
APR	American Poetry Review
Conn. Review	Connecticut Review
EIC	Essays in Criticism
ELH	English Literary History
ES	English Studies
ICarbS	Materials from Southern Illinois University at Carbondale
JPC	Journal of Popular Culture
LC	Library Chronicle (U. of Pennsylvania)
MFS	Modern Fiction Studies
PBSA	Papers of the Bibliographical Society of America
PMASAL	Publication of the Michigan Academy of Science, Arts, and Letters
PMLA	Publications of the Modern Language Association
SR	Saturday Review
SRL	Saturday Review of Literature
TLS	Times Literary Supplement
WAL	Western American Language

Writings about Ernest Hemingway, 1923-1975

1923 A BOOKS - NONE

1923 B SHORTER WRITINGS

1   STEIN, GERTRUDE. "Hemingway: A Portrait," Ex Libris, 1
     (Dec.), 192.
          Poem.

2   _____. "Three Stories and Ten Poems Reviewed," The Paris
     Tribune (27 Nov.).
          Likes Hemingway's work because it is "intelligent"
     and "very pleasantly said."
     Reprinted in The Left Bank Revisited: Selections from the
     Paris Tribune, 1917-1934, edited by Hugh Ford (University
     Park: The Pennsylvania State University Press, 1972),
     p. 257 (See 1972.B28).

1924 A BOOKS - NONE

1924 B SHORTER WRITINGS

1   ANON. Review of Three Stories and Ten Poems, Kansas City Star
     (20 Dec.), p. 6.
          Admiration for the three stories ("the real stuff") be-
     cause they portray reality as it does exist, both in
     Europe and in the Middle West.

2   FORD, FORD MADOX. "A Few Friends," The Paris Tribune
     (24 Feb.).
          Describes In Our Time as "distinguished by a singular,
     an almost unsurpassed, care of handling." Sees Heming-
     way's work following "in the hardest and tightest tra-
     dition of the French."
     Reprinted in The Left Bank Revisited, pp. 258-59 (See
     1972.B28).

1924

3   JOLAS, EUGENE. "Through Paris Bookland," The Paris Tribune
        (1 June).
        Describes meeting Hemingway, watching him box, and ad-
        miring his "Three Stories" which have "a dynamic direct-
        ness and go straight to life."
        Reprinted in The Left Bank Revisited, p. 92 (See 1972.B28).

4   _____. "Open Letter to Ernest Hemingway," The Paris Tribune
        (16 Nov.).
        Praises Hemingway effusively, stating that he was
        "destined to create a new literature on the American con-
        tinent." Prefers his short stories to his poems.
        Reprinted in The Left Bank Revisited, pp. 99-100 (See
        1972.B28).

5   "K. J." Review of Three Stories and Ten Poems, Transatlantic
        Review, 1 (April), 246.
        Finds Hemingway's strength in a realism that convinces
        but does not merely photograph. Is impressed by Heming-
        way's "sensitive feeling for the emotional possibilities
        of a situation."

6   RASCOE, BURTON. A Bookman's Day Book column, New York Herald
        Tribune (15 June), Book section, p. 20.
        Discusses Hemingway with Edmund Wilson, and quotes from
        in our time.

7   "M. R." [MARJORIE REID]. Review of in our time, Transatlantic
        Review, 1 (April), 247-48.
        Admires the intensity of the in our time sketches; finds
        in them the significant moments of universal experience.

8   WILSON, EDMUND. "Mr. Hemingway's Dry-Points," The Dial, 82,
        No. 4 (Oct.), 340-41.
        Discusses in our time and Three Stories and Ten Poems
        as innovative, sharp in line as a dry-point etching.
        Attributes Hemingway's success to Gertrude Stein's example
        in Three Lives.
        Reprinted in Ernest Hemingway: Five Decades of Criticism,
        edited by Linda W. Wagner (East Lansing: Michigan State
        University Press, 1974), pp. 222-23 (See 1974.B3).

1925 A   BOOKS - NONE

2

1925 B SHORTER WRITINGS

1   ANON. Review of In Our Time, New York Times Book Review
        (18 Oct.), p. 8.
            Impressed with the condensation and intensity of Heming-
        way's style. "He makes each word count three or four
        ways."

2   ASHLEY, SCHUYLER. Review of In Our Time, Kansas City Star
        (12 Dec.), p. 6.
            Emphasis on "concrete visualization" and "lean, spare
        sentences" as methods of making scenes have genuine impact.
        Suggests Hemingway's subjects have not yet been worthy of
        his skill.
            Reprinted in Essay Reviews (Kansas City: Lowell Press,
        1929), p. 67 (See 1929.B7).

3   BRICKELL, HERSCHEL. Review of In Our Time, New York Evening
        Post Literary Review (17 Oct.), p. 3.
            Traces Hemingway's skill and subjects to Sherwood Ander-
        son; is most impressed with his effort to understand the
        down-and-out people with whom his writing is concerned.

4   HICKOK, GUY. "Hemingway First Lives Wild Stories Then He
        Writes Them," Brooklyn Daily Eagle (17 May), p. 12.
        Photos.
            Recounts some war experiences of the author, as well as
        some details of the Hemingways' Michigan honeymoon (Sept.
        of 1921).

5   JOLAS, EUGENE. "The Middle West and Mr. Ford Madox Ford,
        etc.," The Paris Tribune (8 March).
            Quotes Ford as saying "Mr. Hemingway writes like an
        Angel; like an Archangel; but his talk--his manner--is
        that of a bayonet instructor."
            Reprinted in The Left Bank Revisited, 241-42 (See
        1972.B28).

6   RASCOE, BURTON. "Contemporary Reminiscences," Arts & Decora-
        tion, 24 (Nov.), 57. Photo.
            Relates Hemingway to his peers.

7   ROSENFELD, PAUL. "Tough Earth," New Republic, 45 (25 Nov.),
        22-23.
            Compares Hemingway's stories to cubist painting in their
        "realization of a picture of the elements of life caught
        in barest, intensest opposition." Admires most "the sheer
        unfeeling barbarity of life, and the elementary humor and
        tenderness lying close upon it" that Hemingway catches.

1925

8   "E. W." [ERNEST WALSH]. Review of In Our Time, This Quarter,
    1 (Autumn-Winter), 319-21.
        Discusses Hemingway's expert use of single words and
    words in patterns, the use of "speech" that is his excel-
    lence. Thematically, Walsh finds a "clarity of heart"
    that also sets Hemingway apart from most contemporary
    writers.

1926 A BOOKS - NONE

1926 B SHORTER WRITINGS

1   ANON. Review of In Our Time, Time, 7 (18 Jan.), 38.
        High praise for these stories which are "often incom-
    plete; just facets of life, color and touch, like
    Katherine Mansfield's 'stories,' only more masculine, and
    (sometimes) brutally natural."

2   ANON. Review of In Our Time, TLS (4 Nov.), p. 766.
        Surprised that the impact of this book is so strong,
    this reviewer points to Hemingway's unconcern with "the
    conventional features of good writing." The stories work
    through "novel and rather puzzling means."

3   ANON. Review of The Sun Also Rises, Chicago Daily Tribune
    (27 Nov.), p. 13.
        Moral indignation that such a gifted writer as Hemingway
    appears to be allows himself to write about "utterly de-
    graded people," wasting his talent on "sensationalism and
    triviality."

4   ANON. Review of The Sun Also Rises, New York Times Book Re-
    view (31 Oct.), p. 7.
        Calls The Sun Also Rises "a truly gripping story, told
    in a lean, hard athletic narrative prose that puts more
    literary English to shame." Speaks of Hemingway's "or-
    ganic" form; calls it "magnificent writing."

5   ANON. Review of The Sun Also Rises, Time, 8 (1 Nov.), 48.
        This reviewer prefers the philosophy evident in In Our
    Time ("Life's great. Don't let it rattle you"). He finds
    The Sun Also Rises more fashionably "soggy," pseudo-roman-
    tic; and Jake Barnes, "very generous, patient, clever and,
    of course, very sad."
        Reprinted in White, pp. 20-21 (See 1969.A11).

6　ANON.　Review of <u>The Torrents of Spring</u>, <u>New York Times Book Review</u> (13 June), p. 8.
　　　Finds the book amusing, a satire of "certain literary affectations."

7　ANON.　Review of <u>The Torrents of Spring</u>, <u>New Yorker</u>, 2 (31 July), 50.
　　　Recognizes that the book burlesques Sherwood Anderson, but finds the comedy sustained and appropriate.

8　ANON.　Review of <u>The Torrents of Spring</u>, <u>SRL</u>, 3 (31 July), 12.
　　　Thinks that because Hemingway parodies Anderson, the latter's place in American literature becomes more assured. Relates the parody novel to the obvious Anderson influence in the stories of <u>In Our Time</u>.

9　ANON.　Review of <u>The Torrents of Spring</u>, <u>Time</u>, 7 (28 June), 31.
　　　Emphasizes that the parody of Anderson also becomes a put-down of the whole "allegedly significant Chicago school of fiction."

10　AIKEN, CONRAD.　Review of <u>The Sun Also Rises</u>, <u>New York Herald Tribune Books</u> (31 Oct.), p. 4.
　　　Impressed with the dialogue--its rhythms and accuracies--and the way Hemingway manipulates it to create character as well as plot.
　　　Reprinted in White, pp. 2-4 (<u>See</u> 1969.A11).

11　ASHLEY, SCHUYLER.　Review of <u>The Sun Also Rises</u>, <u>Kansas City Star</u> (4 Dec.), p. 8.
　　　The sensual nature of Hemingway's description is important to the creation of his style, as well as to the novel proper.

12　BEACH, JOSEPH WARREN.　<u>The Outlook for American Prose</u>. Chicago: University of Chicago Press, pp. 277-78.
　　　Is encouraged by Hemingway's first work, and looks forward to quality and quantity to come.

13　BOYD, ERNEST.　Review of <u>The Sun Also Rises</u>, <u>Independent</u>, 117 (20 Nov.), 594.
　　　Finds Hemingway's technique--a mosaic of seemingly small details and conversation--most effective here, in fact, "fascinating."
　　　Reprinted in White, pp. 5-8 (<u>See</u> 1969.A11).

1926

14   BOYD, ERNEST. Review of The Torrents of Spring, Independent,
         116 (12 June), 694.
            Considers Hemingway's treatment of the parody expert,
         and agrees with the parody, seeing Hemingway as an excel-
         lent literary critic.

15   CHASE, CLEVELAND B. Review of The Sun Also Rises, SRL, 3
         (11 Dec.), 420-21.
            Commenting on the fact that Hemingway seldom uses simi-
         les, Chase praises what he calls the "Shakespearian abso-
         luteness" about Hemingway's writing. "Written in terse,
         precise and aggressively fresh prose, and containing some
         of the finest dialogue yet written in this country, the
         story achieves a vividness and a sustained tension that
         makes it unquestionably one of the events of a year rich
         in interesting books."
         Reprinted in White, pp. 9-11 (See 1969.A11).

16   FITZGERALD, F. SCOTT. "How to Waste Material: A Note on My
         Generation," Bookman, 63 (May), 262-65.
            Argues for the expatriate view of America, as in In Our
         Time. Fitzgerald sees Hemingway's style as "temperamen-
         tally new" and "incorruptible."
         Reprinted in Afternoon of an Author, edited by Arthur
         Mizener. New York: Scribner's, 1958, pp. 117-22.

17   GORMAN, HERBERT S. Review of The Sun Also Rises, New York
         World (14 Nov.), p. 10M.
            Thinks Hemingway's characters live with "an almost pain-
         ful reality" even though the author is so objective as to
         seem unconnected to them.

18   GOULD, GERALD. Review of In Our Time, Observer (7 Nov.), p. 8.
            Speaks of Hemingway's "touch of genius" in that "tech-
         nique follows the vision." Many of the stories appear to
         be cold; a few, however, do reflect feeling, even genuine
         love.

19   HANSEN, HARRY. Review of The Torrents of Spring, New York
         World (30 May), p. 4M.
            Dislikes the fact that Hemingway parodies the very man
         responsible for his introduction to the literary world.
         Also dislikes the parody, which he finds ineffective.

20   KRONENBERGER, LOUIS. Review of In Our Time, SRL, 2 (13 Feb.),
         555.
            Praises the collection because "Mr. Hemingway's stories
         are as much an achievement as they are an experiment.

(KRONENBERGER, LOUIS)
Already he has succeeded in making some of them finished
products, whose form is consonant with their substance."

21 LATIMER, MARGERY. Review of The Torrents of Spring, New York
Herald Tribune Books (18 July), p. 16.
Modified dislike for the parody, which she finds as
boring as the Anderson novel which prompted it.

22 MORRIS, LAWRENCE S. Review of The Sun Also Rises, New Republic, 48 (22 Dec.), 142-43.
Traces Hemingway's progress from In Our Time, where
Hemingway "was molding an idiom of his own to express his
own way of feeling and seeing," to this novel, in which he
recognizes the modern loss of a relevant mythology. "All
contemporary art, that is vital, that has its roots in our
immediate problem, must seem destructive. It is concerned
in realizing this desperate purposelessness by objecti-
fying it."
Reprinted in White, pp. 12-14 (See 1969.A11).

23 _____. Review of The Torrents of Spring, New Republic, 48
(15 Sept.), 101.
Appreciates that the parody is of not only Anderson but
of Stein and Hemingway himself as well; sees the act of
parody as a great compliment to Anderson.

24 O'BRIEN, EDWARD J. Review of In Our Time, Now & Then, No. 21
(Autumn), pp. 30-32.
Sees what he calls Hemingway's "outward brutality" as
the coating of a "very sensitive mind." Finds him a more
important writer than Anderson.

25 RASCOE, BURTON. Review of The Sun Also Rises, New York Sun
(6 Nov.), p. 10.
Impressed by the freshness and liveliness of Hemingway's
writing, Rascoe comments on the real-life identities of
the characters in The Sun Also Rises.

26 TATE, ALLEN. Review of In Our Time, Nation, 122 (10 Feb.),
160-62.
Finds In Our Time one of the great books of American
literature; admires Hemingway's "precise economical
method," "the passionate accuracy of particular observation," and the fusion of style and content.

27 _____. Review of The Sun Also Rises, Nation, 123 (15 Dec.),
642, 644.

1926

(TATE, ALLEN)
Objects to Hemingway's practice of characterizing by
assigning one or two distinctive traits to each person;
finds The Sun Also Rises less effective than In Our Time.
Reprinted in White, pp. 17-19 (See 1969.A11).

28 _____. Review of The Torrents of Spring, Nation, 123
(28 July), 89-90.
Calls the parody "a small masterpiece of American fiction" and Hemingway "the best contemporary writer of
eighteenth-century prose" as he compares The Torrents of
Spring with Joseph Andrews.

29 WOLF, ROBERT. Review of In Our Time, New York Herald Tribune
Books (14 Feb.), p. 3.
Finds Hemingway's scope limited in this book but praises
his "ear for colloquial conversation" and his appreciation
of nature: "Ernest Hemingway has promise of genius."

1927 A   BOOKS - NONE

1927 B   SHORTER WRITINGS

1 ANON. Review of Fiesta, Observer (12 June), p. 8.
Prefers In Our Time to this novel of "maudlin, staccato
conversations" and "bibulous shadows" of characters.

2 ANON. Review of Fiesta, TLS (30 June), p. 454.
Finds Fiesta less interesting than the "vivid impres-
sionism" of In Our Time, although does admire the Spanish
scenes.
Reprinted in White, pp. 22-23 (See 1969.A11).

3 ANON. Review of Men Without Women, New Yorker, 3 (29 Oct.),
92-94.
Considers this collection of "sad and terrible stories"
"a truly magnificent work." Takes issue with Ford's comment that Hemingway writes "like an Angel," saying that
Hemingway writes "like a human being . . . his is a reportorial talent, just as Sinclair Lewis's is. But . . .
Lewis remains a reporter and Hemingway stands a genius because Hemingway has an "unerring sense of selection."

4 ANON. Review of Men Without Women, Time, 10 (24 Oct.), 38.
Photo.
Compares Men Without Women with The Sun Also Rises, en-
joying both for their clarity, precision, and total
objectivity.

5   ANON. Review of <u>The Sun Also Rises</u>, <u>The Dial</u>, 82 (Jan.), 73.
          Objects to the subject matter, particularly the shallow-
     ness of Hemingway's characters (as imaged by their con-
     stant drinking).

6   BARTON, BRUCE. Review of <u>The Sun Also Rises</u>, <u>Atlantic</u>, 139
          (April), 12, 14.
          Admits that the characters drink too much, but insists
     that "they have courage and friendship, and mental honest-
     ness. And they are <u>alive</u>. Amazingly real and alive."

7   CONNOLLY, CYRIL. Review of <u>Men Without Women</u>, <u>New Statesman</u>,
          30 (26 Nov.), 208.
          Mixed review of these "grim little stories" which have
     "no point, no moral and no ornamentation."

8   CURTIS, WILLIAM. Review of <u>Men Without Women</u>, <u>Town & Country</u>,
          82 (15 Dec.), 59.
          Compares this with the best of Kipling, especially "The
     Killers." "Each sentence says something, crisply, sharply,
     incisively."

9   DODD, LEE WILSON. "Simple Annals of the Callous," <u>SRL</u>, 5
          (19 Nov.), 322-32.
          Questions the critical approach of J. E. Spingarn--
     judging the end result by the author's aims--for, using
     that method, he would have to proclaim Hemingway "a master,
     an authentic artist in prose." Demurs, however, because
     of Hemingway's "limited range," although what he does, he
     does "a little better, indeed, than anyone else now writing
     has been able to do it."

10 EISENBERG, EMANUEL. "The Importance of Being Ernest: Irre-
          sponsibly inscribed after a perusal of <u>The Sun Also Rises</u>,"
     <u>New York World</u> (9 May), p. 13.
          Parody.

11 FERGUSON, CHARLES W. "Five Rising Stars in American Fiction,"
          <u>Bookman</u>, 65 (May), 251-57.
          Comments on Hemingway with Eleanor Carroll Chilton, John
     Gunther, Leonard Nason, and Elizabeth Madox Roberts. "By
     far the most interesting thing about <u>The Sun Also Rises</u> is
     its title . . . . the novel as a whole affords good week-
     end diversion."

12 FORD, FORD MADOX. "Some American Expatriates," <u>Vanity Fair</u>,
          28 (1 April), 64, 98. Photos.
          Describes Hemingway's prose style in <u>The Sun Also Rises</u>

1927

(FORD, FORD MADOX)
as "extremely delicate . . . perhaps the most delicate
prose that is today being written," and contends that such
work cannot be done in an inimical atmosphere such as the
U. S. provides.

13 HUTCHISON, PERCY. Review of Men Without Women, New York
Times Book Review (16 Oct.), pp. 9, 27.
Hemingway has carried the reportorial style to the
height of excellence.

14 KRUTCH, JOSEPH WOOD. "The End of Art," Nation, 125 (16 Nov.),
548.
Admires the stories. "Spiritually the distinguishing
mark of Mr. Hemingway's work is a weariness too great to
be aware of anything except sensations; technically it is
an amazing power to make the apparently aimless and incom-
petent talk of his characters eloquent."

15 LAWRENCE, D. H. Review of In Our Time, Calendar of Modern
Letters, 4 (April), 72-73.
Sees that In Our Time is a "series of successive sketches
from a man's life . . . . It is as much as we need know of
the man's life. The sketches are short, sharp, vivid, and
most of them excellent."
Reprinted in Phoenix (London: Heinemann, 1936), p. 365
(See 1936.B10); and in Hemingway: A Collection of Critical
Essays, edited by Robert Weeks. (Englewood Cliffs, N.J.:
Prentice-Hall, Inc., 1962), pp. 93-94 (See 1962.A6).

16 LITTELL, ROBERT. "Notes on Ernest Hemingway," New Republic,
51 (10 Aug.), 303-06.
Criticizes The Torrents of Spring in particular.

17 MUIR, EDWIN. Review of Fiesta, Nation & Athenaeum, 41
(2 July), 450, 452.
Admires Hemingway's technique, but feels that the novel
lacks "artistic significance. We see the lives of a
group of people laid bare, and we feel that it does not
matter to us." Muir is hopeful, however: "this first
novel raises hopes of remarkable achievement."
Reprinted in White, pp. 15-16 (See 1969.A11).

18 POUND, EZRA. Letter. New Republic, 53 (5 Oct.), 177a.
Defends The Torrents of Spring as being "not soggy,"
and wishes that Hemingway's anger had been directed as
well to "American public life, Congress, the bureaucracy,
etc."

19   RASCOE, BURTON. Review of <u>Men Without Women</u>, <u>Bookman</u>, 66
        (Sept.), 90.
             Likes Hemingway's "admirably clean and incisive style"
        and calls "The Killers," "the most talked-of story of the
        year."

20   SMYTH, JOSEPH HILTON. "He Drank With Them, Played With Them,
        Wrote a Book about Them/Ernest Hemingway of Boston [sic]
        Put His Playfellows of Montparnasse Into His Stories,"
        <u>Boston Globe</u> (18 Dec.), Feature section, p. 3. Photo.
             As titled.

21   WALPOLE, HUGH. "Contemporary American Letters," <u>Nation &</u>
        <u>Athenaeum</u>, 41 (4 June), 302-03.
             Refers to Hemingway as "the most interesting figure in
        American letters in the last ten years."

22   WILSON, EDMUND. "The Sportsman's Tragedy," <u>New Republic</u>, 53
        (14 Dec.), 102-03.
             Wilson thinks some reviewers have oversimplified the
        Hemingway world as presented in his fiction. Finds Heming-
        way's attitudes "rather subtle and complicated": "he
        seems so broken in to the human agonies, and, though even
        against his will, so impassively, so hopelessly, resigned
        to them, that the only protest of which he is capable is,
        as it were, the grin and the curse of the sportsman who
        loses the game."
        Reprinted in <u>The Shores of Light</u> (New York: Farrar,
        Straus, and Young, 1952), pp. 339-44 (<u>See</u> 1952.B76).

23   WOOLF, VIRGINIA. "An Essay in Criticism," <u>New York Herald</u>
        <u>Tribune Books</u> (9 Oct.), pp. 1, 8.
             Review of <u>Men Without Women</u>. Traces Hemingway's style
        and manner to France and finds him "modern in manner but
        not in vision; he is self-consciously virile; his talent
        has contracted rather than expanded; compared with his
        novel his stories are a little dry and sterile."
        Reprinted in <u>Granite and Rainbow</u> (New York: Harcourt,
        Brace, 1958), pp. 85-92 (<u>See</u> 1958.B26).

1928 A BOOKS - NONE

1928 B SHORTER WRITINGS

1   BARRETT, RICHMOND. "Babes in the Bois," <u>Harper's Magazine</u>,
        156 (May), 724-36.
             General article about this "adolescent generation."

1928

(BARRETT, RICHMOND)
   Hemingway is called "that brilliant black sheep from the
   Middle West" and The Sun Also Rises a "hard-boiled muscu-
   lar book." Unfortunately, "a crowd of sentimental puppies"
   took it up and distorted its real merits.

2   COWLEY, MALCOLM. "The Hemingway Legend," Brentano's Book Chat
       (Sept.-Oct.), pp. 25-29.
          Sketch of Hemingway by Waldo Pierce. General biographi-
       cal details.

3   HUDDLESTON, SISLEY. Paris Salons, Cafés, Studios: Being
       Social, Artistic and Literary Memories. Philadelphia:
       Lippincott, pp. 121-23. (Published under the title
       Bohemian Literary and Social Life in Paris. London:
       Harrap.)
          Reminiscence of Hemingway during the early Paris years,
       as part of the Ford circle, of his "experiments in prose,"
       "seeking a simple realistic style." Because the "conver-
       sation in novels was too high-falutin," Hemingway "intended
       to make it as he supposed it to be."

4   MATTHEWS, T. S. "Flatteries: Pretty Grand: By a sincere
       flatterer of Ernest Hemingway," New Republic, 53 (8 Feb.),
       323-24.
          Parody.

5   MENCKEN, H. L. Review of Men Without Women, American Mercury,
       14 (May), 127.
          Warns both Hemingway and Thornton Wilder to beware of
       their huge successes. "It is technical virtuosity that
       has won them attention; it is hard and fundamental thinking
       that must get them on, if they are to make good their high
       promise."

6   PAUL, ELLIOTT H. "A Minority Report," The Paris Tribune
       (18 March).
          Defends Hemingway's writing from "careless terminology."
       Paul admires Hemingway's "extraordinary delicacy and his
       patience in putting it into words . . . . his sensitive-
       ness to the currents of human understanding . . . ."
       Reprinted in The Left Bank Revisited, p. 268 (See
       1972.B28).

7   RIDDELL, JOHN COREY FORD. "A Parody Interview with Mr.
       Hemingway," Vanity Fair, 29 (Jan.), 78.
          Caricature of Hemingway by Ralph Barton.

8   ROSENFELD, PAUL. <u>By Way of Art: Criticisms of Music, Litera-</u>
     <u>ture, Painting, Sculpture and the Dance</u>. New York: Coward-
     McCann, pp. 151-63.
         In "Hemingway's Perspective," Rosenfeld describes Heming-
     way as a "prose Goya," "jaded, gifted broadcaster of an
     Age of Hate." Of Hemingway's style, he notices the relent-
     less, "emphatic, condensed declarative sentences: and the
     "rudimentary" and "concrete" vocabulary. Impressive as
     his writing is, however, Rosenfeld feels that "Hemingway
     rarely renders the whole of his situations"; he prefers
     <u>In Our Time</u> to the later work.

9   ROTHMAN, N. L. "Hemingway Whistles in the Dark," <u>The Dial</u>,
     84 (1 April), 336-38.
         "There is a good deal in the writing of Ernest Hemingway
     that is being overlooked." Comments on the characteristic
     understatement which only masks inexpressible anguish.

1929 A BOOKS - NONE

1929 B SHORTER WRITINGS

1   ANON. "Boston Bans Scribner's for July," <u>New York Times</u>
     (29 June), p. 8.
         A second issue of <u>Scribner's Magazine</u> was banned from
     Boston news stands because of the serial <u>A Farewell to</u>
     <u>Arms</u>.

2   ANON. "Boston Police Bar Scribner's Magazine/ Superintendent
     Acts on Objections to Ernest Hemingway's Serial, 'Farewell
     to Arms,'" <u>New York Times</u> (21 June), p. 2.
         "Salacious" was the adjective some readers chose to
     describe <u>A Farewell to Arms</u>.

3   ANON. Review of <u>A Farewell to Arms</u>, <u>Illustrated London News</u>
     (21 Dec.), p. 1092.
         A brilliant book, enhanced by the perfection of details
     and the profound discernment evident in the subject matter.

4   ANON. Review of <u>A Farewell to Arms</u>, <u>Time</u>, 14 (14 Oct.), 80.
         Sees the novel as fulfillment of the prophecy of Heming-
     way's greatness, especially in its "throbbing preoccupation
     with flesh and blood and nerves rather than the fanciful
     fabrics of intellect."

5   ANON. Review of <u>A Farewell to Arms</u>, <u>Times</u> (London)
     (15 Nov.), p. 20.

1929

(ANON.)
Thinks the war has given Hemingway a suitable subject, at long last. Appreciates the "grim dryness of its humour, the sensual realism of its episodes, and the unrelieved pessimism of its view of life." Considers Rinaldi "the most brilliant achievement in a brilliant book."

6 ANON. Review of A Farewell to Arms, TLS (28 Nov.), p. 998.
Considers A Farewell to Arms a powerful novel, with the closing scene its masterpiece. Calls Hemingway "an extremely talented and original artist."
Reprinted in TLS (17 Sept. 1954), p. 87 and in American Writing Today, edited by Allen Angoff, New York, New York University Press, 1957, pp. 370-72 (See 1957.B2).

7 ASHLEY, SCHUYLER. Essay Reviews. Kansas City: Lowell Press.
P. 67: Review of In Our Time, Kansas City Star (12 Dec. 1925), p. 102 (See 1925.B2); Review of The Sun Also Rises, Kansas City Star (4 Dec. 1926) (See 1926.B11).

8 BENNETT, ARNOLD. Review of A Farewell to Arms, Evening Standard (London) (14 Nov.) and Times (London) (15 Nov.), p. 20.
Finds A Farewell to Arms "utterly free of any sentimentality. But imbued through and through with genuine sentiment . . . . a superb performance."

9 BURKE, KENNETH. "A Decade of American Fiction," Bookman, 79 (Aug.), 561-67.
Hemingway gives a "Hollywood conception of glory" in his picture of "the 'lost generation,' contentedly lost." He does, however, "weed out much that is pious, or pompous; he is a good corrective."

10 BUTCHER, FANNY. Review of A Farewell to Arms, Chicago Daily Tribune (28 Sept.), p. 11.
Finds A Farewell to Arms both in technique and in style "the most interesting novel of the year."

11 CANBY, HENRY SEIDEL. "Story of the Brave," review of A Farewell to Arms, SRL, 6 (12 Oct.), 231-32.
Waldo Pierce's drawing of Hemingway. Sees the novel as supplying a philosophy, affirmative if stoic; and finds Hemingway "worthy to be their leader" (of his generation of writers).
Reprinted in Graham, pp. 14-19 (See 1971.A7).

12 CAPERS, JULIAN, JR. Letter to the editor, Scribner's Magazine,
        86 (Sept.), 52-53.
        Regarding Hemingway's work on the Kansas City Star and
    with the ambulance unit in Italy.

13 CARROLL, RAYMOND G. "Hemingway Gives Up Old Life With Literary
        Success," New York Evening Post (18 Nov.), p. 6.
        Describes Hemingway's domestic life with Pauline and
    Patrick, and writes his own parody of the "old" Hemingway.

14 COWLEY, MALCOLM. Review of A Farewell to Arms, New York Herald
        Tribune Books (6 Oct.), pp. 1, 16.
        Claims that A Farewell to Arms is Hemingway's "farewell"
    to a period, an attitude, and ventures to guess that his
    later fiction will be more obviously intellectual. "The
    emotions as a whole are more colored by thought. They
    seem to demand expression in a subtler and richer prose."
    Reprinted in Graham, pp. 3-8 (See 1971.A7).

15 CURTIS, WILLIAM. Review of A Farewell to Arms, Town & Country,
        84 (1 Nov.), 86. Photograph by Helen Breaker.
        Mixed review, with high praise for "The Killers" and
    reticence about the full effect of A Farewell to Arms.

16 De VOTO, BERNARD. Review of A Farewell to Arms, Bookwise, 1
        (Nov.), 5-9.
        Sees in A Farewell to Arms a "passion" and "a kind of
    sublimity" that The Sun Also Rises lacked, at least partly
    because its subject matter is more important. "In A Fare-
    well to Arms Mr. Hemingway for the first time justifies
    his despair and gives it the dignity of a tragic emotion."

17 DOS PASSOS, JOHN. Review of A Farewell to Arms, New Masses, 5
        (1 Dec.), 16.
        Impressed by Hemingway's craftsmanship, Dos Passos com-
    pares A Farewell to Arms to "a piece of wellfinished car-
    penter's work . . . . The stuff will match up as narrative
    prose with anything that's been written since there was
    any English language."

18 FADIMAN, CLIFTON P. Review of A Farewell to Arms, Nation, 129
        (30 Oct.), 497-98.
        Calls A Farewell to Arms Hemingway's "best book to date."
    Sees Hemingway as "anti-intellectual," not as a disparage-
    ment, but in that "the whole book exists on a plane of
    strong feeling," love for a woman and affection for com-
    rades.
    Reprinted in Graham, pp. 20-24 (See 1971.A7).

1929

19   GOULD, GERALD. Review of A Farewell to Arms, Observer
         (17 Nov.), p. 8.
           Considers A Farewell to Arms "not a war-novel." Its key-
         note is "the desperate senselessness of pain," and that re-
         lates to the hero who just happens to be in the war. "I
         have read few books more terrible; but the beauty survives."

20   HARTLEY, L. P. Review of A Farewell to Arms, Saturday Review
         (London), 148 (7 Dec.), 684, 686.
           Put off by the similarity of drinks and dialogue. Hartley
         compares A Farewell to Arms with The Sun Also Rises, but
         decides the new novel is "a much better book." Admires
         the war passages and the Italian officers' characteriza-
         tions.

21   HAZLITT, HENRY. Review of A Farewell to Arms, New York Sun
         (28 Sept.), p. 38. Drawing of Hemingway.
           "Many things in the novel are magnificently done (the
         passage of time is conveyed with uncanny skill)." Admires
         the dialogue but finds unwarranted bare spaces between
         dialogue scenes.

22   HERRICK, ROBERT. "What is Dirt?" Bookman, 70 (Nov.) 258-62.
           Abuses Hemingway for his subject matter and style,
         calling A Farewell to Arms "garbage." For replies to this
         essay see Henry Seidel Canby's Chronicle and Comment column,
         Bookman, 70 (Feb., 1930), 641-47; M. K. Hare's "Is It Dirt
         or Is It Art?" in Scribner's advertisement, Bookman, 71
         (March 1930), xiv-xv; and the foreword, "In Spite of
         Robert Herrick," in Cohn's Bibliography, p. 9.

23   HOPE, EDWARD. The Lantern column, New York Herald Tribune
         (23 Dec.), p. 14.
           This year-end book chronicle includes an appraisal of
         A Farewell to Arms.

24   HUTCHISON, PERCY. Review of A Farewell to Arms, New York
         Times Book Review (29 Sept.), p. 5.
           "A moving and beautiful book," and a revelation of the
         sensitive Hemingway beneath the tough exterior that his
         style tends to suggest.

25   McINTYRE, O. O. "Drop in Again, Ernest!" Kansas City Times
         (9 March), p. 28.
           Gives most coverage to Hemingway's apparent financial
         unconcern for his literary achievements.

26   MATTHEWS, T. S.   "'Nothing Ever Happens to the Brave,'" New
       Republic, 60 (9 Oct.), 208-10.
          Review of A Farewell to Arms. A Farewell to Arms will
       not disappoint the many readers who find Hemingway a master
       of modern fiction. Counters that Hemingway is not a
       realist, and Catherine Barkley is "one of the impossibly
       beautiful characters of modern tragedy."

27   MAUROIS, ANDRÉ. Review of A Farewell to Arms, This Quarter,
       2 (Oct.-Dec.), 212.
          Positive evaluation by an influential European critic.

28   OVERTON, GRANT. An Hour of the American Novel. Philadelphia:
       Lippincott, pp. 142-43.
          Brief comment on Hemingway's fiction.

29   PARKER, DOROTHY. "The Artist's Reward," New Yorker, 5
       (30 Nov.), 28-31.
          Parker stresses Hemingway's interest in craft, his hard
       work, his confidence. Among other things, this essay is
       the origin of the "grace under pressure" phrase, the
       phrase taken from a letter Hemingway wrote to Fitzgerald.

30   "I. M. P." [ISABEL M. PATERSON]. Turns With a Bookworm
       column, New York Herald Tribune Books (24 Nov.), p. 27.
          Mentions the Hemingway-Callaghan boxing match in Paris.
       See Callaghan's reply in the New York Herald Tribune Books
       (8 Dec.), p. 29. This letter to Paterson, denying that
       he ever knocked out Hemingway, is reprinted in That Summer
       in Paris, New York, Coward-McCann, 1963, p. 242 (See
       1963.B7).

31   PRAZ, MARIO. "Un giovane narratore americano," Stampa
       (14 June), p. 3.
          Reprinted in part in Praz' "Hemingway in Italy,"
       Partisan Review, 15 (Oct., 1948). (See 1948.B7.)

32   PRIESTLEY, J. B. Review of A Farewell to Arms, Now & Then,
       No. 34 (Winter), pp. 11-12.
          To this British reviewer, Hemingway's idiomatic language
       is "a curious manner and idiom which are based on charac-
       teristic American speech." Despite that peculiarity, his
       writing is "very vivid and sometimes poignant."

33   RASCOE, BURTON. A Bookman's Daybook. New York: Liveright,
       pp. 253-54.

1929

(RASCOE, BURTON)
Entry for June 5, 1924 ("Ellis, Whitehead and Hemingway"), reprinted from <u>New York Herald Tribune</u>, June 15,
1924 (<u>See</u> 1924.B6).

34 _____. Review of <u>A Farewell to Arms</u>, <u>Arts & Decoration</u>,
32 (Nov.), 124. Photo by Helen Breaker.
". . . a distinguished work of fiction." "The story of
the Italian retreat is superbly done."

35 REDMAN, BEN RAY. "Spokesman for a Generation," <u>Spur</u>, 44
(1 Dec.), 77, 186. Photo.
Discusses <u>The Sun Also Rises</u> and <u>A Farewell to Arms</u>,
with emphasis on Hemingway in Pamplona during the week of
the San Fermin fiesta.

36 ROSS, MARY. Review of <u>A Farewell to Arms</u>, <u>Atlantic</u>, 144
(Nov.), 20.
Admires this novel for its "wider and deeper reach of
emotion than Hemingway has dared before," as well as its
customary laconic dialogue and ability to communicate
through small details.

37 "A. W. S." Review of <u>A Farewell to Arms</u>, <u>New Yorker</u>, 5
(12 Oct.), 120.
Admires the dialogue in the closing scenes of the novel.

38 "E. S." Review of <u>A Farewell to Arms</u>, <u>New Statesman</u>, 34
(30 Nov.), 267.
This "convincing and moving tale" is not about war but
about people, Henry and Catherine. "Mr. Hemingway communicates his experience whole and unimpaired."

39 TODD, B. E. Review of <u>A Farewell to Arms</u>, <u>Spectator</u> (16 Nov.),
727.
Weariness rather than horror dominates <u>A Farewell to
Arms</u>, a "very great war novel" which should be suitable to
counteract a whole shelf of the glory and glamour books.
Reprinted in Graham, pp. 23-24 (<u>See</u> 1971.A7).

40 WALPOLE, HUGH. "The Best Books of 1929," <u>Saturday Review</u>
(London), 148 (21 Dec.), 747-48.
Of the list, "the finest novel of the year for myself is
Ernest Hemingway's <u>A Farewell to Arms</u>, a most moving and
beautiful story."

41 WINTERS, YVOR. "The Extension and Reintegration of the Human
Spirit," <u>The New American Caravan</u>, 3: 361-402.

(WINTERS, YVOR)
    Sees Hemingway's short stories as failures because they
concentrate exclusively on "external data, presenting a
dry skeleton . . . rather than an experience in all its
fullness."
    Reprinted in Yvor Winters: Uncollected Essays and Reviews.
Chicago: The Sparrow Press, 1973, 225-70 (See 1973.B93).

42   WISTER, OWEN. Letter to the editor, Scribner's Magazine, 86
    (July), 27.
        Praises A Farewell to Arms highly.

1930 A BOOKS - NONE

1930 B SHORTER WRITINGS

1   ANON. "Visit by Ernest Hemingway," Kansas City Star (6 July),
    p. 3.
        Interview with Hemingway in Kansas City, enroute to
Wyoming to continue work on Death in the Afternoon.

2   ANDERSON, MARGARET C. My Thirty Years' War: An Autobiography.
    New York: Covici, Friede, pp. 258-60. Photo of Hemingway
by Man Ray.
        Reminisces about Hemingway in Paris in the early 1920's.

3   ATKINSON, J. BROOKS. Review of the play, A Farewell to Arms,
    New York Times (23 Sept.), p. 30.
        Praises Laurence Stallings' adaptation, but thinks no
play could capture the brilliance of the novel, a "vir-
tuoso achievement--fierce, swift, brilliant."

4   CALVERTON, V. F. "Ernest Hemingway and the Modern Temper,"
    Book League Monthly (New York), 3 (January), 165-66.
        Questions the value of Hemingway's fiction, and of his
place in modern literature. Objects to his themes and his
treatment of them.

5   CANBY, HENRY SEIDEL. "Chronicle & Comment," Bookman, 70
    (Feb.), 641-47.
        Thought Herrick's attack fair in some respects, but not
in his calling A Farewell to Arms "garbage." Does find
the love affair reprehensible--"a daydream of extreme
erotic indulgence divorced from the other normal human
emotions." "This is not the stuff of important writing."

1930

6   FERGUSSON, FRANCIS.   Review of the play, <u>A Farewell to Arms</u>,
       <u>Bookman</u>, 72 (Nov.), 296.
          Finds the play moving because the love story is made the
       center of the action, and the play has excellent acting
       and direction.   "It is when one comes to look for the
       Hemingway sensibility, which gives the novel its importance,
       that one is most disappointed.   Mr. Stallings has tried to
       save it by keeping the dialogue intact; but the Hemingway
       laconic remarks lose their flavor when they are not im-
       bedded in the Hemingway prose."

7   GALANTIERE, LEWIS.   Review of <u>A Farewell to Arms</u>, <u>Hound & Horn</u>,
       3 (Jan.-March), 259-62.
          Criticizes the love story because the lovers have little
       motivation: "The war story . . . is much more successful."
       The writing, however, is "the best Hemingway has done."

8   HAMMOND, PERCY.   Review of the play, <u>A Farewell to Arms</u>, <u>New
       York Herald Tribune</u> (23 Sept.), p. 14.
          Thinks the play works relatively well, although not in
       comparison to the novel.

9   HANEMANN, H. W.   <u>The Facts of Life: A Book of Brighter Biogra-
       phy Executed in the Manner of Some of Our Best-Known
       Writers</u> . . . New York: Farrar & Rinehart, pp. 131-59.
          "A Farewell to Josephine's Arms--The Hemingway of All
       Flesh," reprinted in <u>Twentieth Century Parody</u>, edited by
       Burling Lowrey, New York, 1960, pp. 59-70 (<u>See</u> 1960.B14).

10 HICKS, GRANVILLE.   "The World of Hemingway," <u>New Freeman</u>, 1
       (22 March), 40-42.
          Traces the "spiritual history" of the Hemingway hero
       from Nick Adams to Jake Barnes to Frederic Henry.

11 HOFFMAN, LEIGH.   "Mencken Seeks a Naval Holiday in London--
       for Himself--and Purple Spats for Paris," <u>The Paris
       Tribune</u> (5 Jan.).
          Quotes Mencken as praising Hemingway as the most promi-
       nent of younger American authors, with the qualification
       that "he doesn't ring convincingly all the time."
       Reprinted in Hugh Ford, ed., <u>The Left Bank Revisited</u>:
       <u>Selections from the Paris Tribune, 1917-1934</u>.   University
       Park: The Pennsylvania State University Press, 1972,
       p. 168 (<u>See</u> 1972.B28).

12 MENCKEN, H. L.   Review of <u>A Farewell to Arms</u>, <u>American Mercury</u>,
       19 (Jan.), 127.
          With the beginning of his disenchantment with Hemingway,
       Mencken notes that "his tricks begin to wear thin."

*13 ORTON, VREST. "Some Notes Bibliographical and Otherwise on the Books of Ernest Hemingway," <u>Publishers' Weekly</u>, 117 (15 Feb.), 884-86.

14 POUND, EZRA. "Small Magazines," <u>The English Journal</u>, 19, No. 9 (Nov.), 699-706.
Describes Hemingway as an "imagiste" writer, choosing each word with care, polishing, perfecting; and contrasts him with Robert McAlmon, whose writing was either a failure or fine as a whole.

15 REDMAN, BEN RAY. Review of <u>In Our Time</u>, <u>New York Herald Tribune Books</u> (16 Nov.), p. 22.
Positive review of the collection, praising its economy and vivid portraiture.

16 WALDEN BOOKSHOP. <u>Bibliographical Notes on Ernest Hemingway</u>. Chicago: Walden Bookshop. Leaflet, 4 pages.
Contains excerpts from a Hemingway letter about various editions of his work.

17 WARD, ALFRED CHARLES. <u>The Nineteen-Twenties: Literature and Ideas in the Post-War Decade</u>. London: Methuen, pp. 128-29, 146.
Sees Hemingway as "more in step with the despair . . . than either Lewis or Dreiser." Sees his first books as "nakedly and pitilessly hopeless," and his method of characterization unique: "the characters are emotion-registering characters rather than emotion-feeling."

18 WINTERS, YVOR. "Major Fiction," <u>Hound and Horn</u>, 4, No. 2 (1930-1931), 303-05.
Speaks of Hemingway as the most popular of "the contemporary objectivists."
Reprinted in <u>Yvor Winters: Uncollected Essays and Reviews</u>. Chicago: The Swallow Press, 1973, pp. 96-99 (<u>See</u> 1973.B93).

19 YOUNG, STARK. Review of the play, <u>A Farewell to Arms</u>, <u>New Republic</u>, 64 (8 Oct.), 208-09.
Comments on the fact that Hemingway's work is realistic on the surface, even though it may be "at bottom poetic and distilled." Such concentration cannot be transferred to the stage, and therefore the play version is different from the novel. "On the whole I found the play, despite the drag of much of the last act, interesting all through."

1931

1931 A   BOOKS - NONE

1931 B   SHORTER WRITINGS

   1   ANON. "The Ghost of a Writer," <u>Kansas City Star</u> (21 Oct.),
          p. 17.
            Interview with Hemingway in Kansas City, in which he
          tells of an impersonator who has been passing himself off
          as Hemingway in Europe and America.

   2   COHN, LOUIS H. <u>A Bibliography of the Works of Ernest Heming-
          way</u>. New York: Random House.
            Includes pictures of the title pages and some foreign
          entries. "In Spite of Robert Herrick," the foreword, de-
          fends Hemingway's position and his writing.

   3   DEWING, ARTHUR. "The Mistake about Hemingway," <u>North American
          Review</u>, 232, 364-71.
            Dewing admires much of the Hemingway style and method
          ("Not many contemporary writers are as vitally alive") but
          sees no evidence of development in the fiction itself. He
          suggests that Hemingway should either abandon the limited
          narrative method or create an intellectually perceptive
          character like Conrad's Marlowe.

   4   HAZLITT, HENRY. "Salvation for the Modern Soul," <u>Nation</u>, 132
          (10 June), 637.
            Comments on the understatement evident in Hemingway's
          characterization: "The Hemingway character, who only <u>does</u>
          and <u>is</u>, says nothing but the barely and bleakly necessary,
          and despises all subtleties of thought and emotion."

   5   HERBST, JOSEPHINE. "Counterblast," <u>Nation</u>, 132 (11 March),
          275-76.
            Questions the position of Isidor Schneider (<u>Nation</u>,
          Feb. 18, 184-86; <u>See</u> 1931.B11) who criticizes the "Heming-
          way school." Herbst says that Hemingway's "influence" is
          indistinguishable from that of Crane, Chekhov, Balzac, and
          Joyce; therefore Schneider's designation is meaningless.
          She wonders whether or not he should himself be censured
          for what she terms this kind of "menace in loose criticism."

   6   HUDDLESTON, SISLEY. <u>Back to Montparnasse: Glimpses of Broad-
          way in Bohemia</u>. Philadelphia: Lippincott.
            Reminiscence of early little magazine publication, like
          <u>Exile</u>. Quotes Hemingway's "Neothomist Poem."

1932

7   HUXLEY, ALDOUS. <u>Music at Night and Other Essays</u>. London:
         Chatto & Windus.
             In the essay "Foreheads Villainous Low" (111–115),
         Huxley cites phrases from <u>A Farewell to Arms</u> as examples
         of what he calls "stupidity-snobbery" (deliberate non-
         intellectualism). Hemingway reacts to this essay on
         p. 190 of <u>Death in the Afternoon</u>.

8   KUNITZ, STANLEY J. "Dilly Tante," ed. <u>Living Authors: A Book
         of Biographies</u>. New York: Wilson, pp. 175–76. Photo.
         "Ernest Hemingway."
             Biographical sketch with emphasis upon bullring
         activities.

9   O'BRIEN, EDWARD J. <u>The Advance of the American Short Story</u>.
         New York: Dodd, Mead, revised edition, pp. 269–75.
             Names Hemingway as one of three outstanding short story
         writers since Sherwood Anderson: "His work is a triumph
         of sight and hearing." O'Brien also confutes the notion
         that Hemingway's range is "limited."

10   RASCOE, BURTON. A Bookman's Daybook column, "Random Thoughts
         About F. Scott Fitzgerald, Hemingway and Others," <u>New York
         Sun</u> (2 Nov.), p. 37.
             Reminiscence about the important younger writers.

11   SCHNEIDER, ISIDOR. "The Fetish of Simplicity," <u>Nation</u>, 132
         (18 Feb.), 184–86.
             Schneider designates a relatively large group of writers
         as "the Hemingway school" and blames them for "the present
         over-accent on simplicity" and for "the Hemingway picture
         of a hard and disillusioned generation."

12   SCHWARTZ, HARRY and PAUL ROMAINE. <u>Checklists of Twentieth
         Century Authors</u>. Milwaukee: Casanova Booksellers. First
         Series, catalogue, pp. 10–11.
             Brief checklist of Hemingway first editions to 1931.

13   STEFFENS, LINCOLN. <u>The Autobiography of Lincoln Steffens</u>, New
         York: Harcourt Brace. Photo by Helen Breaker.
             Recollections of Hemingway in the early 1920's in Paris,
         and of his cable to the <u>Daily Star</u> which had so much im-
         pressed Steffens.

<u>1932 A BOOKS – NONE</u>

1932

1932 B   SHORTER WRITINGS

1   ANON. Review of Death in the Afternoon, Times (London)
     (16 Dec.), p. 8.
          "If one wishes to understand the technique of the bull-
     fight . . . this is the man and the book." Comments on
     Hemingway's evident understanding of and love for the
     Fiesta Nacional, and the "great felicity" of his treatment.

2   ANON. Review of Death in the Afternoon, Time, 20 (26 Sept.),
     47. Portrait of Hemingway by Luis Quintanilla.
     Positive review.

3   ANON. Review of Death in the Afternoon, TLS (8 Dec.), p. 936.
          Dislikes Hemingway's "supercharged 'he-manishness'" and
     his "irritating" prose style, but finds his concept of the
     bullfight as tragedy valuable. "Praise can scarcely be
     too high" for some parts of Death in the Afternoon.

4   ANON. Review of The Torrents of Spring (Crosby Continental
     Edition), Town & Country, 87 (15 Feb.), 21. Photo.
     Appreciative of the parody.

5   BEACH, JOSEPH WARREN. The Twentieth Century Novel: Studies
     in Technique. New York: Appleton-Century-Crofts,
     pp. 532-37.
          Includes "The Cult of the Simple," and many other refer-
     ences. Finds Hemingway's best effects derived from omis-
     sion: "The movements and words and sensations are re-
     corded; the emotions are left to be inferred."

6   BRICKELL, HERSCHEL. Review of Death in the Afternoon, New
     York Herald Tribune Books (25 Sept.), pp. 3, 12.
          Likes Death in the Afternoon because it is "the essence
     of Hemingway," "teeming with life, vigorous, powerful,
     moving and consistently entertaining."

7   COATES, ROBERT M. Review of Death in the Afternoon, New
     Yorker, 8 (1 Oct.), 61-63.
          Finds this "an expert treatise of bullfighting" with
     "passages of bright, appealing honesty." The book is
     marred, for Coates, however, because Hemingway also "ex-
     presses some pretty bitter opinions on readers, writers,
     and things in general"--to the point of "petulance." Hem-
     ingway's reply to Coates, New Yorker, 8 (5 Nov.).

8   COINDREAU, MAURICE-EDGAR. "L'Amérique et le roman alcoolique,"
     Cahiers du Sud, 19 (April), 166-72.
          A denunciation of Hemingway's work by the French trans-
     lator of A Farewell to Arms and The Sun Also Rises.
     Reprinted in Aperçus de litterature americaine, Paris,
     1946, pp. 76-94.

9   "S. C." [SEWARD COLLINS]. Review of Death in the Afternoon,
     Bookman, 75 (Oct.), 622-24.
          A study of Hemingway's use of the "histrionic aspect of
     the sport." The book contains "plenty of writing that is
     as fine as he has ever done" though marred by some "trucu-
     lent he-manishness."

10   COWLEY, MALCOLM. "A Farewell to Spain," review of Death in
     the Afternoon, New Republic, 73 (30 Nov.), 76-77.
          Considers this book another in a series of "farewells."
     "In a sense, every book he has written has been an elegy."
     Admires the book--even the sections about literary criti-
     cism and Hemingway himself--but feels the need for a change
     in mode.
     Reprinted in Literary Opinion in America, edited by Morton
     Dauwen Zabel, New York, Harper, 1937, pp. 506-11 (See
     1937.B52).

11   DUFFUS, R. L. Review of Death in the Afternoon, New York
     Times Book Review (25 Sept.), pp. 5, 17.
          Has reservations about the style in the book, but finds
     it a "meticulous explanation" of not only the physical
     movement but the spirit of bullfighting.

12   FORD, FORD MADOX. "Introduction" to A Farewell to Arms. New
     York: Scribner's.
          Ford again speaks of Hemingway's vision and his craft,
     each word placed in the context to have surprising impact.

13   GIBBS, WOLCOTT. "Death in the Rumble Seat," New Yorker, 8
     (8 Oct.), 15.
          Parody. Subtitled: "With the usual apologies to Ernest
     Hemingway, who must be pretty sick of this sort of thing."
     Reprinted in Bed of Neuroses, New York, Dodd, Mead, 1937,
     pp. 261-65 (See 1937.B29).

14   HALL, MORDAUNT. "A Hemingway Novel in Film Form," New York
     Times (18 Dec.), x, p. 7.
          Considers Borzage's A Farewell to Arms "an earnest and
     occasionally affecting film," although "the film does not
     capture the spirit of the book."

1932

15   HICKS, GRANVILLE. Review of <u>Death in the Afternoon</u>, <u>Nation</u>,
        135 (9 Nov.), 461.
            Stresses the fact that Hemingway himself plays an inte-
        gral role in the novel; objects to the "premeditated"
        quality of some of these personal revelations.

16   JOHNSON, MERLE. "American First Editions: Ernest Hemingway,"
        <u>Publishers' Weekly</u>, 121 (20 Feb.), 870.
            Brief checklist.

17   LEIGHTON, LAWRENCE. "An Autopsy and a Prescription," <u>Hound &
        Horn</u>, 5 (July-Sept.), 520-39.
            Finds Hemingway's writing "repulsive, sterile, and dead"
        (his condemnation extends to Dos Passos and Fitzgerald
        also); and objects to Hemingway's variety of "tricks" as
        well as his deficient moral view, especially in <u>The Sun
        Also Rises</u>.

18   LEWISOHN, LUDWIG. <u>The Story of American Literature</u>. New York:
        Harper, pp. 518-20.
            Approval of Hemingway's originality and technical pro-
        ficiency.

19   LOVETT, ROBERT MORSE. "Ernest Hemingway," <u>English Journal</u>,
        21, pp. 609-17.
            Sees Hemingway's effect as deriving from contrasts:
        American pioneering and European cosmopolitanism, in-
        genuousness and sophistication, violence and perception.
        Lovett finds Hemingway's chief innovation in his use of
        "realism as the vehicle for animal vitality rather than
        for social denunciation."

20   MACKALL, LEONARD L. Notes for Bibliophiles column, <u>New York
        Herald Tribune Books</u> (31 Jan.), p. 19.
            Review of Louis H. Cohn's <u>Bibliography of the Works of
        Ernest Hemingway</u>.

21   MENCKEN, H. L. Review of <u>Death in the Afternoon</u>, <u>American
        Mercury</u>, 27 (Dec.), 506-07.
            <u>Death in the Afternoon</u> exhibits "his characteristic
        merits and defects." Its excellences as exposition are
        marred by "a gross and irritating cheapness. . . . Take
        out the interludes behind the barn . . . and it would be
        a really first-rate book."

22   PATTERSON, CURTIS. Review of <u>Death in the Afternoon</u>, <u>Town &
        Country</u>, 87 (15 Oct.), 50. Portrait of Hemingway by Luis
        Quintanilla.

(PATTERSON, CURTIS)
   Finds Hemingway's use of the "overlong, highly involved, extremely intricate periodic sentence" ill-chosen. Objects to what he labels "smut" within the book.

23   POUND, EZRA. Letter, "Pound to Rascoe," New York Sun (11 June), p. 36.
   Regarding the merits of Hemingway's work. Also includes a reply by Rascoe, "Rascoe's Riposte," about his own early championing of Hemingway's work.

24   REDMAN, BEN RAY. Review of Death in the Afternoon, SRL, 9 (24 Sept.), 121. Photo.
   Redman finds Hemingway's prose "perfect because it states with absolute precision what it is meant to state, explains what it is meant to explain beyond possibility of misunderstanding, and communicates to the reader the emotion with which it is so heavily charged . . . no reader can put down Death in the Afternoon ignorant of the fact that bullfighting is a tragic art."

25   STALLINGS, LAURENCE. Review of Death in the Afternoon, New York Sun (23 Sept.), p. 34. Photo.
   Finds this "basic treatise on the art of the bullfighter" a "superbly colored and capricious essay on human pride" as well. Connects the book with the "Pagan virtues" rather than Christian moralities.

26   WARD, A. C. American Literature: 1880-1930. London: Methuen; New York: Dial Press, pp. 151-53.
   Compares Hemingway's work with that of his contemporaries.

1933 A   BOOKS - NONE

1933 B   SHORTER WRITINGS

1   ANON. "Hemingway Plans to Hunt Big Game in Tanganyika," New York Herald Tribune, European Edition (17 Nov.), p. 3.
   Interview with Hemingway in Paris where he has been for a month, from Spain.

2   ANON. Review of The Torrents of Spring, TLS (30 March), p. 222.
   The first English publication of The Torrents of Spring with a preface by David Garnett is described as "this amusing mime," "a parody of badness common to a good deal of contemporary fiction: rambling introspection, repetition as padding, shallow lyricism."

1933

3   ANON. Review of <u>Winner Take Nothing</u>, <u>Time</u>, 22 (6 Nov.), 59–60.
         Sees the collection as characteristic, with his subjects
         "always illustrations of the same theme: the sportsman
         caught in an unsportingly tight place and, with various
         versions of the Hemingway stiff upper lip, taking it like
         a sportsman."

4   BEER, THOMAS. "Death at 5:45 P.M.," <u>American Spectator</u>, 1
         (Feb.), 1, 4.
         Review of <u>Death in the Afternoon</u>.
         Reprinted in <u>The American Spectator Yearbook</u>, New York,
         1934, pp. 231–35.

5   CANBY, HENRY SEIDEL. "Farewell to the Nineties," <u>SRL</u>, 10
         (28 Oct.), 217.
         Review of <u>Winner Take Nothing</u>. Sees Hemingway, like
         Ring Lardner, O. Henry, and Kipling, as creating a world
         of imitators. Admires Hemingway's "extraordinary power of
         observation," but regrets the uses to which that observa-
         tion is put.
         Reprinted in <u>Seven Years' Harvest</u>, New York, Farrar & Rine-
         hart, 1936, pp. 150–54 (<u>See</u> 1936.B5).

6   EASTMAN, MAX. "Bull in the Afternoon," <u>New Republic</u>, 75
         (7 June), 94–97.
         Eastman objects to Hemingway's romanticizing the bull-
         fight, thinking that his attitude doesn't reflect his
         fictional premise of telling things the way they are.
         More important, he sees Hemingway's fascination for the
         fights as a symptom of his own psychosis after the killings
         of World War I. This is the essay which provoked the en-
         counter between Hemingway and Eastman in August, 1937.
         <u>See also</u> Eastman's letter, "Red Blood and Hemingway," <u>New</u>
         <u>Republic</u>, 75 (28 June), 184. The essay was reprinted in
         <u>Art and the Life of Action</u>, New York, Knopf, 1934, pp. 87–
         101 (<u>See</u> 1934.B8); and in McCaffery, pp. 66–75 (<u>See</u>
         1950.A1).

7   EDGAR, PELHAM. <u>The Art of the Novel: From 1700 to the</u>
         <u>Present Time</u>. New York: Macmillan, pp. 338–51.
         In Chapter 28 ("Four American Writers: Anderson, Hem-
         ingway, Dos Passos, Faulkner") Edgar admires Hemingway's
         "inspired animalism," his ability to depict sensation, and
         his dialogue ("Low-pitched though it is, it vibrates with
         strange intensity, and carries a surprisingly large pro-
         portion of the weight of the story").

8 "T. S. E." [T. S. Eliot]. "A Commentary," <u>Criterion</u>, 12
(April), 468–73.
General article. Eliot sees Hemingway, usually considered "hard-boiled," as a "writer of tender sentiment,
and true sentiment."

9 ERSKINE, JOHN. Review of <u>Winner Take Nothing</u>, <u>Brooklyn Daily
Eagle</u> (5 Nov.), Sunday Review, p. 17. Portrait of Hemingway by Henry Strater.
Calls <u>Winner Take Nothing</u> "one of the most disagreeable
books I have ever read . . . stories about derelicts, and
waifs, and ne'er-do-wells." Would rather see Hemingway
paint life "as it is." Grants the influence of his work,
however.

10 FADIMAN, CLIFTON. "Ernest Hemingway: An American Byron,"
<u>Nation</u>, 136 (18 Jan.), 63–64.
Both Byron and Hemingway defy conventional morality,
worship the grotesque, exploit athleticism, prefer romantic
localities, and believe that civilization has failed them.
Hemingway also "puts his faith in simple things."

11 _____. "A Letter to Mr. Hemingway," review of <u>Winner Take
Nothing</u>, <u>New Yorker</u>, 9 (28 Oct.), 74–75.
Criticizes the stories in <u>Winner Take Nothing</u> because they
fail to lead to "anything large or profound." Fadiman is
bored with the same themes and subjects, although he admires the stories and considers them "as honest and un-
compromising as anything you've done."

12 FORD, FORD MADOX. <u>It Was the Nightingale</u>. Philadelphia:
Lippincott.
Scattered references, some relating to the <u>Transatlantic
Review</u>, Paris, 1924.

13 FORD, TERENCE. "Men Without Sales; The Trailers of Mr. Hemingway," <u>Bookman</u>, 76 (Feb.), 140.
Parody.

14 GREGORY, HORACE. Review of <u>Winner Take Nothing</u>, <u>New York
Herald Tribune Books</u> (29 October), p. 5.
Depicts the persona of the stories as "the sensitive,
disciplined, entirely civilized person" that the younger
Hemingway character has become.

15 HART, HENRY. "I Come Not to Bury Hemingway," <u>Contempo</u>, 3
(25 Oct.), 1, 2.

1933

(HART, HENRY)
   Discusses the critical turn against Hemingway's work as
   illustrating "the inevitable human necessity to smash the
   idol that has been worshipped."

16   HICKS, GRANVILLE. The Great Tradition: An Interpretation of
     American Literature since the Civil War. New York: Mac-
     millan.
        Interprets "the Hemingway hero" as dual, the first one
     being "a passive rebel." "Never sure of any code of
     values, he let himself drift . . . but he had his own
     conception of the good life." The second hero figure is
     more a "simple, uncritical barbarian." Warns Hemingway
     that his own moral vision must be clarified or his work
     will eventually carry little meaning; uses Death in the
     Afternoon as an example of a diminished power.

17   KIRSTEIN, LINCOLN. "The Canon of Death," Hound & Horn, 6
     (Jan.-March), 336-41.
        Kirstein finds Hemingway's characters either courageous
     or cowardly.
     Reprinted in McCaffery, pp. 59-65 (See 1950.A1).

18   KRONENBERGER, LOUIS. Review of Winner Take Nothing, New York
     Times Book Review (5 Nov.), p. 6.
        Sees Hemingway as creating the new gangster literature
     (and also "so much melodrama disguised as realism or sen-
     timentality disguised as bravado"). Too little real hu-
     manity exists in Hemingway's writing, however.

19   MATTHEWS, T. S. Review of Winner Take Nothing, New Republic,
     78 (15 Nov.), 24.
        Admires Hemingway as one of the "few exciting writers
     we have" and finds that his chief contribution has been
     his excellent characterization of adolescents.

20   QUENNEL, PETER. Review of Torrents of Spring, New Statesman &
     Nation, 5 (18 Feb.), 196.
        Sees the parody of both Anderson and Hemingway himself,
     and sees Hemingway as "perhaps the finest story-teller now
     writing in English."

21   STEIN, GERTRUDE. "Ernest Hemingway and the Post-War Decade,"
     Atlantic, 152 (Aug.), 197-208.
        Many stories of the Paris years in the mid-twenties, as
     revealing of the author as of Hemingway.
     Reprinted, revised, in The Autobiography of Alice B. Toklas,
     New York, Harcourt Brace, 1933, pp. 261-71; in Selected

(STEIN, GERTRUDE)
  Writings of Gertrude Stein, edited by Carl Van Vechten,
  New York, Random House, 1946, pp. 175-82; in McCaffery,
  pp. 25-33 under the title "Hemingway in Paris." (See
  1950.A1.)

22 TROY, WILLIAM. Review of Winner Take Nothing, Nation, 137
    (15 Nov.), 570.
      Questions whether or not Hemingway will be able to "hold
    the championship much longer" since this collection once
    again is based on "action as catharsis," a technique Troy
    feels is over-used.

1934 A BOOKS - NONE

1934 B SHORTER WRITINGS

1 ANON. Review of Winner Take Nothing, Times (London) (9 Feb.),
   p. 9.
     Sees the "ironic bitterness of 'A Natural History of the
   Dead'" as the key to the collection as a whole, "a somewhat gloomy book." Does admire the spirit of Madame Fon-
   tan and the happier mood of "Wine of Wyoming," and thinks
   the book as a whole "will maintain Mr. Hemingway's high
   reputation."

2 ANON. Review of Winner Take Nothing, TLS (8 Feb.), p. 90.
     Finds the title very appropriate because "a melancholy
   note predominates in these tales." Thinks the collection
   inferior to the two earlier short story books, Men Without
   Women and In Our Time.

3 CANBY, HENRY SEIDEL, AMY LOVEMAN, WILLIAM ROSE BENÉT, et al.,
   eds. Designed for Reading: An Anthology Drawn from the
   Saturday Review of Literature--1924-1934. New York: Mac-
   millan, pp. 221-227.
     "Story of the Brave," review of A Farewell to Arms by
   Canby.
   Reprinted from SRL, 4 (12 Oct. 1929). (See 1929.B11.)

4 BENCHLEY, ROBERT. "Why Does Nobody Collect Me?" Colophon,
   Part 18 (Sept.), four-page article, pages unnumbered.
     Humorous account of Hemingway's inscribing the first
   editions of his work in Benchley's collection.
   Reprinted in Carrousel for Bibliophiles, edited by William
   Targ, New York, Duschnes, 1947, pp. 31-35 (See 1947.B16).

1934

5   CHARTERS, JAMES. <u>This Must Be the Place: Memoirs of Mont-
parnasse</u>. Edited by Morrill Cody. London: Herbert
Joseph.
      Reminiscence of the Paris years, Hemingway and his
friends.

6   CONRAD, LAWRENCE H. "Ernest Hemingway," <u>Landmark</u>, 16 (Aug.),
397–400.
      An analysis of what Conrad sees to be the Hemingway value
system.

7   COWLEY, MALCOLM. <u>Exile's Return: A Narrative of Ideas</u>. New
York: W. W. Norton.
      Discussion of the war and <u>A Farewell to Arms</u>, and of
meeting Hemingway at Pound's apartment in Paris, 1923.
      Revised edition under the sub-title <u>A Literary Odyssey of
the 1920s</u>, New York: Viking Press, 1951.

8   EASTMAN, MAX. <u>Art and the Life of Action: with other essays</u>.
New York: Knopf, pp. 87–101.
      "Bull in the Afternoon," reprinted from <u>New Republic</u>,
75 (7 June 1933). (<u>See</u> 1933.B6.)

9   FORSYTHE, ROBERT. "In this Corner, Mr. Hemingway," <u>New Masses</u>,
13 (27 Nov.), 26.
      Another consideration of Hemingway as "king" of modern
writers. Forsythe includes political sympathies in his
critique.

10   GARNETT, DAVID. Review of <u>Winner Take Nothing</u>, <u>New Statesman
& Nation</u>, 7 (10 Feb.), 192.
      Describes Hemingway as "a master of still life who is at
his best in pictures of game and birds, and in describing
the things that he has actually seen with his own eyes.
His weakness is in dramatic effects." Considers <u>Winner
Take Nothing</u> "a disappointing collection," but finds something beautiful in each story.

11   HARTWICK, HARRY. <u>The Foreground of American Fiction</u>. New
York: American Book, pp. 151–59.
      In "Grace Under Pressure," Hartwick calls Hemingway "an
American Byron." Finds that both in his life and his work,
Hemingway "has resigned himself to stoicism . . . . Courage
is man's last refuge, now that he can no longer believe in
God or reason."

12   JAMESON, STORM. "The Craft of the Novelist," <u>English Review</u>,
58:28–43.

(JAMESON, STORM)
> Jameson thinks Hemingway's appeal lies in stimulating "our crudest interests." His technical skill does not save the writing; "it was not worth doing."

13   LEWIS, WYNDHAM. "The Dumb Ox: A Study of Ernest Hemingway," Life & Letters, 10 (April), 33-45.
> Grants that Hemingway is "a very considerable artist in prose-fiction" but aligns him with Rousseau's Noble Savage, "but a white version, the simple American man." This pose would not be so reprehensible if it were not coupled with the "voice of the 'folk,' of the masses, of those to whom things are done, in contrast to those who have executive will and intelligence." Given Hemingway's subject matter, and his method of approach, Lewis finds his writing a dire commentary on modern civilization.
> Reprinted in American Review, 3 (June 1934), pp. 289-312; in Men Without Art, London: Cassell, 1934, pp. 17-40 (See 1934.B13); and Gellens' Twentieth Century Views of A Farewell to Arms, pp. 72-90 (See 1970.A2).

14   LUCCOCK, HALFORD E. Contemporary American Literature and Religion. Chicago: Willett-Clark.
> Luccock finds a lack of any "meaningful significance" in Hemingway's writing, especially The Sun Also Rises.

15   NATHAN, GEORGE JEAN, ERNEST BOYD, THEODORE DREISER, SHERWOOD ANDERSON, JAMES BRANCH CABELL, and EUGENE O'NEILL, eds. American Spectator Year Book. New York: Stokes, pp. 231-35.
> "Death at 5:45 P.M." by Thomas Beer. Review of Death in the Afternoon.
> Reprinted from American Spectator, 1 (Feb. 1933). (See 1933.B1.)

16   PLOMER, WILLIAM. Review of Winner Take Nothing, Now & Then, No. 47 (Spring), pp. 22-23. Photo of Hemingway.
> Links Hemingway to D. H. Lawrence as a creator of "the literature of protest and escape." Finds Hemingway "the most interesting contemporary American short-story writer . . . adroit, and an expert in brevity."

17   RASCOE, BURTON. Review of Winner Take Nothing, Esquire, 1 (Jan.), 86.
> Considers Hemingway a "genius" in his writing, but something less than that as a human being.

1934

18   ROSENE, M. R. "The Five Best American Books Published since
          1900," Writer, 46 (Oct.), 370-71.
             Selects Men Without Women and refers to "The Undefeated"
          as "the best American short story since Crane's 'Open
          Boat.'"

19   SAROYAN, WILLIAM. The Daring Young Man on the Flying Trapeze
          and other stories. New York: Random House, p. 34.
             References to Green Hills of Africa.

20   STEIN, GERTRUDE. "He and They, Hemingway." Portraits and
          Prayers. New York: Random House, p. 193.
             Reprinted, with an interpretation, in The Novel and the
          World's Dilemma by E. B. Burgum, New York, Oxford Univer-
          sity Press, 1947, pp. 171-72 (See 1947.B2).

1935 A BOOKS - NONE

1935 B SHORTER WRITINGS

   1   ANON. Review of Green Hills of Africa, Newsweek, 6 (26 Oct.),
          39-40.
             The subject matter is saved by Hemingway's immense
          writing skill: "Few books have ever brought African
          scenery so vividly to life."

   2   ANON. Review of Green Hills of Africa, Time, 26 (4 Nov.), 81.
             Photo of Ernest and Pauline Hemingway.
             Finds it "a successful experiment. With its swift nar-
          rative and its human conflicts, it is as carefully orga-
          nized as a good novel."

   3   ADAMS, J. DONALD. Review of They Shall Inherit the Earth,
          Morley Callaghan's novel, New York Times Book Review
          (16 Oct.), p. 6.
             Comments on Hemingway's "unfortunate" influence on
          Callaghan's work.

   4   CANBY, HENRY SEIDEL. "Fiction Tells All," Harper's Magazine,
          171 (Aug.), 308-15.
             General article discussing Hemingway, Faulkner, Wolfe.
          Criticizes Hemingway's fiction because "His characters are
          always afraid, afraid often . . . of being afraid" and
          strike Canby as being definite pathological types. He
          concludes, of all three writers' work, "Great literature
          is not nervous."

5   CHAMBERLAIN, JOHN. Review of <u>Green Hills of Africa</u>, <u>New York</u>
        <u>Times</u> (25 Oct.), p. 19.
            Criticizes the book as being "Byronic posturing," a
        refutation of all Hemingway's talk about seeing things
        "truly." Admires some of the images and analogies, but
        finds the book relatively meaningless.

6   COHN, LOUIS H. "A Note on Ernest Hemingway," <u>Colophon</u>, 1, new
        series (Summer), 119-22.
            A listing of the errors and differences in a dummy copy
        of <u>Death in the Afternoon</u> that had been made to look like
        an advance issue and sold to a collector as such.

7   De VOTO, BERNARD. Review of <u>Green Hills of Africa</u>, <u>SRL</u>, 12
        (26 Oct.), 5. Cover photo of Hemingway.
            "A pretty small book for a big man to write." Dislikes
        the book because it is not a work of the imagination, and
        because the sentence length and structure is deficient.
        Reprinted in <u>Forays and Rebuttals</u>, Boston, Little, Brown,
        1936, pp. 340-44 (<u>See</u> 1936.B7).

8   FADIMAN, CLIFTON. Review of <u>Green Hills of Africa</u>, <u>New Yorker</u>,
        11 (2 Nov.), 96, 98.
            Ambivalent review of the mixture of personal, literary,
        and hunting talk that comprises <u>Green Hills of Africa</u>.

9   FORSYTHE, ROBERT [pseudonym of Kyle Crichton]. <u>Redder Than the</u>
        <u>Rose</u>. New York: Covici-Friede, pp. 44-48.
            "In This Corner, Mr. Hemingway," a reply to Hemingway's
        article in <u>Esquire</u>, 2 (Dec. 1934) regarding Heywood Broun.

10 FRANK, WALDO. "Values of the Revolutionary Writer." <u>New</u>
        <u>Masses</u>, 15 (7 May), 19.
            Sees Hemingway as an example of the "over-simplification"
        and "bravado" in American fiction.

11 HAIGHT, ANNE LYON. <u>Banned Books: Informal Notes on Some</u>
        <u>Books Banned for Various Reasons at Various Times and</u>
        <u>in Various Places</u>. New York: Bowker. Second edition;
        1955.
            List of Hemingway's work banned in the U. S. and abroad.
        Notes that in 1938, <u>To Have and Have Not</u> was the only book
        banned in the U. S.

12 HARRIS, PAUL. "Please, Mr. Ernest Hemingway!: A Letter,"
        <u>American Criterion</u>, 1 (Dec.), 13-16.
            Regarding Hemingway's <u>Esquire</u> articles.

1935

13   HATCHER, HARLAN. <u>Creating the Modern American Novel</u>. New
       York: Farrar & Rinehart, pp. 228-33.
       Discusses Hemingway as "the most brilliant novelist of
      the War Generation." Admires <u>The Sun Also Rises</u> because
      "matter and mood go hand in hand with the style" and <u>A
      Farewell to Arms</u> because both the war story and the ro-
      mance are beautifully done.

14   HICKS, GRANVILLE. "Small Game Hunting," <u>New Masses</u>, 17
       (19 Nov.), 23.
      Praises Hemingway as being "the clearest and strongest
      non-revolutionary writer of his generation," but dislikes
      <u>Green Hills of Africa</u> because of its trivial subject mat-
      ter. "If he would just let himself look squarely at the
      contemporary American scene, he would be bound to grow."
      Reprinted in <u>Granville Hicks in the New Masses</u>, edited by
      Jack Alan Robbins. Port Washington, N. Y.: Kennikat
      Press, 1974, pp. 114-16 (<u>See</u> 1974.B12).

15   HOFMANN, W. J. V. Contemporary Portraits, 3: "Ernest Heming-
       way," <u>Literary America</u>, 2 (Feb.), 111-13.
      Caricature of Hemingway by Herbert Fouts.

16   KASHKEEN, J. IVAN. "Ernest Hemingway: A Tragedy of Crafts-
       manship," <u>International Literature</u>, No. 4 (May), pp. 72-90.
      Kashkeen appreciates the delicacy of Hemingway's style
      in relation to his themes ("Hemingway shows us how compli-
      cated he is by his very attempts to be simple") and main-
      tains that the meaning of his work can be found only in an
      overview. Separate works form "a natural cycle," with only
      the earlier works marked by humor.
      Reprinted in part in McCaffery, pp. 76-108 (<u>See</u> 1950.A1).

17   MATTHEWS, T. S. Review of <u>Green Hills of Africa</u>, <u>New Republic</u>,
       85 (27 Nov.), pp. 79-80.
      "It used to be pretty exciting, sitting down to read a
      new book by Hemingway, but now it's damn near alarming."
      Dislikes the apparent casualness and tendency to "gossip"
      in print evident in both <u>Death in the Afternoon</u> and <u>Green
      Hills of Africa</u>.

18   POORE, C. G. Review of <u>Green Hills of Africa</u>, <u>New York Times
       Book Review</u> (27 Oct.), pp. 3, 27.
      Likes the mixture of personal commentary with the story
      of big-game hunting.

19   PRESTON, JOHN HYDE. "A Conversation," <u>Atlantic</u>, 156 (Aug.),
       187-94.

(PRESTON, JOHN HYDE)
Interview with Gertrude Stein, May 3, 1935, during which she said that Hemingway was "not really good after 1925." "Hemingway did not lose it; he threw it away," as he "became obsessed by sex and violent death."

20 SAMUELSON, ARNOLD. "Beating Sharks to a Marlin," Outdoor Life, 75 (June). Photos.
Description of several fishing trips with Hemingway, in marlin waters off Cuba.

21 SHEEAN, VINCENT. Personal History. New York: Doubleday, Doran, pp. 280-81.
Analysis of Hemingway's writing as the aftermath of a meeting with him in Berlin, 1927.

22 SPENDER, STEPHEN. The Destructive Element: A Study of Modern Writers and Beliefs. London: Cape.
Sees even Hemingway's fiction sharing Henry James' puritan view of the past; agrees with Wyndham Lewis' concept that the Hemingway hero is a "dumb ox" because he is acted upon rather than originating the action.

23 STEARNS, HAROLD E. The Street I Know. New York: Furman.
Autobiographical description of Hemingway in Paris in the 1920's.

24 VAN DOREN, CARL. Review of Green Hills of Africa, New York Herald Tribune Books (27 Oct.), p. 3.
Likes the book because it proves Hemingway's sensitivity and subtlety. The personal reflections mar the total effect, but the major parts of the book are excellent.

25 WEEKS, EDWARD. Review of Green Hills of Africa, Atlantic, 46 (Nov.), 30.
Considers the book "a self-portrait" which is "masterful." Enjoys the philosophy of the writer, the landscape passages, and the natural dialogue.

26 WILSON, EDMUND. "Letter to the Russians about Hemingway," New Republic, 85 (11 Dec.), 135-36.
Considers Green Hills of Africa an "instructive experiment" (but a disappointment to Wilson). He wonders whether "something frightful seems to happen to Hemingway as soon as he begins to write in first person--" in that he loses his ability to criticize his own work and becomes maudlin. Wilson continues his argument with Kashkeen about the "moral importance" of Hemingway's work, arguing

1935

(WILSON, EDMUND)
positively that there is a definite moral commitment in
the fiction.
Reprinted in The Shores of Light, New York, Farrar, Straus,
and Young, pp. 616-29 (See 1952.B76).

1936 A BOOKS - NONE

1936 B SHORTER WRITINGS

1   ANON. Review of Green Hills of Africa, Times (London)
         (3 April), p. 10.
         Sees the book as presenting Hemingway's own personal en-
      joyment in living, not only during his time in Africa, but
      elsewhere.

2   ANON. Review of Green Hills of Africa, TLS (4 April), p. 291.
         Likes the book for its four-part design, "each written
      in a rather different mood and tempo." Finds it "the ex-
      pression of a deep enjoyment and appreciation of being
      alive in Africa."

3   BISHOP, JOHN PEALE. "Homage to Hemingway," New Republic, 89
         (11 Nov.), 39-42.
         Recollection of his early meeting with Hemingway in 1922,
      and of the importance of Hemingway's relationship with
      Pound.
         Reprinted in After the Genteel Tradition, edited by
      Malcolm Cowley, New York, W. W. Norton, 1937, pp. 186-201
      (See 1937.B23); in The Collected Essays of John Peale
      Bishop, New York, Scribner's, 1948, pp. 37-46 (See
      1948.B2); and in the New Republic, 131 (22 Nov. 1954),
      109-11.

4   BRUMBACK, THEODORE. "With Hemingway Before A Farewell to Arms,"
         Kansas City Star (6 Dec.), pp. 1 C, 2 C. Photos.
         Recollection of being friends with Hemingway when both
      were reporters on the Kansas City Star. Brumback sailed
      with Hemingway to France, and visited him in the Milan
      hospital.

5   CANBY, HENRY SEIDEL. Seven Years' Harvest: Notes on Contempo-
         rary Literature. New York: Farrar & Rinehart.
         Includes a discussion of Hemingway's style from "Fiction
      Tells All," Harper's Magazine, 171 (Aug., 1935), 150-54
      (See 1935.B4); and "Farewell to the Nineties," review of
      Winner Take Nothing, from SRL, 10 (28 Oct. 1933). (See
      1933.B5.)

6   COOK, C. N. "The Silver Parade," Field & Stream, 41 (June),
       42, 70-71.
          Tuna fishing off Cuba with Hemingway; adventures with
       two tiger sharks.

7   De VOTO, BERNARD. Forays and Rebuttals. Boston: Little
       Brown, pp. 340-44.
          Review of Green Hills of Africa from SRL, 12 (26 Oct.
       1935). (See 1935.B7.)

8   FLEMING, PETER. Review of Green Hills of Africa, Now & Then,
       No. 53 (Spring), pp. 18-19. Photo.
          Admires the "savage poetry" of the account which does
       not romanticize either hunters or hunting.

9   GARNETT, DAVID. Review of Green Hills of Africa, New States-
       man & Nation, 11 (4 April), 529.
          Compares this book with Death in the Afternoon and finds
       it inadequate, partly because of what he terms "the
       author's horizon."

10 LAWRENCE, D. H. Phoenix: The Posthumous Papers of D. H.
       Lawrence, edited by Edward D. McDonald. London: Heine-
       mann, p. 365.
          Review of In Our Time, reprinted from the Calendar of
       Modern Letters, 4 (April 1927). (See 1927.B15.)

11 LEWIS, SINCLAIR. "Rambling Thoughts on Literature as a Busi-
       ness," Yale Literary Magazine, 101 (Feb.), 43-47. Cen-
       tennial Number.
          General article with some incidental criticism of Green
       Hills of Africa and "Lines to a College Professor," a poem
       on Hemingway's use of four-letter words. The verse is re-
       printed in Sinclair Lewis: An American Life, Mark Schorer,
       New York, McGraw-Hill, 1961, p. 617.

12 _____. Short parody of Green Hills of Africa, "Literary
       Felonies: Obtaining Game under False Pretensions," SRL,
       14 (3 Oct.), 3.

13 McINTYRE, O. O. "New Eyes on Key West," Kansas City Times
       (2 June), p. 18.
          Description of Hemingway's home in Key West, his working
       habits, and fishing trips.

14 SLOCOMBE, GEORGE. The Tumult and the Shouting. London:
       Heinemann.

1936

(SLOCOMBE, GEORGE)
Reminisces about meeting Hemingway in 1922 en route to the Genoa Peace Conference, and a visit made by Hemingway, Max Eastman, and himself to Max Beerbohm, in Rapallo, Italy.

15   SYLVESTER, HARRY. "Ernest Hemingway—A Note," Commonweal, 25 (30 Oct.), 10-12.
Regarding Hemingway's conversion to Catholicism and his boxing and war experiences.

16   TAYLOR, WALTER F. A History of American Letters. New York: American Book.
Bibliography of critical studies of Hemingway's work compiled by Harry Harkwick, pp. 596-97.

17   WIMBERLY, LOWRY CHARLES. "Hemingway and Horatio Alger, Jr.," Prairie Schooner, 10 (Fall), 208-11.
Compares passages from "The Killers" with Jed, the Poor House Boy, to establish Alger's influence on Hemingway's style.

1937 A   BOOKS - NONE

1937 B   SHORTER WRITINGS

1   ANON. "Creator's Congress," Time, 29 (21 June), 79-80. Photo.
Report on the Second Writers' Congress, New York, June 4, 1937, including mention of Hemingway's nervousness before his speech. As he spoke of the Spanish Civil War, however, "he warmed up eloquently." For Walter Duranty's letter about the confusion between his and Hemingway's photos, See Time, 30 (12 July), 8.

2   ANON. "Eastman Claims Title," New York Times (16 Aug.), p. 21.
Eastman gives his version of his encounter with Hemingway.

3   ANON. "A Farewell to the Lead-off Man," Esquire, 7 (June), 5.
Regarding Hemingway's writing in the early issues of Esquire.

4   ANON. "Hemingway Links Fate of Democracy with Spain," Los Angeles Times (12 July), p. 1. Photo.
Interview with Hemingway in Los Angeles where the film The Spanish Earth was to be shown for the benefit of the Spanish ambulance corps.

5   ANON. "Hemingway Sees Defeat of Franco," New York Times
         (19 May), p. 10.
            New York interview as Hemingway returned home from Spain.

6   ANON. "Hemingway Slaps Eastman in Face/ Clash in Publisher's
         Office Has to Do with 'Bull' and 'Death' Both 'in After-
         noon,'" New York Times (14 Aug.), p. 15.
            Hemingway discusses his fight with Eastman on August 11
         over the latter's essay "Bull in the Afternoon." See also
         Eastman's Great Companions, New York, Farrar, Straus, and
         Cudahy, 1959, pp. 65-67 (See 1959.B14).

7   ANON. "Hemingway Writes Play in Shell-Rocked Madrid," New
         York Times (15 Nov.), p. 2.
            Hemingway's The Fifth Column was finished here (Madrid)
         today in the Florida Hotel, despite frequent Rebel shells.

8   ANON. "Hot Observation Spot," New York Times (16 Nov.), p. 22.
            Concerning The Fifth Column.

9   ANON. Interview, San Francisco Chronicle (15 July), p. 13.
         Photo.
            Interview with Hemingway on his first visit to San Fran-
         cisco.

10   ANON. Item, Fortune, 16 (Dec.), 224. Photo.
            Brief item about the critics' reception of To Have and
         Have Not.

11   ANON. Item, Newsweek, 10 (21 Aug.), 4. Photo.
            The Hemingway-Eastman encounter.

12   ANON. Item, Time, 30 (23 Aug.), 66.
            The Hemingway-Eastman fight. For John O'Hara's letter
         regarding this, See Time, 30 (6 Sept.), p. 8.

13   ANON. "Literary Slug Fests," New York Times (17 Aug.), p. 18.
            The Hemingway-Eastman meeting.

14   ANON. Review of the film, The Spanish Earth, Time, 30 (23 Aug.),
         48-49.
            Comments on the many famous contributors to the film,
         which this viewer considers fine.

14a ANON. Cover story and review of To Have and Have Not, Time,
         30 (18 Oct.), 79-85. Cover painting of Hemingway by Waldo
         Peirce. Photos.

1937

(ANON.)
A "disconnected and episodic" story whose main character, Harry Morgan, is "his most thoroughly consistent, deeply understandable character."

15   ANON. Review of <u>To Have and Have Not</u>, <u>Times</u> (London) (8 Oct.), p. 20.
Considers Morgan "a plain and unscrupulous rascal" whose adventures, however, are "wonderful . . . the action has an excitement that the novel as a whole lacks."

16   ANON. Review of <u>To Have and Have Not</u>, <u>TLS</u> (9 Oct.), p. 733.
Hemingway's fictional gifts are here in full force. "Within the narrow limits which Mr. Hemingway's scale of values imposes on his material, this is an absorbing and moving story."

17   ANON. "Reviving the practice of salutes to the living," <u>Esquire</u>, 7 (Feb.), 5, 28.
Tribute to Hemingway.

18   ADAMS, J. DONALD. Review of <u>To Have and Have Not</u>, <u>New York Times Book Review</u> (17 Oct.), p. 2.
Thinks <u>To Have and Have Not</u> is "distinctly inferior" to <u>A Farewell to Arms</u>.

19   "E. B." [EARLE BIRNEY]. "The Importance of Being Ernest Hemingway," <u>Canadian Forum</u>, 17 (Dec.), 322–23.
Parody review of <u>To Have and Have Not</u>.

20   BISHOP, JOHN PEALE. "The Missing All," <u>Virginia Quarterly Review</u>, 13 (Winter), 106–21.
Sees Hemingway's prose style as illustrative of his moral stability in a chaotic world. Excellent comments on Hemingway's identity as a Middle-Westerner, as one who had understood death, and who crafted his prose to convey that understanding. Includes his anecdote of Pound's taking him to meet Hemingway.
Reprinted in <u>The Collected Essays of John Peale Bishop</u>, New York, Scribner's, 1948, pp. 66–77 (<u>See</u> 1948.B2); in McCaffery, pp. 292–307 (<u>See</u> 1950.A1).

21   CALVERTON, V. F. "Ernest Hemingway: <u>Primevalite</u>," <u>Modern Monthly</u>, 10 (Dec.), 6–7.
Sees Hemingway's strength in the fact that he is in such complete touch with his own instinctive responses to life.

22   CONNOLLY, CYRIL. Review of <u>To Have and Have Not</u>, <u>New Statesman</u>
      <u>& Nation</u>, 14 (16 Oct.), 606.
         Sees the novel as no advance, almost a parody of his
      characteristic style.

23   COWLEY, MALCOLM, ed. <u>After the Genteel Tradition: American</u>
      <u>Writers Since 1910</u>. New York: W. W. Norton, pp. 186–201.
      Reissued, Carbondale: Southern Illinois University Press,
      1964, Crosscurrents Modern Critiques, pp. 147–58.
         "Homage to Hemingway" by John Peale Bishop, reprinted
      from the <u>New Republic</u>, 89 (11 Nov. 1936). (<u>See</u> 1936.B3.)

24   COWLEY, MALCOLM. "Hemingway: Work in Progress," <u>New Republic</u>,
      92 (20 Oct.), 305–06.
         Review of <u>To Have and Have Not</u>. Finds that <u>To Have and</u>
      <u>Have Not</u> "contains some of the best writing he has ever
      done" but "as a whole it lacks unity and sureness of effect."

25   De VOTO, BERNARD. Editorial, "Tiger, Tiger!" <u>SRL</u>, 16
      (16 Oct.), 8.
         Faulting Hemingway's characters for having a lack of
      consciousness, including those in <u>To Have and Have Not</u>.
      Reprinted in <u>Minority Report</u>, Boston, Little, Brown, 1940,
      pp. 257–61 (<u>See</u> 1940.B17).

26   FADIMAN, CLIFTON. Review of <u>To Have and Have Not</u>, <u>New Yorker</u>,
      13 (16 Oct.), 100–101.
         Admires a few scenes (the bedroom dialogue between Mor-
      gan and his wife for one) but dislikes the novel as a
      whole.

27   FERGUSON, OTIS. Review of the film, <u>The Spanish Earth</u>, <u>New</u>
      <u>Republic</u>, 92 (1 Sept.), 103.
         Not a great film, but a "combination of experience and
      intuition" directs the viewer's attention to the truths
      inherent in it.

28   FORD, COREY. " . . . And So They Lived Happily Ever After.
      Part IV; In the manner of <u>Death in the Afternoon</u>, <u>Death</u>
      <u>Without Women</u>, <u>Death in Esquire</u>. Mr. Ernest Hemingway,"
      <u>Scribner's Magazine</u>, 101 (May), 31.
         Parody.

29   GIBBS, WOLCOTT. <u>Bed of Neuroses</u>. New York: Dodd, Mead,
      pp. 261–65.
         "Death in the Rumble Seat" (With the Usual Apologies to
      Ernest Hemingway) from <u>New Yorker</u>, 8 (8 Oct. 1932). (<u>See</u>
      1932.B13.)

1937

30   HICKS, GRANVILLE. "Hemingway's Pirate," New Masses, 25
        (26 Oct.), 22-23.
           Review of To Have and Have Not. Sees Morgan as Heming-
        way's "most completely realized character," partly because
        "he is placed in a recognizable world." Hicks finds To
        Have and Have Not the fruit of Hemingway's social maturity.
        Reprinted in Granville Hicks in The New Masses, edited by
        Jack Alan Robbins. Port Washington, New York: Kennikat
        Press, 1974, pp. 117-19 (See 1974.B12).

31   KAZIN, ALFRED. Review of To Have and Have Not, New York
        Herald Tribune Books (17 Oct.), p. 3. Photo by Joris
        Ivens.
           Stylistically less sure of himself, "but a good deal
        more intense." Kazin describes the book as "troubled,
        sketchy, feverishly brilliant and flat by turns," pointing
        out that this is the first novel Hemingway had written
        about his own country.

32   KRONENBERGER, LOUIS. Review of To Have and Have Not, Nation,
        145 (23 Oct.), 439-40.
           "Despite a living hero and a handful of superb scenes,
        it is a book with neither poise nor integration, and with
        shocking lapses from professional skill." Objects chiefly
        to the division in the middle, as if Hemingway had realized
        the Morgan story would not stand alone, and had to go back
        and patch other elements onto it.

33   LEWIS, SINCLAIR. Review of To Have and Have Not, Newsweek, 10
        (18 Oct.), 34.
           "Not a novel but a group of thinly connected tales."
        Lewis compares To Have and Have Not ("thin screaming")
        with A Farewell to Arms and comes away disappointed, es-
        pecially with Hemingway's trite moralizing.

34   LOGGINS, VERNON. I Hear America . . . Literature in the
        United States Since 1900. New York: Crowell, pp. 134-38,
        "Dominant Primordial: Frank Norris, Theodore Dreiser,
        Ernest Hemingway and Thomas Wolfe."
           Admires Hemingway's stripped style and the outlook which
        it reflects (Loggins sees it as not pessimistic). Con-
        siders A Farewell To Arms "a very great novel."

35   McCOLE, C. JOHN. "Ernest Hemingway: Spokesman for His Genera-
        tion," Lucifer at Large. London: Longmans, Green,
        pp. 153-72.
           A study of Hemingway's style in A Farewell to Arms and
        "Big Two-Hearted River."
           Bibliographical references.

36   McKAY, CLAUDE. <u>A Long Way From Home</u>. New York: Furman
       pp. 249-52.
       Discusses Hemingway's work and its impact on other
       writers after the publication of <u>in our time</u> in Paris,
       1924.

37   "MacLeish on Spain," <u>Cinema Arts</u>, 1 (Sept.), 59, 104.
       Interview with Archibald MacLeish about the film <u>The
       Spanish Earth</u>.

38   McMANUS, JOHN T. "Down to Earth in Spain," <u>New York Times</u>
       (25 July), pp. x, 4.
       Interview with Joris Ivens regarding the filming of <u>The
       Spanish Earth</u>.

39   "J. T. M." [JOHN T. McMANUS]. Review of the film, <u>The Spanish
       Earth</u>, <u>New York Times</u> (21 Aug.), p. 7.
       Admires the photography (its documentary method) more
       than Hemingway's narrative, which may be "superb" but also
       "a definitely propagandist effort."

40   McMANUS, JOHN T. Review of <u>The Spanish Earth</u>, <u>New York Times</u>
       (22 Aug.), pp. x, 3.
       Comments on Hemingway's "sardonic, vengeful narration,
       reducing the issues to one-syllable dimensions."

41   MUIR, EDWIN. Review of <u>To Have and Have Not</u>, <u>Listener</u>, 18
       (27 Oct.), 925.
       "The contrast between the haves and the have nots is
       unconvincing. But the story of Harry himself is extra-
       ordinary simply as a story."

42   MULLER, HERBERT J. "Apostles of the Lost Generation: Huxley,
       Hemingway," <u>Modern Fiction: A Study of Values</u>. New York:
       Funk & Wagnalls, pp. 383-403.
       Considers <u>The Sun Also Rises</u> "simply a record of a sick
       and lost generation. Its characters have a moral code
       . . . but no faith, no purpose or force to give meaning to
       their existence." Worries about Hemingway's "excessive
       romanticism" and "sterility."

43   PAUL, ELLIOT. "Hemingway and the Critics," <u>SRL</u>, 17 (6 Nov.),
       3-4. Photo.
       A defense of Hemingway against the critics' reception to
       <u>To Have and Have Not</u>. Sees that the book "means a great
       deal to Hemingway" and that he must be "dangerously fond"
       of his characters. Affirms that Hemingway is in many ways
       a positive writer.

1937

(PAUL, ELLIOT)
Reprinted in McCaffery, pp. 109-13 (See 1950.A1). For
Herschel Brickell's reply, see SRL, 17 (20 Nov.), p. 9.

44 PRITCHETT, V. S. Review of To Have and Have Not, Now & Then,
No. 58 (Winter), pp. 29-30.
Finds the weakness in the novel to be Hemingway's own
refusal to think about the social situation underlying the
novel, and the life of every citizen.

45 RAHV, PHILIP. "The Social Muse and the Great Kudu," Partisan
Review, 4 (Dec.), 62-64.
Review of To Have and Have Not. Despite some "superb"
writing, the novel is not successful. Sees the chief dif-
ference between the smugglers and the rich, as Hemingway
presents them, to be the fact that the rich were successful in their buccaneering.

46 REID, JOHN T. "Spain As Seen By Some Contemporary American
Writers," Hispania, 20 (May), 139-50.
General.

47 ROOT, E. MERRILL. "Aesthetic Puritans," Christian Century,
54 (25 Aug.), 1043-45.
Couples Hemingway with H. L. Mencken as an "aesthetic
Puritan," complete with the "old Calvinistic sense of pre-
destination and doom." Even the creative energy is "bleak
and hard with vital thrift" (as Hemingway's style shows).
Fascination with death is also an index of Puritanism.

48 SMITH, FRANCIS. "Hemingway Curses, Kisses, Reads At Sylvia
Beach Literary Session," New York Herald Tribune, European
Edition (14 May), p. 5.
Hemingway read "Fathers and Sons" for the gathering on
May 12, 1937. See facsimile inscription in Winner Take
Nothing, Princeton Alumni Weekly, 65 (16 Feb.), 13.

49 STEVENS, GEORGE. Review of To Have and Have Not, SRL, 16 (16
Oct.), 6-7.
"The idea of the book seems to be that you either live
dangerously or you walk around dead. This idea doesn't
have to be phony . . . and it isn't phony in Hemingway;
but it is less than profound and short of impressive."

50 WEEKS, EDWARD. Review of To Have and Have Not, Atlantic, 160
(Nov.), front section.
Compares Hemingway to Hogarth with his presentation of
brutality and social satire. Finds the book "swift-moving
and wholly absorbing."

51 WRIGHT, DONALD M. "A Mid-Western Ad Man Remembers," <u>Advertis-ing & Selling</u>, 28 (25 March), 54. Photo.
Recalls the 1920 period in Chicago when Hemingway was assistant editor of the <u>Co-operative Commonwealth</u>.

52 ZABEL, MORTON DAUWEN, ed. <u>Literary Opinion in America</u>. New York: Harper, pp. 506-11. Second edition, revised, 1951.
Pp. 444-63: "Hemingway" by Robert Penn Warren (<u>See</u> 1947.B18). "Ernest Hemingway: A Farewell to Spain" by Malcolm Cowley, from <u>New Republic</u>, 73 (30 Nov. 1932).
(<u>See</u> 1932.B10.)

1938 A BOOKS - NONE

1938 B SHORTER WRITINGS

1 ANON. "Adjournment in Book Trial," <u>Detroit News</u> (14 May), p. 2.
Alvin C. Hamer, Detroit book dealer, tries to have the prosecutor's office and the Police Department enjoined from interfering with the sale of <u>To Have and Have Not</u>.

2 ANON. "Hamer Fights Hemingway Ban," <u>Publishers' Weekly</u>, 133 (14 May), 1935.
Covering Hamer's efforts to obtain an injunction to end the ban on <u>To Have and Have Not</u>.

3 ANON. "Hemingway Back from Spain," <u>New York Times</u> (28 Jan.), p. 19.
Interview with Hemingway in Miami.

4 ANON. "Hemingway Back, Sees Food Key to Spanish War," <u>New York Herald Tribune</u> (25 Nov.), p. 3.
Interview with Hemingway in New York.

5 ANON. "Hemingway Returns Tired of War in Spain," <u>New York Times</u> (31 May), p. 12.
Interview with Hemingway in New York.

6 ANON. Item, <u>Publishers' Weekly</u>, 133 (25 June), 2434.
Item about the judge's ruling on <u>To Have and Have Not</u> in Detroit.

7 ANON. Item, <u>Time</u>, 31 (2 May), 24.
Production plans for Hemingway's play <u>The Fifth Column</u>.

1938

8   ANON. "Prosecutor Wins Hemingway Battle," Detroit News
        (19 June), p. 8.
            The judge refused to issue a temporary injunction re-
        straining the Prosecutor and Police from interfering with
        the sale of To Have and Have Not in Detroit.

9   ANON. Review of First 49, Time, 32 (17 Oct.), 75.
            Admires "The Short Happy Life of Francis Macomber" as an
        embodiment of his credo; finds The Fifth Column, in compar-
        ison, "ragged and confused."

10 BAKER, HOWARD. "The Contemporary Short Story," Southern Re-
        view, 3 (Winter), 576-96.
            Of Hemingway's work, discusses "The Snows of Kilimanjaro."

11 BLIXEN-FINECKE, BROR VON. Translated from the Swedish Nyama
        by F. H. Lyon. African Hunter. New York: Knopf.
            Reminiscence about deep-sea fishing with Hemingway,
        during a month spent at Bimini in 1935.

12 BROOKS, VAN WYCK, ARCHIBALD MacLEISH, and THORNTON WILDER.
        Letter to the editor, Nation, 147 (23 July), 96.
            Protesting the banned To Have and Have Not: "the charge
        of obscenity is frivolous." Questions the Detroit Council
        of Catholic Organizations for its part in the injunction.

13 BURGUM, EDWIN BERRY. "Hemingway's Development," New Masses,
        29 (22 Nov.), 21-24.
            Review of First 49. Finds the play interesting for the
        psychological development of the hero; similarly, sees the
        collection of stories as "the record of the road that Hem-
        ingway has traveled through the confusions of modern life
        to a clearer insight into the relation between democracy
        and art."

14 COHN, LOUIS H. "Collecting Hemingway," Avocations, 1 (Jan.),
        346-55. Photos.
            Discussion of rare items and first editions.

15 CONNOLLY, CYRIL. Enemies of Promise. London: Routledge.
            Discussion of Hemingway's style (his "difficulties"
        stem from "the limitations of realism") and his use of the
        colloquial language, which produces work which is "the
        antithesis of fine writing."

16 COWLEY, MALCOLM. "Hemingway in Madrid," New Republic, 96
        (2 Nov.), 367-68.
            Review of First 49. Notes that Hemingway's violence may

(COWLEY, MALCOLM)
    have seemed excessive during the decade that followed
    World War I, but now, once again, "it seems a simple and
    accurate description of the world in which we live."

17   DAVIS, ELMER. Review of First 49, SRL, 18 (15 Oct.), 6.
        Admires the play, and thinks of the story collection
    that "nobody else now living could show forty-nine stories
    that good."

18   FADIMAN, CLIFTON. Review of First 49, New Yorker, 14
        (22 Oct.), 82.
        Considers the play "exciting reading. Some scenes will
    make you gasp and a few, I regret to say, may make you
    snicker." The stories show that Hemingway "is the best
    short-story writer now using English."

*19   FAGIN, BRYLLION. "The Psychological Moment," Step Ladder
        (Chicago), 24 (May), 101-07.
        Unseen.

20   JACK, PETER MONRO. Review of First 49, New York Times Book
        Review (23 Oct.), p. 4.
        Finds the play less than stage-worthy. Senses in the
    stories a more human interest in character, rather than
    method and technique.

21   KAZIN, ALFRED. Review of First 49, New York Herald Tribune
        Books (16 Oct.), p. 5.
        Considers The Fifth Column "an interesting Hemingway
    period piece," but laments Hemingway's own ignorance of
    contemporary drama.

22   McALMON, ROBERT. Being Geniuses Together: An Autobiography.
        London: Secker & Warburg.
        Descriptions of meeting Hemingway, of traveling with him
    to Madrid in 1924, and other Paris occasions.
    Reprinted in McAlmon and the Lost Generation, A Self-
    Portrait, edited by Robert Knoll. Lincoln: University of
    Nebraska, 1962, pp. 225-40. (See 1962.B33.) See also
    McAlmon and Kay Boyle, Being Geniuses Together, 1920-1930.
    Garden City, New York: Doubleday, 1968 (See 1968.B35).

23   MARSH, W. WARD. "One Moment, Please!" Cleveland Plain Dealer
        (24 July), p. 9B.
        Article about Jasper Wood's publication of The Spanish
    Earth and Hemingway's objections to the book.
    Reprinted as pamphlet by the J. B. Savage Co., Cleveland,
    1938.

1938

24 MATTHEWS, HERBERT L. Two Wars and More to Come. New York:
    Carrick & Evans.
       Personal narratives of the Spanish Civil War by the
    foreign correspondent for the New York Times.

25 MIRRIELEES, EDITH. "Those College Writing Courses," SRL, 17
    (15 Jan.), 3-4, 16.
       Discusses the four major influences evident in writing
    courses: O. Henry, Joseph Conrad, Katherine Mansfield,
    and Hemingway. "So far, no writer later than Hemingway
    has established an influence even to be compared with him."

26 PATER, ALAN F. and MILTON LANDAU, eds. What They Said in 1937:
    The Yearbook of Oral Opinion. New York: Paebar, p. 89.
       Quotes Hemingway on the probable duration of the Spanish
    Civil War, from a New York Times interview, May 19, 1937.

27 SCHWARTZ, DELMORE. "Ernest Hemingway's Literary Situation,"
    Southern Review, 3 (Spring), 769-82.
       Schwartz opens his essay by pointing out Hemingway's
    strengths—his style, his accurate portrayal of sensa-
    tions—but faults To Have and Have Not because in it Hem-
    ingway's themes have changed, but his method and style have
    not. The result, according to Schwartz, is that "To Have
    and Have Not is a stupid and foolish book, a disgrace to a
    good writer."
    Reprinted in McCaffery, pp. 114-29 (See 1950.A1).

28 SOLOW, HERBERT. "Substitution at Left Tackle: Hemingway for
    Dos Passos," Partisan Review, 4 (April), 62-64.
       Review of each man's political activities between 1926
    and the present, partly with regard to Communist party
    alliances.

29 STEFFENS, LINCOLN. The Letters of Lincoln Steffens: 1920-
    1936. Vol. 2. Edited by Ella Winter and Granville Hicks.
    New York: Harcourt, Brace.
       Letter to the Committee of Admissions of The Players
    Club, New York, 1930, recommending Hemingway as a member.

30 TINKER, F. G., Jr. Some Still Live. New York: Funk &
    Wagnalls.
       Remembrance of Hemingway in Spain, 1937.

31 WILSON, EDMUND. "Hemingway and the Wars," Nation, 147
    (10 Dec.), 628, 630.
       Review of First 49 and "The Spanish War" dispatches.
    Discounts the play, but is enthusiastic about the four new

(WILSON, EDMUND)
 short stories "which are among the best that Hemingway has
written. 'The Short Happy Life of Francis Macomber' seems
to me to be one of his masterpieces."

1939 A BOOKS - NONE

1939 B SHORTER WRITINGS

1 ANON. Review of <u>First 49</u>, <u>TLS</u> (17 June), p. 359.
  Considers Hemingway "a great technician" but echoes the
"dumb ox" censure, "what the dumb ox says is so peculiarly
uninteresting." "So much blood is tedious." Prefers
"Hills Like White Elephants" and "Big Two-Hearted River."

2 ANON. Review of <u>First 49</u>, <u>TLS</u> (1 July), p. 385.
  Mixed review of the play, pointing out that the espionage
activities, despite the title, hold second place to the
action relating to the war.

3 ADAMS, J. DONALD. "Ernest Hemingway," <u>English Journal</u>, 28
 (Feb.), 87-94.
  "No American writer of his generation has been more
talked about than Ernest Hemingway." Adams admires his
mastery of style and "remarkable talent," but questions
"his attitude toward life," "the mental and emotional
bases on which his work is built." Admires the short
stories most, and thinks <u>The Sun Also Rises</u> has no "universal or lasting value."

4 BESSIE, ALVAH. <u>Men in Battle</u>. New York: Scribner's,
 pp. 135-37.
  Tells of meeting Hemingway and Herbert Matthews during
April 1938 in Spain.

5 BURNETT, WHIT. <u>The Literary Life and the Hell with It</u>. New
 York: Harper.
  Recalls Hemingway's speech for the American Writers'
Congress, 1937, and the relationship between William
Saroyan and Hemingway.

6 CALVERTON, V. F. "Steinbeck, Hemingway and Faulkner," <u>Modern</u>
 <u>Quarterly</u>, 11 (Fall), 36-44.
  Says that Hemingway lost his influence when he "leaped
onto the communist band-wagon," but is still "the most influential writer in the U. S. today" because of his incredible originality.

1939

7   MALONEY, RUSSELL. "A Footnote to a Footnote," New Yorker, 15
    (15 July), 26.
        Regarding Hemingway's footnote on humanism in "A Natural
    History of the Dead," the First 49, p. 543.

8   MELLERS, W. H. Review of First 49, Scrutiny, 8 (Dec.), 335-44.
        Mixed review, regretting the loss of Hemingway's full
    potential, but admiring the qualities that his work does
    evince.

9   MONCHAK, STEPHEN J. Interview with Herbert L. Matthews,
    Editor and Publisher, 72 (4 March), 7.
        Tells the incident in which Hemingway saved war writers
    in Spain from a possible boat crash.

10 MORA, CONSTANCIA DE LA. In Place of Splendor: The Autobiogra-
    phy of a Spanish Woman. New York: Harcourt, Brace,
    pp. 290-91.
        Reminiscence of Hemingway during the Spanish Civil War.

11 ROLFE, EDWIN. The Lincoln Battalion: The Story of the Ameri-
    cans who Fought in Spain in the International Brigades.
    New York: Random House.
        Mention of Hemingway during action.

12 SHEEAN, VINCENT. Not Peace But a Sword. New York: Doubleday,
    Doran.
        Travels with Hemingway and James Lardner in 1938; in-
    cludes the story of the boat crash being averted in Spain.

13 TRILLING, LIONEL. "Hemingway and His Critics," Partisan Re-
    view, 6 (Winter), 52-60.
        Review of First 49. Considers the play inferior because
    it is written by "Hemingway the man"; the stories, however,
    are excellent because they are the products of "Hemingway
    the artist." In both To Have and Have Not and The Fifth
    Column, Hemingway uses first person narration, and that
    device leads to disaster. Trilling also discusses the
    place "critical tradition" holds in Hemingway's career.
    Reprinted in Baker anthology, pp. 61-70 (See 1961.A5).

14 WILSON, EDMUND. "Ernest Hemingway: Bourdon Gauge of Morale,"
    Atlantic, 164 (July), 36-46.
        Wilson summarily discusses each of Hemingway's books,
    beginning with In Our Time, and concludes that rather than
    being apolitical, "his whole work is a criticism of so-
    ciety: he has responded to every pressure of the moral
    atmosphere of the time, as it is felt at the roots of

(WILSON, EDMUND)
    human relations, with a sensitivity almost unrivaled."
    Reprinted in Readings from the Americas: An Introduction
    to Democratic Thought, edited by Guy A. Cardwell (New York:
    Ronald, 1947, pp. 246-48); in Wilson's Eight Essays (Gar-
    den City, New York: Doubleday, 1954, pp. 92-114); in
    Literature in America: An Anthology of Literary Criticism,
    edited by Philip Rahv (New York: Meridian, 1957, pp. 373-
    90) (See 1957.B24); in McCaffery, 236-57 (See 1950.A1);
    and in Wilson's The Wound and the Bow: Seven Studies in
    Literature (Boston: Houghton Mifflin, 1941, pp. 214-42).
    (See 1941.B40.)

1940 A BOOKS - NONE

1940 B SHORTER WRITINGS

1   ANON. "Hemingway Novel a Smash," Publishers' Weekly, 138
        (2 Nov.), 1751.
            Listing of For Whom the Bell Tolls sales.

2   ANON. Review of For Whom the Bell Tolls, Newsweek, 16
        (21 Oct.), 50.
            Discusses the fine suspense built through involving the
        reader with the characters; claims that reading the novel
        "is almost a physical experience. And that is great
        writing."

3   ANON. Review of For Whom the Bell Tolls, Time, 36 (21 Oct.),
        94-95. Photo by Robert Capa.
            For Whom the Bell Tolls is not only a great Hemingway
        love story and a tense story of adventure in war but also
        "a grave and sombre tragedy of Spanish peasants fighting
        for their lives."

4   ANON. Review of the play, The Fifth Column, Life, 8 (25 March),
        100-01. Photos.

5   ANON. Review of the play, The Fifth Column, Time, 35
        (18 March), 65-67.
            Thinks the love affair "flimsy, vaporous, unreal, nearly
        sinks the play." The strength of the conclusion depends
        on "eloquent rhetoric" and that trait is hardly character-
        istic of Hemingway's writing.

6   ADAMS, J. DONALD. Review of For Whom the Bell Tolls, New York
        Times Book Review (20 Oct.), p. 1.

1940

(ADAMS, J. DONALD)
"This is the best book Ernest Hemingway has written,
the fullest, the deepest, the truest . . . . the book of
a man who knows what life is about, and who can convey his
knowledge."

7   ALLEN, HUGH. "The Dark Night of Ernest Hemingway," Catholic
World, 150 (Feb.), 522-29.
Sees Hemingway, and For Whom the Bell Tolls, as without
positive values because Hemingway is bereft of spiritual
understanding.

8   ATKINSON, BROOKS. Review of the play, The Fifth Column, New
York Times (7 March), p. 18.
Despite its unevenness, the play manages "to make a
statement that is always impressive and sometimes poignant
or shattering."

*9   BAKER, CARLOS. "The Hard Trade of Mr. Hemingway," Delphian
Quarterly, 23 (July), 12-17.
Cited in Hanneman bibliography, p. 402 (See 1962.A1).

10   BENÉT, STEPHEN VINCENT and ROSEMARY BENÉT. "Ernest Hemingway:
Byron of Our Day," New York Herald Tribune Books (3 Nov.),
p. 7. Photo.
The romantic elements of the Hemingway legend and life
recalled.

11   BESSIE, ALVAH. Review of For Whom the Bell Tolls, New Masses,
37 (5 Nov.), 25-29.
Critical of the novel for its lack of depth or conception:
there is no searching, no probing, no grappling with the
truths of human life that is more than superficial."
Reprinted in Baker critiques, pp. 90-94 (See 1962.A5);
in Grebstein, pp. 6-15 (See 1971.A8).

12   BROWN, JOHN MASON. Review of the play, The Fifth Column, New
York Post (7 March), p. 10.
Dislikes the play because of the "lack of distinction
and genuine relevance in its writing."

13   BUCKLEY, HENRY. Life and Death of the Spanish Republic.
London: Hamish Hamilton. Photo.
Mention of Hemingway during the Spanish Civil War.

14   CANBY, HENRY SEIDEL. Review of For Whom the Bell Tolls, Book-
of-the Month Club News (Oct.), pp. 2-3.
"Hemingway's best book since A Farewell to Arms."

(CANBY, HENRY SEIDEL)
Admires "one of the most touching and perfect love stories in modern literature--a love story with a tragic ending which lifts rather than depresses the imagination."

15 CHAMBERLAIN, JOHN. Review of For Whom the Bell Tolls, Harper's Magazine, 182 (Dec.), front section.
Thinks this novel is as apt a representation of "the crusading mood of 1940" as The Sun Also Rises and A Farewell to Arms were "brilliant evocations of a post-war mood."

16 _____. Review of For Whom the Bell Tolls, New York Herald Tribune Books (20 Oct.), pp. 1, 2. Photo.
Sees that it combines the qualities of a thriller, a political novel, and a paean to the spirit of Spain.

17 De VOTO, BERNARD. Minority Report. Boston: Little, Brown, pp. 257-61.
"Tiger, Tiger!" on To Have and Have Not, reprinted from SRL, 16 (16 Oct., 1937). (See 1937.B25.)

18 FADIMAN, CLIFTON. "Ernest Hemingway Crosses the Bridge," New Yorker, 16 (26 Oct.), 82-85.
Review of For Whom the Bell Tolls. Likes For Whom the Bell Tolls because it is a "true book," despite the critical quibbling over whether or not it is a "great" one.

19 FISHER, PAUL W. "Back to His First Field," Kansas City Times (26 Nov.), p. 1. Photo.
Interview with Hemingway; recalls his days as reporter and in World War I.

20 GIBBS, WOLCOTT. "Saint Dorothy," New Yorker, 16 (16 March), 44.
Review of the play, The Fifth Column. Likes the theatrical version of Dorothy better than the Hemingway character; finds the play "astonishingly good."

21 GILDER, ROSAMOND. Review of the play, The Fifth Column, Theatre Arts, 24 (May), 310-14.
Thinks the production is structurally better than the Hemingway version, but that much of the effectiveness of the drama is in "the forthright, pungent impact of Hemingway's dialogue."

22 JOHNSON, EDGAR. "Farewell the Separate Peace," Sewanee Review, 48 (July-Sept.), 289-300.

1940

(JOHNSON, EDGAR)
Subtitled "The Rejections of Ernest Hemingway," this
essay stresses Hemingway's intellectual development since
In Our Time. First accepting simple biological persis-
tence, he later rejects that and moves on to an envy of
sophistication (finally also rejected in To Have and Have
Not where he finds a new ideal of humanitas and brother-
hood).
Reprinted in McCaffery, pp. 130-42 (See 1950.A1).

23 JONES, HOWARD MUMFORD. Review of For Whom the Bell Tolls, SRL,
23 (26 Oct.), 5, 19. Cover photo.
"Manner has been replaced by style, and the mere author
has died out in the artist . . . . the finest and richest
novel which Mr. Hemingway has written."
Reprinted in Grebstein, pp. 2-5 (See 1971.A8).

24 KENNEDY, FR. JOHN S. "Hemingway's Latest," Sign, 20 (Dec.),
289.
Sees For Whom the Bell Tolls as another Waste Land and
Hemingway as a "literary garbage collector."

25 KNOX, BERNARD. "I Knew André Marty," New Masses, 37 (19 Nov.),
15, 16.
Reminiscence of the Spanish Civil War political
structure.

26 KRUTCH, JOSEPH WOOD. Review of the play, The Fifth Column,
Nation, 150 (16 March), 371-72.
Faults the play because it "ends stagily as the love
story of a hard-boiled hero whose grandiose gestures may
be authentic but are too familiar."

27 MARSHALL, MARGARET. Review of For Whom the Bell Tolls, Nation,
151 (26 Oct.), 395-96.
Finds the novel superior to A Farewell to Arms, "written
with care and love" and setting "a new standard for Hemingway in characterization, dialogue, suspense, and compassion
for the human being faced with death."

28 MacLEISH, ARCHIBALD. "Post-war Writers and Pre-war Readers,"
New Republic, 102 (10 June), 789.
In a speech presented for the American Association for
Adult Education, MacLeish blamed the war books of Hemingway, Dos Passos, and others for leaving the impression that
not only the war and war issues but all issues, all moral
issues, "were false—were fraudulent." See Hemingway's
letter to Life, 8 (24 June, 1940).

29 NATHAN, GEORGE JEAN. Review of the play, The Fifth Column,
      Newsweek, 15 (18 March), p. 52.
         An occasional effective scene, when the voice of Heming-
      way is most in appearance.

30 PARKER, DOROTHY. Review of For Whom the Bell Tolls, PM
      (20 Oct.), p. 42.
         Admires the book because of its passion and the accuracy
      of its presentation. "It is a great thing to see a fine
      writer grow finer before your eyes."

31 PERKINS, MAX. "Ernest Hemingway," Book-of-the-Month Club News
      (Oct.).
         Biographical sketch; reprinted in Current History &
      Forum, 52 (7 Nov. 1940), 27-28; and in Book-of-the-Month
      Club News (May 1964).

32 RASCOE, BURTON. Review of For Whom the Bell Tolls, American
      Mercury, 51 (Dec.), 493-98.
         Dislikes the novel, calling parts of it "absurdly pre-
      tentious," others, "surprisingly dull."

33 SEAVER, EDWIN. Review of For Whom the Bell Tolls, Direction,
      3 (Oct.), 18-19.
         Finds the novel effective, and considers that Hemingway
      owes a debt to the Spanish Civil War: "it enormously
      deepened his experience" and "saved him from 'death in the
      afternoon.'"

34 SHERWOOD, ROBERT E. Review of For Whom the Bell Tolls,
      Atlantic, 166 (Nov.), front section.
         Calls the novel "a rare and beautiful piece of work,"
      in which Hemingway "achieved the true union of passion and
      reason."

35 THOMPSON, RALPH. Review of For Whom the Bell Tolls, New York
      Times (21 Oct.), p. 15.
         Admires the book for its "incomparable" dialogue and
      superb story, "packed with the matter of picaresque ro-
      mance: blood, lust, adventure, vulgarity, comedy, tragedy."

36 VANDERCOOK, DOROTHY I. Letter, "For Whom the School Bell
      Tolled," Chicago Daily Tribune (3 Dec.), p. 14.
         School chum recalls Wendell Holmes grade school, with
      Hemingway, in Oak Park, Illinois.

37 VAN DOREN, CARL. The American Novel: 1789-1939. New York:
      Macmillan, revised edition.
         Evaluates Hemingway's work in "New Realisms," and

1940

(VAN DOREN, CARL)
describes him as telling "naked stories in a naked language, which was the same--curt, crisp, fresh--whatever
his subject might be." Van Doren stresses, however, that
the Hemingway style is "not so simple as it looks."

38   van GELDER, ROBERT. "Ernest Hemingway Talks of Work and War,"
New York Times Book Review (11 Aug.), p. 2. Photo.
Interview with Hemingway during his July visit to New
York when the final draft of For Whom the Bell Tolls was
being copyread.
Reprinted in Writers and Writing, New York, 1946, pp. 95-
98 (See 1946.B14).

39   VAUGHAN, J. N. Review of For Whom the Bell Tolls, Commonweal,
33 (13 Dec.), 210.
Finds the novel "infinitely inferior to Hemingway's prior
work." The only saving passages in the book are the 34
pages telling of the massacre in the Spanish village.
Reprinted in Grebstein, pp. 16-17 (See 1971.A8).

40   VERNON, GRENVILLE. Review of the play, The Fifth Column,
Commonweal, 31 (22 March), 475-76.
Only the cast saves the "very weak and trite story."

41   WATTS, RICHARD, Jr. Review of the play, The Fifth Column,
New York Herald Tribune (7 March), p. 16.
After a stormy out-of-town history, the play is "sur-
prisingly impressive," particularly the opening scenes.

42   WILSON, EDMUND. Review of For Whom the Bell Tolls, New
Republic, 103 (28 Oct.), 591-92.
Sees the novel as Hemingway's "first attempt to compose
a full-length novel, with real characters and a built-up
story." Admires also his understanding of "social and
political phenomena such as he has hardly given evidence
of before."

43   YOUNG, STARK. Review of the play, The Fifth Column, New
Republic, 102 (25 March), 408.
Ambivalent review, calling attention to the fact that
the added love scenes are in the spirit of Hemingway's
relationships between men and women in the original version.

1941 A BOOKS - NONE

1941 B SHORTER WRITINGS

1 ANON. "Eire Bans Hemingway Book," New York Times (12 June),
       p. 3.
          For Whom the Bell Tolls banned by the censors from cir-
       culation in Ireland.

2 ANON. "Ernest Hemingway Interviewed by Ralph Ingersoll," PM
       (9 June), pp. 6-10.
          Photos and facsimile of a page of the interview edited
       by Hemingway, with penciled revisions. A map, p. 7, shows
       the route of the Hemingways as they traveled, sending
       seven Far East dispatches for PM publication.

3 ANON. "Hemingway Gets Medal for Book," New York Times
       (27 Nov.), p. 21.
          For Whom the Bell Tolls wins Limited Editions Club Award
       as the book most likely to become a classic. Sinclair
       Lewis ranked Hemingway with the half dozen leaders of
       writing at the time, Dreiser, Cather, Maugham, Wells, and
       Jules Romaine (in his address at the presentation luncheon).

4 ANON. "Hemingway, Here for a Visit, Says He'd Think He Was
       Slipping If He Had Won Pulitzer Prize," St. Louis Star &
       Times (23 May), p. 3.
          Hemingway en route to New York.

5 ANON. "Hemingway Novel Wins Critics' Vote," New York Times
       (26 April), p. 13.
          For Whom the Bell Tolls headed a SRL survey (panel of 39
       literary critics) on possible Pulitzer prize winners.

6 ANON. "The Nation's Book Reviewers Nominate Their Pulitzer
       Prize Favorites," SRL, 24 (26 April), 7.
          Although For Whom the Bell Tolls was first choice by a
       large majority, Hemingway did not receive the Pulitzer
       prize for 1940.

7 ANON. Review of For Whom the Bell Tolls, TLS (8 March),
       p. 113.
          Dislikes the use of Spanish and formal English phrases
       in the colloquial matrix; still "Mr. Hemingway holds the
       reader" because "Jordan's personal drama, the drama of a
       civilized soul on the losing side in war with only courage
       to sustain his hope of victory, has pathos and poignancy."

1941

8   BAKER, CHARLES H., Jr. "Tropical Coolers for Torrid Days,"
     Town & Country, 96 (July), 39, 68. Photo.
          Fishing with Hemingway off American Shoals Light; gives
     a recipe for a drink Hemingway called "Death in the Gulf
     Stream."

9   BAREA, ARTURO. The Forge. London: Faber & Faber.
          Brief recollections of Hemingway in Madrid during the
     Spanish Civil War.

10   ____. "Not Spain but Hemingway," Horizon, 3 (May), 350-61.
          Review of For Whom the Bell Tolls. Objects to For Whom
     the Bell Tolls as "deeply untruthful," especially of the
     Spanish people's feelings and reactions to the Civil War.
     Sees Hemingway's misuse of Spanish as indicative of the
     way "Hemingway has failed to grasp certain subtleties of
     Spanish language and psychology."
          Reprinted in Baker anthology, pp. 202-12 (See 1961.A5);
     in The Literary Reputation of Hemingway in Europe, pp. 197-
     210 (See 1965.A3); in Grebstein, pp. 80-90 (See 1971.A8).

11   BATES, H. E. The Modern Short Story: A Critical Survey.
     London: Nelson, pp. 167-78.
          Considers Hemingway the opposite of Lewis' "dumb ox,"
     rather a sensitive and talented craftsman in the Turgenev,
     Maupassant, Anderson, Crane, Defoe, and Biblical tradition.
     Enjoys his "personal rhythm," his stripped-down style, and
     the impact of his delicate stories. Considers Hemingway's
     impact long-lasting because he has "mastered the art of
     implication."
          Reprinted as "Hemingway's Short Stories" in Baker antholo-
     gy, pp. 71-79 (See 1961.A5).

12   BEACH, JOSEPH WARREN. American Fiction: 1920-1940. New
     York: Macmillan.
          "Ernest Hemingway: Empirical Ethics," pp. 69-96,
     traces those ethics from Death in the Afternoon and Green
     Hills of Africa, as applied in The Sun Also Rises, A Fare-
     well to Arms and For Whom the Bell Tolls. Sees Hemingway
     as a moral writer with a definite program for existing.
     "Ernest Hemingway: The Esthetics of Simplicity," pp. 97-
     122; Beach sees that his rejection of abstract concepts
     leads to a new mode in writing per se: "fourth and fifth
     dimensions" (especially apparent in the stories) depend
     on the combination of craft and vision. Admires Heming-
     way's "delicacy of feeling." Partly reprinted in Baker
     critiques, pp. 82-86 (See 1962.A5).

13   CARGILL, OSCAR. Intellectual America: Ideas on the March.
        New York: Macmillan, pp. 351-70: "The Primitivists."
           View of Hemingway as a primitivist and naturalist, con-
        trasting his "hard-boiled cynicism" with Fitzgerald's
        "play-boy disillusionment." Considers Hemingway's
        strengths to be "characterization, naturalness of dialogue,
        and the manipulation of his materials to get the most out
        of them."

14   COWLES, VIRGINIA. Looking For Trouble. New York: Harper.
           Recollections of Hemingway in Spain during the Civil War.

15   COWLEY, MALCOLM. Review of For Whom the Bell Tolls, New
        Republic, 104 (20 Jan.), 89-90.
           For Whom the Bell Tolls as a "very complicated and moral
        document . . . . everything is there if you look for it."
        Sees the novel as an important shift in Hemingway's con-
        cept of subject matter and theme.

16   DAICHES, DAVID. "Ernest Hemingway," English Journal, 30
        (March), pp. 175-86.
           Sees that Hemingway's early writing reflects his "per-
        sonal tradition of living" as developed from war, bull-
        fighting, the American frontier, and his attempts to find
        contemporary substitutes for the tradition. With For Whom
        the Bell Tolls, however, Hemingway expands that personal
        tradition.
           Reprinted in College English, 2 (May), 725-36.

17   FERGUSON, OTIS. "Double-Talk Talks: For Whom is That Bell
        For?" SRL, 24 (27 Sept.), 10.
           Parody.

18   FLOWER, DESMOND. Review of For Whom the Bell Tolls, Observer
        (9 March), p. 4.
           Admires the "sustained effort" of the novel, which he
        sees as a "more mature, more tightly constructed work"
        than A Farewell to Arms. Predicts that For Whom the Bell
        Tolls will be one of the century's great novels.

19   FORSTER, E. M. Review of For Whom the Bell Tolls, Listener,
        26 (10 July), 63.
           A moral statement about wars, "full of courage and bru-
        tality and foul language."

20   GEISMAR, MAXWELL. "No Man Alone Now," Virginia Quarterly Re-
        view, 17 (Autumn), 517-34.
           Sees the basis of Hemingway's early writing as "a total

1941

(GEISMAR, MAXWELL)
   renunciation of all social frameworks," but also finds a
   reversal in the work of the 1930's. Describes Hemingway's
   fascination with death and war as indicative of his similarities with Shakespeare, Kafka, Joyce, and Dostoyevsky,
   and Hawthorne. Sees To Have and Have Not as the most
   satisfying resolution of Hemingway's personal contradic-
   tions, but discusses each of the novels, including For Whom
   the Bell Tolls.
   Enlarged, essay was reprinted in Writers in Crisis, Boston,
   Houghton Mifflin, 1942 (See 1942.B7); reprinted in
   McCaffery, pp. 143-89 (See 1950.A1).

21   GELLHORN, MARTHA. "These, Our Mountains," Collier's, 107
        (28 June), 16-17, 38-44. Photos by Hemingway.
        Description of the Hemingways' trip to the Canton front,
     by plane, truck, motorboat, and horseback.

22   GREENE, GRAHAM. Review of For Whom the Bell Tolls, Spectator,
        166 (7 March), 258.
        Treats the Spanish war with a "subtlety and sympathy"
     which are impressive; this book is not "propaganda first
     and literature only second."
     Reprinted in Grebstein, pp. 21-23 (See 1971.A8).

23   HIGHET, GILBERT. "Thou Tellest Me, Comrade," Nation, 152
        (1 March), 242. Parody.
        Objects to Hemingway's use of Spanish colloquialisms in
     For Whom the Bell Tolls.
     Reprinted in Grebstein, pp. 18-20 (See 1971.A8).

24   INGERSOLL, RALPH. "Hemingway Is on the Way to Far East for
        PM/ Accompanied by Wife, He Returns to the Wars As Our
        Correspondent," PM (31 Jan.), p. 12. Photo.
        While his wife, Martha Gellhorn, was Collier's corre-
     spondent, Hemingway reported for PM.

*25 ISHERWOOD, CHRISTOPHER. "Hemingway, Death, and the Devil,"
        Decision, 1 (Jan.), 58-60.
        Cited in Hanneman bibliography, p. 407 (See 1967.A4).

26   LITTELL, ROBERT. Review of For Whom the Bell Tolls, Yale
        Review, 30 (Winter), vi, viii.
        Pleased that Hemingway can create such involvement, such
     caring, in his readers; considers For Whom the Bell Tolls
     Hemingway's best novel, and one of the best created by any
     American author.

27   "Look Examines: Ernest Hemingway," Look, 5 (8 April), 18,
        20-21. Photos.
        A biographical profile.

28   MACDONALD, DWIGHT. "Reading from Left to Right," Partisan
        Review, 8 (Jan.-Feb.), 24-28.
        Attacks the novel for its "political shortcomings," but
        considers its politics to underlie its technical inade-
        quacies.

29   MALCOLMSON, DAVID. "The Escape from the Devouring Mother,"
        Ten Heroes. New York: Duell, Sloan & Pearce, pp. 156-59.
        Includes a discussion of the death of Robert Jordan's
        father.

30   MELLERS, W. H. Review of For Whom the Bell Tolls, Scrutiny,
        10 (June), 93-99.
        Here Hemingway's usual "reportage" turns to "a small
        kind of art." Mellers would prefer that Hemingway wrote
        only short stories "where the accuracy of his reporter's
        eye and his limitation of emotional range help rather than
        hinder him."

31   PRITCHETT, V. S. Review of For Whom the Bell Tolls, New
        Statesman & Nation, 21 (15 March), 275-76.
        Admires Hemingway's use of Spanish; sees that this mix-
        ture adds to the impact of Hemingway's usually powerful
        dialogue. Finds the political portraits accurate.
        Reprinted in Grebstein, pp. 24-29 (See 1971.A8).

32   SCHORER, MARK. "The Background of a Style," Kenyon Review,
        3 (Winter), 101-05.
        Review of For Whom the Bell Tolls. A pleading for "the
        moral necessity of political violence"; therefore, a dif-
        ferent argument, and a new writer. Sees the change as an
        improvement, reflected in an expansive style.
        Reprinted in Baker critiques, pp. 87-89 (See 1962.A5).

33   SICKELS, ELEANOR M. "Farewell to Cynicism," College English
        3 (Oct.), 31-38.
        Finds "a new spirit of affirmation" in For Whom the Bell
        Tolls.

34   SKINNER, CORNELIA OTIS. Soap Behind the Ears. New York:
        Dodd, Mead, pp. 89-96.
        "When the Gong Sounded."

1941

35 SPENDER, STEPHEN. "Books and the War. Part IV; The Short
        Story To-day," Penguin New Writing, No. 5 (April), pp. 131-
        42.
            General article which includes "Under the Ridge."

36 SQUIRE, SIR JOHN. Review of For Whom the Bell Tolls, Illus-
        strated London News (29 March), p. 420. Photos by Robert
        Capa.
            Bothered by the clipped restrain with which Hemingway
        describes even the love story in the novel: "Think what
        Conrad would have made of this theme!"

37 TRILLING, LIONEL. "An American in Spain," Partisan Review, 8
        (Jan.-Feb.), 63-67.
            Review of For Whom the Bell Tolls. Sees For Whom the
        Bell Tolls as evidence of "a restored Hemingway writing
        to the top of his bent . . . . no one else can make so
        memorable the events of physical experience."
        Reprinted in The Partisan Reader, edited by William
        Phillips and Philip Rahv, New York, Dial Press, 1946,
        pp. 639-44 (See 1946.B11); in Baker critiques, pp. 78-81
        (See 1962.A5).

38 VARGA, MARGIT. Waldo Peirce. New York: Hyperion Press.
            Color reproduction of Peirce's portrait of Hemingway.
        References to the artist's trip to Spain with Hemingway in
        1927, and to his visits to Key West.

39 WALTER, ERICH A. ed. Essay Annual: 1941. Chicago: Scott,
        Foresman, pp. 149-52.
            Review of For Whom the Bell Tolls by Clifton Fadiman,
        reprinted from New Yorker, 16 (26 Oct. 1940). (See
        1940.B17.)

*40 WILSON, EDMUND. "Hemingway: Bourdon Gauge of Morale," The
        Wound and the Bow: Seven Studies in Literature. Boston:
        Houghton Mifflin, pp. 214-42.
        Reprinted from Atlantic, 164 (July 1939), 36-46.

1942 A BOOKS - NONE

1942 B SHORTER WRITINGS

1 ANON. "Out of Oak Park by Madrid," Monthly Letter of the
        Limited Editions Club, No. 149 (Sept.), 4 pages.
            Publication of the illustrated edition of For Whom the
        Bell Tolls, selection of this book club.

2   ANON. Review of <u>Men at War</u>, <u>Newsweek</u>, 20 (16 Nov.), 92.
Subtitled "The Best War Stories of All Time," this is an
excellent collection--"and who is to question Hemingway,
who himself owes his literary life to war."

3   ANDERSON, SHERWOOD. <u>Memoirs</u>. New York: Harcourt, Brace.
Reminiscence of the early years of friendship with
Hemingway and Faulkner, the publication of <u>Torrents of
Spring</u>, and the final meeting between Anderson and Heming-
way.

4   BROOKS, CLEANTH and ROBERT PENN WARREN. "The Killers," <u>Ameri-
can Prefaces</u>, 7 (Spring), 195-209.
Reading of the story as dynamic interchange among all
characters, with focus of attention on Nick.
Reprinted, revised, in <u>Understanding Fiction</u>, New York,
F. S. Crofts, 1943, pp. 316-24.

5   FRANKENBERG, LLOYD. "Themes and Characters in Hemingway's
Latest Period," <u>Southern Review</u>, 7 (Spring), 776-88.
Sees one of Hemingway's continuing themes to be "love
and war don't mix"; by <u>The Fifth Column</u>, "love is now an
irrelevance, if not an impertinence." Particularly dislikes the characterization and style of <u>For Whom the Bell
Tolls</u>.

6   GATES, THEODORE J. and AUSTIN WRIGHT, eds. <u>College Prose</u>.
Boston: D. C. Heath, pp. 416-23.
"Ernest Hemingway Crosses the Bridge," Clifton Fadiman's
review of <u>For Whom the Bell Tolls</u>, reprinted from the <u>New
Yorker</u>, 16 (26 Oct. 1940), 422-23 (<u>See</u> 1940.B18); and "A
Review of <u>For Whom the Bell Tolls</u>" by J. N. Vaughan, re-
printed from <u>Commonweal</u>, 33 (13 Dec. 1940). (<u>See</u> 1940.B39.)

7   GEISMAR, MAXWELL. <u>Writers in Crisis: The American Novel
Between Two Wars</u>. Boston: Houghton Mifflin.
"Ernest Hemingway; You Could Always Come Back," pp. 39-
85, reprinted from <u>Virginia Quarterly Review</u>, 17 (Autumn
1941). (<u>See</u> 1941.B20.)

8   GORMAN, HERBERT. Review of <u>Men at War</u>, <u>New York Times Book
Review</u> (8 Nov.), pp. 1, 37.
Likes the collection for its variety, but dislikes Hemingway's "interesting but badly put together and discursive"
introduction.

1942

9   JONES, HOWARD MUMFORD. Review of Men at War, SRL, 25 (12 Dec.),
        11.
            Finds the collection "shapeless," interesting only as a
        reflection of Hemingway's "curious obsession with death."

10   KAZIN, ALFRED. On Native Grounds: An Interpretation of
        Modern American Prose Literature. New York: Harcourt,
        Brace, pp. 327-41.
            "A superb artist with a minor vision of life," is Kazin's
        judgment. Sees Hemingway as the champion of "preserving
        oneself by preserving and refining one's art." For Heming-
        way, his art was his literal salvation. Kazin finds this
        attitude "the mark of a passionate romanticist who had
        been profoundly disappointed." Assesses the Hemingway in-
        fluence as greater even than that of Dreiser: "Hemingway
        is the bronze god of the whole contemporary literary ex-
        perience in America."
            Reprinted in McCaffery, pp. 190-204 under the title "Hem-
        ingway: Synopsis of a Career" (See 1950.A1).

11   KUNITZ, STANLEY J. and HOWARD HAYCRAFT, eds. Twentieth Century
        Authors: A Biographical Dictionary of Modern Literature.
        New York: Wilson, pp. 635-36. Photo.

12   McHUGH, VINCENT. Review of Men at War, New Yorker, 18
        (24 Oct.), 80-81.
            Most interested in Hemingway's introduction in which he
        says some "profound things" and some less viable.

13   MILLIS, WALTER. Review of Men at War, New York Herald Tribune
        Books (25 Oct.), p. 3.
            Admires the contents of the collection, but found Heming-
        way's introduction to be "angry, chaotic, rambling and
        pointless."

1943 A BOOKS - NONE

1943 B SHORTER WRITINGS

1   ANON. Item, New York Times (10 March), p. 4.
            The Spanish Ambassador to the U. S. protests the pro-
        duction of the movie For Whom the Bell Tolls as propaganda
        against the Franco regime.

2   BAKER, CARLOS. Review of Men at War, Sewanee Review, 51
        (Jan.-March), 160-63.
            Sees the contents of the collection as a compromise

(BAKER, CARLOS)
between Hemingway's high standards and his publishers' ideas of what would sell. Views the introduction as an interesting restatement of Hemingway's literary and personal ideals.

3   FARRELL, JAMES T. "Ernest Hemingway, Apostle of a 'Lost Generation,'" New York Times Book Review (1 Aug.), pp. 6, 14. Photo.
Categorizes The Sun Also Rises as "nihilistic and rather adolescent in character." Moving as the book is, Farrell objects to Hemingway's oversimplification of characters ("simple behaviorism").
Reprinted in The League of Frightened Philistines (New York: Vanguard Press, 1945), pp. 20-24 (See 1945.B6); in McCaffery, pp. 221-25 (See 1950.A1); in Baker critiques, pp. 4-6 (See 1962.A5); in White, pp. 53-57 (See 1969.A11).

4   FENIMORE, EDWARD. "English and Spanish in For Whom the Bell Tolls, ELH, 10 (March), 73-86.
Close analysis of "the suggestive value of words in themselves," which Fenimore takes to be an important reason for Hemingway's use of Spanish in the novel. Defends the shifts in the idioms (from "purely colloquial" to "the most Biblical style") as a rhythmical necessity, and sees that Hemingway's use of Spanish enables him to take liberties with his English as well.
Reprinted in McCaffery, pp. 205-20 (See 1950.A1).

5   KIRKWOOD, M. M. "Value in the Novel Today," University of Toronto Quarterly, 12 (April), 282-96.
General article stressing that in the best novels (For Whom the Bell Tolls, for example) "religion and the state are highly important values in the minds of the characters." Comments on "Hemingway's balanced wisdom in matters of religion and politics" in that novel.

6   LERNER, MAX. "It Tolls for Thee," PM (18 July), p. 2.
Review of the film, For Whom the Bell Tolls. Thinks the novel excels most other fiction, but has reservations about the movie.
Reprinted in Public Journal (New York: Viking Press, 1945), pp. 87-89 (See 1945.B8).

7   STOVALL, FLOYD. American Idealism. Norman: University of Oklahoma Press, pp. 149-52.
From "Contemporary Fiction." Stovall faults Hemingway's writing--except for For Whom the Bell Tolls--because it

1943

(STOVALL, FLOYD)
    shows so little idealism. Contrasts Hemingway and Dos
Passos, saying that Hemingway's "stories are more intense
than comprehensive." Traces Hemingway's cynicism to the
post-war disillusion.

8   WOLFE, THOMAS. <u>The Letters of Thomas Wolfe To His Mother</u>.
    Edited by C. Hugh Holman and Sue Fields Ross. Chapel Hill,
N. C.: The University of North Carolina Press.
    Some mention of Hemingway's work, but Wolfe is more in-
terested in many other writers.

1944 A BOOKS - NONE

1944 B SHORTER WRITINGS

1   ANON. "<u>SRL</u> Poll on Novels and Novelists," <u>SRL</u>, 28 (5 Aug.),
    61. Twentieth Anniversary Issue.
    Hemingway received twice as many votes for the leading
American novelist as Ellen Glasgow, runner-up. Lewis's
<u>Arrowsmith</u> was outstanding novel, with <u>A Farewell to Arms</u>
a close second and <u>For Whom the Bell Tolls</u> fifth choice.
Short biographical and critical note on Hemingway is included.

2   ADAMS, J. DONALD. <u>The Shape of Books to Come</u>. New York:
    Viking Press, pp. 103-13.
    "The Tough Guys" mainly concerns Hemingway. Thinks Hem-
ingway a writer "who gave promise of more than he ful-
filled." Finds in his writing of the 1930's "mental confusion and complete loss of values," at least partly because of inadequate characterization. Of his people,
Adams notes, "They react to stimuli, but they have no
inner life."

3   COWLEY, MALCOLM. "The Generation That Wasn't Lost," <u>College
English</u>, 5 (Feb.), 233-39.
    General essay, saying of Hemingway that his influence
"is so pervasive in recent fiction that critics hardly
bother to mention it any more." Defends recent fiction:
"American fiction between the wars was not on the surface
a literature of ideas, but that wasn't because the novelists did no thinking." Characterizes these novelists,
Hemingway among them, in these terms: (1) international
in their interests, (2) technically adept, (3) lyrical
rather than naturalistic, (4) rebellious but not revolutionary, (5) progressively disillusioned, (6) passive in
mood.

4 _____. "Hemingway at Midnight," New Republic, 111 (14 Aug.), 190-95.
This essay was incorporated into the 1945 Introduction to The Portable Hemingway (See 1945.B4).

5 _____. "Hemingway and the Hero," New Republic, 111 (4 Dec.), 754-58.
Hemingway's four novels "tell a loosely connected story: in effect, a legend of man against society." From A Farewell to Arms, the next three (The Sun Also Rises, To Have and Have Not, and For Whom the Bell Tolls) are all possible sequels to what had already happened at Tagliamento (taking the events in terms of chronology, not in the order the books were written).

6 _____. "Notes for a Hemingway Omnibus: The Pattern of His Work and Its Relation to His Life," SRL, 27 (23 Sept.), 7-8, 23-25.
Also appears in part in the Introduction to The Portable Hemingway (See 1945.B4).

7 De VOTO, BERNARD. The Literary Fallacy. Boston: Little, Brown, pp. 104-08.
According to Hemingway's fiction, life "does not exist above the diaphragm . . . . Intellectual life does not exist even in rudimentary form." From the chapter "Waste Land."

8 GRAVES, ROBERT and ALAN HODGE. The Reader Over Your Shoulder: A Handbook for Writers of English Prose. New York: Macmillan, pp. 304-06.
Examination and comment on a For Whom the Bell Tolls passage in which Spanish colloquialisms are used.

9 HICKS, GRANVILLE. "Twenty Years of Hemingway," New Republic, 111 (23 Oct.), 524, 526.
Review of the Portable Hemingway. Sees Hemingway's importance to lie in his continuing concern with human loneliness and his treatments of man meeting death.

10 LERNER, MAX. "On Hemingway," PM (28 Sept.), p. 2.
Review of the Portable Hemingway. Biographical and critical comments, reprinted in Public Journal, New York, Viking, 1945, pp. 44-46 (See 1945.B8).

11 NORTON, DAN S. "Eclectic Hemingway," New York Times Book Review (8 Oct.), p. 3. Photo.
Review of the Portable Hemingway.

1944

12   WEST, RAY B., Jr. "Ernest Hemingway: Death in the Evening,"
        <u>Antioch Review</u>, 4 (Winter), 569–80.
            Sees Hemingway as closer to the Humanism of Irving
        Babbitt in 1944 than to the realistic or naturalistic pose
        he had earlier assumed. Stresses that Hemingway's impor-
        tance will lie in his short stories, and that their one
        prevalent theme is "that many men achieve their greatest
        victories in the face of death." <u>For Whom the Bell Tolls</u>
        parallels this but adds both faith and mysticism to the
        protagonist's understanding.

<u>1945 A   BOOKS – NONE</u>

<u>1945 B   SHORTER WRITINGS</u>

1   ANON. People Who Read and Write column, "War and Mr. Heming-
        way," <u>New York Times Book Review</u> (8 April), p. 23.
            A war correspondent relates an incident in France and
        describes Hemingway as "about as battle wise as a man can
        be."

2   ANTHEIL, GEORGE. <u>Bad Boy of Music</u>. Garden City, New York:
        Doubleday, Doran.
            Antheil recalls arranging for publication of Hemingway's
        poems in <u>Der Querschnitt</u>, 1925.

3   COWLEY, MALCOLM. "The Middle American Style: Davy Crockett
        to Ernest Hemingway," <u>New York Times Book Review</u> (15 July),
        pp. 3, 14. Photo.
            Sees Hemingway's debt to Gertrude Stein as well as Ander-
        son; says that Stein encouraged Hemingway to write in his
        own Midwestern prose. Instead of looking for synonyms,
        Hemingway learned to base his idiom on patterns of repe-
        titions.

4   ____. "Nightmare and Ritual in Hemingway," Introduction to
        <u>The Portable Hemingway</u>. Edited by Malcolm Cowley. New
        York: The Viking Press.
            Stresses Hemingway's affinity with Poe, Hawthorne, and
        Melville, although his techniques appear to differ. Likes
        Hemingway's "emotional consistency," his returning to the
        same themes throughout his fiction. Besides emphasizing
        the importance of craft to Hemingway, Cowley also notes
        his "instinct for legends, for sacraments, for rituals,
        for symbols . . . ."

5   CRANSTON, HERBERT. "Hemingway's Early Days," [Midland,
        Ontario] Free Press Herald (17 Oct.), p. 2.
            Reminiscences by the editor of the Toronto Star Weekly,
        when Hemingway was on the staff in the early 1920's.

6   FARRELL, JAMES T. The League of Frightened Philistines: and
        other papers. New York: Vanguard Press, pp. 20-24.
            Includes "Ernest Hemingway's The Sun Also Rises," from
        New York Times Book Review (1 Aug., 1943). (See 1943.B3.)

7   FITZGERALD, F. SCOTT. The Crack-Up. Edited by Edmund Wilson.
        New York: Laughlin (New Directions).
            Letter to Hemingway regarding For Whom the Bell Tolls,
        Nov. 8, 1940; references to Hemingway in the Notebooks.

8   LERNER, MAX. Public Journal: Marginal Notes on Wartime
        America. New York: Viking Press.
            Pp. 44-46: "On Hemingway."
        Reprinted from PM (28 Sept. 1944) (See 1944.B10); pp. 87-
        89: "No Man Is An Island," reprinted from PM (18 July
        1943). (See 1943.B6.)

9   [PEIRCE, WALDO]. Waldo Peirce. New York: American Artists
        Group, Monograph No. 5, p. 43.
            Portrait of Hemingway which appeared on the cover of
        Time, 30 (18 Oct. 1937).

*10 SCHNEIDER, MARCEL. "Ernest Hemingway," Espace (June), pp. 98-
        105.
            Cited in Hanneman bibliography, p. 415 (See 1967.A4).

11   SLOCHOWER, HARRY. No Voice Is Wholly Lost: Writers and
        Thinkers in War and Peace. New York: Creative Age Press,
        pp. 36-40.
            In "Bourgeois Bohemia: Huxley and Hemingway," sees
        Hemingway as representative of "the later, disillusioned
        stage of bohemia." By the time of For Whom the Bell Tolls,
        Slochower feels that Hemingway realized that "neutral
        amoralism was anti-human."

12   WEST, RAY B. "Ernest Hemingway: The Failure of Sensibility,"
        Sewanee Review, 53 (Winter), 120-35.
            West finds Hemingway's fiction flawed because he forces
        material to his own ideological end, and moralizes through
        it. Stylistically he is too dependent on understatement.
        Thematically his perspective is limited, but West does ad-
        mire "The Short Happy Life of Francis Macomber."
        Reprinted in Modern American Fiction, edited by Walton

1945

(WEST, RAY B.)
> Litz, New York, Oxford University Press, 1963, pp. 244-55
> (See 1963.B31); Forms of Modern Fiction, edited by William
> Van O'Connor, Minneapolis, University of Minnesota Press,
> 1948, pp. 87-101 (See 1948.B5); The Art of Modern Fiction,
> edited by West and Robert W. Stallman, New York, Holt,
> Rinehart, 1949, pp. 622-34 (See 1949.B20); West's The
> Writer in the Room: Selected Essays, East Lansing,
> Michigan State University Press, 1968, pp. 142-57 (See
> 1968.B66); in Gellens, pp. 15-27 (See 1970.A2); in Weeks,
> pp. 139-51 (See 1962.A6); in Baker critiques, pp. 28-36
> (See 1962.A5).

1946 A BOOKS - NONE

1946 B SHORTER WRITINGS

1   BURLINGAME, ROGER. Of Making Many Books: A Hundred Years of
    Reading, Writing and Publishing, 1846-1946. New York:
    Scribner's.
       Reminiscence of Hemingway's leaving Boni and Liveright
    and becoming associated with Scribner's.

2   COHN, LOUIS HENRY. First Editions of Modern Authors: With a
    Notable Hemingway Collection. New York: House of Books,
    Catalogue, pp. 29-40.
       Includes 118 Hemingway items, among them the manuscript
    of "The Snows of Kilimanjaro." See William White's article
    in American Book Collector, 7 (Nov. 1956). (See 1956.B30.)

3   COWLEY, MALCOLM. "U. S. Books Abroad," Life, 21 (16 Sept.), 6.
       General article in which Cowley claims "Of all American
    authors, Ernest Hemingway is the most widely admired and
    imitated for his technique."

4   HOFFMAN, FREDERICK, J., CHARLES ALLEN, and CAROLYN F. ULRICH,
    eds. The Little Magazine: A History and a Bibliography.
    Princeton: Princeton University Press.
       Attention to Hemingway's contributions, both prose and
    poetry, to the little magazines. Facsimile of the first
    page of "A Divine Gesture," reprinted from the Double
    Dealer, 3 (May 1922), opposite p. 28.

5   FARRELL, JAMES T. "The American Novelist and American Society,
    IV: Ernest Hemingway and Scott Fitzgerald," Institute in
    American Studies, July 15 to July 20 (Minn.: Center for
    Continuation Study, University of Minnesota), pp. 30-32.

(FARRELL, JAMES T.)
Considers Hemingway a "sensationalist in technique" and an adolescent in values. Farrell is disturbed that there is so little growth in Hemingway's fiction.

6 GRAY, JAMES. "Tenderly Tolls the Bell for Three Soldiers," in On Second Thought. Minneapolis: University of Minnesota Press, pp. 74-81.
Sees Fitzgerald, Dos Passos, and Hemingway as similar in their mixture of eagerness and dread, but finds Hemingway unique in his "naive passion for the idiom of ruggedness" and in his use of the "post-graduate 4-H lad" as hero. Considers For Whom the Bell Tolls his best novel. Reprinted in McCaffery, pp. 226-35 (See 1950.A1).

7 GROTH, JOHN. "A Note on Ernest Hemingway," in Men Without Women. Cleveland: The World Publishing Co., pp. 11-16.
The illustrator of sketches for Men Without Women recalls meeting Hemingway in Germany during September of 1944.
Reprinted in McCaffery, pp. 19-24 (See 1950.A1).

8 LINSCOTT, ROGER BOURNE. On the Books column, New York Herald Tribune Book Review (29 Dec.), p. 13.
Interview with Hemingway in New York.

9 McNULTY, JOHN. Review of the film, The Killers, New Yorker, 22 (7 Sept.), 49-50.
Applauds the movie for maintaining the intensity that characterizes Hemingway's stories.

10 MATTHEWS, HERBERT L. The Education of a Correspondent. New York: Harcourt, Brace, pp. 95-106.
Describes the Teruel, December of 1937, attack which he and Hemingway covered together.

11 PHILLIPS, WILLIAM and PHILIP RAHV, eds. The Partisan Reader: Ten Years of Partisan Review, 1934-1944. New York: Dial Press, pp. 639-44.
"An American in Spain" by Lionel Trilling, review of For Whom the Bell Tolls, reprinted from Partisan Review, 8 (Jan.-Feb. 1941). (See 1941.B37.)
Reprinted in Baker critiques, pp. 78-81 (See 1962.A5).

12 SARTRE, JEAN-PAUL. "American Novelists in French Eyes," Atlantic, 178 (Aug.), 114-18.
General article. "To writers of my generation, the publication of the 42nd Parallel, Light in August, A

1946

(SARTRE, JEAN-PAUL)
Farewell to Arms, evoked a reaction similar to the one produced 15 years earlier by the Ulysses of James Joyce. . . .
The greatest literary development in France between 1929
and 1939 was the discovery of Faulkner, Dos Passos, Hemingway, Caldwell, Steinbeck."

13   SAVAGE, D. S. "The Realist Novel in the Thirties: Ernest
Hemingway," Focus, 2, pp. 7-27.
Examines the reasons Hemingway gained fame as a "stylist,"
and then traces what he sees as only a slight development
from early novels to the present. Sees that all of his
characters are marked by "profound spiritual inertia, inner vacancy and impotence," and concludes that Hemingway
has been responsible for the "proletarianization" of literature: "the adaptation of the technical artistic consciousness."
Reprinted in The Withered Branch, London, Eyre & Spottis-
woode, 1950, pp. 29-43 (See 1950.B50).

14   van GELDER, ROBERT. Writers and Writing. New York: Scribner's, pp. 95-98.
"Ernest Hemingway Talks of Work and War," interview reprinted from New York Times Book Review (11 Aug. 1940).
(See 1940.B38.)

1947 A   BOOKS - NONE

1947 B   SHORTER WRITINGS

1   ANON. "Indestructible," Talk of the Town column, New Yorker,
22 (4 Jan.), 20.
Interview with Hemingway in New York.

2   BURGUM, EDWIN BERRY. The Novel and the World's Dilemma. New
York: Oxford University Press.
Includes Stein's "Portrait of Hemingway," (pp. 171-72)
(See 1934.B20); Burgum's "Ernest Hemingway and the Psychology of the Lost Generation," reprinted in McCaffery,
pp. 308-28 (See 1950.A1); and a discussion of the influence
of Hemingway on Richard Wright, from a modified Marxist
perspective. Burgum sees A Farewell to Arms as the
"earliest" of Hemingway's novels, both in style and
philosophy; and The Sun Also Rises and the stories as
his best writing.

3   BUTCHER, FANNY. The Literary Spotlight column, Chicago Sunday
        Tribune (30 March), Magazine of Books, p. 10.
            Visiting with the Hemingways at Finca Vigia.

4   CANBY, HENRY SEIDEL. American Memoir. Boston: Houghton
        Mifflin, pp. 339-44.
            Sees The Sun Also Rises as disturbing because its charac-
        ters lacked any kind of will, as did its author. Canby
        feels, however, that the Hemingway of For Whom the Bell
        Tolls came to doubt his earlier theory of "life without
        principle."

5   CAPA, ROBERT. Slightly Out of Focus. New York: Henry Holt.
        Photos.
            Photographer Capa writes of Hemingway in London in 1944
        and with the 4th Infantry in France, before and after the
        liberation of Paris.

6   DANIEL, ROBERT. "Hemingway and His Heroes," Queen's Quarterly,
        54 (Winter), 471-85.
            Daniel objects to Brooks and Warren's finding a simple
        "code" applicable to each Hemingway hero; he instead uses
        the term "promethean hero," an extraordinary man, possessed
        of special sensitivity and courage.

7   de FELS, MARTHE. "A la recherche d'Hemingway," Bataille
        (16 July), p. 6.
            Interview with Hemingway in Havana.

8   FROHOCK, W. M. "Ernest Hemingway: Violence and Discipline,"
        Southwest Review, 32 (Winter), 89-97, Part I; (Spring),
        pp. 184-93, Part II.
            Sees that Hemingway has "devoted his great talent to
        relatively small subjects." For Whom the Bell Tolls was
        the culmination of his philosophy; in that novel his
        violence had a meaning. Since then, his subject matter
        has not done justice to his great skill. However, every
        younger writer has imitated him, but never successfully.
        Appears in part in "Ernest Hemingway--The River and the
        Hawk," The Novel of Violence in America. (Dallas, Texas:
        Southern Methodist University Press), pp. 166-198 (See
        1950.B23).
            Reprinted in McCaffery, pp. 262-91 (See 1950.A1).

9   GURKO, LEO. The Angry Decade. New York: Dodd, Mead, pp. 187-
        90.
            Concerning Hemingway in the 1930's, Gurko sees that he
        was drawn to the Spanish Civil War by its appropriateness

1947

(GURKO, LEO)
for his pervasive "script, the act of dying." Spain, however, provided "a new kind of dying," that inspired by a
political cause, and it excited Hemingway to heights of
experimentation. The result is a slightly unreal,
idealized Jordan.

10   KEMPTON, KENNETH PAYSON. The Short Story. Cambridge: Harvard
University Press.
Admires Hemingway's dialogue but wishes it were more
often identified. In "The Killers," Kempton responds to
the "overtone," its second meaning, which grows from Hemingway's artistic discipline.

11   MORRIS, LLOYD. Postscript to Yesterday: America: The Last
Fifty Years. New York: Random House, pp. 154-57.
"Salvage," a discussion of Hemingway's view of life as
seen through his characters, "hard-boiled" and mistrustful
of mental processes. Hemingway's view that life was "something to be endured, a kind of penalty" (as in The Sun Also
Rises) was oddly accurate for the perspective that modern
civilization was emasculating. In For Whom the Bell Tolls,
however, Hemingway found a "social faith" and thereby sal-
vaged his belief.

12   PEYRE, HENRI. "American Literature Through French Eyes,"
Virginia Quarterly Review, 23 (Summer), pp. 421-38.
General article, concluding that "the great names of
American fiction are thus in French eyes Hemingway, Stein-
beck, Dos Passos, and Faulkner."

13   PUTNAM, SAMUEL. Paris Was Our Mistress: Memoirs of a Lost
and Found Generation. New York: Viking Press, pp. 127-34.
In "Hard-Boiled Young Man Going Places (Ernest Hemingway)" reminisces on his meetings with Hemingway in Chicago,
in Paris, and elsewhere during the 1920's.

14   RASCOE, BURTON. We Were Interrupted. Garden City, New York:
Doubleday.
In this autobiography, Rascoe recalls meeting Hemingway
in Paris in 1924.

15   SNELL, GEORGE. The Shapers of American Fiction: 1798-1947.
New York: Dutton, pp. 156-72.
In "Ernest Hemingway and the 'Fifth Dimension'" finds
that only in "Snows of Kilimanjaro" does Hemingway achieve
that other dimension. Sees his later work as generally
deficient in the harmony between style and theme that
shaped the earliest writing.

16 TARG, WILLIAM, ed. <u>Carrousel for Bibliophiles</u>. New York:
     Duschnes, pp. 31-35.
        "Why Does Nobody Collect Me?" by Robert Benchley.
     Reprinted from the <u>Colophon</u>, Part 18 (Sept. 1934). (<u>See</u>
     1934.B4.)

17 "Thalia." "Saints Days in Cuba Are Days of Gaiety and Enter-
     tainment," <u>Chicago Sunday Tribune</u> (30 March), Section 7,
     p. 7.
        Includes a description of Finca Vigia.

18 WARREN, ROBERT PENN. "Ernest Hemingway," <u>Kenyon Review</u>, 9
     (Winter), 1-28.
        Thorough discussion of Hemingway's strengths as writer,
     with expert attention to both craft and theme. Warren
     emphasizes <u>A Farewell to Arms</u> but his remarks are appli-
     cable to all Hemingway's writing.
     Reprinted as introduction to Modern Standard Authors
     Edition of <u>A Farewell to Arms</u> (New York: Scribner's,
     1949); in <u>Critiques and Essays on Modern Fiction</u>, edited
     by J. W. Aldridge (New York: Ronald, 1952), pp. 447-73
     (<u>See</u> 1952.B10); in <u>Literary Opinion in America</u>, edited by
     M. D. Zabel (New York: Harper, 1951), pp. 447-60 (<u>See</u>
     1951.B31); in Warren's <u>Selected Essays</u> (New York: Random
     House, 1958), pp. 80-118 (<u>See</u> 1958.B14); and in Wagner,
     pp. 75-102 (<u>See</u> 1974.A3).

1948 A BOOKS - NONE

1948 B SHORTER WRITINGS

 1 BAKER, DENYS VAL, ed. <u>Writers of Today</u>. Vol. 2 (London:
     Sidgwick & Jackson), pp. 3-18.
        "Ernest Hemingway" by Malcolm Cowley, reprinted from the
     Introduction to the Viking <u>Portable Hemingway</u>, pp. vii-
     xxiv (<u>See</u> 1945.B4).

 2 BISHOP, JOHN PEALE. <u>The Collected Essays of John Peale Bishop</u>.
     Edited with an introduction by Edmund Wilson. New York:
     Scribner's, pp. 37-46 and 66-77.
        "Homage to Hemingway," reprinted from <u>New Republic</u>, 89
     (11 Nov. 1936). (<u>See</u> 1936.B3.) Reprinted in <u>After the
     Genteel Tradition</u>, edited by Malcolm Cowley (<u>See</u> 1937.B23),
     and "The Missing All," reprinted from <u>Virginia Quarterly
     Review</u>, 13 (Winter 1937). (<u>See</u> 1937.B20.) Reprinted in
     McCaffery, pp. 292-307 (<u>See</u> 1950.A1).

1948

3   FRIEDE, DONALD. <u>The Mechanical Angel: His Adventures and</u>
<u>Enterprises in the Glittering 1920's</u>. New York: Knopf.
Friede recalls publishing <u>In Our Time</u> and handling the
motion picture sale of <u>For Whom the Bell Tolls</u> in 1940.

4   MacLEISH, ARCHIBALD. <u>Act Five and Other Poems</u>. New York:
Random House.
"Years of the Dog" partially quoted in Baker, p. 19.

5   O'CONNOR, WILLIAM VAN, ed. <u>Forms of Modern Fiction</u>. Minneapolis: University of Minnesota Press.
Includes "Ernest Hemingway: The Failure of Sensibility"
by Ray B. West, Jr., reprinted from <u>The Sewanee Review</u>,
53 (Jan.-March 1945). (<u>See</u> 1945.B12.)

6   ORVIS, MARY BURCHARD. <u>The Art of Writing Fiction</u>. New York:
Prentice-Hall.
Discusses "The Short Happy Life of Francis Macomber,"
<u>A Farewell to Arms</u>, and <u>For Whom the Bell Tolls</u> as useful
samples of writing for various techniques.

7   PRAZ, MARIO. "Hemingway in Italy," <u>Partisan Review</u>, 15 (Oct.),
1086-1100.
Explains the position of Hemingway in Italy and traces
his somewhat negative influence on the work of Elio Vittorini and Giuseppe Berto. Sees Hemingway as a "primitive."
Reprinted in Baker anthology, pp. 116-30 (<u>See</u> 1961.A5).

8   SAVAGE, D. S. "Ernest Hemingway," <u>Hudson Review</u>, 1 (Autumn),
380-401.
Sees <u>For Whom the Bell Tolls</u> as representative of Hemingway's earlier "sickness masquerading as health." Concludes
that the novel contains no social or political insight,
only "peculiar sentimentalism."

9   ·SCHORER, MARK. "Technique as Discovery," <u>Hudson Review</u>, 1
(Spring), 67-87.
General article, emphasizing the modern writer's reliance on organic form. Admires <u>The Sun Also Rises</u> because its form suits its theme so well, theme here being
"the exhaustion of value."

10   WILSON, EARL. It Happened Last Night column, <u>New York Post</u>
(26 Feb.), p. 30.
Details of a visit with the Hemingways at Finca Vigia.

1949 A BOOKS - NONE

1949 B SHORTER WRITINGS

1   ANON. "Giant of the Storytellers," Coronet, 25 (April), 16-17.
     Photographic essay. Biographical profile.

2   BLANKENSHIP, RUSSELL. American Literature: As an Expression
     of the National Mind. New York: Holt, Rinehart & Winston,
     pp. 731-42.
        Discussion of Hemingway as "one of the few original
     writers to arise in America since Mark Twain" in the chap-
     ter "The Present Confusion." Thinks Hemingway's originali-
     ty lies in his having "a characteristic point of view,"
     unique manner of expression, and his uncanny ability to re-
     create "an ordinary incident such as a quail hunt." Makes
     reference to "the authentic Hemingway down to 1937."

3   COWLEY, MALCOLM. "A Portrait of Mister Papa," Life, 25
     (10 Jan.), 86-101. Photos.
        Recounts Hemingway's World War II experiences as he sup-
     posed they related to the in-progress "sea, land, and air"
     epic; biography of the life to date.

4   CRANE, R. S. "Ernest Hemingway: 'The Short Happy Life of
     Francis Macomber,'" English "A" Analyst (Department of
     English, Northwestern University), 16 (1 Nov.).
        Reprinted in Crane, The Idea of the Humanities and Other
     Essays Critical and Historical (Chicago: The University
     of Chicago Press), II, pp. 315-26 (See 1967.B11); and in
     Howell, pp. 129-36 (See 1969.A9).

5   FARRINGTON, S. KIP, Jr. Fishing the Atlantic: Offshore and
     On. New York: Coward-McCann.
        References to fishing with Hemingway.

6   GEISMAR, MAXWELL. "The Position of Ernest Hemingway. Part 2:
     Notes from a Critic on a Novelist's Work," New York Times
     Book Review (31 July), p. 1. Photo.
        In answer to Part 1: "Notes from a Novelist on His
     System of Work--a Letter from Hemingway."

7   GORDON, CAROLINE. "Notes on Hemingway and Kafka," The Sewanee
     Review, 57: 215-226.
        Sees Hemingway as inferior to Kafka because Hemingway is
     concerned mostly with the divinity of man, whereas Kafka
     deals with man's relation to God. Their techniques are
     somewhat the same (dramatic economy, good writing, serious
     subjects) but Hemingway's "reach is not long enough."

1949

8   HACKETT, FRANCIS. "Hemingway: <u>A Farewell to Arms</u>," <u>SRL</u>, 32
(6 Aug.), 32-33.
A reappraisal of the novel, and its metamorphosis in the
twenty years since first publication.

9   HALLIDAY, E. M. "Hemingway's <u>In Our Time</u>," <u>Explicator</u>, 7
(March), Item 35.
Sees no particular order in the arrangement of <u>In Our</u>
<u>Time</u>--more likely, Hemingway was trying "to give an im-
pression of disorder."

10 HEMPHILL, GEORGE. "Hemingway and James," <u>Kenyon Review</u>, 11
(Winter), 50-60.
Sees Hemingway as the writer "everything happens to" and
James, "the man to whom <u>nothing</u> ever happens." Hemphill
finds this dichotomy important because Hemingway's fiction
is so much more immediate, so involved in modern living.
Hemphill thinks that Hemingway "writes moral tracts, for
our times," and uses <u>In Our Time</u> as illustration of that
principle: "The unifying principle of <u>In Our Time</u> is the
author's thematic obsession."

11 KAZIN, ALFRED. Brief appraisal, <u>New York Herald Tribune Book</u>
<u>Review</u> (25 Sept.), p. 25.
Gives reasons for choosing <u>A Farewell to Arms</u> as one of
the three most memorable books of the previous twenty-five
years.

12 LEGMAN, GERSHON. <u>Love and Death: A Study in Censorship</u>. New
York: Breaking Point, pp. 86-90.
Discussion of Hemingway's heroes and heroines.

13 MIZENER, ARTHUR. <u>The Far Side of Paradise: A Biography of F.</u>
<u>Scott Fitzgerald</u>. Boston: Houghton Mifflin.
Letters from Hemingway to Fitzgerald are quoted; also
regarding Fitzgerald's portrayal of Hemingway as Phillipe,
the hero in "The Count of Darkness," published in installments in <u>Redbook</u>.

14 MORRIS, LLOYD. "Heritage of a Generation of Novelists:
Anderson and Dreiser, Hemingway, Faulkner, Farrell and
Steinbeck," <u>New York Herald Tribune Book Review</u> (25 Sept.),
p. 12.
Comments on philosophical similarities.

15 ROSS, LILLIAN. Profile, "El Unico Matador," <u>New Yorker</u>, 25
(12 March), 34-45, Part I; (26 March), 32-56, Part III.
Hemingway was one of the people interviewed for this profile of Sidney Franklin, the American bullfighter.

16   TEDLOCK, E. W., Jr. "Hemingway's 'The Snows of Kilimanjaro,'"
      Explicator, 8 (Oct.), Item 7.
         Sees the leopard (and other symbols) as "perfectly inte-
      grated with the story," with the interior monologues
      "keyed" to these symbols.

17   TRILLING, DIANA. Review of Elio Vittorini's In Sicily, New
      York Times Book Review (27 Nov.), pp. 1, 37.
         Criticizes Hemingway's introduction to the book as "end-
      lessly suggestive, and vulgar."

18   TRILLING, LIONEL. "Contemporary American Literature and Its
      Relation to Ideas," American Quarterly, 1 (Fall), 195-208.
         Finds the writing of Hemingway (and Faulkner) superior
      to that of most moderns because of the intensity, the
      honesty, and the final vision of the writing.
      Reprinted in The American Writer and the European Tradition,
      edited by Margaret Denny and William H. Gilman, Minneapolis,
      University of Minnesota Press, 1950, pp. 146-50 (See
      1950.B20); and under the title "The Meaning of a Literary
      Idea" in The Liberal Imagination (New York: Viking Press,
      1950).

19   WALCUTT, CHARLES C. "Hemingway's 'The Snows of Kilimanjaro,'"
      Explicator, 7 (April), Item 43.
         Sees the leopard as "a symbol of Harry's moral nature";
      the story, the presentation of conflict between Hemingway's
      "fundamental moral idealism" and "the corrupting influence
      of aimless materialism."

20   WARREN, ROBERT PENN. "Introduction" to A Farewell to Arms,
      Modern Standard Authors edition. (New York: Scribner's).
         Describes the original "hypnotic force" of the novel,
      and compares Hemingway with Wordsworth and Stevenson. Ends
      with an overview of the present criticism.
      Reprinted in Three Novels of Ernest Hemingway, New York,
      Charles Scribner's Sons, 1962, iii-xl.

21   WEST, RAY B., Jr. and Robert W. Stallman, eds. The Art of
      Modern Fiction. (New York: Holt, Rinehart), pp. 622-34.
         Analysis of A Farewell to Arms by West: "Ernest Heming-
      way: A Farewell to Arms."

1950 A BOOKS

1   McCAFFERY, JOHN K. M., ed. Ernest Hemingway: The Man and His
     Work (Cleveland: World).

1950

(McCAFFERY, JOHN K. M.)
Contents: pp. 9-15: Introduction by the editor.
pp. 19-24: "A Note on Ernest Hemingway" by John Groth, reprinted from Men Without Women (Cleveland: The Living Library, 1946), pp. 11-16.
pp. 25-33: "Hemingway in Paris" by Gertrude Stein, reprinted from The Autobiography of Alice B. Toklas (New York: Harcourt, Brace, 1933), pp. 261-71.
pp. 34-56: "A Portrait of Mister Papa" by Malcolm Cowley, reprinted from Life, 25 (10 Jan. 1949), revised slightly.
pp. 59-65: "The Canon of Death" by Lincoln Kirstein, reprinted from Hound & Horn, 6 (Jan.-March 1933).
pp. 66-75: "Bull in the Afternoon" by Max Eastman, reprinted from Art and the Life of Action (New York: Knopf, 1934), pp. 87-101.
pp. 76-108: "Ernest Hemingway: A Tragedy of Craftsmanship" by J. Ivan Kashkeen, reprinted from International Literature, No. 5 (May 1935).
pp. 109-113: "Hemingway and the Critics" by Elliot Paul, reprinted from SRL, 17 (6 Nov. 1937).
pp. 114-29: "Ernest Hemingway's Literary Situation" by Delmore Schwartz, reprinted from the Southern Review, 3 (Spring 1938).
pp. 130-42: "Farewell the Separate Peace: The Rejections of Ernest Hemingway" by Edgar Johnson, reprinted from the Sewanee Review, 48 (July-Sept. 1940).
pp. 143-89: "Ernest Hemingway: You Could Always Come Back" by Maxwell Geismar, reprinted from Writers in Crisis (Boston: Houghton Mifflin, 1942), pp. 39-85.
pp. 190-204: "Hemingway: Synopsis of a Career" by Alfred Kazin, reprinted and revised from On Native Grounds (New York: Doubleday, 1942), pp. 327-41.
pp. 205-220: "English and Spanish in For Whom the Bell Tolls," by Edward Fenimore, reprinted from ELH, 10 (March 1943).
pp. 221-25: "The Sun Also Rises" by James T. Farrell, reprinted from The League of Frightened Philistines (New York: Vanguard Press, 1945), pp. 20-24.
pp. 226-35: "Tenderly Tolls the Bell" by James Gray, reprinted from On Second Thought (Minneapolis: University of Minnesota Press, 1946), pp. 74-81.
pp. 236-57: "Hemingway: Gauge of Morale" by Edmund Wilson, reprinted from Atlantic, 146 (July 1939), 39-46.
pp. 258-61: "Hemingway in Spain" by Leo Gurko, reprinted from The Angry Decade (New York: Dodd, Mead, 1947), pp. 187-90.

(McCAFFERY, JOHN K. M.)

pp. 262-91: "Violence and Discipline" by W. M. Frohock, reprinted from The Novel of Violence in America (Dallas: Southern Methodist University Press, 1950), pp. 167-99.

pp. 292-307: "The Missing All" by John Peale Bishop, reprinted from The Collected Essays of John Peale Bishop (New York: Harcourt, Brace, 1948), pp. 66-77.

pp. 308-28: "Ernest Hemingway and the Psychology of the Lost Generation" by Edwin Berry Burgum, reprinted from The Novel and the World's Dilemma (New York: Oxford University Press, 1947), pp. 184-204.

pp. 329-39: "Hemingway and James" by George Hemphill, reprinted from the Kenyon Review, 11 (Winter 1949).

pp. 340-51: "Hemingway's Women" by Theodore Bardacke. Not previously published. Finds the heroines in Hemingway's writing very important because, for Hemingway, "heterosexual intercourse symbolizes love" just as war and bull fights symbolize death. Sees Catherine Barkley as the completely subjugated woman, Hemingway's ideal, contrasted with the unfulfilling emancipation of Brett Ashley. Another kind of ideal woman appears in the characters of Marie Morgan (To Have and Have Not) and Maria (For Whom the Bell Tolls). Reissued in 1969, New York, Cooper Square Publishers.

1950 B   SHORTER WRITINGS

1   ANON. "British Call Hemingway Book 'Evil, Adolescent,'" Chicago Sun Tribune Magazine of Books (17 Sept.), p. 14.
    Surveys the British critics' reception to Across the River and Into the Trees.

2   ANON. Editorial, "and New Champion," Collier's, 126 (18 Nov.), 86.
    Includes caricature of Hemingway.

3   ANON. Item, Commonweal, 52 (22 Sept.), 572-73.
    Survey of critical reception to Across the River and Into the Trees.

4   ANON. Item, Time, 54 (30 Oct.), 44.
    Quotes from Evelyn Waugh's criticism of Hemingway's critics in the Tablet, 196 (30 Sept. 1950). For William Faulkner's letter supporting Waugh, See Time, 56 (13 Nov. 1950), 6.

5   ANON. "The New Hemingway," Newsweek, 36 (11 Sept.), 90-95.
    Photos.

1950

(ANON.)
Article and review of <u>Across the River and Into the Trees</u>. Sees Hemingway as having "mastered a new subject and a new style." <u>Across the River and Into the Trees</u> is a study in shadows, "quiet talk, a sense of ease and friendliness, suddenly captured and suddenly lost, against the magical loveliness of the ancient city."

6   ANON. "Profile: Ernest Hemingway," <u>Observer</u> (10 Sept.), p. 2.
Biographical profile.

7   ANON. Review of <u>Across the River and Into the Trees</u>, <u>Time</u>, 56 (11 Sept.), 110, 113.
Although calling the famed Hemingway style a "parody of itself," this review recognizes that the novel does have powerful moments.

8   ANON. Review of <u>Across the River and Into the Trees</u>, <u>TLS</u> (6 Oct.), p. 628.
Sees the novel as completely controlled, with Hemingway being the old master competent, in charge of his skill and his passion.

9   ANON. "Shapers of the Modern Novel: A Catalogue of an Exhibition," <u>Princeton University Library Chronicle</u>, 12 (Spring), 134-41.
Fifteen Hemingway items listed on pp. 136-37.

10   ADAMS, J. DONALD. Speaking of Books column, <u>New York Times Book Review</u> (24 Sept.), p. 2.
Regarding the critics' reception of <u>Across the River and Into the Trees</u>.

11   ANGOFF, CHARLES. Review of <u>Across the River and Into the Trees</u>, <u>American Mercury</u>, 71 (Nov.), 619-25.
Unfavorable review of <u>Across the River and Into the Trees</u> as an incredible example of "his brand of realism."

12   "M. B." Review of <u>Across the River and Into the Trees</u>, <u>Saturday Night</u>, 65 (3 Oct.), 24.
Despite the absence of plot, <u>Across the River and Into the Trees</u> reveals Hemingway's "unique power of presenting a picture of universal sadness without a coincidental feeling of futility." "Here is the sure touch of the literary artist."

13   BREIT, HARVEY. "Talk With Mr. Hemingway," <u>New York Times Book Review</u> (17 Sept.), p. 14.
Informal interview.

14 BRERETON, GEOFFREY. Review of <u>Death in the Afternoon</u>, <u>New Statesman & Nation</u>, 39 (24 June), 716-17.
    Sees the book as "a minor monument to its epoch" and discusses the fascination Spain held for many writers.

15 BUTCHER, FANNY. Review of <u>Across the River and Into the Trees</u>, <u>Chicago Sunday Tribune</u> (17 Sept.), Magazine of Books, pp. 3, 14. Photo.
    Speaks of Hemingway's "old black magic with words, a magic which his imitators have dreamed of but which is truly his alone." Finds great power of technique in <u>Across the River and Into the Trees</u>, a novel dominated by its ending.

16 CLARK, GREGORY. "Hemingway Slept Here," <u>Montreal Standard</u> (4 Nov.), pp. 13-14.
    Reminiscences by the Feature Editor of the <u>Toronto Star Weekly</u> about Hemingway's writing for the paper in the early 1920's.

17 CONNOLLY, CYRIL. Review of <u>Across the River and Into the Trees</u>, <u>Sunday Times</u> (London), (3 Sept.), p. 3.
    Considers the novel "lamentable," though he points out that nearly every great writer has written at least one bad book. Finds most offensive Hemingway's "false sense of values."

18 "N. C." [NORMAN COUSINS]. Editorial, "Hemingway and Steinbeck," <u>SRL</u>, 33 (28 Oct.), 26-27.
    Compares <u>Across the River and Into the Trees</u> with Steinbeck's <u>Burning Bright</u>, and decides that Steinbeck "reveals moral values where Hemingway reveals monomaniac meanderings."

19 COWLEY, MALCOLM. Review of <u>Across the River and Into the Trees</u>, <u>New York Herald Tribune Book Review</u> (10 Sept.), pp. 1, 16.
    Beautifully polished so far as the writing is concerned, <u>Across the River and Into the Trees</u> is, however, "still below the level of his earlier novels, which we studied so eagerly and from which we learned so much." Calls the novel "a tired book," and waits for Hemingway's next "big book."

20 DENNY, MARGARET and WILLIAM H. GILMAN, eds. <u>The American Writer and the European Tradition</u>. Minneapolis: University of Minnesota Press.
    Includes Lionel Trilling's discussion of the importance

1950

(DENNY, MARGARET and WILLIAM H. GILMAN)
of ideas in the fiction of both Faulkner and Hemingway.
Reprinted from American Quarterly, 1 (Fall 1949). (See
1949.B18.) Also includes Harry Levin's "Some European
Views of Contemporary American Literature," in which
Levin quotes Cyril Connolly's "envy" of America for
having "Hemingway as a novelist, Edmund Wilson as a critic,
and E. E. Cummings as a poet," pp. 168-84.

21 DRISCOLL, JOSEPH. "Hemingway Takes Shine Off High Brass," St.
Louis Post-Dispatch (1 Oct.), p. 2G.
This article, subtitled, "Author Ranks Ten Best Generals
in New Book," quotes largely from Across the River and
Into the Trees.

22 ENGSTROM, ALFRED G. "Dante, Flaubert, and 'The Snows of Kilimanjaro,'" Modern Language Notes, 65 (March), 203-05.
Sees that death holds the same symbolic importance for
Hemingway that righteousness held for Dante, and art main-
tained for Flaubert.

23 FROHOCK, WILBUR M. The Novel of Violence in America: 1920-
1950. Dallas: Southern Methodist University Press,
pp. 167-99. Drawing of Hemingway.
"Ernest Hemingway: The River and the Hawk," reprinted
from Southwest Review, 32 (Winter and Spring 1947). (See
1947.B8.)

24 GALLUP, DONALD C. "The Making of The Making of Americans,"
New Colophon, 3: 54-74.
Quotes from correspondence between Gertrude Stein and
Hemingway in the early 1920's, regarding publication of
her book in Transatlantic Review. Facsimile of Hemingway
letter, p. 65.

25 GANNETT, LEWIS. Review of Across the River and Into the Trees,
New York Herald Tribune (7 September), p. 23.
Has reservations about the novel because even at its
best, it is not Hemingway at his best; and parts of it are
very bad. Objects to the typical Hemingway "dream girl,"
the good shooting, the contrived plot.

26 GARDINER, HAROLD C., S.J. Review of Across the River and Into
the Trees, America, 83 (16 Sept.), 628, 630.
Considers this "an utterly trivial book," dominated by
an "unmanly atmosphere of griping and whining." Does admire "the sense of human fellowship" and "the bitter realization of the futility of war."

27   GEISMAR, MAXWELL. Review of Across the River and Into the
         Trees, SRL, 33 (9 Sept.), 18, 19. Photo.
              Sees the book as "not only Hemingway's worst novel" but
         also "the synthesis of everything that is bad in his pre-
         vious work." Another adjective Geismar uses is "dreadful."

28   HANSEN, HARRY. "Hemingway Back, Carrying His Hush-Hush Manu-
         script," Chicago Sunday Tribune (9 April), 4, p. 10.
              Hemingway arrived in New York, conferring with Wallace
         Meyer, his Scribner's editor, about changes in Across the
         River and Into the Trees for book publication.

29   HICKS, GRANVILLE, "The Critics Have Never Been Easy on Heming-
         way," New York Times Book Review (15 Oct.), pp. 5, 32.
         Review of McCaffery. (See 1950.A1.)

30   HOLMES, JOHN and CARROLL S. TOWLE, eds. A Complete College
         Reader. Boston: Houghton Mifflin, pp. 244-47.
         Reprinted "A Farewell to Arms, A Review" by Henry Seidel
         Canby, from SRL, 6 (12 Oct. 1929). (See 1929.B11.)

31   HUTCHENS, JOHN K. "Nobody on the Fence," New York Herald
         Tribune Book Review (24 Sept. 1950), p. 3.
              Points out the universal (almost) negative reaction to
         Across the River and Into the Trees.

32   JACKSON, JOSEPH HENRY. Review of Across the River and Into
         the Trees, San Francisco Chronicle (7 Sept.), p. 18.
              Sees the novel as important but not so great as most of
         his earlier books.

33   KAZIN, ALFRED. Review of Across the River and Into the Trees,
         New Yorker, 26 (9 Sept.), 101-03.
              Thinks the novel was written under great tension and in
         haste, and is waiting for the next novel. This one "can
         only distress anyone who admires Hemingway."

34   LEWIS, WYNDHAM. Rude Assignment: A narrative of my career
         up-to-date. London: Hutchinson.
              Appraises Hemingway's work as limited by his choice of
         characters and his own attitudes toward them. Quotes a
         letter from Hemingway.

35   LYONS, LEONARD. The Lyons Den column, New York Post (30 March),
         p. 30.
              Quotes a letter from Hemingway listing his five "home
         towns" as being Paris, Venice, Ketchum, Key West, and
         Havana.
              Partially reprinted in Time, 55 (10 April), 36.

1950

36   MEYER, BEN F.   "Hemingway Novel of Venice Completed at Home in
            Cuba," Kansas City Star (10 Sept.), p. 1C.
            Interview with Hemingway at Finca Vigia.

37   MILLER, LEE G.   The Story of Ernie Pyle.   New York: Viking
            Press.
                References to Hemingway when he and Pyle (and other war
            correspondents) lived in a press camp near Omaha Beach,
            Normandy, June 1944.

38   O'HARA, JOHN.   Review of Across the River and Into the Trees,
            New York Times Book Review (10 Sept.), pp. 1, 30-31.
            Photos.
                High praise for the novel and for Hemingway: "The most
            important author living today, the outstanding author since
            the death of Shakespeare . . . . out of the millions of
            writers who have lived since 1616."   For replies to this
            review, see New York Times Book Review (1 Oct.), p. 37.

39   PAUL, ELLIOT.   Review of Across the River and Into the Trees,
            Providence Sunday Journal (10 Sept.), 6, p. 8.
                Finds the novel "familiar, touching, sad."   "Thanks to
            Ernest and nuts to his disparagers."

40   PERKINS, MAXWELL E.   Editor to Author: The Letters of Maxwell
            E. Perkins.   Edited by John Hall Wheelock.   New York:
            Scribner's.
                Included are 15 letters to Hemingway, written between
            1932 and 1945.

41   POORE, CHARLES.   Review of McCaffery, New York Times (30 Sept.),
            p. 15.
                (See 1950.A1.)

42   _____.   Review of Across the River and Into the Trees, New
            York Times (7 Sept.), p. 29.
                Sees the book as "proof positive that he is still the
            old master," complete with "stinging comedy" and "his
            profoundly tragic sense of life."

43   POUND, EZRA.   The Letters of Ezra Pound: 1907-1941.   Edited by
            D. D. Paige.   New York: Harcourt, Brace.
                Mentions Hemingway as protege; letter to Hemingway in
            1936, commending an Esquire article.

44   RAHV, PHILIP.   Review of Across the River and Into the Trees,
            Commentary, 10 (Oct.), 400-02.
                Sees the book as "egregiously bad" and "a parody" of the

(RAHV, PHILIP)
usual Hemingway. "The story turns on no significant principle of honor or valor or compassion such as invested
some of Hemingway's earlier narratives with value and
meaning."
Reprinted in Image and Idea, New York, New Directions,
1957, pp. 188-92 (See 1957.B24); and The Myth and the
Powerhouse, New York, Farrar, Straus and Giroux, 1964,
pp. 193-98 (See 1964.B43).

45   REDMAN, BEN RAY. "The Champ and the Referees," SRL, 33
(28 Oct.), 15-16, 38.
     Assesses the diverse reception accorded Across the River
and Into the Trees, and feels that reviewers are reading
Hemingway too much as Cantwell. Sees that Hemingway remains "one of our greatest living authors."

46   REED, HENRY. Review of Across the River and Into the Trees,
Listener, 44 (9 Nov.), 515.
     Compares Across the River and Into the Trees with Al-
berto Moravia's Disobedience. Finds "an honestly earned
richness and certainty in Moravia; in Hemingway there is
only an affected roughness which suggests a quick-return
evasion of all difficult problems."

47   ROSS, LILLIAN. Profile, "How Do You Like It Now, Gentlemen?"
New Yorker, 26 (13 May), 36-62.
     Drawing of Hemingway by Reginald Marsh. Controversial
portrait of Hemingway in which he discusses drinking,
writing, friendship, and the present life he leads. "I
wake up in the morning and my mind starts making sentences,
and I have to get rid of them fast--talk them or write
them down."
     Reprinted, somewhat revised, in Portrait of Hemingway, New
York, Simon and Schuster, 1961 (See 1962.A6); in Weeks,
pp. 17-39 (See 1962.A6).

48   ROVERE, RICHARD H. Review of Across the River and Into the
Trees, Harper's Magazine, 201 (Sept.), 104-16.
     Finds the book "disappointing." "It is an incredibly
talky book . . . almost garrulous." Suspects that Hemingway "is here using dialogue not as a tool of narrative but
simply as a means for the author to unburden himself of
opinions."

49   RUGOFF, MILTON. "Much Smoke, Some Sparks," New York Herald
Tribune Book Review (15 Oct.), p. 12.
     Review of McCaffery. (See 1950.A1.)

1950

50   SAVAGE, DEREK S. The Withered Branch: Six Studies in the
       Modern Novel. London: Eyre & Spottiswoode, pp. 23-43.
       Reprinted "Ernest Hemingway" from Focus, 2 (1946). (See
       1946.B13.)

51   SIMON, KATE. Review of Across the River and Into the Trees,
       New Republic, 123 (18 Sept.), 20-21.
           Reads the novel as "a slight, sad book, quieter and more
       muted than his others," whose phrasing blurs "the border
       between prose and poetry." "The mixture is, on a minor
       scale, as before and still magical; the Hemingway spell
       still holds."

52   SMITH, HARRISON. "A Titan To Task," SRL, 33 (28 Oct.), 17, 39.
       Review of McCaffery. (See 1950.A1.)

53   STEGNER, WALLACE. "Fiction: A Lens on Life," SRL, 33
       (22 April), 9-10, 32-33.
           Sees individuality as the key to any author's greatness:
       "The world that results in Hemingway's fiction may not be
       a world we like, but it is unmistakably a world."

54   STEIN, LEO. Journey Into the Self. Edited by Edmund Fuller.
       New York: Crown.
           In a 1934 letter to Dr. Trigant Burrow, Stein finds
       Hemingway's writing illustrative of the effect Cézanne's
       painting may have on the written word.

55   STRONG, L. A. G. Review of Across the River and Into the
       Trees, Spectator, 185 (8 Sept.), 279.
           States that Hemingway's "great gifts survive. The
       descriptive writing is assured, the dialogue, as always,
       excellent." Has reservations about the novel, however,
       because "the colonel is immature," and his reaction to the
       threat of death is to drink himself toward it; therefore,
       he is no tragic figure.

56   WALLENSTEIN, MARCEL. "A Tip from Gertrude Stein Started Hem-
       ingway to Top," Kansas City Times (5 Jan.), p. 13.
           Reminiscence about Hemingway in Paris in the 1920's,
       when Stein advised him to give up newspaper work.

57   WARSHOW, ROBERT. Review of Across the River and Into the
       Trees, Partisan Review, 17 (Nov.-Dec.), 876-84.
           This compilation of Hemingway's usual themes and situa-
       tions is, however, here "so vulgarized that one wonders
       how the writer himself can possibly be taken in . . . .
       the saddest story Hemingway has written."

58   WAUGH, EVELYN. "The Case of Mr. Hemingway," <u>Commonweal</u>, 53
        (3 Nov.), 97-98.
            A defense of <u>Across the River and Into the Trees</u> and a
        question as to the reason critics and reviewers are anti-
        Hemingway. Waugh claims they have found in Hemingway a
        quality they abhor--"Decent Feeling," exemplified in this
        novel as "respect for women, pity for the weak, love of
        honor."
        Reprinted in <u>Commonweal</u>, 99 (16 Nov. 1973), 195-97.

59   _____. Review of <u>Across the River and Into the Trees</u>, <u>Tablet</u>,
        196 (30 Sept.), 290, 292.
            Cuts through all the critical furor and states, "What,
        in fact, Hemingway has done is to write a story entirely
        characteristic of himself, not his best book, perhaps his
        worst, but still something very much better than most of
        the work to which the same critics give their tepid
        applause." Finds its strength in the fact that it is
        "largely a monologue" and therefore the unique Hemingway
        vernacular excels.

60   WEEKS, EDWARD. Review of <u>Across the River and Into the Trees</u>,
        <u>Atlantic</u>, 186 (Oct.), 80, 81.
            Finds the book good for Hemingway's treatment of various
        kinds of love--for the Infantry, for Venice and the Vene-
        tians, for sea food and wine, and gondolas and Renata.

61   WHITE, E. B. "Across the Street and Into the Grill," <u>New
        Yorker</u>, 26 (14 Oct.), 28.
            Parody.
        Reprinted in <u>The Second Tree from the Corner</u>, New York,
        Harper, 1954, pp. 140-43 (<u>See</u> 1954.B50).

62   WILLIAMS, TENNESSEE. "A Writer's Quest for a Parnassus," <u>New
        York Times Magazine</u> (13 Aug.), pp. 16, 35. Caricature.
            General article, mentioning <u>Across the River and Into
        the Trees</u> and Hemingway's relationship with Venice.

63   WILLIAMS, WILLIAM CARLOS. <u>A Beginning on the Short Story
        (Notes)</u>. New York: Alicat Bookshop Press.
            Praises "Big, Two-Hearted River"; traces Hemingway's
        excellence in part to his sitting "at the feet of Gertrude
        Stein and Ezra Pound. They taught him a lot,"
        Reprinted as essay in <u>Selected Essays of William Carlos
        Williams</u>, New York, Random House, 1954, pp. 295-310.

64   WILSON, EDMUND. <u>Classics and Commercials: A Literary
        Chronicle of the Forties</u>. New York: Farrar, Straus,
        pp. 3-9.

1950

    (WILSON, EDMUND)
       Commentary on Archibald MacLeish's article in the <u>New
    Republic</u>, 102 (10 June 1940) in which MacLeish criticized
    the war novels of Hemingway and Dos Passos as lacking in
    terms of conviction and belief. (<u>See</u> 1940.B28.)

65   YOUNG, PHILIP. Review of <u>Across the River and Into the Trees</u>,
    <u>Tomorrow</u>, 10 (Nov.), 55-56.
      Sees problems with the situation and the character of
    the novel, but since so many other touches are characteris-
    tic of Hemingway, Young cannot explain why <u>Across the River
    and Into the Trees</u> is "a pretty bad book."

66   ZABEL, MORTON DAUWEN. Review of <u>Across the River and Into the
    Trees</u>, <u>Nation</u>, 171 (9 Sept.), 230.
      Views the book with "exasperated depression."

<u>1951 A BOOKS - NONE</u>

<u>1951 B SHORTER WRITINGS</u>

1   ADAMS, J. DONALD. Speaking of Books column, <u>New York Times
    Book Review</u> (25 Oct.), p. 2.
      More discussion of <u>Across the River and Into the Trees</u>.

2   ALDRIDGE, JOHN W. <u>After the Lost Generation: A Critical Study
    of the Writers of Two Wars</u>. New York: McGraw-Hill.
      Several chapters dealing with Hemingway: "Hemingway:
    Nightmare and the Correlative of Loss" and "The Neo-Heming-
    ways: and the Failure of Protest." Aldridge feels that
    Hemingway spoke to this generation and created "traditions"
    for them. Although this period is over, both chronologi-
    cally and philosophically, Aldridge thought it was a good
    time to be alive.
    Reprinted as "Homage to Hemingway" in <u>The Devil in the
    Fire: Retrospective Essays on American Literature and
    Culture, 1951-1971</u>, New York, Harper's Magazine Press,
    1972, pp. 83-85 (<u>See</u> 1972.B4).

3   BAKER, CARLOS. "The Mountain and the Plain," <u>Virginia
    Quarterly Review</u>, 27 (Summer), 410-18.
      Discussion of the symbolic value in the plain and the
    mountains which are visible from the house at the be-
    ginning of <u>A Farewell to Arms</u>.
    Reprinted as part of Chapter 5 in <u>Hemingway: The Writer
    as Artist</u>, Princeton, Princeton University Press, 1952
    (<u>See</u> 1952.A2).

4 _____. "Twenty-five Years of a Hemingway Classic," New York
    Times Book Review (29 April), pp. 5, 31.
       Reappraisal of The Sun Also Rises as even more important
    than it appeared in 1926.

5 BEACH, JOSEPH WARREN. "How Do You Like It Now, Gentlemen?"
    The Sewanee Review, 59 (Spring), 311-28.
       Concerning the "fourth and fifth dimensions" in prose
    that Hemingway described in Green Hills of Africa, Beach
    suggests that the fourth dimension is related to an
    "esthetic factor" created by the hero's participation in
    some traditional ritual; and that the fifth may be an
    "ethical factor" achieved by his "participation in the
    moral order of the world."
    Reprinted in Baker anthology, pp. 227-44 (See 1961.A5).

6 BESSIE, ALVAH, ed. The Heart of Spain: An Anthology of
    Fiction, Non-fiction and Poetry. New York: Veterans of
    the Abraham Lincoln Brigade, p. 6.
       Commentary in the Preface concerning the reasons for
    omitting work by Hemingway. Compare "The Abraham Lincoln
    Brigade Revisited" by Brock Brower in Esquire, 57 (March
    1962).

*7 BOAL, SAM. "I Tell You True," Park East, 10 (Dec. 1950), 18-
    19, 46-47, Part I; and 11 (Jan. 1951), 36, 48-49, Part II.
    Cited in Hanneman, p. 433 (See 1967.A4).

8 CARROLL, JOCK. "I Never Knocked Out Hemingway," Montreal
    Standard (31 March), pp. 9, 25.
    Interview with Morley Callaghan.

9 FARRINGTON, CHISIE. Women Can Fish. New York: Coward-McCann.
    Photo.
       References to Hemingway's fishing at Bimini, in the
    1930's.

10 FRYE, NORTHROP. Review of Across the River and Into the Trees,
    Hudson Review, 3 (Winter), 611-12.
       Sees a relationship to Mann's "Death in Venice" and re-
    grets that the theme was not better handled. Finds promise
    in the opening and closing of the book: "in between, how-
    ever, the story lies around in bits and pieces with no
    serious effort to articulate it."

11 GARDINER, HAROLD C., S.J., ed. Fifty Years of the American
    Novel: A Christian Appraisal. New York: Charles
    Scribner's Sons. Michael F. Maloney, "Ernest Hemingway:
    The Missing Third Dimension," pp. 183-96.

1951

(GARDINER, HAROLD C.)
    Sees Hemingway as "the most considerable figure in Ameri-
can fiction in the past quarter of a century," but dislikes
Across the River and Into the Trees. Admires Hemingway's
"sense of the tragic," his "love of the good earth," and
his "narrative gifts" but finds that his weaknesses include his philosophy--or lack of it--and the fact that
his characters "live in a world beyond moral good and evil."
Compares Hemingway's heroes with Nietzschean supermen.
Reprinted in Baker anthology, pp. 180-91 (See 1961.A5).

12   HEMINGWAY, MARY. "Life with Papa," Flair, 2 (Jan.), 29, 116-17.
    Photo.
    Biography and description of life at Finca Vigia.

13   HOFFMAN, FREDERICK J. The Modern Novel in America: 1900-1950.
    Chicago: Regnery, pp. 89-103.
    Sees that Hemingway's "chief virtue was his dedication
to the art of writing within his own candidly recognized
limitations. He was not a man of ideas." Hoffman finds
Hemingway an expert in his early work, but temperamentally
ill-suited to create the more searching literature of the
1930's.

14   LEVIN, HARRY. "Observations on the Style of Hemingway,"
    Kenyon Review, 13 (Autumn), 581-609.
    Centers on Hemingway's fictional method of using a series
of images (like moving pictures) to create the feeling of
immediacy and sequence in time. Other parts of the Hemingway style--sentence and paragraph structure, for example--
are very simple.
    Reprinted in his Contexts of Criticism, Cambridge, Harvard
University Press, 1957 (See 1957.B20); Baker anthology,
pp. 93-115 (See 1961.A5); and Weeks, pp. 72-85 (See
1962.A6).

15   MALLETT, RICHARD. Literary Upshots or Split Reading. London:
    Cape, pp. 44-47.
    Parody, "Purple Bits of Hemingway: A sort of reminis-
cence of Green Hills of Africa."

16   MEHRING, WALTER. The Lost Library: The Autobiography of a
    Culture. Translated from the German by Richard and Clara
Winston. Indianapolis: Bobbs-Merrill, pp. 190-91.
    Describes the American cultural background from which
Hemingway came to become enamored of Latin culture.

17 MORROW, ELISE. "The Hemingway View of His Critics," St. Louis
    Post-Dispatch (15 Jan.), p. 1C.
        Quotes a letter from Hemingway regarding the critics'
    reception of Across the River and Into the Trees.

18 ORROK, DOUGLAS HALL. "Hemingway, Hugo, and Revelation,"
    Modern Language Notes, 66 (Nov.), 441-45.
        Answers Engstrom's notion that Hemingway had borrowed
    from Flaubert; proposes instead that the concept of
    mountain to symbolize moral superiority may have come from
    Hugo's William Shakespeare. Reads "The Snows of Kiliman-
    jaro" as "a fable of literary integrity."

19 PAPAJEWSKI, HELMUT. "The Question of Meaningfulness in Heming-
    way," Anglia, 70: 186-200.
        Sees Across the River and Into the Trees as symptomatic
    of the generally declining literary situation, the Ameri-
    can novelists' interest in "life-analysis" which leads to
    repetitiousness and boredom. Points out that the main
    characters of Across the River and Into the Trees remind
    us of other, earlier Hemingway protagonists, but without
    the verve and originality. Instead of simplicity, Heming-
    way gives us "pseudo-primitivism." Includes Hemingway's
    Nobel prize acceptance speech.

20 POORE, CHARLES. Brief review of Lee Samuels' A Hemingway
    Check List, New York Times (27 July), p. 17.

21 QUINN, ARTHUR HOBSON, ed. The Literature of the American
    People: An Historical and Critical Survey. New York:
    Appleton-Century-Crofts, pp. 882-84, from George F.
    Whicher's chapter "The Twentieth Century."

22 ROSENFELD, ISAAC. "A Farewell to Hemingway," Kenyon Review,
    13 (Winter), 147-55.
        Review of Across the River and Into the Trees. Sees
    that Hemingway expresses a "false attitude toward life"
    as a rule, but in the characterization of Cantwell, he
    touches reality. "This is the most touching thing that
    Hemingway has done."
    Reprinted in An Age of Enormity, Cleveland, World, 1962,
    pp. 258-67 (See 1962.B45).

23 SAMUELS, LEE. A Hemingway Check List. New York: Scribner's.
    Listing of items from 1922 to 1950, with some annotation.

24 SCHEVILL, JAMES. Sherwood Anderson: His Life and Work.
    Denver, Colorado: University of Denver Press.

1951

(SCHEVILL, JAMES)
   Regarding Hemingway's early relationship with Anderson,
   Torrents of Spring, and the letter Hemingway wrote Anderson
   after the book was published.

25   SPENDER, STEPHEN. World Within World. New York: Harcourt,
     Brace.
       Describes a conversation with Hemingway in Spain in which
     Hemingway impressed him with his aesthetic sense.

26   STRAUMANN, HEINRICH. American Literature in the Twentieth
     Century. New York: Harper & Row.
       Traces many of Hemingway's "essential qualities" to "Up
     in Michigan"--the use of the hunting motif, death, personal
     isolation. Sees each of Hemingway's novels, even Across
     the River and Into the Trees, as central to the experience
     of its age, written with a variety of techniques.

27   WEST, RAY B. Jr. "Three Methods of Modern Fiction: Ernest
     Hemingway, Thomas Mann, Eudora Welty," College English,
     12 (Jan.), 194-96.
       An explication of "The Short, Happy Life of Francis
     Macomber" using new critical methods.
     Reprinted in West, The Writer in the Room, East Lansing,
     Michigan, Michigan State University Press, 1968 (See
     1968.B66).

28   WHIT, JOSEPH. "Hemingway's 'The End of Something,'" Explicator,
     9 (June), Item 58.
       Speculates that the heavy narrative emphasis on Bill at
     the end of the story carries a homosexual suggestion.

29   WILLIAMS, WILLIAM CARLOS. The Autobiography of William Carlos
     Williams. New York: Random House.
       Recollections of Hemingway in Paris in 1924.

30   WYLDER, DEB. Review of Across the River and Into the Trees,
     Western Review, 15 (Spring), 237-40.
       Criticizes the dialogue as sounding "like an imitation
     of Hemingway's worst imitators," which in some ways Wylder
     finds appropriate since the Colonel himself is also "un-
     believable."

31   ZABEL, MORTON D., ed. Literary Opinion in America. New York:
     Harper.
       Includes Robert Penn Warren, "Ernest Hemingway,"
     pp. 447-60 (See 1947.B18).

1952 A BOOKS

1   ATKINS, JOHN. The Art of Ernest Hemingway: His Work and
       Personality. London: Peter Nevill. Photos.
          General survey of Hemingway's life with special attention
       to what Atkins feels are "significant events," and a corre-
       lation between these biographical items and the fiction.
       Appendix A, pp. 233-34, includes a partial checklist of
       Hemingway's work; appendix B, pp. 235-39, discusses Heming-
       way's view of the English; appendix C, pp. 240-45 is an
       essay by Bernard Raymund, "Old Soldier Goes Sour," in which
       he states that Hemingway actively disliked war. Revised in
       1964, London: Spring Books.

2   BAKER, CARLOS. Hemingway: The Writer as Artist. Princeton:
       Princeton University Press.
          A close reading of much of Hemingway's fiction from the
       perspective that Hemingway was first a craftsman whose
       every detail and image was chosen for usefulness in several
       perspectives. Baker's study involves many close readings
       of both the novels and the stories. Appended is a "Working
       Check-List of Hemingway's Prose, Poetry, and Journalism--
       with Notes," pp. 299-310. Excerpts from the study have
       been reprinted widely (See individual essay collection
       listings, by year). Revised and enlarged, 1956, 1963,
       and 1972.

3   YOUNG, PHILIP. Ernest Hemingway. New York: Rinehart (Rine-
       hart Critical Studies).
          A critical analysis of Hemingway's work through the Nick
       Adams (and other heroes) persona. Young places the fiction
       in the direct line from the writing of Mark Twain, as part
       of the American mythic response to adversity and life. His
       attempt to locate Hemingway's work in a larger tradition
       continues to be important. Revised and enlarged in 1966,
       University Park, Pennsylvania: The Pennsylvania State
       University Press. Excerpts from the study have been re-
       printed widely (See individual essay collection listings
       by year).

1952 B SHORTER WRITINGS

1   ANON. Editorial, "A Great American Storyteller," Life, 33
       (1 Sept.), 21. Cover photo by Alfred Eisenstaedt.
          The Old Man and the Sea appeared in full in this issue.
       See Life, 33 (22 Sept.), 12, 14, for letters from William
       Saroyan and A. N. Brabrook respectively.

1952

2   ANON. "Hemingway Gets Medal," New York Times (24 Sept.), p. 7.
    Hemingway received the Medal of Honor from the Cuban
    Tourist Institute for The Old Man and the Sea; speaking in
    Spanish, he accepted the award "in the name of all commer-
    cial fishermen of the north coast of Cuba."

3   ANON. Item, "About 'the old man' and his book," Publishers'
    Weekly, 162 (13 Sept.), p. 1011.

4   ANON. Review excerpts, Now & Then, No. 87 (Autumn), pp. 10-11.
    Excerpts from reviews of The Old Man and the Sea which
    appeared previously in British periodicals.

5   ANON. Review of The Old Man and the Sea, Newsweek, 40
    (8 Sept.), 102-03.
    Likes the story, except when Hemingway takes it from a
    moving and simple account of the fisherman's adventure to
    "tragic intensity."

6   ANON. Review of The Old Man and the Sea, Time, 60 (8 Sept.),
    114.
    Sees the similarities between this novel and the earlier
    Hemingway; argues with those who find it radically dif-
    ferent. Does find "perhaps a new underlying reverence for
    the Creator of such wonders."

7   ANON. Review of The Old Man and the Sea, Times (London)
    (13 Sept.), p. 8.
    Mentions the "limited" scope of Hemingway's writing, but
    finds The Old Man and the Sea a masterpiece within that
    scope. Stresses its "biblical simplicity and purity," its
    great care and polish.

8   ANON. Review of The Old Man and the Sea, TLS (12 Sept.),
    p. 593.
    Finds the novel sometimes marred by the "precious" in
    its occasional "ponderous simplicity and tendency to imply
    an inner meaning."

9   ADAMS, J. DONALD. Speaking of Books column, New York Times
    Book Review (21 Sept.), p. 2.
    Discussion of The Old Man and the Sea.

10 ALDRIDGE, JOHN W., ed. Critiques and Essays on Modern Fiction:
    1920-1951. New York: Ronald Press.
    Pp. 447-73: "Ernest Hemingway" by Robert Penn Warren
    (See 1947.B18); pp. 588-91: Robert W. Stallman's selected
    bibliography of critical studies of Hemingway's work.

11   BAKER, CARLOS. "The Marvel Who Must Die," <u>SR</u>, 35 (6 Sept.), 10-11. Cover drawing of Hemingway by Norkin.
     Review of <u>The Old Man and the Sea</u>. Stresses the similarities between Santiago and the other Hemingway heroes, particularly at the end of the novel. Mentions that here Hemingway has included "the further power of Christian symbolism" and concludes "<u>The Old Man and the Sea</u> is a great short novel, told with consummate artistry and destined to become a classic in its kind."

12   _____. "Hemingway's Wastelanders," <u>Virginia Quarterly Review</u>, 28 (Summer), 373-92.
     This essay became part of Chapter 4 of <u>Hemingway: The Writer as Artist</u>, Princeton, 1952 (<u>See</u> 1952.A2).

13   BISHOP, JIM. <u>The Mark Hellinger Story: A Biography of Broadway and Hollywood</u>. New York: Appleton-Century-Crofts.
     Pp. 312-18: describing Hellinger's production of "The Killers" and Hemingway's pleased reaction to the film. Pp. 347-52: Hellinger's trips to confer with Hemingway about film rights, to Havana and Sun Valley, Idaho.

14   BLACKMUR, R. P. <u>Language as Gesture: Essays in Poetry</u>. New York: Harcourt, Brace, pp. 341-43.
     Compares the sensibilities of Hemingway and Tate as he reviews Allen Tate's <u>Reactionary Essays on Poetry and Ideas</u>, 1936.

15   BREEN, MELWYN. Review of <u>The Old Man and the Sea</u>, <u>Saturday Night</u>, 68 (13 Sept.), 26.
     Sees the novella as similar to Hemingway's other work, "the same pre-occupation with suffering, violence, and death." Control is, however, "superb," "Hemingway at his most stripped, exercising the peculiar discipline he inherited with a difference from Flaubert."

16   BREIT, HARVEY. Review of <u>The Old Man and the Sea</u>, <u>Nation</u>, 175 (6 Sept.), 194.
     Sees this as another instructive novel, and part of Hemingway's ethic that he be teaching whenever he writes. "It has little to do with pedantry; it has everything to do with reality and concreteness." This device, Breit sees, leads Hemingway "into universal meanings."

17   _____. "Talk with Ernest Hemingway," <u>New York Times Book Review</u> (7 Sept.), p. 20.
     "A set of answers to a set of questions that Hemingway himself devised," among them "I have always been happy when I am working."

1952

(BREIT, HARVEY)
Reprinted in The Writer Observed, Cleveland, World, 1956,
pp. 263-65 (See 1956.B8).

18 BROOKS, VAN WYCK. The Confident Years: 1885-1915. New York:
Dutton, pp. 570-76.
Comments on Hemingway's work in the chapter "The Religion
of Art."

19 BUTCHER, FANNY. Review of The Old Man and the Sea, Chicago
Sunday Tribune (7 Sept.), Magazine of Books, p. 1.
Sees the novella as an important come-back for Hemingway.

20 CALDER-MARSHALL, ARTHUR. Review of The Old Man and the Sea,
Listener, 48 (18 Sept.), 477.
"The Old Man and the Sea is not only the finest long
short story which Mr. Hemingway has ever written, but one
of the finest written by anyone anywhere." Points out that
there is no suspense in the story, that Hemingway does not
need that tool: "What holds us is the perfection of composition and execution." Compares the novella to a lyric
poem.

21 CALVO, LINO NOVÁS. "A Cuban Looks at Hemingway," Américas,
4 (Nov.), 37-38.
Review of The Old Man and the Sea. Discounts the fact
that Hemingway has lived in Cuba; sees his work as universal. Admires The Old Man and the Sea for its presentation of Santiago's "moral courage."

22 CANBY, HENRY SEIDEL. "A Report on The Old Man and the Sea,"
Book-of-the-Month Club News (Aug.), pp. 2-3.
Chosen as part of a dual selection for September, 1952,
The Old Man and the Sea is described by Canby as an "un-
forgettable picture of man against the sea and man against
fate."
Reprinted as 4-page leaflet which was sent to subscribers.

23 CANNON, JIMMY. Jimmy Cannon Says column, New York Post
(29 Aug.), p. 54.
Identifies with Hemingway because he too is "a sports
writer," and praises The Old Man and the Sea for its good
qualities. Calls Hemingway "the greatest writer."

24 CARY, JOYCE. "I Wish I Had Written That," New York Times Book
Review (7 Dec.), p. 4.
In this essay by various authors, Cary writes on The
Old Man and the Sea as a revelation of Hemingway, rather

(CARY, JOYCE)
than an exposure. Sees Hemingway, through the novella, as "an exacting artist, a visionary of nature and human nature, a man committed to self-reliance jusqu'au feu and beyond."

25   CONNOLLY, CYRIL. Review of The Old Man and the Sea, Sunday Times (London) (7 Sept.), p. 5.
Calls the novella "the best story Hemingway has ever written . . . . no page of this beautiful master-work could have been done better or differently." Mentions that Hemingway is a writer who can describe action precisely whereas most writers are limited to description.

26   COURNOS, JOHN and SYBIL NORTON. Famous Modern American Novelists (Famous Biographies for Young People). New York: Dodd, Mead, photo, pp. 129-35: "Ernest Miller Hemingway: Fighting Author."

27   COWLEY, MALCOLM. "Hemingway's Novel Has the Rich Simplicity of a Classic," New York Herald Tribune Book Review (7 Sept.), pp. 1, 17. Photo by Lee Samuels.
Review of The Old Man and the Sea. Sees the novella as classic prose because of the care given to each word. Notes that Hemingway types his manuscripts with several vertical spaces following each word, setting each word off as if for emphasis. "That is what the words seem to do in The Old Man and the Sea."

28   CRANSTON, HERBERT. "When Hemingway Earned Half a Cent a Word on the Toronto Star," New York Herald Tribune Book Review (13 Jan.), p. 6.
Reminiscences by the editor of the Toronto Star Weekly when Hemingway was on the staff in the early 1920's.

29   DAVIS, ROBERT GORHAM. Review of The Old Man and the Sea, New York Times Book Review (7 Sept.), pp. 1, 20.
Describes the book as "hard," "disciplined," "superbly told"; likes it particularly because the novella contains "new indications of humility and maturity and a deeper sense of being at home in life which promise well for the novel in the making."

*30   DUTOURD, JEAN. Review of The Old Man and the Sea, Arts (17 Oct.), p. 5.
Cited in Hanneman, 1967.A4, p. 446.

1952

31 FAULKNER, WILLIAM. Review of The Old Man and the Sea, Shenan-
    doah, 3 (Autumn), 55.
        "His best. Time may show it to be the best single piece
    of any of us, I mean his and my contemporaries. This time,
    he discovered God, a creator."
    Reprinted in Essays, Speeches & Public Letters, New York,
    Random House, 1965, p. 193 (See 1965.B14).

32 FENTON, CHARLES A. "Hemingway's Kansas City Apprenticeship,"
    New World Writing, No. 2 (1952), pp. 316-26.
        Became part of Chapter II of The Apprenticeship of
    Ernest Hemingway, New York, Farrar, Straus, and Young,
    1954 (See 1954.A1).

33 _____. "No Money for the Kingbird: Hemingway's Prizefight
    Stories," American Quarterly, 4 (Winter), 339-50.
        Sees most of the Hemingway attitudes in these stories,
    although without extensive verbalization. Claims that
    these stories, for all their apparent subject matter, con-
    tradict the "dumb ox" theory.
    Reprinted, with changes, in Fenton (See 1954.A1); and in
    Benson, pp. 53-63 (See 1975.A3).

34 FRANKLIN, SIDNEY, "Bullfighter from Brooklyn," Town & Country,
    106 (Feb.), 112-15, 126-34, Part II; (April), 74-77, 130-
    34, Part IV. Photos.
        Description of touring the bullfights with Hemingway in
    1929. Notes the impression Anna Pavlova made on Hemingway
    when she danced for them in Sevilla. Part IV describes
    Franklin's 1937 trip to cover the Spanish Civil War with
    Hemingway.
    Reprinted, with revisions, in Bullfighter from Brooklyn,
    New York, Prentice-Hall, 1952.

35 GARDINER, HAROLD C., S.J. Review of The Old Man and the Sea,
    America, 87 (13 Sept.), 569.
        Admires the novella for its clean style and the feeling
    of kinship between the two elemental creatures--"fisher-
    man and fish--each noble in his own way." Finds, however,
    a pathetic fallacy inherent in the treatment, and thinks
    this "militates against true greatness."
    Reprinted in In All Conscience, Garden City, New York,
    Hanover House, 1959, pp. 125-26 (See 1959.B20).

36 GILL, BRENDAN. Review of The Old Man and the Sea, New Yorker,
    28 (6 Sept.), 115.
        Sees the novella as revealing an "unprecedented tender-
    ness" in Hemingway. Warns against reading the book as a

(GILL, BRENDAN)
parable; says we must take the story "on its own spare
terms; its dimensions and meanings will prove as big and
as many as he can make them."

37   GURKO, LEO. "The Achievement of Ernest Hemingway," College
English, 13 (April), 368-75.
Sees Hemingway as responsible for both a stylistic revolution and a philosophical one. Thinks that Hemingway's
attitude toward the world is as relevant in 1952 as it was
thirty years before. Finds many parallels between Santiago
and Jake Barnes.
Reprinted in English Journal, 41 (June), 291-98.

38   HALLIDAY, E. M. "Hemingway's Narrative Perspective," Sewanee
Review, 60 (April-June), 202-18.
A lucid essay which relates Hemingway's use of first and
third person narrative methods to the variety of his subjects.
Reprinted in Baker critiques, pp. 174-82 (See 1962.A5);
and in Modern American Fiction, edited by A. Walton Litz,
New York, Oxford University Press, 1963, pp. 215-27 (See
1963.B31).

39   HICKS, GRANVILLE. "Hemingway's 'Happy Conspiracy with Per-
manence,'" New York Times Book Review (12 Oct.), p. 4.
Review of Carlos Baker's Hemingway: The Writer as
Artist. Photo of the original dust jackets of The Sun
Also Rises, A Farewell to Arms, Across the River and Into
the Trees, and The Old Man and the Sea.

40   HIGHET, GILBERT. Review of The Old Man and the Sea, Harper's
Magazine, 205 (Oct.), 102, 104.
Relates the novella to Hemingway's essay "On the Blue
Water" in 1936 Esquire.

41   HOBSON, LAURA Z. Trade Winds column, "Momentary Scoop," SR,
35 (23 Aug.), 4.
Item regarding the circumstances which gave Life magazine publication of The Old Man and the Sea.

42   HORMEL, OLIVE BEANE. Review of The Old Man and the Sea,
Christian Science Monitor (11 Sept.), p. 11.
Comments upon the confusion readers will have with the
novella. Reads it herself as "a triumph for the old man,"
and as a "definite advance" in Hemingway's philosophy.
"His god, however, is still only 'the principle of good
sportsmanship.'"

1952

43   HOWARD, MILTON. "Hemingway and Heroism," <u>Masses and Mainstream</u>,
        5 (Oct.), 1-8.
           Howard criticizes the isolation of Santiago from any
        social or class struggle.
           Reprinted in Jobes, p. 119 (<u>See</u> 1968.A9).

44   HUGHES, RILEY. Review of <u>The Old Man and the Sea</u>, <u>Catholic</u>
        <u>World</u>, 176 (Nov.), 151.
           Considers the book "Hemingway at his best" because of the
        unity in the work as a whole.

45   HUTCHENS, JOHN K. On the Books column, "'Luck' and Mr. Heming-
        way," <u>New York Herald Tribune Book Review</u> (22 June), p. 2.
           Item about the forthcoming <u>The Old Man and the Sea</u>, with
        a brief quotation from a Hemingway letter.

46   JACKSON, JOSEPH HENRY. Review of <u>The Old Man and the Sea</u>, <u>San</u>
        <u>Francisco Chronicle</u> (7 Sept.), pp. 20, 22.
           Drawing of Hemingway by Bert Buel. Sees that in this
        "fishing yarn" Hemingway is talking about courage, about
        the fact that "it is the striving that is important."

47   KRIM SEYMOUR. Review of <u>The Old Man and the Sea</u>, <u>Commonweal</u>,
        56 (19 Sept.), 584-86.
           Sees the novella as another embellishment on the earlier
        Hemingway reputation, again, restricted by his limited
        range. Within that range, however, Krim contends that
        Hemingway is as "intense and brilliant" as even Faulkner.

48   LYONS, LEONARD. The Lyons Den column, "Lunch at Papa Heming-
        way's," <u>New York Post</u> (7 Jan.), p. 22.
           Describing a visit to Finca Vigia.

49   MAYBERRY, GEORGE. "Truth and Poetry," <u>New Republic</u>, 127
        (13 Oct.), 21-22.
           Review of <u>Baker</u> (1952.A2). Finds Baker's textual exami-
        nation of Hemingway "illuminating but essentially sterile,"
        that this tactic does not come close to touching the
        poetry of the great writing. But for explication, Baker's
        is a good book.

50   MIZENER, ARTHUR. "Prodigy Into Peer," <u>SR</u>, 35 (18 Oct.), 25.
           Review of <u>Baker</u> (1952.A2). Terms the study a "fine,
        sensible book." Stresses that Baker recognizes "Heming-
        way's lifelong commitment to an ideal of fiction not un-
        like Eliot's objective correlative."

51   MUIR, EDWIN. Review of <u>The Old Man and the Sea</u>, <u>Observer</u>
        (7 Sept.), p. 7.

(MUIR, EDWIN)
Sees Hemingway as an "imaginative writer," not a "tough" one, and finds that in the novella "his imagination has never displayed itself more powerfully than in this simple and tragic story."

52 OPPEL, HORST. "Hemingway's <u>Across the River and Into the Trees</u>," <u>Neueren Sprachen</u>, No. 11, translated from the German by Joseph M. Bernstein.
Re-evaluates <u>Across the River and Into the Trees</u> as being in some ways similar to the other fiction (style, characterizations, dialogue) but more interesting because the theme of facing death is posed as a "deep, inner challenge." Oppel finds the theme of purgation central. Reprinted in Baker anthology, pp. 213-26 (<u>See</u> 1961.A5).

53 PARKER, ALICE. "Hemingway's 'The End of Something,'" <u>Explicator</u>, 10 (March), Item 36.
Sees Nick's relationship with Marjorie as based on their "tutorial" symbiosis.

54 PARSONS, LOUELLA O. "Hemingway's Magic Touch," <u>Cosmopolitan</u>, 133 (Oct.), 15-16. Photo.
Describing the movie version of "The Snows of Kilimanjaro."

55 PHILLIPS, WILLIAM. "Male-ism and Moralism: Hemingway and Steinbeck," <u>American Mercury</u>, 75 (Oct.), 93-98.
Contrasts the two writers, finding more evident positive moral value in the recent Steinbeck fiction than in that of Hemingway.

56 PICKREL, PAUL. Review of <u>The Old Man and the Sea</u>, <u>Yale Review</u>, 42 (Autumn), viii.
Describes <u>The Old Man and the Sea</u> as providing "an image of life, intense and passionate, its meaning self-contained yet universal."

57 PORTUONDO, JOSÉ ANTONIO. "The Old Man and Society," <u>Américas</u>, 4 (Dec.), 6-8, 42-44. Photos.
Assesses Hemingway's contributions to literature.

58 POWERS, CLARE. Review of <u>The Old Man and the Sea</u>, <u>Sign</u>, 32 (Nov.), 63-64.
Feels that Hemingway lacked "the inspiration, the vision to uncover anything in life beyond an animal struggle for existence."

1952

59 PRESCOTT, ORVILLE. Review of The Old Man and the Sea, New
        York Times (28 Aug.), p. 21.
            Describes Hemingway as "the master technician."

60 _____. In My Opinion: An Inquiry into the Contemporary Novel.
        Indianapolis: Bobbs-Merrill, pp. 65-71.
            From the chapter "Squandered Talents: Lewis, Steinbeck,
        Hemingway, O'Hara," Prescott laments the misuse of high
        technical proficiency in less-than-moral literature.

61 QUINN, PATRICK F. "Measure of Hemingway," Commonweal, 56
        (24 Oct.), 73-75.
            Review of Baker (1952.A2).

62 RAHV, PHILIP. "Hemingway in the 1950's," Commentary, 14
        (Oct.), 390-91.
            Review of The Old Man and the Sea. Remarks on the in-
        feriority of Across the River and Into the Trees, but has
        some praise for The Old Man and the Sea. Rahv thinks it
        a minor story, however, with no overt symbolism. Con-
        siders Hemingway to be at the same place philosophically
        as he was in the 1920's.
        Reprinted in Rahv's Image and Idea, New York, New Direc-
        tions, 1957, pp. 192-95 (See 1957.B24); in The Myth and
        the Powerhouse, New York, Farrar, Straus & Giroux, 1964,
        pp. 193-201 as "Hemingway in the Early 1950's" (See
        1964.B43); in Literature and the Sixth Sense, Boston,
        Houghton Mifflin, 1969, pp. 351-57 (See 1969.B61); and in
        Jobes, pp. 110-12 (See 1968.A9).

63 ROBINSON, DONALD. The 100 Most Important People in the World
        Today. Boston: Little, Brown, pp. 364-67.
            Pen portrait. "Ernest Hemingway." Biographical sketch.

64 RODMAN, SELDEN. "Ernest Hemingway," Book-of-the-Month Club
        News (Aug.), pp. 6-7.
            Recalls a visit with Hemingway in Cuba.

65 RUGOFF, MILTON. "A Major Work of Literary Evaluation," New
        York Herald Tribune Book Review (23 Nov.), p. 8.
            Review of Baker (1952.A2). Praises the study for its
        accuracy, care, and conscientiousness.

66 SAMPSON, EDWARD C. "Hemingway's 'The Killers,'" Explicator,
        11 (Oct.), Item 2.
            Sees the confusion about Mrs. Bell and Mrs. Hirsch as
        another detail, another "mistake" in the prevailing pat-
        tern of errors: individuality has been lost, no one
        "knows" even the simplest facts.

106

67 SANN, PAUL. Review of The Old Man and the Sea, New York Post
        (31 Aug.), p. 12M.
        Parody.

68 SCHERMAN, DAVID E. and ROSEMARIE REDLICH. Literary America:
        A Chronicle of American Writers with Photographs of the
        American Scene that Inspired Them. New York: Dodd, Mead,
        pp. 152-54.
        Scenes in Key West, Florida, and Horton Bay, Michigan,
        which were the settings for To Have and Have Not and some
        short stories.

69 SCHORER, MARK. "With Grace Under Pressure," New Republic,
        127 (6 Oct.), 19-20.
        Review of The Old Man and the Sea. Terms Hemingway "the
        greatest craftsman in the American novel in this century."
        Finds that much of the power in the novella comes from its
        parable-like quality.
        Reprinted in Baker critiques, pp. 132-34 (See 1962.A5).

70 SCHWARTZ, DELMORE. Review of The Old Man and the Sea, Partisan
        Review, 19 (Nov.-Dec.), 702-03.
        Finds the novella disappointing because in it Hemingway
        treats the same theme as he did in "The Undefeated" and
        the retreat from Caporetto in A Farewell to Arms. Thinks
        Santiago's introspection the weakest part of the novella.

71 TINKLE, LON. "Year of the Long Autumn: A Reviewer Wanders
        Through 1952," SR, 35 (27 Dec.), 7-9.
        Survey of many books, with a comment on The Old Man and
        the Sea as having a vestige of Christian wisdom. "It
        remained for Carlos Baker in the Saturday Review (in what
        was probably the best book review of the year) to state
        most clearly the symbols of Hemingway's present brooding
        over Christian thought."

72 WAGENKNECHT, EDWARD C. Cavalcade of the American Novel. New
        York: Holt, pp. 368-81.
        Chapter XX: "Ernest Hemingway: Legend and Reality,"
        compares the "living legend" which Hemingway has become
        with the "sharply defined limitations" of his philosophi-
        cal view. Wagenknecht is disturbed by "the adolescent
        overemphasis" on action, at the expense of moral reflec-
        tion and choice.

73 WEEKS, EDWARD. Review of The Old Man and the Sea, Atlantic,
        190 (Sept.), 72.
        Admires the "stripped, lean, objective narrative" of
        Hemingway at his best.

1952

74   WEST, RAY B., Jr.   The Short Story in America: 1900-1950.
        Chicago: Regnery. Pp. 85-106.
          Chapter IV: "Hemingway and Faulkner: Two Masters of
        the Modern Short Story," West sees these writers as central
        to modern fiction because they provided "revaluation, re-
        examination of the moral and aesthetic principles upon
        which both American life and American art had been es-
        tablished." Sees the similarities between Faulkner and
        Hemingway to outweigh the differences, and their influence
        on modern writing to be indisputable.
        Reprinted in Benson, pp. 2-14 (See 1975.A3).

75   WHITE, WILLIAM. "Father and Son: Comments on Hemingway's
        Psychology," Dalhousie Review, 31 (Winter), 276-84.
          Acknowledges that much of Hemingway's writing is auto-
        biographical and marked by his interest in violence, but
        thinks that these two traits stem from the fact that his
        work is probably motivated by his relations with his
        father, not so much his World War I experience or living
        abroad.

76   WILSON, EDMUND. The Shores of Light: A Literary Chronicle
        of the Twenties and Thirties. New York: Farrar, Straus &
        Young, pp. 115-24.
          "Emergence of Ernest Hemingway" contains three letters
        from Hemingway to Wilson, 1923-24, and Wilson's Dial re-
        view of Three Stories and Ten Poems and in our time (See
        1924.B8).
        Reprinted in Baker anthology, pp. 55-60 (See 1961.A5);
        pp. 339-44: "The Sportsman's Tragedy," reprinted from
        New Republic (Dec. 14, 1927). (See 1927.B22.) Pp. 616-29:
        "Letter to the Russians About Hemingway," reprinted from
        New Republic (Dec. 11, 1935) with a prefatory note ex-
        plaining how the essay came to be written (See 1935.B26).

77   YOUNG, PHILIP. "Hemingway's In Our Time," Explicator, 10
        (April), Item 43.
          Sees that the connections between both the stories and
        the vignettes are important, and are generally chronologi-
        cal. He admits that they are "less aesthetic than per-
        sonal" but claims that they are highly significant to
        Hemingway's "peculiarly autobiographical method."

1953 A   BOOKS - NONE

1953 B SHORTER WRITINGS

1 ANON. "Concerning Mr. Hemingway," TLS (20 Feb.), p. 122.
        Review of John Atkins' The Art of Ernest Hemingway and
        Baker (1952.A2).

2 ANON. Editorial, "A Souvenir from a Pulitzer Prize Novelist,"
        Life, 34 (11 May), 25.
        Quotes from a letter from Hemingway regarding The Old
        Man and the Sea as the epitome of his craft.

3 ANON. "Hemingway Awarded Pulitzer Prize," New York Times
        (5 May), pp. 1, 24. Photo of Hemingway by Lee Samuels.
        First Pulitzer prize, for The Old Man and the Sea.

4 ANON. Item, Time, 61 (2 March), 33.
        Quotes a letter from Hemingway to high school students
        in Louisville, Kentucky, about The Old Man and the Sea.

5 ABERG, GILBERT. "White Hope--Somewhat Sunburned: The
        Maturity of Hemingway," Chicago Review, 7 (Spring), 18-24.
        "Morality--that is the real clue to an understanding of
        Ernest Hemingway" (even in his apparent immorality). Dis-
        likes The Old Man and the Sea, however, because there are
        so few real characters; the book is more of an allegory.

6 ALDRIDGE, JOHN W. Review of The Old Man and the Sea, Virginia
        Quarterly Review, 29 (Spring), 311-20.
        Grants that the novella is "a remarkable advance" over
        Across the River and Into the Trees, but sees it as "dis-
        tinctly minor" and wonders at the "prevailing wild en-
        thusiasm."

7 ANDERSON, SHERWOOD. Letters, edited by Howard Mumford Jones
        and Walter B. Rideout. Boston: Little, Brown.
        Letters to Gertrude Stein introducing the Hemingways,
        and concerning the blurb he wrote for the dust jacket of
        In Our Time.

8 BAKER, CARLOS. "When the Warriors Sleep," SR, 36 (4 July), 13.
        A reassessment of The Sun Also Rises: finds that it re-
        mains "fresh" because of its language, its "devotion to
        fact," its "skill in the evocation and manipulation of
        emotional atmospheres," and its "symbolic landscape."
        Locates the greatness of the book in the way Hemingway
        handled the contrasting philosophical attitudes and moral
        atmospheres within the book.

1953

9   BARNES, LOIS L. "The Helpless Hero of Ernest Hemingway," Science and Society, 17 (Winter), 1–25.
       Sees Santiago as another of Hemingway's common heroes, "helpless" because he does not think. Says that Hemingway does not understand people, and has no real interest in them; therefore, Barnes finds him incapable of writing tragedies.

10   BEAVER, JOSEPH. "'Technique' in Hemingway," College English, 14 (March), 325–28.
       Refers not to stylistic matters but to the "technique" of performing some job properly. Sees that this quality makes heroes of Hemingway's characters. "Most of them have no philosophy except the philosophy of performing something correctly."

11   BELLOW, SAUL. "Hemingway and the Image of Man," Partisan Review, 20 (May–June), 338–42.
       Review of Young's Ernest Hemingway. Sees that Hemingway wants to "create an image of manhood," to impose himself both fictionally and personally as a guide for his culture. Bellow feels this kind of responsibility is beyond the author's province.

12   BLACK, FREDERICK. "The Cuban Fish Problem," New Mexico Quarterly, 23 (Spring), 106–08.
       Parody review of The Old Man and the Sea.

13   BROOKS, VAN WYCK. The Writer in America. New York: Dutton.
       Occasional references to Hemingway as an expatriate writer whose concern remained with this country.

14   BROWN, DEMING. "Hemingway in Russia," American Quarterly, 5 (Summer), 143–56.
       Concerns the Russian translations of Hemingway's work, and also the critical response.
       Reprinted in Baker anthology, pp. 145–61 (See 1961.A5).

15   BUCHWALD, ART. "For Whom the Bloody Marys Toll," New York Herald Tribune, European Edition (5 Aug.), p. 6.
       Interview with Hemingway, enroute from Spain to Africa by way of Paris.

16   CONNOLLY, CYRIL. "Earnest Work," Sunday Times (London), (8 Feb.), p. 5.
       Review of Atkins' The Art of Ernest Hemingway and Baker (1952.A2).

17 COTTEN, LYMAN. "Hemingway's The Old Man and the Sea,"
        Explicator, 11 (March), Item 38.
            The change in Manolin from the opening to the closing of
        the novella is significant and indicates his maturity
        through his concern for Santiago.

18 CRANSTON, J. HERBERT. Ink On My Fingers. Toronto: Ryerson
        Press, pp. 107-10.
            Chapter 27: "His Hero Was a Matador," reminiscences by
        the editor of the Toronto Star Weekly when Hemingway wrote
        for the paper, 1920-23.

19 CROSBY, CARESSE. The Passionate Years. New York: Dial Press.
            The account of Hemingway's giving permission for Crosby's
        Black Sun Press to re-issue several of his novels, and
        other reminiscences of the friendship in Paris.

20 DANIEL, ROBERT. Review of Baker (1952.A2), Yale Review, 42
        (Spring), 443-45.
            Favorable.

21 DUGGAN, FRANCIS X. "The Obsession of Violence," Commonweal,
        57 (13 March), 583-84.
            Review of Young's Ernest Hemingway. Summary review,
        stressing that Young relates the Hemingway hero to both
        Hemingway himself and Huck Finn.

22 DUPEE, F. W. "Hemingway Revealed," Kenyon Review, 15 (Winter),
        150-55.
            Review of The Old Man and the Sea. Sees that Across the
        River and Into the Trees may be accepted eventually as
        less disappointing than it originally was felt to be.
        Likes Santiago as "the preeminently natural man who is
        . . . entirely human." The Old Man and the Sea is a suc-
        cess, a predictable one, but is glad Hemingway has recovered
        his powers.

23 _____. Review of The Old Man and the Sea, Perspectives U.S.A.,
        No. 3 (Spring), pp. 127-30.
            Considers the novella "a first-rate example of that
        literature of the big hunt to which so many American
        writers have contributed, affirming through this image the
        frontier virtues and the natural basis of our life." Sees
        the character of Santiago as illustration of "that humane
        naturalism" common to Faulkner and other American writers.

24 DWORKIN, MARTIN S. "A Dead Leopard and an Empty Grail: Three
        Ernest Hemingways," Humanist, 13 (July-Aug.), 164-65.
            Review of the film The Snows of Kilimanjaro.

1953

25   FRASER, G. S. The Modern Writer and His World. London:
       William Clowes and Sons.
          Locates Hemingway as one of the "novelists of action"
       whose work is marked by "the glum plugging away at episodes
       of violence, with a direct appeal to sinister impulses in
       the reader."

26   FREEHOF, SOLOMON B. Review of The Old Man and the Sea,
       Carnegie Magazine, 27 (Feb.), 44–48.
          Admires its "unintended tenderness" and its "dynamic
       prose which is unequalled." Laments, however, Hemingway's
       ultimate meaning: "What is he trying to say in all these
       powerfully written novels? . . . There is no introspection,
       there is only outer action."

27   FREY, LEONARD H. "Irony and Point of View in 'That Evening
       Sun,'" Faulkner Studies, 2, No. 3 (Autumn), 33–40.
          Compares the Faulkner story to "The Killers" in that both
       protagonists are exposed to a tragic situation over which
       they have no control. Hemingway, however, does not place
       the emphasis of the plot on the tragic object; Frey there-
       fore feels that the Faulkner story succeeds more fully.

28   FROHOCK, W. M. "Mr. Hemingway's Truly Tragic Bones," South-
       west Review, 38 (Winter), 74–77.
          Review of The Old Man and the Sea. Considers The Old
       Man and the Sea a "poem," and a tragic one at that because
       "its principal themes are human endurance and the defeat
       of human endurance." The novella follows the pattern of
       classical tragedy. Finds the book perhaps the best
       Hemingway.

29   GURKO, LEO. Heroes, Highbrows and the Popular Mind. Indianapo-
       lis: Bobbs-Merrill.
          Includes discussions of the Hemingway hero, and the "dis-
       belief in human improvability" evident in A Farewell to
       Arms and To Have and Have Not.

30   HALLIDAY, E. M. "Hemingway's Hero," University of Chicago
       Magazine, 45 (May), 10–14.
          Discusses the various qualities of the composite which
       he finds to be the Hemingway hero.

31   HEMINGWAY, MARY. The Man I Married series, "Ernest Hemingway,"
       Today's Woman (Feb.), pp. 30–31, 46–48. Photos.
          Biographical account.

32   HOFFMAN, FREDERICK J. "No Beginning and No End: Hemingway and
        Death," Essays in Criticism, 3 (Jan.), 73-84.
            Sees Hemingway's use of death as therapeutic (compare
        with Cather's use in Death Comes for the Archbishop), and
        also a literary landmark. "It was Hemingway's task to
        describe its circumstance and to give it its first and
        most incisive literary statement and judgment."

33   HOTCHNER, A. E. "Hemingway Ballet: Venice to Broadway," New
        York Herald Tribune (27 Dec.), pp. IV, 3.
            An account of the four years preparation for the adapta-
        tion of "The Capital of the World" into a ballet.

34   HYMAN, STANLEY EDGAR. "A Hemingway Sampler," New York Times
        Book Review (13 Sept.), p. 28.
            Review of The Hemingway Reader. Stresses Hemingway's
        fictional versatility.

35   LEWIS, R. W. B. Review of The Old Man and the Sea, Hudson
        Review, 6 (Spring), 146-48.
            Admires the "rare and gentle humanities" in the novella,
        but doubts that it can "bear the amount of critical weight
        already piled upon it." Finds some passages corrupted
        from excellence into the stuffy and pretentious.

36   McCLENNEN, JOSHUA. "Ernest Hemingway and His Audience,"
        Michigan Alumnus Quarterly Review, 59 (Summer), 335-40.
            Sees that Hemingway's "world of violence" is used in pre-
        senting what is really a Greek view of the universe rather
        than a Christian. Discusses "The Killers," pointing out
        that the effect when the story is read would be very dif-
        ferent from its impact as a film.

37   McCORMICK, JOHN. "Hemingway and History," Western Review, 17
        (Winter), 87-98.
            Traces some of Hemingway's work to Henry James. Sees
        Hemingway's career as uneven, partly because it is tied
        more intimately than is usually recognized to history.
        A Farewell to Arms was important because it presented the
        initiation theme so vividly: The Sun Also Rises "presented
        a meaningful political attitude" toward the continuing
        trauma which followed World War I. Contends that Heming-
        way should not be condemned for his experimentation, for
        through it he is trying to express his times.

38   POORE, CHARLES. "Foreword" to The Hemingway Reader. New York:
        Charles Scribner's Sons, XI-XX.
            Stresses Hemingway's stylistic excellences ("a body of

1953

(POORE, CHARLES)
work that has changed the course of storytelling") as well
as his "clarity," "intensity," "humor," "valor," "grace,"
and "love of life."

39   REDMAN, BEN RAY. "Gallantry in the Face of Death," SR, 36
(6 June), 18.
Reviews the new Scribner's editions of The Sun Also Rises,
A Farewell to Arms, To Have and Have Not, and Green Hills
of Africa, seeing that one common theme is the omnipresence
of death and the characters' reactions to its threat.

40   RUARK, ROBERT C. "Papa in Spain," New York World-Telegram &
Sun (10 Aug.), p. 13.
Account of Hemingway at Pamplona.

41   ST. JOHN, ROBERT. This Was My World. Garden City, N. Y.:
Doubleday.
Recollections of his boyhood in Oak Park, Illinois, in-
cluding incidents in which Hemingway took part.

42   STEIN, GERTRUDE. The Flowers of Friendship: Letters Written
to Gertrude Stein, edited by Donald C. Gallup. New York:
Knopf.
Includes several letters from Hemingway, written in
Paris, in 1924.

43   STOBIE, MARGARET. "Ernest Hemingway, Craftsman," Canadian
Forum, 33 (Nov.), 179, 181-82.
Describes the effect of Hemingway's writing as a "prose
pointillisme"--its most salient feature the juxtaposition
of facts and images. Perhaps his craft is less sensational
than that of Joyce and Stein, but it may be farther
reaching.

44   STRAGE, MARK. "Ernest Hemingway: Wars, Women, Wine, Words,"
Pageant, 8 (April), 18-29. Photos.
A popularized account of the legend.

*45 STRAUSS, STUART H. "Hemingway and Tomorrow," Kansas Magazine
(1953), pp. 31-32.
Unseen.

46   TERRY, WALTER. Review of the ballet, "The Capital of the
World," New York Herald Tribune (28 Dec.), p. 14.
Presented by the Ballet Theatre at the Metropolitan
Opera House on December 27, 1953. Score by George Antheil;
choreography by Eugene Loring. The work was commissioned
by the Ford Foundation's Television Workshop and first presented on Omnibus, December 6.

47   VANDERCOOK, DOROTHY POWELL. "Pictures with a Past," <u>Saturday</u>
      <u>Evening Post</u>, 226 (21 Nov.), 17.
         Photo of Hemingway at 14, dressed in a Japanese kimono
      for a Sunday school play.

48   WEST, RAY B., JR. "The Sham Battle over Ernest Hemingway,"
      <u>Western Review</u>, 17 (Spring), 234-40.
         Reviews of <u>The Old Man and the Sea</u>, <u>Baker</u>, and Young's
      <u>Ernest Hemingway</u>. Finds that criticism is in a "confused
      and unhappy state," but likes <u>The Old Man and the Sea</u>.
      Considers the range of Hemingway's fiction and concludes
      by wishing that Hemingway were more capable of surprising
      his readers, and himself; in that respect, were more like
      Faulkner.

49   WHICHER, GEORGE F. Review of <u>The Hemingway Reader</u>, <u>New York</u>
      <u>Herald Tribune Book Review</u> (27 Sept.), p. 21.
         Favorable review.

50   WHITFIELD, E. "Hemingway: The Man," <u>Why</u>, 1 (April), 10-19.
         A psychoanalytical study of his supposed characteristics,
      based on both his fiction and his public persona.

51   WYRICK, GREEN D. <u>The World of Ernest Hemingway: A Critical</u>
      <u>Study</u>. Emporia, Kansas: Graduate Division of the Kansas
      State Teachers College (Emporia State Research Studies,
      11). 32 pp., bibliographic footnotes.
         Survey of the major fiction, with attention to the formu-
      lation of Hemingway's own fictional world.

1954 A   BOOKS

1   FENTON, CHARLES A. <u>The Apprenticeship of Ernest Hemingway:</u>
      <u>The Early Years</u>. New York: Farrar, Straus & Young.
         Thorough study of Hemingway's early work, with close
      attention to the composition of <u>In Our Time</u>. Fenton's
      analysis of Hemingway's journalism and the <u>In Our Time</u>
      materials remains valuable.

1954 B   SHORTER WRITINGS

1   ANON. "Career Marked by Wars," <u>New York Times</u> (29 Oct.), p. 10.
         Biographical sketch in conjunction with announcement of
      Nobel Prize for Literature.

2   ANON. Cover story, "An American Storyteller," <u>Time</u>, 64
      (13 Dec.), 70-77. Photos. Cover drawing of Hemingway by
      Artzybasheff.
         For the background of this article, <u>See</u> Robert Manning's

1954

(ANON.)
"Hemingway in Cuba" in Atlantic, 216 (Aug. 1965) and let-
ters from Philip Young in Time, 65 (3 Jan. 1955), 2 and
George Sumner Albee in Time, 65 (10 Jan. 1955), 2, 4.

3   ANON. "Cuba Honors Hemingway," New York Times (22 July), p. 3.
The Order of Carlos Manuel de Céspedes, the highest
award that Cuba gives a foreigner, was presented to Hemingway on his fifty-fifth birthday.

4   ANON. "Ernest Agent," Newsweek, 43 (4 Jan.), 35.
Spruille Braden, former Assistant Secretary of State,
disclosed that Hemingway's wartime duty in the Caribbean
was part of a counterespionage organization whose purpose
was to help American agents discover saboteurs who were
sinking Allied ships.

5   ANON. "Ernest Hemingway's School Days," Chicago, 1 (Aug.),
57-60. Photos.
Contains the Senior Tabula Class Prophecy which Hemingway wrote for the yearbook, June, 1917.

6   ANON. "Gave Up On Hemingway," Kansas City Times (15 May),
p. 7.
Report on the extended injuries Hemingway received in
the African plane crashes.

7   ANON. "Hemingway Is the Winner of Nobel Literature Prize,"
New York Times (29 Oct.), p. 1. Photo.
Hemingway, at Finca Vigia, received the news that he had
been awarded the Nobel prize for literature for 1954. The
gold medal and $35,000 were to be presented in Stockholm,
December 10.

8   ANON. "Hemingway: Making of a Master," Newsweek, 43 (17 May),
104, 106. Photo.
Review of Fenton's Apprenticeship (See 1954.A1).

9   ANON. "Heroes: Life with Papa," Time, 64 (8 Nov.), 27.
Photo.
Regarding Hemingway's life and his receiving the Nobel
prize.

10   ANON. "Homage to the Old Man," Reporter, 11 (18 Nov.), 6-7.
Regarding the Nobel prize and Hemingway's writing career.

11   ANON. "A Medal for Hemingway," New York Times (24 March),
p. 55.

(ANON.)
>   Hemingway received the Award of Merit medal and $1000
>   from the American Academy of Arts and Letters.

12   ANON.   "1954 Nobel Prizes Awarded by King/ Hemingway, Unable
>   to Attend in Stockholm, Asserts That Writing Is a Lonely
>   Life," New York Times (11 Dec.), p. 5.
>   Quotes from Hemingway's Nobel prize acceptance speech.

13   ANON.   "Nobel's Hemingway: The Rock," Newsweek, 44 (8 Nov.),
>   88-89. Photo.

14   ANON.   "The Old Man Lands the Biggest Fish," Life, 37 (8 Nov.),
>   25-29. Photos.
>   Regarding Hemingway's being awarded the Nobel prize.

15   ANON.   Photographic essay, "Sportsman: Ernest Hemingway,"
>   Sports Illustrated, 1 (4 Oct.), 9-10.
>   See Winston McCrea's letter regarding Hemingway's trips
>   to Sun Valley, Idaho in Sports Illustrated, 1 (1 Nov.), 79.

16   ANON.   Talk of the Town column, "Dead or Alive," New Yorker,
>   29 (6 Feb.), 21.
>   Surveys the newspapers' obituary notices about Hemingway,
>   when he was believed dead in the plane crash in East Africa,
>   January 23, 1954.

17   ALDRIDGE, JOHN W.   "Before the Sun Began to Rise," New York
>   Times Book Review (11 July), p. 4.
>   Review of Fenton's Apprenticeship. Summary and dis-
>   cussion of Fenton's approach and findings.

18   _____.   "Hemingway: The Etiquette of the Berserk," Mandrake,
>   2 (Autumn-Winter), 331-41.
>   In what Aldridge considers to be Hemingway's best fic-
>   tion, The Sun Also Rises and A Farewell to Arms, a wounded
>   hero lives through his code of conduct to save himself
>   from destruction: Hemingway shows how the loss of soul or
>   consciousness, the berserk condition, occurs in the sym-
>   bolic terms of the breakdown of the code.
>   Reprinted in In Search of Heresy, New York, McGraw-Hill,
>   1956, pp. 149-65 (See 1956.B4).

19   BACHE, WILLIAM B.   "Hemingway's 'The Battler,'" Explicator,
>   13 (Oct.), Item 4.
>   Nick arrives at a fuller and more complicated under-
>   standing of the nature of the world.

1954

20 BAKER, CARLOS. "The Palmy Days of Papa," <u>SR</u>, 37 (29 May), 14–
    15.
        Review of Atkins' <u>The Art of Ernest Hemingway</u> and Fen-
    ton's <u>Apprenticeship</u>. Laments the "oversimplification,"
    "obtuse judgments," and "speleological nonsense" of
    Atkins' book, but approves of Fenton wholeheartedly.

21 BOWERS, CLAUDE G. <u>My Mission to Spain: Watching the Rehearsal</u>
    <u>for World War II</u>. New York: Simon & Schuster.
        The former U. S. Ambassador to Spain (1933–39) describes
    his meetings with Hemingway both in Madrid and Teruel.

22 BREIT, HARVEY. "The Sun Also Rises in Stockholm," <u>New York</u>
    <u>Times Book Review</u> (7 Nov.), p. 1. Photo.
        Telephone interview with Hemingway regarding the Nobel
    prize.
        Reprinted in <u>The Writer Observed</u>, Cleveland, World, 1956,
    pp. 275–79 (<u>See</u> 1956.B8).

23 BROWN, DEMING B. and GLENORA BROWN. <u>A Guide to Soviet Russian</u>
    <u>Translations of American Literature</u>. New York: King's
    Crown Press (Columbia University).
        P. 21: notes that stories and excerpts from Hemingway's
    novels "appeared at least 25 times in Soviet periodicals
    from 1934 to 1939." Pp. 92–95: Checklist of Russian
    translations of Hemingway's work.

24 BROWN, [ERNEST] FRANCIS, ed. <u>Highlights of Modern Literature:</u>
    <u>A Permanent Collection of Memorable Essays from The New</u>
    <u>York Times Book Review</u>. New York: New American Library,
    pp. 106–09.
        "Twenty–Eight Years of a Hemingway Classic" by Carlos
    Baker, reprinted <u>New York Times Book Review</u> (29 April
    1951). (<u>See</u> 1951.B3.)

25 CARPENTER, FREDERICK I. "Hemingway Achieves the Fifth
    Dimension," <u>PMLA</u>, 69 (Sept.), 711–18.
        Connecting Hemingway's phrase "fifth dimension" with
    Henri Bergson's two kinds of "time" and P. D. Ouspensky's
    "fifth dimension," Carpenter sees it as a further descrip-
    tion of William James' "radical empiricism" (immediate or
    pure experience). Always one to avoid abstract theorizing
    when possible, Hemingway created narrative structures,
    especially in <u>For Whom the Bell Tolls</u> and <u>The Old Man and</u>
    <u>the Sea</u>, that embody his fifth dimension.
        Reprinted in <u>American Literature and the Dream</u>, New York,
    The Philosophical Library, 1955, pp. 185–93 (<u>See</u> 1955.B11);
    in Baker anthology, pp. 192–201 (<u>See</u> 1961.A5); in Waldhorn
    pp. 83–91 (<u>See</u> 1973.A7); and in Wagner, pp. 279–87 (<u>See</u>
    1974.A3).

26   COOKE, ALISTAIR. "Hemingway: Master of the Mid-West Vernacu-
         lar," Guardian (Manchester) (11 Nov.), p. 7.
         Attributes much of Hemingway's force as writer to his
         natural, colloquial realism, a diction not always appealing
         to readers more accustomed to formal levels of expression.

27   COWLEY, MALCOLM. The Literary Situation. New York: Viking
         Press, pp. 184-85.
         Discusses Hemingway's disciplined working habits.

28   CUNLIFFE, MARCUS. The Literature of the United States. London:
         Penguin.
         Views Hemingway as a writer of "remarkable gifts." His
         simple men need not be simpletons. Cunliffe admires the
         earlier work more than the later.

29   DUPEE, F. W. Item in Perspectives U. S. A., No. 9 (Autumn),
         pp. 154-55.
         Regarding Hemingway's award from the National Institute
         of Arts and Letters.

30   Ernest Hemingway: A Bibliography. U. S. Information Agency,
         Office of the U. S. High Commissioner for Germany. Bonn.
         Includes German translations of Hemingway's work, as well
         as standard biographical, bibliographical, and critical
         items. In English.

31   FENTON, CHARLES A. "Hemingway's Apprenticeship," Saturday
         Night, 70 (18 Dec. 1954), 17-19; (25 Dec. 1954), pp. 14-
         18; (1 Jan. 1955), pp. 11-12; (8 Jan. 1955), pp. 14-18;
         (15 Jan. 1955), pp. 16-18. Photos.
         Serialization in five parts from Fenton's book.

32   _____. "Ernest Hemingway: The Young Years," Atlantic, 98
         (March), 25-34, Part I; (April), 49-57, Part II: (May),
         39-44, Part III.
         Cover drawing of Hemingway by Russell Carpenter.
         Reprinted in Fenton (1954.A1).

33   FUSSELL, EDWIN. "Hemingway and Mark Twain," Accent, 14
         (Summer), pp. 199-206.
         Finds the chief similarity between Twain and Hemingway
         to be in their "emotional integrity," their interest in
         it, their attempts to capture it, both in their writing
         and their experiences.

1954

34 GARNETT, E. B. "A New Book Tells of Work on the Star That
       Helped Hemingway to Fame," Kansas City Star (16 May),
       p. 4D.
          Review of Fenton's Apprenticeship.

35 GEISMAR, MAXWELL. "Hemingway and the Nobel Prize," SR, 37
       (13 Nov.), 24, 34.
          Because Hemingway tends to neglect social forces and
       dwell morbidly on his own psyche, Geismar finds his best
       work that of the 1930's and perhaps The Fifth Column and
       the First Forty-Nine Stories. Says the prize was given
       for the wrong book. Admits that Hemingway is an expert
       "chronicler of intense emotional states."
          Reprinted in American Moderns, New York, Hill & Wang,
       1958, pp. 61-64. See letter from Emmett B. McGeever in
       SR, 37 (25 Dec.), 21.

36 GOULD, JACK. Radio in Review column, "NBC Salutes Hemingway
       as Man Who 'Lived it Up to Write it Down,'" New York Times
       (22 Dec.), p. 34.
          Review of the hour-long documentary "Meet Ernest Heming-
       way," NBC, Dec. 18, 1954. Participants included Lester
       Pearson, narrator, Charles A. Fenton, James T. Farrell,
       John Mason Brown, Max Eastman, Leonard Lyons, and Malcolm
       Cowley. Marlon Brando read excerpts from The Old Man and
       the Sea, and a tape was played of Hemingway reading his
       Nobel prize acceptance speech.

37 HARLING, ROBERT. "A Journey to Hemingway," Sunday Times
       (London) (19 Dec.), p. 10. Photo by Leonard McCombs.
          Interview with Hemingway at Finca Vigia.

38 HECHT, BEN. A Child of the Century. New York: Simon and
       Schuster, p. 232.
          Sees Hemingway as the best of Sherwood Anderson's
       "imitators," but one whose eye was too often on the "box-
       office."

39 LAIRD, LANDON. About Town column, Kansas City Times (30 Jan.),
       p. 5.
          Herbert R. Schindler recalls Hemingway's bravery in the
       no-man's-land of the Huertgen Forest, during World War II.

40 LEARY, LEWIS. Articles on American Literature: 1900-1950.
       Durham, N. C.: Duke University Press, pp. 137-39.
          Checklist of critical studies of Hemingway's work.

41 LYONS, LEONARD. "Papa," New York Post (25 Jan.), p. 20.
      Reminiscences of his friendship with Hemingway.

42 MacLENNAN, HUGH. "Homage to Hemingway" in Thirty & Three,
      edited by Dorothy Duncan. Toronto: Macmillan, pp. 85-96.
      Account of Hemingway's contributions to modern writing
      as well as biographical items.

43 MATTHEWS, HERBERT L. "Winner Rules Out Trip to Stockholm,"
      New York Times (29 Oct.), p. 10.
      Interview with Hemingway with mention of his injuries
      from the two African plane crashes and his plans to keep
      working through the winter in Cuba.

44 O'HARA, JOHN. Sweet and Sour: Comments on Books and People.
      New York: Random House, pp. 39-44.
      Chapter 7 on Hemingway warns against the hangers-on and
      bums who claim Hemingway's friendship; laments his not
      having won the Nobel prize: "Ernest Hemingway's work will
      be read as long as there are people around to read."

45 POORE, CHARLES. "Hemingway's Quality Built on a Stern Appren-
      ticeship," New York Times (29 Oct.), p. 10.
      Cites the nearly thirty years of writing in which Heming-
      way has never slighted his craft as important to his re-
      ceiving the Nobel prize.

46 SCHORER, MARK. "Mr. Hemingway and His Critics," New Republic,
      131 (15 Nov.), 18-20.
      Along with reviewing books by Atkins and Fenton,
      Schorer declares that The Sun Also Rises "may yet prove
      to be the most remarkable of American novels."

47 SOBY, JAMES THRALL. "Hemingway and Painting," SR, 37 (4 Dec.),
      60-61.
      Description of some of Hemingway's affinities with
      modern painting.

48 SULLIVAN, ED. "Papa Was Overdue: New Yorkers Glad Famed
      Nobel Prize went to Hemingway," St. Louis Globe-Democrat
      (28 Nov.), p. 1F.

49 WAGENKNECHT, EDWARD C. A Preface to Literature. New York:
      Holt, pp. 341-44.
      Review of The Old Man and the Sea by Carlos Baker, re-
      printed from SR, 35 (6 Sept. 1952). (See 1952.B11.)

1954

50 WHITE, E. B. "Across the Street and Into the Grill," <u>The</u>
    <u>Second Tree from the Corner</u>. New York: Harper and Row,
    pp. 140-43.
        A parody sketch of the Cantwell-Renata relationship in
    <u>Across the River and Into the Trees</u>, as seen during a
    lunch at Schrafft's.
        Reprinted from <u>New Yorker</u>, 26 (14 Oct. 1950). (<u>See</u>
    1950.B61.)

51 WILSON, EARL. "Fans Hail Hemingway As Invulnerable 'Papa,'"
    <u>New York Post</u> (25 Jan.), p. 3.
        Reactions after plane crashes.

1955 A BOOKS - NONE

1955 B SHORTER WRITINGS

1   ANON. "Cuba Decorates Hemingway," <u>New York Times</u> (28 Oct.),
    p. 15.
        Hemingway received the Order of San Cristobal in recog-
    nition of his interest in Cuba.

2   ANON. Photographic essay, "The Old Man by the Sea," <u>Pageant</u>,
    10 (March), 114-19.
        Photos by Hans Malmberg.

3   ALLEN, CHARLES A. "Ernest Hemingway's Clean, Well-Lighted
    Heroes," <u>Pacific Spectator</u>, 9 (Autumn), 383-93.
        Sees that the heroes' stoicism and courage comprise a
    kind of "defense mechanism" prompted perhaps by parental
    rejection and feelings of inadequacy. Rituals and sani-
    tation are other primary defenses. Santiago's code is the
    final and culminating statement.

4   BACKMAN, MELVIN. "Hemingway: The Matador and the Crucified,"
    <u>Modern Fiction Studies</u>, 1 (August), 2-11.
        Sees that in Hemingway's two dominant motifs, adminis-
    tering and receiving death, "the matador represents a
    great force held in check, releasing itself proudly in a
    controlled yet violent administering of death. The cruci-
    fied stands for the taking of pain . . . so that it be-
    comes a thing of poignancy and nobility." Backman con-
    tends that the two motifs are synthesized in Santiago.
    Reprinted in Baker anthology, pp. 245-58 (<u>See</u> 1961.A5);
    and Baker critiques, pp. 135-43 (<u>See</u> 1962.A5).

5   [BARTLETT'S]. <u>Familiar Quotations by John Bartlett: A Col-</u>
    <u>lection of Passages, Phrases and Proverbs Traced to Their</u>

([BARTLETT'S])
Sources in Ancient and Modern Literature. Boston: Little,
Brown, Thirteenth and Centennial Edition, pp. 982-83.
Short quotations from Death in the Afternoon, Green Hills
of Africa, For Whom the Bell Tolls, Men at War, Baker
(1952.A2), and others.

6 BECK, WARREN. "The Shorter Happy Life of Mrs. Macomber," MFS,
1 (Nov.), 29-32.
Beck questions Wilson's credibility as narrator, and
reads the story as a positive description of Mrs. Macomber.
Reprinted in Howell, pp. 119-28 (See 1969.A9).

7 BEEBE, MAURICE. "Criticism of Ernest Hemingway: A Selected
Checklist with an Index to Studies of Separate Works,"
MFS, 1 (August), 36-45.

8 BREIT, HARVEY. "A Walk with Faulkner," New York Times Book
Review (30 Jan.), pp. 4, 12.
Regarding Faulkner's listing Hemingway last (of five)
when asked to name the five best contemporary writers.

9 BROOKS, CLEANTH, ed. Tragic Themes in Western Literature.
New Haven: Yale University Press, 153-54.
"The Saint as Tragic Hero" by Louis L. Martz. Uses the
rain in A Farewell to Arms as symbolic of physical human
isolation in much literature.
Reprinted in Gellens, pp. 55-56 (See 1970.A2).

10 BURNAM, TOM. "Primitivism and Masculinity in the Work of
Ernest Hemingway," MFS, 1 (Aug.), 20-24.
Of Hemingway's "primitivism" in his two latest books,
Burnam places Hemingway's appeal in "man's most primal
doubts, conflicts, and triumphs."

11 CARPENTER, FREDERICK I. American Literature and the Dream.
New York: Philosophical Library, pp. 185-93.
Chapter 20: "Hemingway Achieves the Fifth Dimension,"
reprinted from PMLA, 69 (Sept., 1954). (See 1954.B25.)

12 CLOETE, STUART. The African Giant: the Story of a Journey.
Boston: Houghton Mifflin.
Recollections of Hemingway recuperating in Nairobi after
the two African plane crashes in 1954.

13 COLVERT, JAMES B. "Ernest Hemingway's Morality in Action,"
American Literature, 27 (Nov.), 372-85.
Finds a definite moral system in Hemingway's fiction, a

1955

(COLVERT, JAMES B.)
new system of "morality in action," in search of which
some of Hemingway's heroes founder. In his fiction,
morality "is always implicitly--and sometimes very ex-
plicitly--related to feeling and emotion." Colvert compares the Hemingway hero to Crane's Henry Fleming.

14   DIETRICH, MARLENE. "The Most Fascinating Man I Know," This
Week (13 Feb.), pp. 8-9. Photo.
Relates her meeting with Hemingway on the Ile de France
in 1934, and their subsequent friendship.

15   EDEL, LEON. "The Art of Evasion," Folio, 20 (Spring), 18-20.
Edel finds that style must embody substance, and--until
1955--he thinks Hemingway's writing adolescent, of little
interest. "Hemingway is an artist of the small space, the
limited view."
Reprinted in Weeks, pp. 169-71 (See 1962.A6). See Young's
"A Defense," Ibid., pp. 20-22 (See 1962.A6).

16   FALK, ROBERT P., ed. American Literature in Parody. New
York: Twayne, pp. 241-44.
"When the Gong Sounded" by Cornelia Otis Skinner, reprinted from Soap Behind the Ears, New York, Dodd, Mead,
1941, pp. 89-96 (See 1941.B34).

17   FIEDLER, LESLIE. An End to Innocence: Essays on Culture and
Politics. Boston: Beacon Press.
Sees The Old Man and the Sea as a return to Hemingway's
earlier excellence because of its technical skill and its
avoidance of dealing with mature emotions. By omitting
women, Hemingway can enjoy "that 'safe' American Romance
of the boy and the old man."

18   FLANAGAN, JOHN. "Hemingway's Debt to Sherwood Anderson,"
Journal of English and German Philology, 54 (Oct.), 507-20.
Sees Hemingway indebted in that both men wrote simply,
concretely; both included sex; both worked from plot
structures; both preferred simple characters and an honest
revelation of the protagonist.

19   GURKO, LEO. "The Heroic Impulse in The Old Man and the Sea,"
English Journal, 44 (Oct.), 377-82.
Sees The Old Man and the Sea as recording the liberation
of the human spirit through the challenges of nature; it
gives off a buoyant tone of relief that is new to Hemingway.

(GURKO, LEO)
>   Reprinted in College English, 17 (Oct.), 11-15 as "The
>   Old Man and the Sea" and in Jobes, pp. 64-71 (See 1968.A9).

20   HOFFMAN, FREDERICK J. The Twenties: American Writing in the
>   Postwar Decade. New York: Viking Press, pp. 66-76,
>   Chapter 2: "The Unreasonable Wound" and pp. 80-85,
>   Chapter 2: "The Text: Hemingway's The Sun Also Rises."
>   Hoffman presents reinforcement of the psychic wound idea,
>   manifested in Hemingway's fiction as the "unreasonable
>   wound," forcing people to accept the most unrational of
>   circumstances with grace and "moral improvisation." Sees
>   The Sun Also Rises as a "moral novel," and, Hoffman be-
>   lieves, Hemingway's best.

21   HOLMAN, C. HUGH. "Hemingway and Emerson: Notes on the Con-
>   tinuity of an Aesthetic Tradition," MFS, 1 (Aug.), 12-16.
>   Hemingway shares Emerson's position on organic form,
>   "the significance of the thing itself," art as microcosm,
>   language, and the "ultimate equation of beauty and truth";
>   therefore Holman sees them as "parts of a continuing
>   aesthetic tradition."

22   KLINEFELTER, R. A. "Estimate of Hemingway," Catholic Mind,
>   53 (Nov.), 681-84.
>   Even after The Old Man and the Sea, Klinefelter believes
>   that Hemingway had "spelled his doom . . . by omitting
>   from his writings all concept of universal values."

23   KUNITZ, STANLEY J. and VINETA COLBY, eds. Twentieth Century
>   Authors. New York: Wilson, first supplement, pp. 433-34.

24   LEWIS, R. W. B. The American Adam: Innocence, Tragedy and
>   Tradition in the Nineteenth Century. Chicago: University
>   of Chicago Press, p. 115.
>   Aligns Hemingway with Poe, Cooper, and Hawthorne as
>   viewing "initiation" more appropriately as denitiation,
>   "not initiation into society, but, given the character of
>   society, an initiation away from it."

25   MacLEISH, ARCHIBALD. "Presentation to Ernest Hemingway of the
>   Award of Merit Medal for the Novel," American Academy of
>   Arts and Letters and the National Institute of Arts and
>   Letters Proceedings, New York, Second Series, No. 5,
>   pp. 28-29.

26   MAUROIS, ANDRÉ. "Ernest Hemingway," Revue de Paris, 62
>   (March), 3-16.

1955

(MAUROIS, ANDRÉ)
   Declares Hemingway a great writer, but one committed to
   writing about violence and death. Psychological study of
   his origins, his wound, the marriages, and the writing.
   Traces his debt to Twain, Kipling ("The capital sin is to
   be afraid"), and Proust.
   Reprinted, translated into English, in Baker anthology,
   pp. 38-54 (See 1961.A5).

27 MOYLAN, THOMAS J. "Violence in Hemingway," Catholic World,
      181 (July), pp. 287-93. Photo.
      Makes use of his personal acquaintance with Hemingway
   to discuss multi-level significance of violence in Hemingway's fiction. For Hemingway, "life is brutal; but men
   are brave, and can win, even without God."

28 OLDSEY, BERNARD S. "Hemingway's Old Men," MFS, 1 (Aug.),
      31-35.
      Points out that Hemingway has shown increasing interest
   in the old and aging (older characters pride themselves
   on the same things the young ones do, however). Sees a
   progression in Morgan, Jordan, and Anselmo's acceptance
   of social dependence. Then, Cantwell represents a full
   turnabout, and Santiago "a majestic return to nada."

29 PHILLIPS, WILLIAM L. "Sherwood Anderson's Two Prize Pupils,"
      University of Chicago Magazine, 47 (Jan.), 9-12. Photo.
      Regarding Anderson's influence on Hemingway and Faulkner,
   in regard to both themes and methods.

30 PRITCHETT, V. S. "Ernest Hemingway," New Statesman and Nation,
      50 (30 July), 137-38.
      Sees that Hemingway omits the "civilized regions" of
   American characters, but that he still uses many things
   traditionally American: "nostalgia, the . . . passion
   for techniques," and the power to describe seemingly real
   characters. Pritchett wonders why Hemingway could not
   live in the country he obviously has affection for. Reply
   by H. Quiller, New Statesman and Nation, 50 (6 Aug., 1955),
   163.

31 RUSSELL, H. K. "The Catharsis in A Farewell to Arms," MFS, 1
      (Aug.), 25-30.
      Finds that Henry's "sacrificial" role in the retreat at
   Caporetto causes pity and fear, both for him and for our-
   selves. We don't want him to win the challenge to his
   world because his winning would mean only chaos, and a
   meaningless world.

32 SARTRE, JEAN-PAUL. Literary and Philosophical Essays. New
York: Criterion Books, pp. 34, 35, 38.
Compares Albert Camus's style with that of Hemingway.

33 SCHWARTZ, DELMORE. "The Fiction of Ernest Hemingway," Perspectives U. S. A., 13 (Autumn), 70-88.
Labeling Hemingway "moral historian of the American
dream," Schwartz discusses his style in terms of Hemingway's own masculine identity (seeing reticence and tough-
ness closely related). A sympathetic view of Hemingway's
characters, claiming that their desire for sensation is
not sensuality but a striving for individuality.

34 SMITH, THELMA M. and WARD L. MINER. Transatlantic Migration:
The Contemporary American Novel in France. Durham, N. C.:
Duke University Press.
Pp. 99-121: Chapter 8, "Ernest Hemingway," pp. 221-27.
Checklist of translations, critical articles, and reviews
of Hemingway's work appearing in French periodicals.

35 SPILLER, ROBERT E. The Cycle of American Literature: An Essay
in Historical Criticism. New York: Macmillan, pp. 269-74,
"Full Circle: O'Neill, Hemingway."
Sees that Hemingway's contribution was his "mastery of
the art of fiction, a mastery which gave his relatively
limited themes their universality. Ranks Hemingway with
T. S. Eliot and William Faulkner.

36 SPIVEY, TED R. "Hemingway's Pursuit of Happiness on the Open
Road," Emory University Quarterly, 11 (Dec.), 240-52.
Sees an affinity between Hemingway's writing and that of
Whitman, but since Hemingway's world is less stable, one
of his themes is the brevity of comradeship and the re-
sulting suffering.

37 STARRETT, VINCENT. Best Loved Books of the Twentieth Century.
New York: Bantam Books, pp. 125-27.
Comments on A Farewell to Arms.

38 UNTERMEYER, LOUIS. Makers of the Modern World: The Lives of
Ninety-two Writers, Artists, Scientists, Statesmen, In-
ventors, Philosophers, Composers, and other Creators Who
Formed the Pattern of Our Century. New York: Simon &
Schuster, pp. 717-25: "Ernest Hemingway."

39 WAGGONER, HYATT H. "Ernest Hemingway," Christian Scholar, 38
(June), 114-20.
Sees Hemingway's view as not anti-Christian but

1955

(WAGGONER, HYATT H.)
anti-Victorian because his works "sharpen the issues,
clarify the alternatives, cut away the fuzziness that gives
us the illusion that we need not choose whom we will serve."

40 WILLIAMS, STANLEY T. The Spanish Background of American Literature, Vol. 1. New Haven: Yale University Press.
Sees Hemingway's interest in Spain as prompted by "his
obsession with violence, with the physical life of men and
women, and with a kind of pseudo primitivism."

41 WILSON, EARL. "Hemingway . . . About to Bank Another Book,"
New York Post (9 Nov.), p. 17.
Regarding a visit to the Hemingways.

42 WYRICK, GREEN D. "Hemingway and Bergson: The Élan Vital,"
MFS, 1 (Aug.), 17-19.
Sees that for Hemingway the "real thing" parallels
Bergson's "élan vital," action or movement in time with
creation as a result.

43 YOUNG, PHILIP. "A Defense," Folio, 20 (Spring), 20-22.
Answer to Leon Edel's "The Art of Evasion," Ibid.,
pp. 18-20. Young defends Hemingway's style and what Edel
considers the superficial themes.
Reprinted in Weeks, pp. 172-74 (See 1962.A6).

1956 A BOOKS

1 BAKER, CARLOS. Hemingway: The Writer as Artist. Princeton:
University Press.
Enlarged second edition includes a chapter on The Old
Man and the Sea, pp. 289-310, which novel Baker views as
the culmination of Hemingway's fascination with "Wahrheit."
Santiago is an exemplary hero, with many parallels to
Jesus; he differs from earlier Hemingway heroes in that he
never loses touch with nature. And, as Baker sees it,
Hemingway's "tragic view of life comes out in his peren-
nial contrast of the permanence of nature and the evanes-
cence of man."

1956 B SHORTER WRITINGS

1 ANON. "Campaigning," Newsweek, 48 (29 Oct.), 57.
Quotes Hemingway letter to students at the University of
Glasgow, who had nominated him for job of honorary Lord
Rector.

2   ANON. "Hemingway's Big Catch," St. Louis Post-Dispatch
        (4 May), p. 6A.
            After a 45-minute fight, Hemingway landed a 750 pound
        black marlin as cameramen recorded for The Old Man and the
        Sea film, in Cabo Blanco, Peru.

3   ANON. "Papa with Old Man Ramirez," Time, 67 (18 June), 47.
        Photo.
            Hemingway and Miguel Ramirez, the old Cuban fisherman,
        partial model for Santiago in The Old Man and the Sea.

4   ALDRIDGE, JOHN W. In Search of Heresy: American Literature in
        an Age of Conformity. New York: McGraw-Hill, pp. 149-65,
        Chapter 6.
            "Hemingway: the Etiquette of the Berserk," reprinted
        from Mandrake, 2 (Autumn-Winter 1954-55). (See 1954.B18.)

5   BACHE, WILLIAM B. "Craftsmanship in 'A Clean, Well-Lighted
        Place,'" Personalist, 37 (Winter), 60-64.
            The three characters of Hemingway's story symbolize
        youth, middle age, and old age; taken collectively, they
        represent the dilemma of modern man.

6   BERNHEIM, KURT. "Ernest Hemingway," McCall's Visits series,
        McCall's (May), pp. 6, 8, 10. Photos.
            Interview at Finca Vigia.

7   BOVE, CHARLES F., with DANA LEE THOMAS. A Paris Surgeon's
        Story. Boston: Little, Brown, pp. vii, 60.
            Recollections of Hemingway in Paris, mid-1920's.

8   BREIT, HARVEY. The Writer Observed. Cleveland, World. Pp.
        263-65: An interview with Hemingway, reprinted New York
        Times Book Review (7 Sept. 1952). (See 1952.B16.)
        Pp. 275-79: Interview with Hemingway, reprinted New York
        Times Book Review (7 Nov. 1954). (See 1954.B22.)

9   COCKBURN, CLAUD. A Discord of Trumpets: An Autobiography.
        New York: Simon & Schuster, pp. 302-03.
            The British journalist writes of Hemingway in Spain
        during the Civil War.

10 D'AGOSTINO, NEMI. "Ernest Hemingway," Balfagor, 11 (Jan.),
        54-73.
            An English translation titled "The Later Hemingway"
        appeared in Sewanee Review, 68 (Summer 1960), 482-93 (See
        1960.B4); and was reprinted in Weeks, pp. 152-60 (See
        1962.A6).

1956

11   GOODHEART, EUGENE. "The Legacy of Ernest Hemingway," <u>Prairie Schooner</u>, 30 (Fall), 212-18.
      Sees the code of violence and "blood and guts" as an adolescent one: "hard, defiant, swaggering . . . but at bottom impatiently fearful of the great world."

12   HALLIDAY, E. M. "Hemingway's Ambiguity: Symbolism and Irony," <u>American Literature</u>, 28 (March), 1-22.
      Sees Hemingway as subordinating his symbolism to his realism, whereas his pervasive use of irony clearly makes his fiction great. "The ironic gap between expectation and fulfillment, pretense and fact, intention and action . . . -- this has been Hemingway's great theme from the beginning; and it has called for an ironic method to do it artistic justice."
      Reprinted in Baker critiques, pp. 174-82 (<u>See</u> 1962.A5); in Weeks, pp. 52-71 (<u>See</u> 1962.A6); in Gellens, pp. 64-71 (<u>See</u> 1970.A2); and in Waldhorn, pp. 35-55 (<u>See</u> 1973.A7).

13   HEMINGWAY, MARY, JOHN O'HARA, MALCOLM COWLEY, JOHN GROTH, et al. "Who the Hell is Hemingway?" <u>True</u>, 36 (Feb.), 14-19, 25-31, 68. Cover drawing and photos.
      A symposium comprised of reprinted excerpts.

14   HERTZEL, LEO. "Hemingway and the Problem of Belief," <u>Catholic World</u>, 184 (Oct.), 30-31.
      Sees Hemingway as thinking a professed Catholicism is a satisfying state of mind; envies Catholics their "spiritual security."

15   HOLMAN, C. HUGH. "Hemingway and <u>Vanity Fair</u>," <u>Carolina Quarterly</u>, 8 (Summer), 31-37.
      Considers some of Hemingway's writing in direct line with late Victorian conservatism.

16   HUGHES, LANGSTON. <u>I Wonder as I Wander</u>. New York: Rinehart, pp. 362-65, "A Hemingway Story."
      Hughes tells the real-life episode of a shooting in the Aquarium Bar in Madrid, the beginning of Hemingway's story "The Butterfly and the Tank."

17   ISHI, ICHIRO. "Understanding of E. Hemingway," <u>Hototogisu</u>, 5 (Feb.), 12-13.
      Sees as one of Hemingway's fictional premises the belief that no one can write convincingly about experiences without having had them. His most impressive fiction results from his own living and his gradually broadening philosophy of life.

18 KASHKEEN, IVAN. "Alive in the Midst of Death," Soviet Litera-
        ture, 7 (1956), 160-72.
        Sees Hemingway's heroes motivated by "real life, work,
        and creative power." Sees Hemingway as a realist because
        "again and again the major problems of life crop up in his
        books." His values are the importance of work, the
        struggle for a decent life, and the solidarity of honest
        men and women.
        Reprinted in Baker anthology, pp. 162-79 (See 1961.A5).

19 MERTENS, GERARD M. "Hemingway's Old Man and the Sea and Mann's
        The Black Swan," Literature and Psychology, 6 (Aug.), 96-
        99.
        Each book has a hero who wages brave but unsuccessful
        battle; both of whom feel betrayed by fate, and have one
        true friend. Each story contains a mystic dream element.

20 O'CONNOR, WILLIAM VAN. "Two Views of Kilimanjaro," History of
        Ideas Newsletter, 2 (Oct.), 76-80.
        Compares a poem titled "Kilimandjaro" by Bayard Taylor
        with the Hemingway story, and concludes that Taylor's
        vision has "a far greater assurance of strength and abiding
        influence."

21 O'FAOLAIN, SEAN. The Vanishing Hero: Studies in Novelists of
        the Twenties. London: Eyre & Spottiswoode, pp. 137-65,
        "Ernest Hemingway or Men Without Memories."
        Sees many of Hemingway's characters as in reality
        affirming human dignity.

22 OLDFIELD, COL. BARNEY. Never a Shot in Anger. New York:
        Duell, Sloan & Pearce.
        References to Hemingway as war correspondent during
        World War II.

23 PAOLINI, PIER FRANCESCO. "Lo Hemingway dei grandi racconti,"
        Letteratura Moderne, 6 (Nov.-Dec.), 742-50.
        Finds Hemingway at his best in the long short stories
        and The Old Man and the Sea, fiction that taken collective-
        ly can both define his world and his philosophy. Close
        comparison of The Old Man and the Sea and "The Undefeated."
        Translated into English by Joseph M. Bernstein and re-
        printed in Baker anthology, pp. 131-44 (See 1962.A5).

24 PARKS, EDD WINFIELD. "Hemingway and Faulkner: The Pattern of
        Their Thought," Dagens Nyheder (12 Feb.), pp. 4-5. English
        translation in South Atlantic Bulletin, 22 (March 1957),
        1-2.
        See 1957.B23.

1956

25 RIDEOUT, WALTER B. <u>The Radical Novel in the United States</u>,
    <u>1900–1954</u>. Cambridge: Harvard University Press.
    Brief references to Hemingway's involvement in the
    Spanish Civil War, and his fiction as bone of contention
    for both <u>New Masses</u> and <u>Partisan Review</u>. Reissued in 1966
    from Hill & Wang.

26 SOSIN, MILT. "Novelist Hemingway Puts Books in 'Bank,'"
    <u>Miami Daily News</u> (22 May), p. 2. Photo, p. 1.
    Interview with Hemingway in Miami as plane arrives from
    Peru.

27 TAYLOR, WALTER FULLER. <u>The Story of American Letters</u>. Chica-
    go: Regnery, pp. 400–406, Chapter 2: "Pioneers of the
    Second Generation: F. Scott Fitzgerald (1896–1940) and
    Ernest Hemingway (1899–   )."
    Surveys Hemingway's career through <u>Across the River and</u>
    <u>Into the Trees</u> as "an expression of the naturalistic view
    of man and the naturalistic way in art." Grants Heming-
    way's influence among writers, but terms his "limitation
    of vision" "truly astonishing."

28 WALCUTT, CHARLES CHILD. <u>American Literary Naturalism, A</u>
    <u>Divided Stream</u>. Minneapolis: University of Minnesota
    Press, pp. 270–80; Chapter 11: "Later Trends in Form:
    Steinbeck, Hemingway, Dos Passos."
    Though some tenets of naturalism apply to Hemingway's
    fiction, Walcutt points out that Hemingway "is not con-
    tained by them." Sees <u>For Whom the Bell Tolls</u> as a "re-
    integration of spirit," "the most explicit, sustained, and
    triumphant reunion of its divided stream that American
    naturalism has seen." Sees <u>The Old Man and the Sea</u> as
    similarly triumphant.

29 WALDMEIR, JOSEPH. "<u>Confiteor Hominem</u>: Ernest Hemingway's
    Religion of Man," <u>PMASAL</u>, 42: 277–81.
    Convincing discussion of the opinion that Hemingway made
    no major changes in order to write <u>The Old Man and the Sea</u>;
    his religion was evident throughout his work, but it was a
    religion of the brotherhood among men rather than a formal
    and isolating deity–man relationship.
    Reprinted in Baker critiques, pp. 144–49 (<u>See</u> 1962.A5);
    in Weeks, pp. 161–68 (<u>See</u> 1962.A6); in Wagner, pp. 141–52
    (<u>See</u> 1974.A3).

30 WHITE, WILLIAM. "On Collecting Hemingway," <u>American Book</u>
    <u>Collector</u>, 7 (Nov.), 21–23.
    <u>See also</u> letters from Fraser Drew, <u>ABC</u>, 7 (Dec.), 2 and
    Adrian Goldstone, <u>ABC</u>, 7 (Feb. 1957), 20.

31   WILSON, COLIN. The Outsider. London: Gollancz, pp. 31-39.
         Discussion of the importance of Hemingway's work to the
         problem of the "existentialist outsider."

32   WOLFE, THOMAS. The Letters of Thomas Wolfe, edited by Eliza-
         beth Nowell. New York: Charles Scribner's Sons.
         P. 468: Wolfe's comment on Hemingway's Green Hills of
         Africa attack on him; p. 655: on writing methods. Other
         scattered references.

1957 A   BOOKS - NONE

1957 B   SHORTER WRITINGS

1   ANDERSON, CARL L. The Swedish Acceptance of American Litera-
         ture. Stockholm: Almqvist & Wiksell, pp. 98-99.
         Hemingway's influence on Swedish authors, especially in
         the short story.

2   ANGOFF, ALLAN, ed. American Writing Today: Its Independence
         and Vigor. New York: New York University Press, pp. 370-
         72.
         Review of A Farewell to Arms, reprinted from Times
         Literary Supplement (28 Nov. 1929). (See 1929.B6.)

3   BACHE, WILLIAM B. "Nostromo and 'The Snows of Kilimanjaro,'"
         Modern Language Notes, 72 (Jan.), 32-34.
         Sees that Nostromo served Hemingway as "a thematic
         inspiration, a critical model, and a source" so far as
         "The Snows of Kilimanjaro" is concerned.

4   BARTLETT, PHYLLIS. "Other Countries, Other Wenches," MFS,
         3 (Winter), 345-49.
         Both Hemingway and Faulkner (and others) borrow Eliot's
         version of a quotation from Marlowe's The Jew of Malta.

5   BRIGGS, ELLIS O. Shots Heard Round the World: An Ambassador's
         Hunting Adventures on Four Continents. New York: Viking
         Press, pp. 55-73; Chapter 4, "No Hasta El Postre: Meaning
         You Can't Throw Rolls until Dessert."
         Describing Hemingway's submarine hunting activities in
         the Caribbean in 1943, and his forty-fourth birthday party
         at Finca Vigia.

6   CHASE, RICHARD. The American Novel and Its Tradition. Garden
         City, New York: Doubleday.
         P. 144: Sees Frederic Henry as "impervious to trans-
         formation and tragic awareness," and therefore considers

1957

(CHASE, RICHARD)
A Farewell to Arms something other than an "initiation"
novel. Pp. 159-60: points out that most American
novelists--Hemingway among them--ask readers to judge
characters by "what they are at heart" rather than the
way they react to social situations.

7 CODMAN, COL. CHARLES R. Drive: The General Patton Story.
Boston: Little, Brown, pp. 255-56.
The author recalls a dinner conversation about The Sun
Also Rises with Hemingway, in Paris, in 1945.

8 CONNOLLY, THOMAS E. The Personal Library of James Joyce: A
Descriptive Bibliography. Buffalo: University Bookstore,
p. 19.
Regarding an inscribed copy of A Farewell to Arms, in
which Hemingway had filled in the publisher's dashes with
the original obscenities.

9 FAGAN, EDWARD R. "Teaching Enigmas of The Old Man and the Sea,"
English Record, 8 (Autumn), 13-20.
Finds the book especially adaptable to a heterogeneous
classroom. Discusses the variety of interpretation--
story, allegory, symbol--and its applicability to a student-
oriented discussion.

10 FENTON, CHARLES A. "The Writers Who Came Out of the War," SR,
40 (3 Aug.), 5-7.
Sees this generation absorbing their technique from the
early Hemingway, their values from the later Hemingway:
"The twin themes of combat and personal subjugation per-
sist in the fiction of this later post-war generation."

11 FRIEDRICH, OTTO. "Ernest Hemingway: Joy through Strength,"
The American Scholar, 26 (Autumn), 470, 518-30.
Finds Hemingway's early work so despairing that suicide
is its "only logical conclusion," but does see some alle-
viation of that nada in To Have and Have Not and The Old
Man and the Sea.
Reprinted in Graham, pp. 46-54 (See 1971.A7).

12 FROHOCK, W. J. The Novel of Violence in America. Dallas:
Southern Methodist University Press.
Sees A Farewell to Arms as closer to being a good movie
than a good novel, because of its visual appeal, dialogue,
symbols, and foreshortened time.

13   GORDON, CAROLINE. <u>How to Read a Novel</u>. New York: Viking
Press, pp. 78-79, 99-102, 146-47.
"Today Is Friday" and <u>A Farewell to Arms</u> are used as
examples of the "effaced narrator."

14   HART, ROBERT C. "Hemingway on Writing," <u>College English</u>, 18
(March), 314-20.
Describes various Hemingway approaches to craft; sees as
basic his notion of "truth--the illusion of real life ex-
perience--" and his methods of attaining it.

*15   KASHKEEN, IVAN. "Hemingway on the Path to Mastery," <u>Voprosi
Literaturi</u> (Moscow), No. 6 (Sept.), 184-204.
In Baker anthology bibliography, p. 285. (<u>See</u> 1961.A5.)

16   KELLY, FRANK K. <u>Reporters Around the World</u>. Boston: Little,
Brown, pp. 155-66. Juvenile biography.
"Under Fire in Italy, Hemingway Finds He Is Mortal."

17   KNOLL, ROBERT E. <u>Robert McAlmon: Expatriate Publisher and
Writer</u>. Lincoln: University of Nebraska Studies, No. 18,
pamphlet.
References to Hemingway in Paris in the 1920's.

18   KREYMBORG, ALFRED. "Exit Vachel Lindsay--Enter Ernest Hemingway," <u>Literary Review</u>, 1 (Winter), 208-19.
Mostly an account of Kreymborg's friendship with Lindsay,
followed by an anecdote of one meeting with Hemingway.

19   LARRABEE, ERIC, ed. <u>American Panorama: Essays by Fifteen
American Critics on 350 Books Past and Present which Por-
tray the U. S. A. in its Many Aspects</u>. New York: New
York University Press, p. 155: "The Short Stories of
Ernest Hemingway" by "C.F." (Clifton Fadiman).
Thinks the stories his best work: "With them he started
a new school of writing." Finds that "posturing and belli-
cosity occasionally mar his longer works."

20   LEVIN, HARRY. <u>Contexts of Criticism</u>. Cambridge: Harvard
University Press.
Pp. 140-67, Chapter 10: "Observations on the Style of
Ernest Hemingway," reprinted from <u>Kenyon Review</u>, 13
(Autumn 1951), 581-609 (<u>See</u> 1951.B13); and in Weeks,
pp. 72-85, abridged (<u>See</u> 1962.A6); in Baker anthology,
pp. 93-115 (<u>See</u> 1961.A5). Pp. 190-207, Chapter 12: "Sym-
bolism and Fiction," reprinted from book of same title,
Charlottesville, University of Virginia Press, 1956.

1957

21 LYONS, LEONARD. "Last Day in Europe," New York Post (21 Jan.),
    p. 26. Photo, p. 2.
       Relates spending a day in Paris with the Hemingways.

22 McCORMICK, JOHN. Catastrophe and Imagination: An Interpreta-
    tion of the Recent English and American Novel. London:
    Longmans, Green.
       Pp. 95-96: Discussion of Henry James' influence on
    Hemingway's work as being "a single-minded insistence upon
    moral behaviour." Pp. 208-14: Discussion of Hemingway's
    war novels in which Hemingway reversed the usual order:
    The Sun Also Rises dealt with the idea of war; A Farewell
    to Arms, with the fact of it.

23 PARKS, EDD WINFIELD. "Faulkner and Hemingway--Their Thought,"
    South Atlantic Bulletin, 22 (March), 1-2.
       Both Faulkner and Hemingway have changed attitudes from
    the earliest hopelessness to an awareness that man alone
    is responsible and can be destroyed but not defeated.

24 RAHV, PHILIP. Image and Idea: Twenty Essays on Literary
    Themes. New York: New Directions.
       Pp. 188-92: Review of Across the River and Into the
    Trees, reprinted from Commentary, 10 (Oct. 1950). (See
    1950.B44.) Pp. 192-95: Review of The Old Man and the Sea,
    reprinted from Commentary, 14 (Oct. 1952). (See 1952.B62.)
    And reprinted in Jobes, pp. 110-12 under the title "Heming-
    way in the 1950's" (See 1968.A9).

25 ROBERT, MacLEAN. "An Afternoon with Papa Hemingway," Bachelor,
    2 (May), 38-41, 72. Photos.
       Interview at the Finca Vigia.

26 SCOTT, ARTHUR L. "In Defense of Robert Cohn," College English,
    18 (March), 309-14.
       Sees that the society portrayed in The Sun Also Rises is
    at fault and considers Cohn "the most normal character in
    the book."

27 SEYPPEL, JOACHIM H. "Two Variations on a Theme: Dying in
    Venice," Literature and Psychology, 7 (Feb.), 8-12.
       Thomas Mann's Death in Venice and Hemingway's Across the
    River and Into the Trees both reflect the "tragic experience
    of the 'mystical union' of beauty and death, and of sex and
    death, with which psychologists have long been familiar."

28 SHOCKLEY, MARTIN STAPLES. "Hemingway's Moment of Truth,"
      Colorado Quarterly, 5 (Spring), 380-88.
        Sees "Death in the Afternoon" as Hemingway's supreme
      revelation, his moment of truth.

29 SIMPSON, JAMES BEASLEY. Best Quotes of '54, '55, '56. New
      York: Crowell, pp. 8-10, 267-68.
        Hemingway is quoted concerning the African plane crashes,
      the Nobel prize, etc.

30 SMITH, REX, ed. Biography of the Bulls. New York: Rinehart,
      pp. 369-71.
        "Papa Goes to the Fights," by Robert Ruark, reprinted
      from New York World Telegram & The Sun (10 Aug. 1953).
      (See 1953.B40.)

31 THODY, PHILIP. "A Note on Camus and the Contemporary American
      Novel," Comparative Literature, 9 (Summer), 243-49.
        Compares Camus' L'Etranger and Meursault with Jake Barnes
      and quotes Camus' statement that he "was imitating and
      criticizing not the finely balanced descriptive prose of
      Hemingway, but the rather crude idea of what this prose
      was like which had been popularized by writers and trans-
      lators." Does find them alike in that they write in "cer-
      tain defined limits" without being "overly ambitious."

32 WAGNER, VERN. "A Note for Ernest Hemingway," College English,
      18 (March), 327.
        A parody of phrases from contemporary literature.

33 WEEKS, ROBERT. "Hemingway and the Spectatorial Attitude,"
      Western Humanities Review, 11 (Summer), 277-81.
        Sees that Hemingway's objectivity stemmed from his ex-
      periences as journalist; eventually the Hemingway hero be-
      came "a detached spectator in a violent world."

34 WEEKS, ROBERT P. "Hemingway and the Uses of Isolation,"
      University of Kansas City Review, 24 (Dec.), 119-25.
        Locates the Hemingway heroes' need to stand alone as
      being not withdrawal but a resolute and disciplined stance.

35 _____. "Hemingway's 'The Killers,'" Explicator, 15 (May),
      Item 53.
        Mrs. Bell's chief function is to intensify Ole Andreson's
      isolation.

36 WILLIAMS, WILLIAM CARLOS. The Selected Letters, edited by
      John C. Thirlwall. New York: McDowell, Obolensky.

1957

(WILLIAMS, WILLIAM CARLOS)
Some reference to knowing Hemingway in Paris in 1924; an analysis of Hemingway's "cloak of vulgarity" in order to "protect a Jamesian sensitivity to detail."

37 WILSON, EARL. "A Visit with 'Papa,'" New York Post (26 May), p. M3.
Interview from Havana.

38 ZABEL, MORTON DAUWEN. Craft and Character in Modern Fiction: Texts, Method and Vocation. New York: Viking Press.
Pp. 317-21: "Hemingway: 1950 and 1952," review of Across the River and Into the Trees, reprinted from the Nation, 171 (9 Sept. 1950). (See 1950.B66.) Pp. 321-26: Essay on The Old Man and the Sea, based on material from the TLS (17 Sept. 1954).

1958 A   BOOKS - NONE

1958 B   SHORTER WRITINGS

1 ATKINS, JOHN. "Hemingway and the American Novel," Wisdom, 3 (June), 4-9.
Hemingway gives us another view of the Waste Land in his own terms. He has moved from a concern with fear, its uses and abuses, to the comfort of discipline. Most recently, "he stresses the importance of communion." Sees his realism giving way to mysticism.

2 BEATTY, JEROME, Jr. "Hemingway vs. Esquire," SR, 41 (28 Aug.), 9-11, 36.
As a result of Hemingway's court action against Esquire (later settled out of court) to prevent the reprinting of three of his stories from Esquire, 1938, Hemingway got back his copyrights and Esquire got publicity for their collection.

3 CORIN, FERNAND. "Steinbeck and Hemingway: A Study in Literary Economy," Revue des Langues Vivantes, 24: 60-75 and 153-60.
Sees some similarities in each author's tendency to create parables, but finds Hemingway's The Old Man and the Sea more effective than Steinbeck's The Pearl because "the materials have been organized and disciplined so as to express the theme."

4 DAWSON, WILLIAM. "Ernest Hemingway: Petosky Interview," Michigan Alumnus Quarterly Review, 64 (Winter), 114-23.

(DAWSON, WILLIAM)
   Dawson interviews people in the area who had known Hemingway, and makes some observations on the Nick Adams
stories.

5   DREW, FRASER B. Thirty-five Years of Ernest Hemingway: A
   Catalogue of the Hemingway Collection of Dr. Fraser B.
   Drew. 8 mimeographed pages.
      Exhibited in the Edward H. Butler Library of the State
   University of New York College for Teachers at Buffalo,
   Nov. 1-19, 1958. Ninety-eight items, including inscribed
   first editions, periodicals with first appearances, letters,
   photos, and translations.

6   DRUMMOND, ANN. "The Hemingway Code as Seen in the Early Short
   Stories," Discourse, 1 (Oct.), 248-52.
      Sees that Hemingway demands a "definite and positive
   code of behavior from his fictional beings." The code is
   based on individual responsibility for one's own actions
   and salvation.

7   EVANS, OLIVER. "The Protagonist of Hemingway's 'The Killers,'"
   Modern Language Notes, 73 (Dec.), 589-91.
      Sees that Nick is used as a narrative device, and that
   the story remains Andreson's.

8   FIEDLER, LESLIE, ed. The Art of the Essay. New York: Crowell,
   pp. 86-92.
      Excerpt about Hemingway from Stein's The Autobiography
   of Alice B. Toklas, pp. 261-71 (See 1933.B21).

9   FRIEDMAN, NORMAN. "Criticism and the Novel: Hardy, Hemingway,
   Crane, Woolf, Conrad," Antioch Review, 18 (Fall), 343-70.
      Concentrates on each novel from its texture, imagery
   patterns, symbolic associations, and archetypal structures.
   Considers A Farewell to Arms "as a wasteland archetype,"
   but finds through this exercise that critically "we have
   no commonly-accepted body of terms, principles, and distinction for grasping satisfactorily the literal action of
   a novel."

10   _____. "What Makes a Short Story Short?" MFS, 4 (Summer),
   103-17
      Works from two premises, that a story is short because
   the material itself may be of small compass or it may be
   treated economically. Admires "Hills Like White Elephants"
   and "Ten Indians" for the latter reason; finds For Whom the
   Bell Tolls is too long for "the size of its action."

1958

11   GEISMAR, MAXWELL. "Ernest Hemingway: At the Crossroads,"
      in American Moderns: From Rebellion to Conformity. New
      York: Hill & Wang, pp. 54-58.
         Sees Hemingway's writing as "a sort of literary catalyst
      which has affected the entire course of American writing
      . . . it has remained untouched by and superior to all the
      imitations of it."
      Reprinted from New York Times Book Review (31 July 1949)
      under the title "Notes from a Critic on a Novelist's Work,"
      (See 1949.B6); pp. 59-61: "A Year Later," review of Across
      the River and Into the Trees, reprinted from SRL, 33
      (9 Sept. 1950). (See 1950.B27). Pp. 61-64: "The Nobel
      Prize," reprinted from SR, 37 (13 Nov. 1954). (See
      1954.B35.)

12   GREBSTEIN, SHELDON NORMAN. "Controversy," The American
      Scholar, 27 (Spring), 229-31.
         In answer to Friedrich, Grebstein defends Hemingway as
      being neither superficial nor unreal: "few writers in our
      time have shown the philosophical and artistic development
      that is apparent in Hemingway between In Our Time and The
      Old Man and the Sea."

13   [GUFFEY, DON CARLOS]. First Editions of English and American
      Authors: The Library of Dr. Don Carlos Guffey. New York:
      Parke-Bernet Galleries, auction catalogue, Oct. 14.
         Facsimiles of manuscript pages from Death in the After-
      noon, and of inscription to Dr. Guffey on p. 31; pp. 26-
      41: "An Important Collection of Ernest Hemingway Features
      the Major Portion of the manuscript of Death in the After-
      noon."

14   LUDOVICI, LAURENCE, J., ed. Nobel Prize Winners. London:
      Arco, pp. 85-100.
         "Ernest Hemingway" by M.J.C. Hodgart stresses "one of
      the most poetic" of novelists," a writer who had "already
      become an institution" by the time he had won the Nobel
      prize: "'Hemingway' had long been an adjective to describe
      a personality, an attitude, a style."

15   MOORE, HARRY T. "An Earnest Hemingwaiad," Encounter, 10
      (June), 15-18.
         Traces the origins of Hemingway's style to Twain, Lard-
      ner, Anderson, Stein, Pound; then surveys his career and,
      in mock heroic couplets, counts him out.
      Reprinted in Age of the Modern and Other Literary Essays,
      Carbondale, S. Illinois University Press, 1971, pp. 23-27.

16   MORRIS, WRIGHT. "The Ability to Function: A Reappraisal of
          Fitzgerald and Hemingway" in New World Writing, No. 13.
          New York: The New American Library, pp. 34-51.
             Sees Hemingway's impact to be stylistic, an accurate
          representation of the modern man: "His style . . . sounds
          the note of enchantment to the very disenchantment it an-
          ticipates." Hemingway writes from an oversimplified posi-
          tion: "Man is a mess, but Nature will prevail . . . Man
          finitely simple, and Nature infinitely complex."
          Reprinted in The Territory Ahead, New York, Atheneum, 1963,
          pp. 43-51, as "Hemingway: The Function of Style" (See
          1963.B34).

17   NORTH, JOSEPH. No Men Are Strangers. New York: International
          Publishers.
             Relates an argument on communism which he had with Hem-
          ingway in Madrid, 1938, and quotes from the article Heming-
          way wrote for the 1936 issue of New Masses.

18   PLIMPTON, GEORGE. "The Art of Fiction, 21: Hemingway," Paris
          Review, No. 18 (Spring), pp. 61-89.
             Much information about Hemingway's writing habits and
          theories including the "iceberg" principle is given.
          Reprinted in Writers at Work: The Paris Review Interviews,
          Second Series, New York, Viking, 1963, pp. 215-39 (See
          1963.B38); in Baker anthology, pp. 19-37 (See 1961.A5);
          in Wagner, pp. 21-37 (See 1974.A3).

19   RICHARDSON, H. EDWARD. "The 'Hemingwaves' in Faulkner's Wild
          Palms," MFS, 4 (Winter), 357-60.
             Reads the novel as "an independent satirical comment on
          Hemingway."

20   SHAPIRO, CHARLES, ed. Twelve Original Essays on Great American
          Novels. Detroit: Wayne State University Press.
             Pp. 238-56, "The Death of Love in The Sun Also Rises"
          by Mark Spilka. Sees the theme as common to other post-
          war novels, but finds The Sun Also Rises the most effective
          treatment of it because it provides an "extensive parable."
          Cohn, for example, is "the last chivalric hero," and Pedro
          "the real hero of the parable, the final moral touchstone."
          Reprinted in Baker anthology, pp. 80-92 (See 1961.A5); in
          Weeks, pp. 127-38 (See 1962.A6); in Baker critiques, pp.
          18-25 (See 1962.A5); and in White, pp. 73-85 (See 1969.A11).

21   STEPHENS, ROBERT O. "Hemingway's Across the River and Into the
          Trees: A Reprise," Texas Studies in English, 37: 92-101.
             A view of Cantwell as a continuation of earlier Hemingway

1958

(STEPHENS, ROBERT O.)
heroes, here caught in bleak social disillusionment that
forces him to create his own values, to ritualistically
return to the site of his wounding, and to perpetuate himself through Renata, the woman he loves.

22 STEWART, RANDALL. <u>American Literature and Christian Doctrine</u>.
Baton Rouge: Louisiana State University Press.
Sees as positive Hemingway's insistence on "ritualistic
discipline" in "A Clean, Well-Lighted Place" and "Big Two-
Hearted River."

*23 TODD, HAROLD W., Jr. "Natural Elements in Hemingway's Novels,"
<u>Wingover</u>, 1 (Autumn-Winter), 25-27.
Cited in Baker anthology bibliography, p. 289 (<u>See</u>
1961.A5).

24 WARREN, ROBERT PENN. "Ernest Hemingway," in <u>Selected Essays</u>.
New York: Random House, pp. 80-118.
Reprinted from <u>Kenyon Review</u>, 9 (Winter 1947). (<u>See</u>
1947.B18.)

*25 WOOD, DEAN C. "The Significance of Bulls and Bullfighters in
<u>The Sun Also Rises</u>," <u>Wingover</u>, 1 (Fall-Winter), 28-30.
Cited in Baker anthology bibliography, p. 297 (<u>See</u>
1961.A5).

26 WOOLF, VIRGINIA. "An Essay in Criticism," in <u>Granite and
Rainbow: Essays</u>. London: Hogarth, pp. 85-92.
Review of <u>Men Without Women</u>, reprinted from <u>New York
Herald Tribune Books</u> (9 Oct. 1927). (<u>See</u> 1927.B23.)

1959 A BOOKS

1 YOUNG, PHILIP. <u>Ernest Hemingway</u>. Minneapolis: University of
Minnesota Press (Pamphlets on American Writers, No. 1).
Approaches the entire Hemingway canon from the perspective of Nick Adams. Sees Nick as Hemingway's most significant protagonist, and the subjects of "the wound, the
break from society, and the code" as pervasive in all his
writing. Relates his work—both stylistically and thematically—to Twain. Bibliographical references, pp. 42-44.
Reprinted, revised, in <u>Seven Modern American Novelists</u>,
edited by William Van O'Connor, Minneapolis, University
of Minnesota Press, 1964, pp. 153-88 (<u>See</u> 1964.B40).

1959 B   SHORTER WRITINGS

1   ADAMS, RICHARD. "Sunrise Out of the Waste Land," Tulane
        Studies in English, 9: 119-31.
            Traces the influence of The Waste Land, Ulysses, and The
        Great Gatsby on The Sun Also Rises, which Adams sees as
        Hemingway's affirmative answer to the post-war mood.
        Reprinted in Wagner, pp. 241-51 (See 1974.A3).

2   BAKER, SHERIDAN. "Hemingway's Two-Hearted River," Michigan
        Alumnus Quarterly Review, 65 (28 Feb.), 142-49.
            Geographical observations about Hemingway's Fox River,
        Seney, and other Michigan towns.
        Reprinted in Benson, pp. 150-59 (See 1975.A3).

3   BEACH, SYLVIA. Les Années Vingt, Les Écrivains Américains á
        Paris et leurs amis: 1920-1930. Paris: Centre Culturel
        Americain. Photos.
            Catalogue of the Exposition sponsored by the American
        Cultural Center of the U. S. Embassy, March 11 to April 25,
        1959, in Paris. Pp. 102-04: List of photos, letters,
        inscribed books, and periodical pieces by Hemingway.

4   _____. Shakespeare and Company. New York: Harcourt, Brace.
        Photos.
            Pp. 77-83: Chapter 9, "My Best Customer," refers to
        Hemingway's mid-1920's patronage of the Paris bookshop;
        pp. 219-20: Chapter 23, "Hemingway Liberates the Rue de
        l'Odéon," describes Hemingway's arrival during the libera-
        tion of Paris, August 1944.

5   BEAVER, HAROLD, ed. American Critical Essays: Twentieth
        Century. London: Oxford University Press, pp. 286-313.
            "Observations on the Style of Ernest Hemingway" by Harry
        Levin, reprinted from Contexts of Criticism, Cambridge,
        Harvard University Press, 1957, pp. 140-67 (See 1957.B20).

6   BLUEFARB, SAMUEL. "The Sea--Mirror and Maker of Character in
        Fiction and Drama," English Journal, 48 (Dec.), 501-10.
            Thematic and psychological analysis of the sea as
        shaping image in O'Neill, Melville, and Hemingway. In The
        Old Man and the Sea, the sea is "indifferent" and some-
        times "malicious" in its interference, highlighting the
        protagonist's struggle, defeat, and transcendence.

7   BRINNIN, JOHN MALCOLM. The Third Rose: Gertrude Stein and
        Her World. Boston: Atlantic-Little, Brown, photos by
        Man Ray, pp. 249-63.

1959

(BRINNIN, JOHN MALCOLM)
    Stein recounts meeting Hemingway in Paris in 1922; her influence on his writing and their references to each other in their later books.

8   BROOKS, CLEANTH and ROBERT PENN WARREN. "The Killers," Understanding Fiction. New York: Appleton-Century-Crofts, pp. 303-12.
    A structuralist reading, with extensions to Hemingway's other characters, portrayed as sensitive, disciplined and understated.
    Reprinted in Benson, pp. 187-96 (See 1975.A3).

9   BURY, JOHN PATRICK. "Hemingway in Spain," Contemporary Review, No. 1118 (Feb.), pp. 103-05.
    Sees that Death in the Afternoon, The Sun Also Rises, and For Whom the Bell Tolls express Hemingway's homage to Spain where he had found a good life and important spiritual values: courage, the permanence of earth, and the need for personal responsibility.

10   CARPENTER, FREDERICK I. "'The American Myth': Paradise (To Be) Regained," PMLA, 74 (Dec.), 599-606.
    Sees The Old Man and the Sea as an example of the American myth: "The American Adam kills the wild thing that he loves, but learns thereby a deeper wisdom . . . . a wiser innocence."
    Reprinted partially in Jobes, p. 103 (See 1968.A9).

11   COHEN, JOSEPH. "Wouk's Morningstar and Hemingway's Sun," South Atlantic Quarterly, 58 (Spring), 213-24.
    Wouk's Marjorie Morningstar parallels The Sun Also Rises: Robert Cohn is to Noel Airman as Brett Ashley is to Marjorie. Hemingway's code of "morality in action" is transmuted to Wouk's theme of "morality in tradition."

12   COLBURN, WILLIAM E. "Confusion in 'A Clean, Well-Lighted Place,'" College English, 20 (Feb.), 241-42.
    Questions the unnecessary inconsistencies in the dialogue between the waiters.

13   COUSINS, NORMAN. "For Whom the Bells Ring in Russia," SR, 42 (22 Aug.), 18.
    Although Hemingway's novels are not Marxist, he is esteemed in Russia, perhaps because the Russian reader looks for his fiction "to be epic in scope, to deal with grand themes, with color and movement."

14 EASTMAN, MAX. "The Great and the Small in Ernest Hemingway,"
    SR, 42 (4 April), 13-15, 50-51.
        Reminiscences about the Eastman-Hemingway fight in Max-
    well Perkins' office, as well as their last meeting in
    1946.

15 _____. "The Great and Small in Ernest Hemingway," in Great
    Companions: Critical Memoirs of Some Famous Friends.
    New York: Farrar, Straus & Cudahy, pp. 41-76. Photo.
        Partially reprinted in SR, 42 (4 April 1959). (See
    1959.B14.) Includes a letter from Hemingway, regarding
    the essay.

16 ELLMANN, RICHARD. James Joyce. New York: Oxford University
    Press.
        P. 543: Letter from Hemingway to Sherwood Anderson
    about Ulysses; p. 598: Letter protesting the pirating of
    Ulysses; p. 708: an evaluation of Hemingway by Joyce.

17 FEIDELSON, CHARLES, Jr. and PAUL BRODTKORB, Jr., eds. Inter-
    pretations of American Literature. New York: Oxford
    University Press, pp. 297-331.
        E. M. Halliday's "Hemingway's Ambiguity: Symbolism and
    Irony," reprinted from American Literature, 28 (March 1956),
    320-331 (See 1956.B12); Frederick J. Hoffman's "No Begin-
    ning and No End: Hemingway and Death," reprinted from
    Essays in Criticism, 3 (Jan. 1953). (See 1953.B32.)

18 FIEDLER, LESLIE. Love and Death in the American Novel. New
    York: Stein and Day, pp. 304-09 and 350-52.
        Sees Hemingway as comfortable only in presenting men
    with men, in searching for life in the uninhibited "West,"
    mythic or real. Women, for Hemingway, are only bitches,
    inhibitors, or castration symbols.
        Reprinted as "Men Without Women" in Weeks, pp. 86-92 (See
    1962.A6).

19 FREEDMAN, RICHARD. "Hemingway's Spanish Civil War Dispatches,"
    Texas Studies in Literature and Language, 1 (Summer), 171-
    80.
        Sees that Hemingway's NANA dispatches were written with-
    out bias, and that Hemingway rarely used the material so
    covered in his later fiction.

20 GARDINER, HAROLD C., S.J. In All Conscience: Reflections on
    Books and Culture. Garden City, N. Y.: Hanover House.
        Pp. 124-25: "He-Man Whimpering," review of Across the

145

1959

(GARDINER, HAROLD C., S.J.)
River and Into the Trees, reprinted from America, 83
(16 Sept. 1950). (See 1950.B26.) Pp. 125-26: "Pathetic
Fallacy," review of The Old Man and the Sea, reprinted
from America, 87 (13 Sept. 1952). (See 1952.B35.)

21 GARLINGTON, JACK. "The Intelligence Quotient of Lady Brett
    Ashley," San Francisco Review, 1 (Sept.), 23-28.
        Premise is that "Hemingway's characters aren't very
    bright" as shown by analysis of dialogue (since characters
    cannot even express themselves) and by their failure finan-
    cially and socially. Expresses the assumption that only
    idiots believe in animism.

22 GWYNN, FREDERICK L. and JOSEPH L. BLOTNER, eds. Faulkner in
    the University: Class Conferences at the University of
    Virginia, 1957-1958. Charlottesville: University of Vir-
    ginia Press.
        Scattered references to Hemingway as an important writer,
    with some excellences, and other limitations.

23 HAGOPIAN, JOHN V. "Style and Meaning in Hemingway and
    Faulkner," Jahrbuch für Amerikastudien, 4: 170-79.
        Stylistic analysis of each writer's work, concluding
    that "Hemingway's taut sentences and simple diction embody
    the sense of restraint . . . the nervous tension of charac-
    ters unable to release their emotions fully," whereas
    Faulkner's "rolling sentences and rich diction" suggest "a
    full exploration" of all the multifariousness of life.

24 HOLMAN, C. HUGH. "Ernest Hemingway" from Louis D. Rubin,
    "Modern Novelists and Contemporary American Society: A
    Symposium," Shenandoah, 10 (Winter), 4-11 of 3-31.
        Sees that Hemingway has been critical of American values
    from the beginning (one reason for his fictional choice of
    other locations); Cantwell in Across the River and Into
    the Trees is the culmination of this attitude.

25 HOTCHNER, A. E. "Hemingway Talks to American Youth," This
    Week Magazine (18 Oct.), pp. 10-11, 24-26.

26 JOHNSON, JAMES W. "The Adolescent Hero: A Trend in Modern
    Fiction," Twentieth Century Literature, 5 (April), 3-11.
        Sees Nick Adams as an adolescent protagonist, part of a
    current trend to romanticize childhood. In Hemingway's
    fiction, "life is seen as a chaotic, transitional process
    lost between some vanished pattern of values and an un-
    known future."

27 JONES, JOHN A. "Hemingway: The Critics and the Public Legend,"
      Western Humanities Review, 13 (Autumn), 387-400.
         Sees the drift of criticism since 1950 changing to con-
      centrate on Hemingway as artist rather than as man; viewed
      most often as "a naturalistic symbolist" or "a poet," and
      concludes that "the best thing about him is his personal
      lyricism rather than the conflict of his characters."

28 KARSH, YOUSUF. Portraits of Greatness. London: Nelson,
      pp. 96-97. Photo.
         An account of his visit to Finca Vigia in 1957 to photo-
      graph Hemingway.
      Reprinted, with revisions, from Atlantic, 200 (Dec. 1957).

29 KINNAMON, KENETH. "Hemingway, the Corrida, and Spain," Texas
      Studies in Literature and Language, 1 (Spring), 44-61.
         Correlates Hemingway's pervasive use of the bullfight
      and Spain as setting for stories and novels with attitudes
      about morality and tragedy from the Spanish culture.
      Kinnamon believes Hemingway adopted these attitudes early.
      He also traces the influence of El Greco, Goya, and Velás-
      quez.
      Reprinted in Wagner, pp. 57-74 (See 1974.A3).

30 KROEGER, FREDERICK P. "The Dialogue in 'A Clean, Well-Lighted
      Place,'" College English, 20 (Feb.), 240-41.
         Sees the waiters' dialogue as muddled, but attempts to
      straighten it out.

31 LABOR, EARLE. "Crane and Hemingway: Anatomy of Trauma,"
      Renascence, 11 (Summer), 189-96.
         Frederic Henry and Henry Fleming are both representative
      modern heroes, but Fleming finds a pattern that gives him
      stature.

32 LEVY, ALFRED J. "Hemingway's The Sun Also Rises," Explicator,
      17 (Feb.), Item 37.
         The devastation of the normal human relationship is
      dramatized between Jake's pick-up of Georgette and his
      first scene with Brett alone.

33 LOEB, HAROLD. The Way It Was. New York: Criterion.
         Reminiscence of meeting Hemingway, Paris, 1923; going
      to Pamplona in 1924; and the subsequent events described
      in The Sun Also Rises.
      Reprinted as "With Duff at Ascain" in Sarason, pp. 136-44
      (See 1972.A8).

1959

34   LUDWIG, RICHARD M., ed. <u>Literary History of the U. S.:</u>
      <u>Bibliography Supplement</u>. New York: Macmillan, pp. 137–39.
          Checklist of biographical and critical studies on Heming-
      way from 1947 to 1957.

35   McCULLERS, CARSON. "The Flowering Dream: Notes on Writing,"
      <u>Esquire</u>, 52 (Dec.), 162–64.
          Describes Hemingway as a "cosmopolitan" writer and thinks
      that "Emotionally he is a wanderer."

36   MAILER, NORMAN. <u>Advertisements for Myself</u>. New York: Berkley.
          Respect for Hemingway's early writing colors Mailer's
      view of the master, though he finds the later novels dis-
      appointing and minor.

37   MORRIS, WILLIAM E. "Hemingway's 'The Killers,'" <u>Explicator</u>,
      18 (Oct.), Item 1.
          The lunchroom clock's being 20 minutes fast is a realistic
      detail which forces reader involvement.

38   MOSES, W. R. "Water, Water Everywhere! <u>Old Man</u> and <u>A Farewell</u>
      <u>to Arms</u>," <u>MFS</u>, 5 (Summer), 172–74.
          Sees as parallels between the novels (Richardson to the
      contrary) the fact that the master image for both Faulkner
      and Hemingway is water, the protagonists in both books are
      forced into unwanted activities, and the rhythm of tension
      in both corresponds closely.

39   MOYNIHAN, WILLIAM T. "The Martyrdom of Robert Jordan," <u>College</u>
      <u>English</u>, 21 (Dec.), 127–32.
          Sees that the plot of <u>For Whom the Bell Tolls</u> is arranged
      to emphasize the sacrifice of Jordan, and from the charac-
      terization stems the "mighty theme" of the book, the one-
      ness of mankind.
      Reprinted in Grebstein, pp. 94–101 (<u>See</u> 1971.A8).

40   REGLER, GUSTAV. <u>The Owl of Minerva: Autobiography</u>. London:
      Hart-Davis, translated from the German by Norman Denny,
      pp. 290–99.
          Recollections of Hemingway during the Spanish Civil War.

41   REINERT, OTTO. "Hemingway's Waiters Once More," <u>College</u>
      <u>English</u>, 20 (May), 417–18.
          Discounts the fact that typographical mistakes may occur,
      but wants assurance that Hemingway was not himself confused
      in the "thematic function" of the two men.

42 WARD, J. A. "'The Blue Hotel' and 'The Killers,'" CEA Critic,
    21 (Sept.), 1, 7-8.
        Sees the stories as similar in their themes of imperson-
    ality and the inevitability of evil: "In neither story is
    murder an isolated event, but a demonstration of the evil
    inherent and inevitable in human society, of the violence
    beneath the tranquil surface of modern civilization."

43 ZINK, CAPT. D. D. Ernest Hemingway. [Denver]: U. S. Air
    Force Academy Library, Special bibliography series, No. 8.
    Pamphlet, 8 pages.
        A selective checklist of critical studies of Hemingway's
    work.

1960 A BOOKS

1   KILLINGER, JOHN. Hemingway and the Dead Gods: A Study in
    Existentialism. Lexington: University of Kentucky Press.
        A study of the fictional world of Hemingway as it is re-
    lated to the world view of existentialism, both attitudes
    stemming at least in part from the experiences of war.

2   LANIA, LEO [pseudonym of LAZAR HERRMANN]. Hemingway: eine
    Bildbiographie. Munich: Kindler. Translated into English
    by Joan Bradley, as Hemingway: a pictorial biography.
    New York: Viking Press, 1961.
        Chronology, pp. 129-31.

1960 B SHORTER WRITINGS

1   ALSOP, JOSEPH. "A Cuban Visit with Hemingway," New York
    Herald Tribune (9 March), p. 18.
        Interview.

2   ARNOLD, AEROL. "Hemingway's 'The Doctor and the Doctor's Wife,'"
    Explicator, 18 (March), Item 36.
        Interprets the doctor as being inadequate in the world of
    adults so he turns to his child and to nature, a solace to
    the child who is too young to understand his weakness.

3   BURHANS, CLINTON S., Jr. "The Old Man and the Sea: Heming-
    way's Tragic Vision of Man," American Literature, 31
    (Jan.), 446-55.
        Sees that Hemingway has reaffirmed man's oldest moral
    values--"courage, love, humility, solidarity and interde-
    pendence"--in The Old Man and the Sea, creating it in
    "perfectly realized symbolism and irony."

1960

(BURHANS, CLINTON S., Jr.)
Reprinted in Baker anthology, pp. 259-68 (See 1961.A5);
in Baker critiques, pp. 150-55 (See 1962.A5); and in Jobes,
pp. 72-80 (See 1968.A9).

4   D'AGOSTINO, NEMI. "The Later Hemingway," Sewanee Review, 68
(Summer), 482-93.
Reprinted from Balfagor, 11 (Jan. 1956), 54-73 (See
1956.B10).

5   DURHAM, PHILIP and TAUNO F. MUSTANOJA. American Fiction in
Finland: An Essay and Bibliography. Helsinki: Societe
Neophilologique.
Comments on Hemingway's influence in Finland.

6   GRAHAM, JOHN. "Ernest Hemingway: The Meaning of Style," MFS,
6 (Winter), 298-313.
Sees that the vitality of Hemingway's fiction lies at
least partly in the movement of the work and the vibrant
characterization. Discusses his methods of achieving movement and convincing characterization.
Reprinted in Graham, pp. 88-105 (See 1971.A7); in Baker
critiques, pp. 183-92 (See 1962.A5); in Waldhorn, pp. 18-
34 (See 1973.A7).

7   GUTTMANN, ALLEN. "Mechanized Doom: Ernest Hemingway and the
Spanish Civil War," Massachusetts Review, 1 (May), 541-61.
Finds the heart of Hemingway's presentation of conflict
in both The Spanish Earth and For Whom the Bell Tolls to
lie in his confrontation of men with machines.
Reprinted in Baker critiques, revised, pp. 95-107 (See
1962.A5) and in Grebstein, pp. 71-79 (See 1971.A8).

8   HARADA, KEIICHI. "The Marlin and the Shark: A Note on The
Old Man and the Sea," Journal of the College of Literature
(Aoyama Gakuin University, Tokyo), No. 4 (March).
Discusses Hemingway's "multi-layeredness" and its achieve-
ment through images, symbols, and archetypal patterns.
Reprinted in Baker anthology, pp. 269-76 (See 1961.A5).

9   HARRISON, JAMES M. "Hemingway's In Our Time," Explicator, 18
(May), Item 51.
In the introductory vignette, the "I" is a British
officer, the "he" the author, and acts as a preview of the
action.

10 HOFFMAN, FREDERICK J. "The Temper of the Twenties," The Minnesota Review, 1, No. 1 (Fall), 36-45

(HOFFMAN, FREDERICK J.)
Sees Hemingway as an integral and formative part of "the temper of the 20's, a milieu influenced terrifically by World War I. Notes his audacious self-confidence, comic self-consciousness, philosophical flexibility, informality, and search for the "new."

*11   KUPPUSWAMY, B. "Hemingway on Insomnia," Literary Half-Yearly, 1 (July), 58-60.
Cited in Benson bibliography, p. 359 (See 1975.A3).

12   LAIR, ROBERT L. "Hemingway and Cézanne: An Indebtedness," MFS, 6 (Summer), 165-68.
Discusses the apparent borrowings in terms of building character and landscape, and the uses of montage.

13   LEHAN, RICHARD. "Camus and Hemingway," Wisconsin Studies in Contemporary Literature, 1 (Spring-Summer), 37-48.
Sees that Camus' familiarity with Hemingway's work probably helped him translate "philosophical motives into dramatic terms."

14   LOWREY, BURLING, ed. Twentieth Century Parody: American and British. New York: Harcourt, Brace.
Pp. 59-70: "A Farewell to Josephine's Arms--The Hemingway of All Flesh" by H. W. Hanemann, reprinted from The Facts of Life, New York, Farrar & Rinehart, 1930, pp. 131-59 (See 1930.B9); pp. 265-67: "Thou Tellest Me, Comrade" by Gilbert Highet, reprinted from the Nation, 152 (1 March 1941). (See 1941.B23.)

15   MACDONALD, DWIGHT. Parodies: From Chaucer to Beerbohm--and After. New York: Random House.
Pp. 248-50: "Death in the Rumble Seat" by Wolcott Gibbs, reprinted from More in Sorrow, New York, 1958, pp. 20-23 (See 1932.B14); pp. 251-54: "Across the Street and Into the Grill" by E. B. White, reprinted from The Second Tree from the Corner, New York, Harper, 1954, pp. 140-43 (See 1954.B50).

16   MAZZARO, JEROME L. "George Peele and A Farewell to Arms: A Thematic Tie?" Modern Language Notes, 75 (Feb.), 118-19.
Changes in character caused by love and war (a shift from the profane to the spiritual) are the theme of both Peele's poem and Hemingway's novel of the same title.

1960

17   OWEN, CHARLES A., JR. "Time and the Contagion of Flight in
     'The Killers,'" Forum (Houston), 3 (Fall-Winter), 45-46.
          Sees the heart of the story to lie in the moment of trans-
     fer during the contact between Andreson and Nick.

18   PATMORE, DEREK. Private History: An Autobiography. London:
     Cape, pp. 99-101.
          Relates a visit to the Hemingways in the rue Notre Dame
     des Champs with Ezra Pound, in 1925.

19   [PENNSYLVANIA, UNIVERSITY OF]. Index to Articles on American
     Literature: 1951-1959. Prepared in The Reference Depart-
     ment, University of Pennsylvania, University Library:
     Philadelphia, pp. 228-35.
          Listing of critical studies and biographical articles on
     Hemingway.

*20 RAO, K. S. NARAYANA. "Women, Violence and Darkness in the World
     of Hemingway's Short Stories," Literary Criterion, 4
     (Winter), 32-38.
          Cited in Benson bibliography, p. 326 (See 1975.A3).

21   RUBENSTEIN, ANNETTE T. "Brave and Baffled Hunter," Mainstream,
     13: 1-23.
          Sees Hemingway as at his best in the early writing, when
     war provided his focus and impetus, and again in The Old
     Man and the Sea. The work between is mixed, never fully
     developed.

22   SANDERS, DAVID. "Ernest Hemingway's Spanish Civil War Experi-
     ence," American Quarterly, 12 (Summer), 133-43.
          Sees For Whom the Bell Tolls as an anti-fascist, not pro-
     Communist novel, with more attention given to Spain the
     country than to any political entity.
          Reprinted in Grebstein, pp. 32-42 (See 1971.A8).

23   SOUCIE, GARY. "Reflections on Hemingway," Carolina Quarterly,
     12 (Spring), 57-63.
          Unhappy with much Hemingway criticism, Soucie gives a
     historical, analytical picture of Hemingway's work, seeing
     "the search theme" as a key to the later books, the quest
     satisfied finally in The Old Man and the Sea.

24   SPILKA, MARK. "The Necessary Stylist: A New Critical Revision,"
     MFS, 6 (Winter), 283-92.
          Criticizes New Criticism because it separates the author
     from his work and such separation is difficult when style
     is concerned. Language and structure, the most important
     components of style for Spilka, are then used in discussing
     "The Short, Happy Life of Francis Macomber."

25 SPILLER, ROBERT E., WILLARD THORP, THOMAS H. JOHNSON, and
    HENRY SEIDEL CANBY. Literary History of the United States.
    New York: Macmillan.
    See also the Bibliography Supplement.

26 SPRINGER, ANNE M. The American Novel in Germany. Hamburg:
    Cram, de Gruyter.
        A study of the importance of eight American novelists--
    including Hemingway--in Germany, during the period between
    the two World Wars.

27 STEIN, WILLIAM BYSSHE. "Ritual in Hemingway's 'Big, Two-
    Hearted River,'" Texas Studies in Literature and Language,
    1 (Winter), 555-61.
        Aligns Nick's ritual of fishing with the Fisher King
    myth; also initiation; also Christianity. Correlates pat-
    terns with The Old Man and the Sea as well.

28 STEPHENS, ROBERT O. "Hemingway's Riddle of Kilimanjaro: Idea
    and Image," American Literature, 32 (March), 84-87.
        Sees the imagery in "Snows" to indicate that Hemingway
    stresses "man's attempt to transcend his animal nature and
    to reach a spiritual plane of existence, no matter what
    the cost."
    Reprinted in Howell, pp. 93-94 (See 1969.A9).

29 TATE, ALLEN. "Random Thoughts on the 1920's," Minnesota Re-
    view, 1, No. 1 (Fall), 46-56.
        Sees writers today as more skillful and knowledgeable
    than writers in the 1920's, but, in the case of Hemingway,
    "nobody is as good as he is." Much material on Ford Madox
    Ford, Hemingway's intelligence, and the devotion of the
    writers to their art. Contradicts Stein's "lost genera-
    tion" concept.

30 THORP, WILLARD. American Writing in the Twentieth Century.
    Cambridge: Harvard University Press, pp. 185-95.
        Discusses naturalism as "basic" to Hemingway's work.
    Sees Hemingway as "the least bookish of the new primi-
    tivists," with his short stories among the best written
    anywhere.

31 THURSTON, JARVIS, O. B. EMERSON, CARL HARTMAN, and ELIZABETH
    V. WRIGHT. Short Fiction Criticism: A Checklist of In-
    terpretation since 1925 of Stories and Novelettes (Ameri-
    can, British, Continental) 1800-1958. Denver: Alan
    Swallow, pp. 82-90.
        Checklist of explications of Hemingway's stories.

1960

32   TYNAN, KENNETH. "Papa and the Playwright," Tynan Right and
     Left. New York: Atheneum.
       Repeats the story of Tennessee Williams and Hemingway,
     also recounted in "A Visit to Havana," Holiday, 27 (Feb.),
     pp. 50-58.

1961 A BOOKS

1   ARONOWITZ, ALFRED G. and PETER HAMILL. Ernest Hemingway: The
     Life and Death of a Man. New York: Lancer, original
     paperback. Cover drawing of Hemingway by Oscar Liebman.
       Sections of this superficial biography are reprinted
     from a series of eleven articles which appeared in the New
     York Post, July 3-16, 1961.

2   ROSS, LILLIAN. Portrait of Hemingway (pamphlet). New York:
     Simon & Schuster. Photo of Hemingway by Paul Radkai.
     Reprinted, with revisions, from the Profile in the New
     Yorker, 26 (13 May 1950); new preface, pp. 11-19.

3   SANDERSON, STEWART F. Ernest Hemingway. London: Oliver &
     Boyd (Writers and Critics series, No. 7).
       A critical study of Hemingway's work, useful for intro-
     ductory purposes. More summary of works than interpreta-
     tion. Sanderson sees that Hemingway ends his career as a
     "poet," at the peak of his writing promise.

4   SINGER, KURT D. Hemingway: Life and Death of a Giant. Los
     Angeles: Holloway House, paperback original. Illustrated
     by Ben Kudo.
       Biographical study.

5   BAKER, CARLOS, ed. Hemingway and His Critics: An International
     Anthology. New York: Hill & Wang.
       Contents: pp. 1-18: "Introduction: Citizen of the
     World" by the editor. Reviews the international scope of
     Hemingway's publication and reputation, from the 1920's to
     the present. Sees that even Hemingway's subjects have an
     international interest, not a parochial: "fishing,
     hunting, bullfighting, and war" but that he works from the
     concrete to the symbolic, so that in the broader context of
     meaning, he also crosses national boundaries.
       pp. 19-37: "An Interview with Ernest Hemingway" by
     George Plimpton, reprinted from Paris Review, 5 (Spring
     1958).
       pp. 38-54: "Ernest Hemingway" by André Maurois, reprinted
     from Revue de Paris, 62 (March 1955), translated from the
     French by Joseph M. Bernstein.

5   ALGREN, NELSON. "Hemingway: The Dye That Did Not Run,"
    Nation, 193 (18 Nov.), 387-90.
       "No American writer since Walt Whitman has assumed such
    risks in forging a style." Algren sees the style as in-
    tegral with Hemingway's life, and thereby containing a
    tension that no mere literary exercise could have achieved.

6   ALLEN, JOHN J. "The English of Hemingway's Spaniards," South
    Atlantic Bulletin, 27 (Nov.), 6-7.
       Sees that the unorthodox Spanish idiom used in For Whom
    the Bell Tolls gives an exotic cast to all the Spanish
    characters and the novel as a whole.
       Reprinted in Grebstein, pp. 91-93 (See 1971.A8).

7   ANDERSON, CHARLES R. "Hemingway's Other Style," Modern
    Language Notes, 76 (May), 434-42.
       Sees that juxtaposition is crucial to Hemingway's effects,
    as in A Farewell to Arms when Hemingway uses the brief
    dream sequence during the retreat from Caporetto. "Rare
    and brief as they are," these lyric passages "achieve a
    special resonance by being sounded against the hard
    polished surface of his typical prose."
       Reprinted in Baker critiques, pp. 41-46 (See 1962.A5).

8   BACHE, WILLIAM B. "The Red Badge of Courage and 'The Short
    Happy Life of Francis Macomber,'" Western Humanities Re-
    view, 15 (Winter), 83-84.
       Sees that Hemingway's short story echoes the pattern of
    Crane's novel.

9   BAKER, CARLOS. "Hemingway," SR, 44 (29 July), 10-13.
       Emphasizes Hemingway's world stature, and attributes his
    greatness to his sensual alertness, to his ability to see
    subjects whole, and to his interest in the eternal veri-
    ties, "courage, love, honor, endurance, suffering, and
    death."

10 BETSKY, SEYMOUR. "A Last Visit," SR, 44 (29 July), 22.
       Betsky and Leslie Fiedler visited Hemingway in Ketchum,
    Idaho in November, 1960, and found him fragile, inarticu-
    late, and reluctant to talk about his work.

11 BODE, CARL, ed. The Great Experiment in American Literature:
    Six Lectures. New York: Frederick Praeger.
       Pp. 135-51: "The Two Hemingways" by Arthur Mizener.
    Because Hemingway so distrusts the abstracting intellect,
    he works almost entirely from what he feels (scenes and
    images carry his fiction). When this tactic works, it

1961

(BODE, CARL)
succeeds well; when it misfires, the effect (as in For Whom the Bell Tolls) is mechanical and disspirited.

12 BOOTH, WAYNE C. The Rhetoric of Fiction. Chicago: University of Chicago Press.
Pp. 151-52: "The Killers" is used as an example of the undramatized narrator. Pp. 299-300: "A Clean, Well-Lighted Place" is used to illustrate the use of the reliable narrator in a "nihilistic" short story.

13 BRADY, CHARLES A. "Portrait of Hemingway," America, 105 (22 July), 546-48.
Finds his greatness in his "grace under pressure," "compassion for the human condition," and "utter honesty of intention and effect."

14 CIARDI, JOHN. "The Language of an Age" ("Manner of Speaking" column), SR, 44 (29 July), 32.
Discusses Hemingway's dialogue--"art is what makes the impossible look easy." Disagrees with Faulkner's famed ranking of Hemingway; will not put Hemingway at the bottom of any list.

15 EHRENBURG, ILYA. "The World Weighs a Writer's Influence: USSR," SR, 44 (29 July), 20.
Explains Hemingway's immense following in Russia since the mid-1930's as based on his understanding of people. Compares Hemingway with Chekhov, Joyce, and Gide.

16 ELLISTON, STEPHEN. "Hemingway and the Next Generation," University College Quarterly, 7 (Nov.), 23-27.
Lists qualities that Hemingway represents, and sees him set in contrast to "Acquisitive Society."

17 EVANS, OLIVER. "'The Snows of Kilimanjaro': A Revaluation," PMLA, 76 (Dec.), 601-07.
Finds that Harry's real sickness is his inability to love. The story contrasts life-in-death (the leopard and mountain) and death-in-life (Helen and the physical illness). Reprinted in Howell, pp. 150-57 (See 1969.A9).

18 F[INKELSTEIN], S[IDNEY]. "Ernest Hemingway: 1898-1961," Mainstream, 14, No. 8, pp. 6-10.
Sees Hemingway apart from most writers of the 1920's in his concern for "ordinary human beings," and these are the people who mourn his death.

1961

19 FORREY, ROBERT. "The Old Man and the Fish," Mainstream, 14
       (June), pp. 31-38.
          Continues Santiago's story after the Cuban revolution
       (in imitation Hemingway style).

20 GABRIEL, JOSEPH F. "The Logic of Confusion in Hemingway's 'A
       Clean, Well-Lighted Place,'" College English, 22 (May),
       539-46.
          Sees that the "inconsistency of the dialogue is deliberate,
       an integral part of the pattern of meaning."

21 GEORGE, MANFRED. "Ernest Hemingway's Nachlass," Universitas,
       16 (Oct.), 1129-31.
          Description of the unpublished materials and the process
       of locating them.

22 GERSTENBERGER, DONNA and GEORGE HENDRICK. The American Novel,
       1789-1959: A Checklist of Twentieth-Century Criticism.
       Denver: Alan Swallow, pp. 119-28.
          Listing of Hemingway materials.

23 GLASSER, WILLIAM. "Hemingway's A Farewell to Arms," Explicator,
       20 (Oct.), Item 18.
          Considers the strength of the novel Henry's life set in
       "sharp opposition to the natural world around him."

24 GOLDEN, HARRY L. Carl Sandburg. Cleveland: The World Pub-
       lishing Co.
          P. 171: quotes Hemingway as saying, on receiving the
       1954 Nobel Prize, that Sandburg was more worthy of it;
       p. 172: cites Sandburg's great love of Hemingway's work.

25 GREBSTEIN, SHELDON NORMAN. "Sex, Hemingway, and the Critics,"
       Humanist, 21 (July-Aug.), 212-18.
          Defends Hemingway's use of sex as filling a function
       "far more serious and meaningful than most have given him
       credit for."

26 HASSAN IHAB. Radical Innocence. Princeton, N. J.: Princeton
       University Press, p. 48.
          Traces the dark Romanticism of a Marlon Brando or James
       Dean to Nick Adams, a limited but affirmative hero. "The
       code stands him in good stead, and narrow though it may be,
       it is still viable . . . . But the wound, the tragic aware-
       ness, is always there."

1961

27   HEIMBURG, CAROL. Etched Portraits of Ernest Hemingway.
       Northampton, Mass.: Apiary Press, pamphlet.
       Seven etchings, brief excerpt from "Banal Story."

28   HICKS, GRANVILLE. "A Feeling About Life," SR, 44 (29 July),
       30, 38.
         Although his work tended to symbolize an age of violence,
       his greatness transcended his personal legend in expressing
       courage, endurance, and honor.

29   HOWE, IRVING. "Hemingway: The Conquest of Panic," New Republic,
       145 (24 July), 19-20.
         Comments on the dichotomy that, although his fiction
       seemed violent and fatalistic, reading it served to incite
       one to "personal resistance and renewal, possible endurance
       and companionship in stoicism." See Lillian Ross's reply,
       New Republic, 145 (7 Aug.), 30-31.

30   HUMMEL, EDWIN. The Calculus of Hemingway. Drawing of Heming-
       way by author, privately printed.
         Traces the "true, lifelong influence" on Hemingway as
       Frank Norris' Essays on Authorship.

31   KEELER, CLINTON. "A Farewell to Arms: Hemingway and Peele,"
       Modern Language Notes, 76 (Nov.), 622-25.
         Sees that the relationship is an ironic one because
       Peele's courtier has a firm belief and Henry never finds
       any belief.

32   KELLY, JOHN C. "Ernest Hemingway (1899-1961): Formulating
       the Data of Experience," Studies (Dublin), 50 (Autumn),
       312-26.
         Sees Hemingway as a great writer, and attempts to place
       him in the preconceptions of "dull" literature. Comments
       on style, on his vision, and his story-telling ability.
       Lists a ten-point story-teller's "credo."

33   KNIGHT, ARTHUR. "Hemingway into Film," SR, 44 (29 July),
       33-34.
         Lists 14 movies made from Hemingway stories or novels,
       stressing that making movies from his writing is difficult
       because his obvious simplicity does not translate well.

34   LEVI, CARLO. "The World Weighs a Writer's Influence: Italy,"
       SR, 44 (29 July), 19.
         Compares Hemingway with Stendhal, although Stendhal's
       "voluptuousness" is replaced in Hemingway by "arid pity
       for the world."

35 LIGHT, JAMES F. "The Religion of Death in A Farewell to Arms,"
    MFS, 7 (Summer), 169–73.
        Sees the novel as "illustrative of four ideals of service:
    to God (the Priest), country (Gino), beloved (Catherine),
    or mankind (Rinaldi)." All such service fails, however,
    and Hemingway opts for bravery and stoicism.
    Reprinted in Baker critiques, pp. 37–40 (See 1962.A5); in
    Graham, pp. 39–45 (See 1971.A7).

36 LOEB, HAROLD. "The Young Writer in Paris and Pamplona," SR,
    44 (29 July), 25–26.
        Recollections of the early friendship with Hemingway,
    described as a "warm, vital individual who could love and
    hate, work and play with . . . glorious exuberance."

37 LYDENBERG, JOHN. "American Novelists in Search for a Lost
    World," Revue des Langues Vivantes, 27: 306–21.
        Sees the tendency to yearn for a lost golden age as
    peculiarly American, and identifies Hemingway with Dos
    Passos, Twain, Cooper, Salinger, Henry James, and Faulkner
    in this longing.

38 MacLEISH, ARCHIBALD. "His Mirror Was Danger," Life, 51
    (14 July), 71–72.
        Moving tribute to Hemingway as writer and man, stressing
    the fact that his life was in many ways non-literary, that
    he used danger as a means of revealing truths about the
    human condition, and that as a result, he caught the
    highest aim of art—that fusion of knowledge and experience
    and art—for which every writer aims.
    Reprinted as "Ernest Hemingway" in A Continuing Journey,
    Boston, Houghton Mifflin, 1968, pp. 307–312 and in Ernest
    Hemingway/William Faulkner, Life Educational Reprint, 6,
    New York, Life Education Program, 1968, pp. 22–23.

39 MADARIAGO, SALVADOR DE. "The World Weighs a Writer's Influence:
    Spain," SR, 44 (29 July), 18.
        Sees Hemingway as important in revealing to the world
    many aspects of Spanish culture previously misunderstood.

40 MARCUS, MORDECAI. "A Farewell to Arms: Novel into Film,"
    Journal of the Central Mississippi Valley American Studies
    Association, 2 (Spring), 69–71.
        Many of the changes made in the film version show not
    only how but why Hemingway's vision of life was almost
    completely excluded from the film.

1961

41 MONTGOMERY, MARION. "The Leopard and the Hyena: Symbol and
    Meaning in 'The Snows of Kilimanjaro,'" University of
    Kansas City Review, 27 (Summer), 277-82.
        Sees that Hemingway's narrative technique in the story
    causes problems in interpretation; thinks his use of the
    hyena is skillful, but that of the leopard and mountain,
    inefficient.
    Reprinted in Howell, pp. 145-49 (See 1969.A9).

42 MORAES, FRANK. "The World Weighs a Writer's Influence: India,"
    SR, 44 (29 July), 18-19.
        In India, for a number of reasons, Hemingway's recent
    death has created little interest.

43 MORRIS, WRIGHT. "One Law for the Lion," Partisan Review, 28,
    No. 5-6, pp. 541-51.
        "With such a writer, appraisal and reappraisal never
    end." Death only increases his complexity. "We shall
    not soon forget how he looked, and never how he wrote."

44 NORMAN, CHARLES. Ezra Pound. New York: Macmillan.
        Scattered references to the Paris years and p. 322, to
    Hemingway's last visit with Pound, in Paris, 1934.

45 NYREN, DOROTHY, ed. A Library of Literary Criticism: Modern
    American Literature. New York: Ungar.
        Sixteen short excerpts from critical studies of Hemingway
    are included.

46 O'FAOLAIN, SEAN. "'A Clean, Well-Lighted Place,'" Short
    Stories: A Study in Pleasure. Boston: Little, Brown,
    pp. 76-79.
        Reads it as a story of "unexpected depths," enhanced by
    Hemingway's "kindness and tenderness": "He is a delicate
    sculptor of great muscle."
    Reprinted in Weeks, pp. 112-13 (See 1962.A6).

47 PARSONS, THORNTON H. "Hemingway's Tyrannous Plot," University
    of Kansas City Review, 27 (Summer), 261-66.
        Sees that, structurally, the "fierce concentration upon
    the bridge is the great strength of the novel For Whom the
    Bell Tolls, the source of unity."
    Reprinted in Grebstein, pp. 107-112 (See 1971.A8).

48 PRYCE-JONES, ALAN. "The World Weighs a Writer's Influence:
    England," SR, 44 (29 July), 21.
        Sees Hemingway's influence as great ("there is not a
    living writer in England who has been unaffected by the

(PRYCE-JONES, ALAN)
   laconic speed of his dialogue, the subtle revelation of
   character that lies behind a spoken phrase") although
   admits that his subjects and range of emotion were "utterly
   alien" to British fiction.

49   RIDEOUT, WALTER B. and JAMES K. ROBINSON, eds. A College Book
        of Modern Fiction. Evanston, Ill.: Row, Peterson,
        pp. 552-65.
        "Hills Like White Elephants" and "Ten Indians" are used
        as examples in Norman Friedman's "What Makes a Short Story
        Short," reprinted from Modern Fiction Studies, 4 (Summer
        1958). (See 1958.B9.)

50   ROSS, DANFORTH. The American Short Story. Minneapolis:
        University of Minnesota Press (pamphlets on American
        writers, No. 14), pp. 34-36.
        Sees that Hemingway's achievement lies in the way he
        polishes his stories. Thematically they either "give an
        uninitiated character illumination or show a character
        battling forces in such a way as to gain dignity. The
        first sort of story is really a preparation for the second."

51   SCHORER, MARK. Sinclair Lewis: An American Life. New York:
        McGraw-Hill. Photo.
        Pp. 616-17: Lewis's essay on Green Hills of Africa;
        pp. 671-72: his first meeting with Hemingway, 1940, and
        their trip to Cuba; pp. 780-81: the Hemingways' meeting
        Lewis in Venice, 1949, and the lampoon of Lewis in Across
        the River and Into the Trees.

52   SCHROETER, JAMES. "Hemingway's The Sun Also Rises," Explicator,
        20 (Nov.), Item 28.
        The "nightmare" atmosphere of the novel results from
        Hemingway's "combination of opposites within a given
        character."

53   SEIDENSTICKER, EDWARD. "The World Weighs a Writer's Influence:
        Japan," SR, 44 (29 July), 21-22.
        Although translations of Hemingway's work were available
        early, his chief vogue has occurred since World War II,
        and he has influenced a "stream of hard-boiled writing
        among young Japanese writers," not in the sense that they
        copy his discipline, but rather that they murder the
        language.

54   STALLMAN, R. W. The Houses That James Built and Other Literary
        Studies. East Lansing: Michigan State University Press.

1961

(STALLMAN, R. W.)
Pp. 173-93: "The Sun Also Rises--But No Bells Ring," a study of the narrator's biased point of view and the way The Sun Also Rises would read from Robert Cohn's perspective. Pp. 193-99: "A New Reading of 'The Snows of Kilimanjaro'" emphasizes its "design": scenes of external reality alternate with juxtaposed scenes of internal monologue. Both, however, relate thematically.

55 STEIN, WILLIAM BYSSHE. "Hemingway's 'The Short Happy Life of Francis Macomber,'" Explicator, 19 (April), Item 47.
Sees that Macomber's "coming of age" is not based on Wilson's model (a paradigm of "the ruthless and selfish philosophy of British imperialism").

56 _____. "Love and Lust in Hemingway's Short Stories," Texas Studies in Literature and Language, 3 (Summer), 234-42.
Defends Hemingway's vision of moral reality; sees that characters are not lost, but that each must "climb his own particular hill of Calvary."

57 STEPHENS, ROBERT O. "Hemingway's Don Quixote in Pamplona," College English, 23 (Dec.), 216-18.
Sees The Sun Also Rises as a wise, if inconclusive, statement of the movement between the lost philosophy and the spiritually certain.

58 _____. "Hemingway's Old Man and the Iceberg," MFS, 7 (Winter), 295-304.
Sees Santiago as the only one of Hemingway's heroes to triumph by his ability to understand the fate he cannot biologically avoid. Instead of not thinking, here, man thinks. Stephens also analyzes Christian and natural imagery, especially in relation to man's trying to relinquish his own animal nature.

59 TAYLOR, J. GOLDEN. "Hemingway on the Flesh and the Spirit," Western Humanities Review, 15 (Summer), 273-75.
Sees "The Snows of Kilimanjaro" as a composite, in secular terms, of elements of the "Parable of talents," the "Parable of the Prodigal Son," Pilgrim's Progress, Everyman, and Paradise Lost, and is religious in that it tells of man's struggle toward achieving ideal spiritual ends.

60 THOMAS, HUGH. The Spanish Civil War. New York: Harper.
References to Hemingway during the war; excerpts from his dispatches.

61 TOYNBEE, PHILIP. "Hemingway," Encounter, 17, No. 4 (Oct.),
    86–88.
        Sees The Old Man and the Sea as a "stuffed book,"
    "meritricious," "insufferable," and "sentimental." "The
    book is doctor-bait, professor-bait." Suggests that one
    read "The Killers" or "The Undefeated," and then muse about
    this "genuine literary tragedy."
        Reprinted in Jobes, p. 112 (See 1968.A9).

62 WALKER, WARREN S., ed. Twentieth-Century Short Story Explica-
    tion: Interpretations, 1900–1960 Inclusive, of Short
    Fiction Since 1800. Hamden, Conn.: Shoe String Press,
    pp. 146–60.
        Checklist of explications of Hemingway's short stories.

63 WATERMAN, ARTHUR E. "Hemingway's 'The Short Happy Life of
    Francis Macomber,'" Explicator, 20 (Sept.), Item 2.
        The primitive world strips the Macombers of hypocrisy
    and transforms them into a basically honest guy and a
    "bitch," a "hysterical savage who murders her mate in
    blind, primitive hate."

64 WHEELER, JOHN. I've Got News for You. New York: Dutton,
    pp. 183–87.
        Brief comments on Hemingway's NANA dispatches; includes
    a letter from Hemingway regarding publication of "Fifty
    Grand."

65 WHITE, WILLIAM. "Ernest Hemingway: Violence, Blood, Death,"
    Orient/West, 6 (Nov.), 11–23.
        Sees that his fictional preoccupation with violence and
    "a death cult" stems from his boyhood experiences.

66 _____. Ernest Hemingway (21 July 1899–2 July 1961): Guide to
    a Memorial Exhibition. Detroit: University of Detroit
    Library, July 14–August 12, 1961. 8 pp.
        Catalogue of an exhibition of manuscripts and presenta-
    tion copies of books from the collection of Charles F.
    Feinberg, and of periodicals, translations, and ephemera
    from White's collection.

67 WRENN, JOHN H. John Dos Passos. New York: Twayne, passim.
        Scattered biographical references, with Wrenn making the
    point that, although both writers created relatively auto-
    biographical characters, Hemingway admired his and Dos
    Passos didn't; therefore, the characters of Dos Passos are
    less appealing.

1961

68 WRIGHT, AUSTIN McGIFFERT. <u>The American Short Story in the</u>
    <u>Twenties</u>. Chicago: University of Chicago Press.
        Pp. 391-93, Appendix D: "The Use of First Person in
    'Cross-Country Snow' and 'An Alpine Idyll.'
        Pp. 400-01, Appendix H: "A Scene from 'The Doctor and
    the Doctor's Wife.'"
        Pp. 401-02, Appendix I: "The Chronology of 'In Another
    Country.'"

<u>1962 A BOOKS</u>

1 HEMINGWAY, LEICESTER. <u>My Brother, Ernest Hemingway</u>. Cleveland: World Publishing Co. Photos.
       An informal biography which makes some use of primary
   Hemingway materials; first appeared in <u>Playboy</u>, 8 (Dec.
   1961) and 9 (Jan., Feb., March 1962).

2 MACHLIN, MILT. <u>The Private Hell of Hemingway</u>. New York:
   Paperback Library. Cover photo of Hemingway by Yousuf
   Karsh.
       Inaccurate biography with emphasis on sensational
   elements.

3 RINK, PAUL. <u>Ernest Hemingway: Remaking Modern Fiction</u>.
   Chicago: Encyclopaedia Britannica Press (Britannica
   Bookshelf: Great Lives for Young Americans).
       Juvenile readers' biography, illustrated by Robert
   Boehmer.

4 SANFORD, MARCELLINE HEMINGWAY. <u>At the Hemingways: A Family</u>
   <u>Portrait</u>. Boston: Atlantic-Little, Brown. Photos.
       Description of childhood in Oak Park and Northern Michi-
   gan, with attention to the family response to his writing
   and his life. First appeared serialized in <u>Atlantic</u>, 208
   (Dec. 1961); 209 (Jan. and Feb. 1962).

5 BAKER, CARLOS, ed. <u>Ernest Hemingway: Critiques of Four Major</u>
   <u>Novels</u>. New York: Scribner's (A Scribner Research
   Anthology).
         Contents: p. 1: Introduction by editor.
       pp. 4-6: "<u>The Sun Also Rises</u>" by James T. Farrell,
   reprinted from <u>The League of Frightened Philistines</u>, New
   York, Vanguard Press, 1945, pp. 20-24.
       pp. 7-10: "<u>The Sun Also Rises</u>: A Commentary" by Philip
   Young, reprinted from <u>Ernest Hemingway</u>, New York, Rinehart,
   1952, pp. 54-60.

(BAKER, CARLOS)

pp. 11-17: "Place, Fact, and Scene in The Sun Also Rises" by Carlos Baker, reprinted from Hemingway: The Writer as Artist, Princeton, 1956 (second edition), pp. 48-59.

pp. 18-25: "The Death of Love in The Sun Also Rises" by Mark Spilka, reprinted from Twelve Original Essays on Great American Novels, edited by Charles Shapiro, Detroit, Wayne State University Press, 1958, pp. 238-56.

pp. 28-36: "A Farewell to Arms" by Ray B. West, Jr., reprinted from The Art of Modern Fiction, New York, Rinehart, 1949, pp. 622-33.

pp. 37-40: "The Religion of Death in A Farewell to Arms" by James F. Light, reprinted from MFS, 7 (Summer 1961).

pp. 41-46: "Hemingway's Other Style" by Charles R. Anderson, reprinted from Modern Language Notes, 76 (May 1961).

pp. 47-60: "The Mountain and the Plain" by Carlos Baker, reprinted from Ibid., pp. 94-116.

pp. 61-74: "Hemingway's Ambiguity: Symbolism and Irony" by E. M. Halliday, reprinted from American Literature, 28 (March 1956).

pp. 75: The Original Conclusion to A Farewell to Arms.

pp. 78-81: "An American in Spain" by Lionel Trilling, reprinted from The Partisan Reader, edited by William Phillips and Philip Rahv, New York, Dial Press, 1946, pp. 639-44.

pp. 82-86: "Style in For Whom the Bell Tolls" by Joseph Warren Beach, reprinted from American Fiction, New York, Macmillan, 1941, pp. 111-119.

pp. 87-89: "The Background of a Style" by Mark Schorer, reprinted from Kenyon Review, 3 (Winter 1941).

pp. 90-94: Review of For Whom the Bell Tolls by Alvah C. Bessie, reprinted from New Masses, 37 (5 Nov. 1940).

pp. 95-107: "'Mechanized Doom': Ernest Hemingway and the American View of the Spanish Civil War" by Allen Guttmann, reprinted with revisions from Massachusetts Review, 1 (May 1960).

pp. 108-30: "The Spanish Tragedy" by Carlos Baker, reprinted from Ibid., pp. 223-63.

pp. 132-34: "With Grace Under Pressure" by Mark Schorer, reprinted from New Republic, 127 (6 Oct. 1952).

pp. 135-43: "Hemingway: The Matador and the Crucified" by Melvin Backman, reprinted with corrections from MFS, 1 (Aug. 1955).

pp. 144-49: "Confiteor Hominem: Ernest Hemingway's Religion of Man" by Joseph Waldmeir, reprinted from PMASAL, 42 (1956).

1962

(BAKER, CARLOS)
    pp. 150–55: "The Old Man and the Sea: Hemingway's
Tragic Vision of Man" by Clinton S. Burhans, Jr., reprinted
from American Literature, 31 (Jan. 1960).
    pp. 156–72: "Hemingway's Ancient Mariner" by Carlos
Baker, reprinted with revisions from Ibid., pp. 289–320.
    pp. 174–82: "Hemingway's Narrative Perspective" by
E. M. Halliday, reprinted from Sewanee Review, 60 (Spring
1952).
    pp. 183–92: "Ernest Hemingway: The Meaning of Style"
by John Graham, reprinted from MFS, 6 (Winter 1960–61).

6 WEEKS, ROBERT P., ed. Hemingway: A Collection of Critical
    Essays. Englewood Cliffs, N. J.: Prentice-Hall, Twentieth
    Century Views series.
    Contents: pp. 1–16: introduction by editor.
    pp. 17–39: "How Do You Like It Now, Gentlemen?" by
Lillian Ross, reprinted from New Yorker, 26 (13 May 1950).
    pp. 40–51: "Nightmare and Ritual in Hemingway" by
Malcolm Cowley, reprinted from the introduction to the
Viking Portable Hemingway, pp. vii–xxiv.
    pp. 52–71: "Hemingway's Ambiguity: Symbolism and Irony"
by E. M. Halliday, reprinted from American Literature, 28
(March 1956).
    pp. 72–85: "Observations on the Style of Ernest Heming-
way" by Harry Levin, reprinted abridged from Contexts of
Criticism, Cambridge, Harvard University Press, 1957,
pp. 140–67.
    pp. 86–92: "Men Without Women" by Leslie Fiedler, re-
printed from Love and Death in the American Novel, New York,
Stein and Day, 1959, pp. 304–09; 350–52.
    pp. 93–94: "In Our Time: A Review" by D. H. Lawrence,
reprinted from Phoenix, New York, Viking Press, 1936,
p. 365.
    pp. 95–111: "Adventures of Nick Adams" by Philip Young,
reprinted from Ernest Hemingway, New York, Rinehart, 1952,
pp. 1–27.
    pp. 112–13: "'A Clean, Well-Lighted Place'" by Sean
O'Faolain, reprinted from Short Stories: A Study in
Pleasure, Boston, Little, Brown, 1961, pp. 76–79.
    pp. 114–117: "The Discovery of Evil: An Analysis of
'The Killers,'" by Cleanth Brooks and Robert Penn Warren,
reprinted from Understanding Fiction, New York, Appleton-
Century-Crofts, 1959, pp. 303–12.
    pp. 118–126: "The Two African Stories" by Carlos Baker,
reprinted from Hemingway: The Writer as Artist, Princeton
University Press, 1952, pp. 186–96.

(WEEKS, ROBERT P.)
    pp. 127-138: "The Death of Love in The Sun Also Rises" by Mark Spilka, reprinted from Twelve Original Essays on Great Novels, edited by Charles Shapiro, Detroit, Wayne State University Press, 1958, pp. 238-56.
    pp. 139-151: "The Biological Trap" by Ray B. West, Jr., reprinted from The Art of Modern Fiction, New York, Rinehart, 1949, pp. 622-634.
    pp. 152-160: "The Later Hemingway" by Nemi D'Agostino, reprinted from Sewanee Review, 68 (Summer 1960).
    pp. 161-168: "Confiteor Hominem: Ernest Hemingway's Religion of Man" by Joseph Waldmeir, reprinted from PMASAL, 42 (1956).
    pp. 169-71: "The Art of Evasion" by Leon Edel, reprinted from Folio, 20 (Spring 1955).
    pp. 172-174: "Hemingway: A Defense" by Philip Young, reprinted from Folio, 20 (Spring 1955).
    pp. 175-76: Chronology of Important Dates
    pp. 179-180: Selected Bibliography.

1962 B SHORTER WRITINGS

1   BAKER, CARLOS. Introduction to The Old Man and the Sea, Three Novels of Ernest Hemingway. New York: Charles Scribner's Sons, pp. iii-xvii.
    Biographical account of the novella, placing it as "the epilogue to all Hemingway's writing" because "its 'virtues and implicaciones' made it representative of his true forte in the writing of fiction." Relates the story to Christian symbolism as well.

2   _____. "Two Rivers: Mark Twain and Hemingway," Mark Twain Journal, 11 (Summer), 2.
    Compares Hemingway's description of a river in A Farewell to Arms, Chapter 31, with that of Twain in Chapter 19 of Huckleberry Finn.

3   BARNES, ROBERT J. "Two Modes of Fiction: Hemingway and Greene," Renascence, 14 (Summer), 193-98.
    Greene views man from the perspective of the Christian tradition and therefore discounts time; Hemingway, conversely, conveys his ideas by means of devices "in which the time-sense is paramount."

4   BARRETT, C. WALLER. Italian Influence on American Literature. New York: Grolier Club. An Address and A Catalogue of an Exhibition of Books, Manuscripts and Art showing this influence on American Literature and Art, held October 17 to December 10, 1961, p. 49.
    Lists Hemingway items.

1962

5   BELL, NEIL. "Of the Company," <u>Mark Twain Journal</u>, 11 (Summer),
     18.
          Lists Hemingway "of the company" of storytellers.

6   BROCKI, SISTER MARY DAMASCENE, CSSF. "Faulkner and Hemingway:
     Values in a Modern World," <u>Mark Twain Journal</u>, 11 (Summer),
     5-9, 15.
          Compares "The Bear" and <u>The Old Man and the Sea</u> as being
     similar in intention and in plot.

7   BROWN, DEMING. <u>Soviet Attitudes toward American Writing</u>.
     Princeton: Princeton University Press, pp. 297-315.
          "Ernest Hemingway," revised version of the essay "Heming-
     way in Russia," <u>American Quarterly</u>, 5 (Summer 1953). (<u>See</u>
     1953.B14.)

8   BRYHER, WINIFRED. <u>The Heart to Artemis</u>. New York: Harcourt,
     Brace and World.
          Recounts some memories of the Paris years when Adrienne
     Monnier predicted that Hemingway would be the best-known
     of them all because he cared for his craft (pp. 213-14).
     Bryher agrees, stressing that Hemingway was not a "tough
     writer" but rather "the last of the great Victorians who
     still believed in loyalty and honor."

9   CAMPBELL, HARRY M. "Comments on Mr. Stock's <u>Nada</u> in Heming-
     way's 'A Clean Well-Lighted Place,'" <u>Midcontinent American</u>
     <u>Studies Journal</u>, 3 (Spring), 57-59.
          Points out some of Stock's "shaky premises."

10   CLENDENNING, JOHN. "Hemingway's Gods, Dead and Alive," <u>Texas</u>
     <u>Studies in Literature and Language</u>, 3 (Winter), 489-502.
          Criticizing Killinger's <u>Hemingway and the Dead Gods</u>,
     Clendenning points out that Hemingway's gods are both
     alive and dead, and that the action often stems from the
     hero's efforts to resolve the ambiguity. Most of the
     fiction is considered.

11   COTTER, JANET M. "<u>The Old Man and the Sea</u>: An 'Open'
     Literary Experience," <u>English Journal</u>, 51 (Oct.), 459-63.
          The applicability of many teaching methods to the
     novella.

12   COWLEY, MALCOLM. "'Commencing with the Simplest Things,'"
     introduction to <u>The Sun Also Rises</u> in <u>Three Novels of</u>
     <u>Ernest Hemingway</u>. New York: Charles Scribner's Sons,
     pp. ix-xxviii.

1962

(COWLEY, MALCOLM)
Biographical and critical comments, placing The Sun Also Rises in the exciting milieu of the 1920's. Sees his use of understatement and omission as pivotal in creating "something like a revolution in American prose fiction." Reprinted in White, pp. 91-106 (See 1969.A11).

13 DIECKMANN, EDWARD A., JR. "The Hemingway Hypnosis," Mark Twain Journal, 11 (Summer), 3-4, 16.
Traces Hemingway's style to Twain, Crane and London.

14 DREW, FRASER. "Hemingway's Generosity and Humility," Mark Twain Journal, 11 (Summer), 19.
Quotes from a letter from Hemingway: "If I hadn't gone where I've been and made mistakes and learned and taken chances of being very wrong I could not have had the knowledge from which I invent."

15 _____. "Pupil, Teacher and Hemingway," New York State Education (March), pp. 16-17, 37.

16 DUDLEY, LAVINIA P. and JOHN J. SMITH, eds. The Americana Annual: 1962. New York: Americana, pp. 333-34. Photos.
"Ernest Miller Hemingway" by Carlos Baker.

17 EVANS, OLIVER. "The Arrow Wounds of Count Mippipopoulos," PMLA, 77 (March), 175.
"One of us" is not only meant to refer to sharing our code, but also "one of the damned."

18 FIEDLER, LESLIE. "An Almost Imaginary Interview: Hemingway in Ketchum," Partisan Review, 29 (Summer), 395-405.
Recounting of the saddening visit with Hemingway in Ketchum, Idaho, the fall before his suicide.

19 FLOOR, RICHARD. "Fate and Life: Determinism in Ernest Hemingway," Renascence, 15 (Fall), 23-27.
Hemingway creates a "new stage of conflict" from the dreary inevitableness of life; he judges characters "by how much they wring from the slender piece of life they are given."

20 GERSTENBERGER, DONNA. "The Waste Land in A Farewell to Arms," Modern Language Notes, 76 (Jan.), 24-25.
Refers to Chapter 23 of A Farewell to Arms where Hemingway quotes from Andrew Marvell, and less directly to The

1962

  (GERSTENBERGER, DONNA)
    Waste Land, to achieve "a meaningful relationship between
    the situation of his lovers and the modern situation
    diagnosed by Eliot."

21 HAGOPIAN, JOHN V. "Symmetry in 'Cat in the Rain,'" College
    English, 24 (Dec.), 220–222.
      Calls it "Hemingway's best made short story."
    Reprinted in Benson, pp. 230–232 (See 1975.A3).

22 HALE, NANCY. "Hemingway and the Courage to Be," Virginia
    Quarterly Review, 38 (Autumn), 620–39.
      Sees that for Hemingway "courage is an individual
    solution to the collective dilemma," but criticizes his
    philosophy because it omits so much: "The Hemingway hero
    has not come to terms with woman, with home, or with his
    life."
    Reprinted in The Realities of Fiction, Boston, Little,
    Brown, 1962, pp. 85–112.

23 HELMSTADTER, FRANCES. Picture Book of American Authors. New
    York: Sterling (Visual History Series), pp. 55–57.
    "Ernest Hemingway." Photo. Juvenile.

24 HERZBERG, MAX J., ed. The Reader's Encyclopedia of American
    Literature. New York: Crowell, pp. 450–56. Photo.
    "Ernest (Miller) Hemingway" by Philip Young.

25 HOLMAN, C. HUGH. "Ernest Hemingway: A Tribute," Books Abroad,
    36 (Winter), 5–8.
      Sees the autobiographical elements in Hemingway's work
    as "not a source of strength but a momentary hindrance to
    its success."

26 KRAUSE, SYDNEY J. "Hemingway's 'My Old Man,'" Explicator, 20
    (Jan.), Item 39.
      Butler was honest, and the boy should be condemned for
    disbelieving in him.

27 KROCK, ARTHUR. "Previous Veto of a Pulitzer Board Award,"
    New York Times (May 11), p. 30.
      Discussion of the fact that the Pulitzer Prize Advisory
    Board recommended For Whom the Bell Tolls for 1941 prize,
    and Nicholas Murray Butler vetoed.

28 KRUSE, HORST. "Hinrich Kruses Weg un Ümweg und die Tradition
    der Short Story Ernest Hemingways," Germanisch-Romanische

1962

(KRUSE, HORST)
Monatsschrift, 43 (July), 286–301.
An analysis of Hemingway's influence on Kruse's collec-
tion of stories.

29 KRZYZANOWSKI, JERZY R. "For Whom the Bell Tolls: The Origin
of General Golz," Polish Review, 7: 69–74.
Sees that Golz, despite his infrequent appearances, is
important to the structure and tone of the novel for "his
tragedy is greater than Jordan's." Golz is based on General
Karol Swierczewski.
Reprinted in Grebstein, pp. 50–55 (See 1971.A8).

30 LAND, MYRICK. The Fine Art of Literary Mayhem: A Lively
Account of Famous Writers and Their Feuds. New York: Holt,
Rinehart & Winston, pp. 180–204.
"Mr. Hemingway Proves a Good Sport--but Only to Himself,"
describes Hemingway's controversies with Sherwood Anderson,
Gertrude Stein, Harold Loeb, Morley Callaghan, and Max
Eastman.

31 LID, RICHARD W. "Hemingway and the Need for Speech," MFS, 8
(Winter), 401–07.
Sees the struggle for speech as important for the reality
of Hemingway's characters, even though in his fiction "the
barriers to speech seem insuperable."

32 McALEER, JOHN J. "A Farewell to Arms: Frederic Henry's Rejected Passion," Renascence, 14 (Winter), 72–79.
Finds a "detailed and sustained parallel between the
events of Christ's Passion and Henry's actions."

33 McALMON, ROBERT. McAlmon and the Lost Generation: A Self-
Portrait, edited by Robert E. Knoll. Lincoln: University
of Nebraska Press. Photos.
Reminiscence of Hemingway in Paris and on vacation in
Pamplona and Burguette, pp. 226–40.

34 MACDONALD, DWIGHT. "Ernest Hemingway," in Against the American
Grain: essays on the effects of mass culture. New York:
Random House, pp. 167–84.
Considers his work after 1930 inferior; finds Hemingway's
real importance as a stylistic innovator, chiefly great in
the short story.
Reprinted from Encounter, 18 (Jan. 1962), pp. 179–84.
Appendix: "Dissenting Opinion," letter from George
Plimpton.

1962

35   McNEIR, WALDO F., ed. Studies in Comparative Literature.
        Baton Rouge: Louisiana State University Press, pp. 260,
        262-63, 268.
            Horst Oppel discusses Hemingway in the chapter "American
        Literature in Postwar Germany: Impact or Alienation?"

36   MARCUS, FRED H. "A Farewell to Arms: The Impact of Irony and
        the Irrational," English Journal, 51 (Nov.), 527-35.
            Filled with bitter ironies, A Farewell to Arms is domi-
        nated by the irrational. From it all will come Henry's
        assumption of "the strong hero's stance: awareness,
        acceptance, and busying oneself with simple sensory
        satisfaction."

37   MARSHALL, S. L. A. "How Papa Liberated Paris," American
        Heritage, 13 (April), 4-7, 92-101.
            Brigadier General Marshall's recollections of events of
        August 25, 1944, when Paris was occupied. Marshall's
        account differs considerably from Hemingway's report in
        Collier's.

38   MONTGOMERY, MARION. "Hemingway's 'The Gambler, the Nun, and
        the Radio': A Reading and a Problem," Forum (Houston), 3
        (Winter), 36-40.
            Frazer is forced to see that the radio "is his personal
        form of opium." This realization leads to "stoical per-
        severance."
        Reprinted in Benson, pp. 203-210 (See 1975.A3).

39   MOSELEY, EDWIN M. Pseudonyms of Christ in the Modern Novel:
        Motifs and Methods. Pittsburgh: University of Pittsburgh
        Press, pp. 205-13: "Christ as the Old Champion: Heming-
        way's The Old Man and the Sea."
            Sees The Old Man and the Sea as "an example of neo-
        orthodoxy" although Hemingway's use of Christ is only "one
        symbol among symbols." Finds Hemingway's acceptance of
        this mode appropriate for the mature writer.

40   NEWMAN, PAUL B. "Hemingway's Grail Quest," University of
        Kansas City Review, 28 (Summer), 295-303.
            Finds the mood of The Sun Also Rises indebted to Eliot
        and Jessie Weston.

41   O'CONNOR, WILLIAM VAN. "Faulkner's One-Sided 'Dialogue' with
        Hemingway," College English, 24 (Dec.), 208, 213-15.
            Draws parallels between the lives and the work of the
        two novelists.

42   _____. The Grotesque: An American Genre and Other Essays.
         Carbondale: Southern Illinois University Press (Cross-
         currents Modern Critiques), pp. 119-124.
            Chapter 11: "Two Views of Kilimanjaro," reprinted from
         History of Ideas Newsletter, 2 (Oct. 1956). (See 1956.B20).

43   RANDALL, DAVID A. "Dukedom Large Enough," Papers of the Biblio-
         graphical Society of America, 56: 346-53.
            Discussion of changes and editing done for foreign
         editions of Hemingway's work, of Hemingway's manuscripts,
         and of personal anecdotes.

44   RODRIGUES, EUSEBIO L. "'Hills Like White Elephants': An
         Analysis," Literary Criterion, 5: 105-09.
            Sees the entire story to be "the crisis in the life of
         this girl" and her resulting "despair but not her defeat."

45   ROSENFELD, ISAAC. An Age of Enormity: Life and Writing in the
         Forties and Fifties, edited by Theodore Solotaroff. Cleve-
         land: World, pp. 258-67.
            "A Farewell to Hemingway," reprinted from Kenyon Review,
         13 (Winter 1951). (See 1951.B22.)

46   SCHAFER, WILLIAM J. "Ernest Hemingway: Arbiter of Common
         Numerality," Carleton Miscellany, 3 (Winter), 100-104.
            Parody of modern criticism, using Hemingway's "The Light
         of the World" as subject.

47   SCHÜCK, H. R. SOHLMAN, A. ÖSTERLING, G. LILJESTRAND, A. WEST-
         GREN, M. SIEGBAHN, A. SCHOU, and N. K. STAHLE, Nobel, The
         Man and His Prizes. Amsterdam: Elsevier Publishing Co.,
         p. 123.
            On reasons for awarding the 1954 Nobel Prize for Litera-
         ture to Hemingway.

48   SPILLER, ROBERT E., ed. A Time of Harvest: American Litera-
         ture, 1910-1960. New York: Hill & Wang, pp. 73-82: "The
         'Lost Generation,'" by Arthur Mizener.
            General survey.

49   STEVENSON, PHILIP. "A Note on Ernest Hemingway," Monthly Re-
         view, 13 (Feb.), 475-79.
            Sees that Hemingway's understatement is sometimes bother-
         some, not so much from a stylistic perspective but a
         thematic one: Stevenson finds his interest in the art of
         killing "absurd if not despicable."

50   STOCK, ELY. "Nada in Hemingway's 'A Clean, Well-Lighted
         Place,'" Midcontinent American Studies Journal, 3 (Spring),
         53-57.

1962

(STOCK, ELY)
>Defines the term nada as "a mystical concept, uniting
>. . . the quality of ineffability . . . and the noetic
>quality."

51 STONE, EDWARD. "Hemingway's Waiters Yet Once More," American
>Speech, 37 (Oct.), 239-40.
>>Perhaps the puzzling dialogue could be better understood
>>if it were to represent a translation from Spanish.

52 SUTHERLAND, WILLIAM O. S., JR., ed. Six Contemporary Novels:
>Six Introductory Essays in Modern Fiction. Austin: De-
>partment of English, University of Texas, pp. 58-75, Chap-
>ter 4. Drawing of Hemingway by Cyril Satorsky.
>>William J. Handy, "A New Dimension for a Hero: Santiago
>>of The Old Man and the Sea," contends that Hemingway is not
>>a naturalistic writer, that he instead creates "an internal
>>world of singular human values" which, hopefully, contra-
>>dicts the aim of the generally malevolent universe. Santi-
>>ago, in these terms, is a successful hero.

53 TANSELLE, G. THOMAS. "Hemingway's 'Indian Camp,'" Explicator,
>20 (Feb.), Item 53.
>>Although concerned with other themes, Hemingway also
>>dramatizes the gradual supplanting of the Indian culture
>>by the white.

54 TURNBULL, ANDREW. "Fitzgerald and Ernest Hemingway," Esquire,
>57 (March), 110-13, 115-24.
>>Account of the friendship between the two writers, in-
>>cluding some of the most memorable anecdotes.

55 _____. Scott Fitzgerald. New York: Scribner's.
>>Many references, especially to the Paris years and "The
>>Snows of Kilimanjaro."

56 WARREN, ROBERT PENN. Introduction to A Farewell to Arms in
>Three Novels of Ernest Hemingway. New York: Charles
>Scribner's Sons, pp. iii-xl.
>>Reprinted from A Farewell to Arms, Modern Standard Authors
>>edition, New York, Scribner's, 1949.

57 WEEKS, ROBERT. "Fakery in The Old Man and the Sea," College
>English, 24 (Dec.), 188-92.
>>Weeks points out what he believes to be errors in Heming-
>>way's descriptions of both Santiago's fishing process and
>>nature itself; he further sees this failure of realism as
>>evidence that Hemingway's world view has "gone soft."
>>Reprinted in Jobes, pp. 34-40 (See 1968.A9).

58   WEEKS, ROBERT P. "The Power of the Tacit in Crane and Heming-
     way," <u>MFS</u>, 8 (Winter), 415–18.
          Compares four episodes from <u>For Whom the Bell Tolls</u> and
     <u>The Red Badge of Courage</u>, concluding that Hemingway, by
     having more faith than Crane in "the immense power of the
     tacit," achieves effects that are both more complex and
     more subtle.
          Reprinted in Grebstein, pp. 102–06 (<u>See</u> 1971.A8).

59   WHITE, WILLIAM. "Hemingway-iana: Annotated," <u>Mark Twain</u>
     <u>Journal</u>, 11 (Summer), 11–13.
          A chronological list of all the books on Hemingway.

60   _____. "Some Thoughts on the Hemingway Racket," <u>New Republic</u>,
     146 (26 March), 24–25.
          Corrects impressions and lambasts some of the current
     popular biographies of Hemingway as "cheap and vulgar."

61   WOODRESS, JAMES. <u>Dissertations in American Literature: 1891–</u>
     <u>1955. With Supplement: 1956–1961</u>. Durham, N. C.: Duke
     University Press, pp. 23, 93.
          Checklists of dissertations on Hemingway's work.

1963 A   BOOKS

1   BAKER, CARLOS. <u>Hemingway: The Writer as Artist</u>. Princeton:
    Princeton University Press, 3rd edition.
         Includes a new last chapter covering the last decade of
    Hemingway's life and work, pp. 329–48.

2   DeFALCO, JOSEPH. <u>The Hero in Hemingway's Short Stories</u>.
    Pittsburgh: University of Pittsburgh Press.
         Using a mixed Jungian and mythic perspective, DeFalco
    claims many new readings for the Hemingway stories. In
    particular, he sees the heroes of these stories as illus-
    trative of "the primal conflicts which all men through all
    ages have experienced." Is interested in Hemingway's use
    of the young hero, the Nick Adams figure, and points to
    the several significances of his name. Pp. 25–39 reprinted
    in Benson, pp. 159, 67.

3   ROVIT, EARL. <u>Ernest Hemingway</u>. New York: Twayne (United
    States Authors Series, No. 41).
         A perceptive analysis of Hemingway's achievements and
    his significance in literary history. Locates much of his
    philosophy in American transcendentalism. Excerpts widely
    re-published.

1963

4   SINGER, KURT and JANE SHERROD. Ernest Hemingway, Man of
     Courage: A Biographical Sketch of a Nobel Prize Winner in
     Literature. Minneapolis: Denison (Men of Achievement
     Series). Cover photo.
     Juvenile.

1963 B SHORTER WRITINGS

1   BAKER, CARLOS. "Letters from Hemingway," Princeton University
     Library Chronicle, 24 (Winter), 101-07.
          An interim report on the acquisition of Hemingway's let-
     ters by the Princeton library.

2   BELFRAGE, SALLY. "The Haunted House of Ernest Hemingway,"
     Esquire, 59 (Feb.), 66.
          Describes the Havana house as permeated with the presence
     of its owner.

3   BROADUS, ROBERT N. "The New Record Set by Hemingway's Old
     Man," Notes and Queries, 10 (April), 152-53.
          Sees the fact that Santiago goes 84 days without a catch
     as a reference to Western novelist Zane Grey's "unbeatable"
     record of having gone 83 days without a catch.

4   BROOKS, CLEANTH. The Hidden God: Studies in Hemingway,
     Faulkner, Yeats, Eliot, and Warren. New Haven: Yale
     University Press, pp. 6-21.
          "Ernest Hemingway: Man on His Moral Uppers." Brooks'
     moderate view of Hemingway's search for religious belief
     sets the writer in the context of other modernist authors.
     Brooks sees Hemingway as attempting to substitute secular
     values for more traditionally religious ones.

5   _____. William Faulkner, The Yoknapatawpha Country. New
     Haven: Yale University Press.
          Compares Hemingway's praise of the earth in For Whom the
     Bell Tolls with Faulkner's in "The Bear." Sees Sartoris
     as the novel closest to the Hemingway mode.

6   BRYAN, JAMES E. "Hemingway as Vivisector," University Review,
     30 (Oct.), 3-12.
          Explains Hemingway's interest in big-game hunting as
     that of the scientist's; sees Africa as "a vivisector's
     laboratory where he can study the effects of 'violent
     death' in the interests of his art."

7   CALLAGHAN, MORLEY. That Summer in Paris: Memories of Tangled
     Friendships with Hemingway, Fitzgerald, and some others.

(CALLAGHAN, MORLEY)
New York: Coward-McCann. Photo.
Recollections of Hemingway in Toronto in 1923 and in
Paris during the summer of 1929.

8 CHILDS, BARNEY. "Hemingway and the Leopard of Kilimanjaro,"
American Notes and Queries, 2 (Sept.), 3.
Traces the epigraph for "The Snows of Kilimanjaro" to a
passage in H. W. Tilman's Snow on the Equator (1938).

9 CHRISTENSEN, FRANCIS. "A Lesson from Hemingway," College
English, 25 (Oct.), 12-18.
Christensen quotes John Erskine's belief that "the
modifier is the essential part of any sentence." She then
proceeds by linguistic analysis to discuss "The Undefeated."
Reprinted in Notes Toward a New Rhetoric, New York, Harper
& Row, 1967, pp. 24-37 and in Benson, pp. 121-29 (See
1975.A3).

10 CROSBY, JOHN. With Love and Loathing. New York: McGraw-Hill,
pp. 11-15.
"Aranjuez, Spain" describes an afternoon at the bullfights with Hemingway, watching Antonio Ordonez.
Reprinted from New York Herald Tribune (8 June and 10 June,
1959).

11 DAVIDSON, DONALD. The Spyglass: Views and Reviews, 1924-1930.
Selected and edited by John Tyree Fain. Nashville, Tenn.:
Vanderbilt University Press, pp. 75-79.
"Tragedy of Limitation: Tarkington and Hemingway," re-
view of Men Without Women. Relegates Hemingway to the
naturalist camp, and denigrates his style. Admits, how-
ever, that "you cannot ignore Mr. Hemingway, even if you
dislike him."
Reprinted from Nashville Tennessean (28 Jan. 1928).
Pp. 88-92: "Perfect Behavior," review of A Farewell to
Arms, criticizes Hemingway's so-called "scientific method"
which allows no vulgarity, no improbability; objects to
A Farewell to Arms on grounds both thematic and stylistic.
Reprinted from Nashville Tennessean (3 Nov. 1929).

12 DILLINGHAM, WILLIAM B. "Hemingway and Death," Emory University
Quarterly, 19 (Summer), pp. 95-101.
Sees as unfortunate for him personally that he was obsessed with death, but finds that theme giving Hemingway
his strongest fiction.

1963

13   DODD, MARTHA. "Hemingway in Cuba--A Home Away from Home,"
      Mainstream, 16 (Feb.), 25-30.
         Views Hemingway's living in Cuba as proof of his hatred
      for the bourgeoisie, his sympathy for the poor, and his
      "warm friendship" for Fidel.

14   EISINGER, CHESTER E. Fiction of the Forties. Chicago: The
      University of Chicago Press.
         Many references to Hemingway as (p. 4) one of the major
      writers whose talent was diminishing as the decade opened.
      Even in Across the River and Into the Trees, his sensibility
      was different (p. 23) in that it was less acute than the
      perceptions of other war novelists. Pp. 25-26, 41, 331:
      as influence on younger writers.

15   FIEDLER, LESLIE. "The Death of the Old Men," Arts and Sciences
      (Winter), pp. 1-5.
         In viewing both Faulkner and Hemingway, Fiedler claims
      that both "were essentially comic or quasi-comic writers,"
      first caricaturing the world, and finally themselves.

16   FITZGERALD, F. SCOTT. The Letters of F. Scott Fitzgerald,
      edited by Andrew Turnbull. New York: Scribner's.
      Pp. 295-313.
         Part IV: "Letters to Ernest Hemingway" includes 18 let-
      ters, dated Nov. 30, 1925 to Nov. 8, 1940.

17   GELFANT, BLANCHE. "Language as a Moral Code in A Farewell to
      Arms," MFS, 9 (Summer), 173-76.
         Sees Hemingway's use of the cliché as a moral index to
      character, as well as plot. Through language, "style,
      character, and structure reinforce each other."
      Reprinted in Graham, pp. 83-87 (See 1971.A7).

18   GOLDHURST, WILLIAM. F. Scott Fitzgerald and His Contemporaries.
      Cleveland: World.
         A study of the part Edmund Wilson, H. L. Mencken, Ring
      Lardner and Hemingway played in Fitzgerald's life and
      career. Pp. 155-216: Chapter 5, "Ernest Hemingway" in-
      cludes comparative readings to show the reciprocal in-
      fluences of Hemingway and Fitzgerald on each other's work.

19   GRAY, JAMES. "Hemingway in Piggott," Approach, No. 48
      (Summer), 30-32.
         Recalls Hemingway's living in Piggott twice, once while
      working on A Farewell to Arms.

1963

20   GRIGSON, GEOFFREY, ed. The Concise Encyclopedia of Modern
      World Literature. New York: Hawthorn Books, pp. 205-06:
      "Hemingway." Photo.

21   HANDY, WILLIAM J. Kant and the Southern New Critics. Austin:
      University of Texas Press.
          Considers Hemingway's prose style--especially in dialogue
      and scene--an example of the modernist poetics stress on
      "meaning being presentational and immediate." Handy de-
      scribes the "sharp demarcation" between scenes in Heming-
      way's fiction as being like the juxtaposition of single
      images in a poem (pp. 86-88).

22   HOFFMAN, FREDERICK, J. The Modern Novel in America. New York:
      Regnery, pp. 98-111.
          "Hemingway's chief virtue was his dedication to the art
      of writing within his own candidly recognized limitations."
      Hoffman sees Hemingway's interest in simplicity, craft,
      and control as his most important contribution to American
      fiction.

23   HOFLING, CHARLES K. "Hemingway's The Old Man and the Sea and
      the Male Reader," American Image, 20 (Summer), 161-73.
          Santiago's victory-in-defeat may recall "some of the
      favorable aspects of latency."

24   HOLDER, ALAN. "The Other Hemingway," Twentieth Century Litera-
      ture, 9: 153-57.
          Studies Hemingway's sympathetic presentation of women;
      claims criticism has overlooked such stories as "Hills
      Like White Elephants" and "Cat in the Rain" in seeing
      Hemingway as anti-female.
      Reprinted in Wagner, pp. 103-09 (See 1974.A3).

25   HOWE, IRVING. A World More Attractive: A View of Modern
      Literature and Politics. New York: Horizon Press,
      pp. 59-76.
          Chapter 3: "The Quest for Moral Style." Studies Heming-
      way's writing and influence in which Howe sees Hemingway's
      importance as being his ability to do without a set value
      system. Hemingway's strength in finding "an honorable
      style of survival," however, is in some ways misleading,
      and Howe questions the fact that Hemingway "rarely attempted
      a frontal or sustained representation of life in the U. S."
      "Hemingway was always a young writer, and always a writer
      for the young."
      Reprinted in Decline of the New, New York, Harcourt, Brace
      and World, 1970, pp. 151-66 (See 1970.B61).

1963

26   KILLINGER, JOHN. The Failure of Theology in Modern Literature.
      New York: Abingdon Press.
          Scattered references; sees that Hemingway uses a
      renascence-by-water motif and also relies on light and
      dark symbolism in much of his fiction. Such symbolism
      frequently relates to a wish to believe in something.
      Killinger agrees with Hyatt Waggoner that Hemingway's
      world is "sub-Christian" rather than "anti-Christian."
      Sees The Old Man and the Sea as "the Moby Dick of our
      time."

27   LAGIOS, SOCRATES A. "The Old Man and the Sea--1932 and 1952,"
      Exercise Exchange, 10 (March), 12-13.
          Compares the stories from the novella and the Esquire
      account.

28   LAUTER, PAUL. "Plato's Stepchildren, Gatsby and Cohn," MFS,
      9 (Winter), 338-46.
          Thinks that the parallels between Gatsby and Cohn are
      so numerous and so pervasive that they cannot be entirely
      accidental.

29   LEWIS, WYNDHAM. The Letters of Wyndham Lewis, edited by W. K.
      Rose. Norfolk, Conn.: New Directions.
          Many references to his early friendship with, and later
      criticism of, Hemingway. P. 433, contrasts the 1940's with
      the 1920's: "It was a blessed situation, when Joyce, Eliot,
      Hemingway, and myself began. The reference was in alto-
      gether different directions--towards scientific, or artis-
      tic, truth." Admires Hemingway's dialogue. Considers For
      Whom the Bell Tolls his "first bad book."

30   LINNEMANN, WILLIAM R. "Faulkner's Ten-Dollar Words," American
      Speech, 38 (May), 158-59.
          In comparing word use by Faulkner and Hemingway, Linne-
      mann notes that Faulkner uses a significantly larger number
      of Latin borrowings, which bears out Florence Leaver's
      point that "'Faulkner prefers abstract words, whereas Hem-
      ingway has an aversion to them.'"

31   LITZ, A. WALTON, ed. Modern American Fiction: Essays in
      Criticism. New York: Oxford University Press.
          Pp. 201-14. "Hemingway: The Matador and the Crucified"
      by Melvin Backman, reprinted from MFS, 1 (Aug. 1955) (See
      1955.B4); pp. 215-27: "Hemingway's Narrative Perspective"
      by E. M. Halliday, reprinted from Sewanee Review, 60 (April-
      June 1952) (See 1952.B38); pp. 228-43: "First Forty-five
      Stories" by Carlos Baker, reprinted from Baker, pp. 117-27

(LITZ, A WALTON)
(See 1952.A2); pp. 244-55: "Ernest Hemingway: The Failure
of Sensibility" by Ray B. West, Jr., reprinted from Sewanee
Review, 53 (Jan.-March 1945). (See 1945.B12.)

32 MERIWETHER, JAMES B. "The Text of Ernest Hemingway," Papers
of the Bibliographical Society of America, 58: 403-21.
Meriwether describes the problems of working with Hemingway materials (unpublished, unavailable, widely-scattered
and unindexed).

33 MOORE, GEOFFREY. "The Sun Also Rises: Notes Toward an Extreme
Fiction," Review of English Literature, 4 (Oct.), 31-46.
For stylistic and philosophical reasons The Sun Also
Rises may be considered the high point of Hemingway's
literary career.

34 MORRIS, WRIGHT. The Territory Ahead. New York: Atheneum,
pp. 133-46.
Reprinted "The Ability to Function: A Reappraisal of
Fitzgerald and Hemingway" from New World Writing, No. 13,
New York, The New American Library, pp. 34-51.

35 O'CONNOR, FRANK. The Lonely Voice: A Study of the Short
Story. Cleveland: World, pp. 156-69.
"'A Clean, Well-Lighted Place,'" traces Hemingway's
methods to Joyce's in Dubliners, as well as to Stein's,
especially in matters of repetition (single words, inter-
vals, structures). While he admires the method, he feels
that Hemingway never found appropriate subjects for his
craft.

36 OLDSEY, BERN. "The Snows of Ernest Hemingway," Wisconsin
Studies in Contemporary Literature, 4 (Spring-Summer),
172-98.
Because the novels and over one-third of the stories
contain snow, ice, cold, white, and/or light imagery,
Oldsey contends that these (not rain or mountains) are the
major natural and symbolic elements of Hemingway's fictional
world, appropriate to his pervasive interest in death and
in viewing man at moments of greatest tension. Oldsey also
distinguishes between Hemingway's more imagistic use of objects and a symbolistic approach.
Reprinted in Waldhorn, pp. 56-82 (See 1973.A7).

37 PAGE, ALEX. "Pakistan's Hemingway," Antioch Review, 23
(Summer), 203-11.
Sees in Hemingway's great popularity a contradiction;

1963

(PAGE, ALEX)
what is seen as valuable in his work supports deeply-held
Pakistani beliefs; what is criticized supports "the standard
charges against the West and against America in particular."

38 [PLIMPTON, GEORGE]. Writers at Work: The Paris Review Interviews, second series.
Introduced by Van Wyck Brooks. New York: Viking Press,
pp. 215-39, "Ernest Hemingway," reprinted from Paris Review, 5 (Spring 1958). (See 1958.B18.)

39 RAY, MAN. Self Portrait. Boston: Atlantic-Little Brown.
Reminiscences of Hemingway in Paris during the 1920's.

40 REID, STEPHEN A. "The Oedipal Pattern in Hemingway's 'The
Capital of the World,'" Literature and Psychology, 13
(Spring), 37-43.
Sees that the Oedipal pattern suggests the organization
and the story's resultant power.

41 WELLS, ARVIN R. "A Ritual of Transfiguration: The Old Man
and the Sea," University Review, 30 (Dec.), 95-101.
Santiago is "the apotheosis of the code hero; his experience is not only a confirmation of personal dignity
and courage but what is perhaps best called a ritual of
transfiguration."
Reprinted in Jones, pp. 56-63 (See 1968.A9).

42 WEST, PAUL. The Modern Novel. London: Hutchinson, pp. 220-
27 and passim.
Sees Hemingway as a realistic mid-Westerner who has merely
re-located his characters and ethics. Objects to the way
Hemingway "petrifies" his characters' minds, except in The
Old Man and the Sea, "the most moving and most heartening
of Hemingway's books."

43 WILSON, EDMUND. Review of Callaghan's That Summer in Paris,
New Yorker, 39 (23 Feb.), 139-42, 145-58.
Wilson adds his reminiscence of the three--Hemingway,
Fitzgerald, and Callaghan--and terms Callaghan's picture
"perfectly accurate." Adds his own analysis of Hemingway
as a man subject to an "ominous self-distrust."
Reprinted in The Bit Between My Teeth, New York, Farrar,
Straus & Giroux, 1965, pp. 515-25. See New Yorker, 39
(16 March), 160, 162-3 for Mary Hemingway's reply.

44 WOODWARD, R. H. "Hemingway's 'On the Quai at Smyrna,'"
Exercise Exchange, 10 (March), 11-12.
Note on this addition to In Our Time.

45   YUNCK, JOHN A.   "The Natural History of a Dead Quarrel: Heming-
         way and the Humanists," South Atlantic Quarterly, 62
         (Winter), 29-42.
            Sees Hemingway and Humanist Irving Babbitt as more alike
         than different: both believed that "valor is inward," and
         thus Hemingway's "code" parallels the Humanists' "decorum."

1964 A BOOKS

1   ISABELLE, JULANNE.   Hemingway's Religious Experience.   New York:
         Vantage Press.
            A somewhat effusive study of Hemingway's religious be-
         liefs and their representation in his fiction. Isabelle
         sees Hemingway as "a religiously oriented man" whose "beauty
         and courage" kept him writing masterpieces with spiritual
         conviction.

1964 B SHORTER WRITINGS

1   ANON.   "Fifty Pounds of Hemingway," Newsweek, 63 (6 Jan.), 67.
            Interview with Mary Hemingway regarding Hemingway's un-
         published manuscripts; photo.

2   ADLER, JACK.   "Theme and Character in Hemingway: For Whom the
         Bell Tolls," University Review, 30 (June), 293-99.
            Notes that the minor characters contribute to two of the
         most important themes, "insubordination and courage."

3   ALLEN, WALTER.   The Modern Novel.   New York: E. P. Dutton,
         pp. 92-98.
            Compares Hemingway with Conrad and Malraux as being "the
         dramatist of the extreme situation." His almost obsessive
         concern is with honor, personal honor; and from In Our Time
         forward, this was his subject.

4   BEEBE, MAURICE.   Ivory Towers and Sacred Founts: The Artist
         as Hero in Fiction from Goethe to Joyce.   New York: New
         York University Press, pp. 306-07.
            Uses Hemingway as an illustration of "the triumph of art
         over life." Sees For Whom the Bell Tolls as a poem to
         death rather than life; notes that Jordan responds to
         Maria only partially, and terms the book a "nihilistic,
         perhaps arrogant novel which affirms only the success of
         the artist."

5   BROUSSARD, LOUIS.   "Hemingway as a Literary Critic," Arizona
         Quarterly, 20 (Autumn), 197-204.

1964

(BROUSSARD, LOUIS)
　　Finds the core of Hemingway's aesthetic theories in "Mr.
and Mrs. Elliott" and The Torrents of Spring, especially
his displeasure with the "waste land" theme.

6　BROWN, ERNEST FRANCIS, ed. Opinions and Perspectives: From
　　The New York Times Book Review. Boston: Houghton Mifflin,
　　passim and pp. 162-68.
　　　　"Was 'Papa' Truly a Great Writer?" by Maxwell Geismar,
　　reprinted from New York Times Book Review (1 July 1962).

7　CONNOLLY, CYRIL. Previous Convictions. London: Hamish Hamil-
　　ton, pp. 290-92.
　　　　"Ernest Hemingway: 1," review of Across the River and
　　Into the Trees, reprinted from Sunday Times (London)
　　(3 Sept. 1950). Pp. 293-98: "Ernest Hemingway: 2,"
　　memorial essay, reprinted from Sunday Times (London)
　　(9 July 1961).

8　COOPERMAN, STANLEY. "Death and Cojones: Hemingway's A Fare-
　　well to Arms," South Atlantic Quarterly, 63 (Winter),
　　85-92.
　　　　Sees Hemingway not as an existentialist but as one ob-
　　sessed with the ritual of death; the existentialist is
　　more concerned with living well.

9　CUNNINGHAM, DONALD H. "Hemingway's 'The Snows of Kilimanjaro,'"
　　Explicator, 22 (Feb.), Item 41.
　　　　Hemingway's persistent references to whiteness during the
　　latter part of the story reveal his symbolic intentions.

10　DANBY-SMITH, VALERIE. "Reminiscence of Hemingway," SR, 47
　　(9 May), 30-31, 57.
　　　　The author worked for Hemingway in the summer of 1959
　　and then for the Hemingway estate; discusses the manuscript
　　and final preparation of A Moveable Feast.

11　DAVIDSON, DONALD, ed. Concise American Composition and Rheto-
　　ric. New York: Scribner's, pp. 90-92.
　　　　"Landscape in Gorizia" by Carlos Baker, reading of A
　　Farewell to Arms, Chapter 1, reprinted from Baker, pp. 94-
　　96 (See 1952.A2).

12　DOS PASSOS, JOHN. "Old Hem Was a Sport," Sports Illustrated,
　　20 (29 June), 58-67.
　　　　Reminiscence of fishing with Hemingway in Key West in
　　the 1930's, complete with mention of Hemingway's scorn for

1964

(DOS PASSOS, JOHN)
Dos Passos' shell collection. Tells the story of Hemingway's playing a giant tuna all day, only to have it eaten
by sharks.

13 EHRENBURG, ILYA. Memoirs: 1921-1941. Cleveland: World,
pp. 383-91.
Regarding his meeting with Hemingway in Madrid, March
1937, during the Spanish Civil War.

14 ELLISON, RALPH. "The World and the Jug," New Leader, 47
(3 Feb.).
Claims that Hemingway was more important to the development of his writing than Richard Wright ("Wright was . . .
a 'relative'; Hemingway an 'ancestor'") "because he appre-
ciated the things of this earth which I love . . . .
weather, guns, dogs, horses, love and hate and impossible
circumstances which to the courageous and dedicated could
be turned into benefits and victories."
Reprinted in Shadow and Act, New York, Random House, 1964,
pp. 107-43.

15 FIEDLER, LESLIE. Waiting for the End. New York: Stein & Day.
Many references to Hemingway, but mentions that Hemingway's importance lies in being "the exploiter of the self-
pity of the first in a long series of American Lost Generations." Preferring Hemingway's first books, Fiedler claims
the late writing is "unreal" because Hemingway had himself--
through publicity and his own psychology--become unreal.
In Chapter 1: "The Death of the Old Men," Fiedler describes
Hemingway and Faulkner as "great presences who made possible
both homage and blasphemy, both imitation and resistance,"
reprinted from Arts & Sciences, 64 (Winter 1963-64), (See
1963.B16).

16 GALANTIERE, LEWIS. "A Moveable Feast," New York Times Book
Review (11 May), p. 1.
Considers the memoir "a true triumph of Hemingway's art."

17 GUÉRARD, ALBERT J., MACLIN B. GUÉRARD, JOHN HAWKES, and CLAIRE
ROSENFIELD. The Personal Voice: A Contemporary Prose
Reader. Philadelphia: Lippincott.
Pp. 431-44: "Observations on the Style of Ernest Heming-
way" by Harry Levin, reprinted from Contexts of Criticism,
Cambridge, Harvard University Press, 1957, pp. 140-67 (See
1957.B20). Pp. 444-55: "Nightmare and Ritual in Heming-
way" by Malcolm Cowley, reprinted from Introduction to
Portable Hemingway, pp. vii-xxiv (See 1945.B3).

1964

18   HAGOPIAN, JOHN V. "Tidying Up Hemingway's Clean, Well-Lighted
      Place," <u>Studies in Short Fiction</u>, 1 (Winter), 140-46.
         By calling one line of dialogue in the story an obvious
      typographical error, the confusion disappears.

19   HALVERSON, JOHN. "Christian Resonance in <u>The Old Man and the
      Sea</u>," <u>English Language Notes</u>, 2 (Sept.), 50-54.
         Sees the novella to embody "the lesson of faith, hope,
      and charity" through Santiago's example, which is "pro-
      foundly Christian."

20   HARDY, JOHN EDWARD. "<u>A Farewell to Arms</u>: The Death of
      Tragedy," in <u>Man in the Modern Novel</u>. Seattle: University
      of Washington Press, pp. 123-36.
         Sees the weakness of this novel as pervading all the
      subsequent writing, Hemingway's failure to establish the
      characters as believable people. Notes that Henry is
      laconic because he is "fearful of the emotional conse-
      quences of eloquence," that he is grudging in his personal
      relationships because he is a romantic, and that ultimately,
      "of all modern heroes, Hemingway's is most uncertain of
      his identity."

21   HEMINGWAY, LEICESTER. "Ernest Hemingway's Boyhood Reading,"
      <u>Mark Twain Journal</u>, 12, No. 2, pp. 4-5.
         Stresses the debt to Twain, summarizing that Hemingway
      read "boys books."

22   HEMINGWAY, MARY. "The Making of a Book: A Chronicle and a
      Memoir," <u>New York Times Book Review</u> (10 May), pp. 26-27.
         Describes the writing and editing of <u>A Moveable Feast</u>.

23   HERTZEL, LEO J. "The Look of Religion: Hemingway and Catholi-
      cism," <u>Renascence</u>, 17 (Winter), 77-81.
         Sees Hemingway as a naturalist, treating the Catholic
      Church as just another bullfight, a "colorful institution."

24   HOFFMAN, FREDERICK J. <u>The Mortal No: Death and the Modern
      Imagination</u>. Princeton, N. J.: Princeton University
      Press.
         Pp. 153-54: considers Hemingway's use of the bullfight
      a successful image for postwar tension, and Hemingway's
      heroes as people accustomed to the shock of violence, not
      precipitators of it; more victims than victimized (p. 171).
      Pp. 215-18: comments that Hemingway's style is marked by
      what Erich Kahler calls "New Factuality"--abruptness,
      neutrality, and an emphasis on fact that becomes nearly
      symbolic.

25   HOHENBERG, JOHN. <u>Foreign Correspondence: The Great Reporters</u>
     <u>and Their Times</u>. New York: Columbia University Press,
     pp. 283-84.
          On Hemingway's seriousness as a journalist, and <u>passim</u>.

26   HUTTON, VIRGIL. "The Short Happy Life of Macomber," <u>University</u>
     <u>Review</u>, 30 (June), 253-63.
          Sees Hemingway's treatment of Wilson as satire, and
     offers several explanations for Wilson's face being de-
     scribed as red.
          Reprinted in Benson, pp. 239-50 (<u>See</u> 1975.A3).

27   KASHKEEN, IVAN. "Another View," <u>American Dialogue</u>, 1, No. 2
     (Oct.-Nov.), 14.
          Excerpt from his book on Hemingway. Basically a Leftist,
     politico-social view of Hemingway, with praise for the
     commitment of his writing of the 1930's.

28   KAZIN, ALFRED. "Ernest Hemingway as His Own Fable," <u>Atlantic</u>,
     213 (June), 54-57 and <u>Cornhill</u>, 174 (Summer), 139-47.
          Treats <u>A Moveable Feast</u> as fiction, as "the Growth and
     Development of the Writer" done in an unusual memoirs
     structure. Explains that Hemingway had no mercy for the
     poor writers who disappointed him because Hemingway him-
     self worked so hard at his writing.

29   KNIEGER, BERNARD. "The Concept of Maturity in Hemingway's
     Short Stories," <u>CLA Journal</u>, 8 (Dec.), 149-56.
          Defines maturity as being "brave before imminent death,"
     "competent and self-sufficient," "knowledgeable," "de-
     cisive," and accepting the "responsibility for his own
     acts."

30   MacBETH, GEORGE. "The Sick Rhetoric of War," <u>Critical Quar-</u>
     <u>terly</u>, 6: 154-63.
          Relates that Hemingway was fascinated by D'Annunzio in
     the Italian campaign of 1918. Opposite in their views and
     attitudes toward war, D'Annunzio was a Romantic and a
     rhetorician.

31   MacLEISH, ARCHIBALD. <u>The Dialogues of Archibald MacLeish and</u>
     <u>Mark Van Doren</u>. Edited by Warren V. Bush. New York:
     Dutton, pp. 85-87, 147.
          MacLeish speaks of his friendship with Hemingway in the
     1920's and of Hemingway's visit to his farm in Massachu-
     setts in 1930.

1964

32   MEAKER, M. J. Sudden Endings. Garden City, New York:
         Doubleday, pp. 1-25.
         "A Wow at the End," studies Hemingway's work as related
         to his suicide.

33   MERIWETHER, JAMES B. "The Dashes in Hemingway's A Farewell to
         Arms," Papers of the Bibliographical Society of America,
         58 (Oct.-Dec.), 449-57.
         Obscenities in the manuscript of A Farewell to Arms,
         deleted in the first edition, "played a significant part
         in establishing the tone of the scenes in which they origi-
         nally appeared."

34   MILLER, PATRICK. "Hemingway's 'A Way You'll Never Be,'"
         Explicator, 23 (Oct.), Item 18.
         Sees that Nick's metaphor for locusts for bait reflects
         his own anxiety personally.

35   MIZENER, ARTHUR. "The American Hero as Leatherstocking: Nick
         Adams," in The Sense of Life in the Modern Novel. Boston:
         Houghton Mifflin, pp. 205-26.
         Mizener thinks of the Hemingway hero as an isolato:
         "The Hemingway hero's real life is lived alone." Mizener
         relates the fictional hero to the author, describing Hem-
         ingway as "a cross between Teddy Roosevelt and a character
         invented by Richard Harding Davis." Finds Hemingway's
         anti-intellectualism his chief weakness: "there are limits
         to what even the most powerful unanalyzed responses can do
         to give formal order."

36   MOSS, SIDNEY P. "Character, Vision, and Theme in The Sun Also
         Rises," Iowa English Yearbook, No. 9 (Fall), 64-67.
         Sees Hemingway's world as without meaning, held together
         by violence, terror, and disaster.

37   MOTOLA, GABRIEL. "Hemingway's Code: Literature and Life,"
         MFS, 10 (Winter), 319-29.
         The manner of Hemingway's death might seem inconsistent
         with his professed code, but Motola sees the code as more
         "elastic" than readers might realize.

38   MUDRICK, MARVIN. "A Farewell to Spring and Paris," Hudson
         Review, 17 (Winter), 572-79.
         Sees A Moveable Feast as Hemingway's "masterpiece,"
         Traces Hemingway's writing from the stories of Nick (the
         "nightmare stories") to the "know-how stories" to what he
         sees as "self-parody." A Moveable Feast, however, is a
         fresh beginning, an honest recounting of youth and love.

1964

(MUDRICK, MARVIN)
Reprinted, revised, in On Culture and Literature, New York,
Horizon Press, 1970, pp. 117-27.

39   NORTH, JOSEPH. "Hemingway: The Man and the Writer," American
Dialogue, 1, No. 2 (Oct.-Nov.), 7.
    North's basic contention is that brave men lead brave
lives. Hemingway was a brave man; ergo, his is a brave
life.

40   O'CONNOR, WILLIAM VAN, ed. Seven Modern American Novelists:
An Introduction. Minneapolis: University of Minnesota
Press, pp. 153-88.
    "Ernest Hemingway" by Philip Young (revised from the
Pamphlet on American Writers, 1959). (See 1959.A1.)

41   PARKER, STEPHEN JAY. "Hemingway's Revival in the Soviet Union:
1955-1962," American Literature, 35 (Jan.), 485-501.
    Hemingway enjoyed great popularity in Russia until For
Whom the Bell Tolls, which displeased the people. Following The Old Man and the Sea, Hemingway was officially
reinstated.
    Reprinted in The Literary Reputation of Hemingway in
Europe, pp. 177-95 (See 1965.A3).

42   PEDEN, WILLIAM. The American Short Story: Front Line in the
National Defense of Literature. Boston: Houghton,
Mifflin.
    Uses Hemingway's "Indian Camp" to illustrate one end of
the range of the American short story. The study does not
include much discussion of Hemingway (whom Peden calls,
with Faulkner, "the greatest American short story writer
of the twentieth century") because he wrote so few stories
after 1940.

43   RAHV, PHILIP. The Myth and the Powerhouse. New York: Farrar,
Straus & Giroux, pp. 193-201.
    Reprinted of "Hemingway in the Early 1950's" from Commen-
tary, 14 (Oct. 1952). (See 1952.B62.)

44   ROSS, LILLIAN. Reporting. New York: Simon & Schuster.
    Pp. 144-83: regarding Hemingway in the Profile of
Sidney Franklin, New Yorker, 25 (12 and 26 March 1949).
(See 1949.B15.)
    Pp. 187-94: Preface from Portrait of Hemingway (book).
    Pp. 194-222: "Portrait of Hemingway," reprinted from
New Yorker, 26 (13 May 1950). (See 1950.B47.)

1964

45   SEVAREID, ERIC.   "Mano a Mano," in This Is Eric Sevareid.   New
         York: McGraw-Hill, pp. 296-303.
         Describes his meeting with the Hemingways in Málaga,
         reprinted from Esquire, 52 (Nov. 1959).

46   SIMPSON, HERBERT.   "The Problem of Structure in A Farewell to
         Arms," Forum (Houston), 4 (Spring-Summer), 20-24.
         Finds the plot of A Farewell to Arms "structurally un-
         satisfactory" and Hemingway's using war as a symbol--and
         a symptom--of "man's eternal chaos." Love, as Hemingway
         uses it, represents a respite, a "way of achieving what
         limited kind of good life one can."

*47   TANNER, TONY.   "Hemingway y Fitzgerald," Casa de Las Americas,
         4 (Dec.), 99-105.
         Cited in Hemingway Notes, III.

48   _____.   "Tough and Tender," Encounter, 23 (July), 71-75.
         Reviews Fitzgerald's Letters and A Moveable Feast.

49   TAUBE, MYRON.   "The Nada and Plato's Cave," CEA Critic, 26
         (May), 5-6.
         For both Plato and Hemingway, the reality lies outside.
         In Hemingway's fiction, darkness symbolizes that sense of
         reality, lying outside.

50   [TEXAS, UNIVERSITY OF].   A Creative Century: Selections from
         the Twentieth Century Collections at the University of
         Texas.   Austin: University of Texas.
         Catalogue of an Exhibit held in Nov. 1964, Academic
         Center and Undergraduate Library, pp. 29-30: quotation
         from a Hemingway letter to "Dear Old Carper," Howell G.
         Jenkins.

51   WAGNER, GEOFFREY.   "A Moveable Feast," Commonweal (29 May),
         p. 302.
         Says of the book, "for all the good it is likely to do
         Hemingway's reputation [it] could have stayed in Cuba
         permanently."

52   WEATHERHEAD, A. K.   "Romantic Anachronism in The Alexandria
         Quartet," MFS, 10 (Summer), 128-36.
         Compares Durrell's Quartet with The Sun Also Rises in
         its concern with deracinés, casual sexual unions, its
         female protagonist and, in connection with her, a great
         city. Sees Durrell's solution as unacceptable, however.

53   WEBSTER, HARVEY CURTIS. "Ernest Hemingway: The Pursuit of
         Death," Texas Quarterly, 7 (Summer), 149-59.
            Describes Hemingway's interest in death as an alternative
         to man's condition: "Man is an inspired, entangled animal,
         with possibilities he probably will not reach. Death, and
         its limiting possibilities, lies above all of us."

54   WESTBROOK, MAX. "Necessary Performance: The Hemingway Col-
         lection at Texas," Library Chronicle of the University of
         Texas, 7 (Spring), 26-31.

55   WHITE, WILLIAM. "Novelist as Reporter: Ernest Hemingway,"
         Orient/West, 9, No. 5, pp. 77-92.
            Describes Hemingway's journalism as unorthodox "instead
         of the objective reporting we normally associate with
         daily journalism." Points out that in some cases the same
         piece was published as both fiction and journalism, "with
         no change whatever."

56   WITHAM, W. TASKER. The Adolescent in the American Novel, 1920-
         1960. New York: Frederick Ungar Publishers.
            References to Nick Adams, in his romances (usually
         idyllic), his parental relationships, his wandering in
         search of his own independence, and his hunting.

57   WOLFF, MILTON. "We Met in Spain," American Dialogue, 1, No. 2
         (Oct.-Nov.), 8-9.
            Met Hemingway in Spain several times (Wolff is former
         commander of the Lincoln Brigade) and saw the first drafts
         of Fifth Column. Includes several short letters from Hem-
         ingway, one of which is his reaction to Wolff's negative
         response ("attack") to For Whom the Bell Tolls.

58   YOUNG, PHILIP. "Our Hemingway Man," Kenyon Review, 26
         (Autumn), 676-706.
            Describes his "role" as the first (controversial) Heming-
         way critic, and reviews 32 books and pamphlets from the
         early 1960's, in personal essay style.
         Reprinted as "The End of Compendium Reviewing" in Three
         Bags Full, Essays in American Fiction, New York, Harcourt,
         Brace, 1972, pp. 30-54 (See 1972.B114).

1965 A BOOKS

  1   KILEY, JED. Hemingway: An Old Friend Remembers. New York:
         Hawthorne Books. Photos.
            Memories of Hemingway in Paris during the 1920's and

1965

(KILEY, JED)
 later in Bimini and Key West, Fla. First published in
 eight installments as "Hemingway: a title bout in ten
 rounds" in Playboy, 3 (Sept. 1956), pp. 19, 28, 34-38;
 (Oct.), pp. 55-56; (Nov.), pp. 67, 70, 84-86; (Dec.),
 pp. 61-62, 75; 4 (March 1957), pp. 51-52, 60, 66; (April),
 pp. 63, 66; (Aug.), pp. 45-46, 50, 52, 60, 66-67; (Sept.),
 pp. 65-66.

2 LEWIS, ROBERT W., JR. Hemingway on Love. Austin: University
 of Texas Press, pp. 229-35. Selected Reading List.
 A study to "consider the subject of love as treated by
 Hemingway in major and representative works." Using the
 patterns of eros and agape from the Tristan-Iseult story,
 Lewis emphasizes a rigidity that is questionable in the
 novels taken collectively.

3 ASSELINEAU, ROGER, ed. The Literary Reputation of Hemingway
 in Europe. Paris: Minard (Lettres Modernes, No. 5).
 This collection of essays is from a symposium on the
 critical reception of Hemingway's work (Sept. 1960) held
 at the Villa Serbelloni in Bellagio, Italy; two other
 essays--Parker's and Barea's--have been added.
 Contents: pp. 3-7: Introduction by Heinrich Straumann.
 pp. 9-36: "Hemingway's English Reputation by D. S. R.
 Welland; notes, pp. 36-38.
 pp. 39-65: "French Reactions to Hemingway's Work between
 the two World Wars" by Roger Asselineau; notes, pp. 66-72.
 pp. 73-91: "The Critical Reception of Hemingway's Work
 in Germany since 1920" by Helmut Papajewski; notes, pp. 91-
 92.
 pp. 93-123: "Hemingway in Italy" by Mario Praz; notes,
 pp. 124-125.
 pp. 127-148: "Hemingway in Norway" by Sigmund Skard;
 notes, pp. 148-49.
 pp. 151-170: "Hemingway in Sweden" by Lars Ahnebrink;
 notes, pp. 171-74; checklist of Swedish translations,
 p. 175.
 pp. 177-193: "Hemingway's Revival in the Soviet Union:
 1955-1962" by Stephen Jan Parker, reprinted from American
 Literature, 35 (Jan. 1964); notes, pp. 193-195.
 pp. 197-210: "Not Spain but Hemingway" by Arturo Barea,
 reprinted from Horizon, 3 (May 1941).

1965 B SHORTER WRITINGS

1 ANON. "Papa's Poems," Time, 86 (30 July), 33.
 Commentary on the "Poems to Mary" published in Atlantic.

194

1965

(ANON.)
   While this reviewer does not think the poems have much
literary worth, he does quote Mrs. Hemingway as saying
there are enough poems to "fill a book one-half inch
thick."

2   ADAMS, J. DONALD. <u>Speaking of Books--and Life</u>. New York:
   Holt, Rinehart & Winston, pp. 174-76.
      "The Sun Also Sets," reprinted from <u>New York Times Book
   Review</u> (16 July 1961).

3   ALGREN, NELSON. <u>Notes from a Sea Diary: Hemingway All the
   Way</u>. New York: Putnam.
      Many references in this general defense of Hemingway
   against certain critics, mixed with an account of a trip
   to the Orient.

4   BERNARD, KENNETH. "Hemingway's 'Indian Camp,'" <u>Studies in
   Short Fiction</u>, 2 (Spring), 291.
      Sees that the story suggests that Uncle George is the
   father of the baby, to create more symbolic meanings.

5   BIGSBY, C. W. E. "Two Types of Violence," <u>University Review</u>,
   32 (Winter), 129-36.
      Sees that Hemingway's fiction clearly expresses the two
   types of violence most common to American life: formal,
   "the result of violence conducted to a formal code of
   rules" (law, bullfights) and informal, "exhibits a lack of
   control and is conducted to no code."

6   BROWNE, RAY B. and MARTIN LIGHT, eds. <u>Critical Approaches to
   American Literature</u>, Vol. 2. New York: Crowell, pp. 275-
   91.
      "The Hero and the Code" by Philip Young, reprinted from
   <u>Ernest Hemingway</u>, New York, Rinehart, 1952, pp. 28-50
   (<u>See</u> 1952.A3).

7   CALLAGHAN, MORLEY. "Legends of the Old Man," <u>SR</u>, 48 (28 Aug.),
   43.
      Reviews Kiley's <u>Hemingway: An Old Friend Remembers</u> and
   Algren's <u>Notes from a Sea Diary</u>, and terms the latter "a
   passionate, honest, and moving defense."

8   CANADAY, NICHOLAS, JR. "Is There Any Light in Hemingway's
   'The Light of the World'?" <u>Studies in Short Fiction</u>, 3
   (Fall), 75-76.
      Terms the title of the story ironic, and in the emphasis
   on place rather than character, Hemingway creates further
   irony.

1965

9   COLLINS, LARRY and DOMINIQUE LAPIERRE. Is Paris Burning?
       New York: Simon and Schuster.
         Scattered references to Hemingway's intelligence work at
       Rambouillet and the liberation of Paris, 1944.

10   CONNOLLY, CYRIL. The Modern Movement: One Hundred Key Books
       from England, France and America, 1880-1950. London:
       Hamish Hamilton/Andre Deutsch.
         No. 50, p. 53: "Ernest Hemingway, The Sun Also Rises."
       With this novel, Hemingway became one of the "few men of
       action" within the Modern Movement, becoming "an immediate
       symbol of an age." No. 60, p. 60: "Ernest Hemingway, A
       Farewell to Arms." So successful was this book that it
       "ended Hemingway's influence as a writer. After it one
       could no more imitate that musical crystal-clear style."

11   COOPERMAN, STANLEY. "Hemingway and Old Age: Santiago as
       Priest of Time," College English, 27 (Dec.), 215-220.
        Sees the novella as a return to the theme of isolation,
       and an unfortunate refusal on the author's part to see
       "old age in any other terms but the values of pride,
       sacrifice, and endurance."

12   DAVIES, PHILLIPS G. and ROSEMARY R. DAVIES. "Hemingway's
       'Fifty Grand' and the Jack Britton-Mickey Walker Prize
       Fight," American Literature, 37 (Nov.), 251-58.
        The story seems to have been based on newspaper accounts
       of the welterweight championship fight at Madison Square
       Garden, Nov. 1, 1922.

13   DRINNON, RICHARD. "In the American Heartland: Hemingway and
       Death," Psychoanalytic Review, 52 (Summer), 5-31.
        Sees Hemingway's pre-occupation with death, war, violence,
       and masculine companionship in the context of castration
       fears and American prairies.

14   FAULKNER, WILLIAM. Essays, Speeches and Public Letters,
       edited by James B. Meriwether. New York: Random House.
        P. 193, review of The Old Man and the Sea, reprinted from
       Shenandoah, 3 (Autumn 1952). (See 1952.B31); pp. 210-11,
       letter regarding Evelyn Waugh's view of Across the River
       and Into the Trees, reprinted from Time, 56 (13 Nov. 1950).
       (See 1950.B4.)

15   FLANNER, JANET. Paris Journal, 1944-1965, edited by William
       Shawn. New York: Atheneum.
        Description of an exhibit based largely on Sylvia Beach's
       holdings, including many Hemingway items.

16   FORD, FORD MADOX. <u>Letters of Ford Madox Ford</u>, edited by
      Richard M. Ludwig. Princeton, N. J.: Princeton University
      Press.
        Many references show Ford's consistent support of Heming-
      way and his work. In a 1930 letter, he lists Hemingway as
      one of "my babies." In a 1932 letter he asks Hemingway for
      a word of praise for Pound's <u>Cantos</u>.

17   FUCHS, DANIEL. "Ernest Hemingway, Literary Critic," <u>American</u>
      <u>Literature</u>, 36 (Jan.), 431-51.
        A comprehensive account of Hemingway's aesthetic prin-
      ciples, and some of the major influences on his writing--
      Conrad, Flaubert, Twain, Joyce, Fielding, Cervantes. Fuchs
      sees much of Hemingway's fiction in "the novel in burlesque
      tradition" . . . "from explicit parody to implicit criti-
      cism."
      Reprinted in Waldhorn, pp. 92-111 (<u>See</u> 1973.A7); and
      Wagner, pp. 38-56 (<u>See</u> 1974.A3).

18   GADO, FRANK. "The Curious History of the Hemingway Hero,"
      <u>Symposium</u> (Union College), 4 (Winter), 18-22.
        Surveys the kind of description the so-called Hemingway
      hero has received during the years.

19   GINGRICH, ARNOLD. <u>The Well-Tempered Angler</u>. New York:
      Knopf, pp. 20-27.
        "Horsing Them in with Hemingway." These recollections
      of fishing at Key West and Bimini with Hemingway, during
      the 1930's, are reprinted from <u>Playboy</u>, 12 (Sept. 1965).

20   GRANT, DOUGLAS. <u>Purpose and Place: Essays on American</u>
      <u>Writers</u>. London: Macmillan.
        Pp. 169-74: "Ernest Hemingway, 1: The Bruiser and the
      Poet," a review of <u>A Moveable Feast</u>, reprinted from <u>TLS</u>
      (21 May 1964); pp. 175-182: "Ernest Hemingway, 2: <u>Men</u>
      <u>Without Women</u>."

21   HEINEY, DONALD. <u>Barron's Simplified Approach to Ernest</u>
      <u>Hemingway</u>. Woodbury, N. Y.: Barron's Educational Series.

22   HEMINGWAY, MARY. "Circumstances in which 'To Mary in London'
      and 'Second Poem to Mary' were written," <u>Atlantic</u>, 216
      (Aug.), 96.
        Reminiscence of her relationship with Hemingway during
      World War II.

23   _____. "Havana" in "The Lost Resorts" series, <u>SR</u>, 48 (2 Jan.),
      40-41, 70-74.

1965

(HEMINGWAY, MARY)
Reminiscence of Havana as a resort, including hotels and foods Hemingway enjoyed.
Reprinted in The Saturday Review Sampler of Wit and Wisdom, edited by Martin Levin, New York, Simon & Schuster, 1966, pp. 288-94.

24 _____. "To Parajiso with Papa and 'Pilar,'" Sports Illustrated, 23, No. 2 (12 July), 62-68, 70.
Remembrance of trips with Hemingway in the Caribbean, off Peru, and Africa, using old diaries. Stresses Hemingway's love for the "Pilar." Describes a favorite island (Megano de Casegua) which Hemingway called "Parajiso."

25 HOFFMAN, FREDERICK J. "Hemingway and Fitzgerald" in American Literary Scholarship: An Annual, 1963, edited by James Woodress. Durham, N. C.: Duke University Press, pp. 81-91.
Surveys criticism on both authors published during 1963.

26 HOFFMANN, GERHARD. "'The Gambler, the Nun, and the Radio'-- Untersuchung zur Gestaltungsweise Hemingways," Germanisch-Romanische Monatsschrift, 15 (Oct.), 421-29.
Uses the story to analyze Hemingway's mature narrative technique.

27 HOVEY, RICHARD B. "Hemingway's 'Now I Lay Me': A Psychological Interpretation," Literature and Psychology, 15 (Spring), 70-78.
Because the story bears striking resemblance to what happens in psychoanalytic treatment, it sheds light on the conflicts in other Hemingway stories, with the mother portrayed as destroyer. Here too wounding is linked with the rejection of marriage.
Reprinted in Benson, pp. 180-87 (See 1975.A3).

28 _____. "The Torrents of Spring: Prefigurations in Early Hemingway," College English, 26 (March), 460-64.
Even in a minor work, Hemingway's preoccupation with wounds, and their relation to love, is evident.

29 KORGES, JAMES. "Curiosities: Nin and Miller, Hemingway and Seager," Critique, 7, No. 3 (Spring-Summer), 66-81.
In his review of A Moveable Feast, Korges sees Hemingway's great fault as being an absence of either humor or charity, and describes his characteristic nastiness to writers to whom he was indebted.

30 KRAUSS, WILLIAM A. "Footnote from Hemingway's Paris, 1964,"
Harper's, 231 (Aug.), 91–95.
Reminiscence of a pilgrimage to the places Hemingway and
his friends frequented in the 1920's.

31 LEARY, LEWIS, ed. The Teacher and American Literature: Papers
Presented at the 1964 Convention of the National Council of
Teachers of English. Champaign, Ill.: National Council of
Teachers of English.
Pp. 149–56: "Recent Scholarship on Faulkner and Heming-
way" by Richard P. Adams. Pp. 157–62: "Faulkner and Hem-
ingway: Implications for School Programs" by John N.
Terrey.

32 LeBOST, BARBARA A. "'The Way It Is': Something Else on Hemingway," Journal of Existentialism, 6 (Winter), 175–80.
Sees Hemingway as "a major existentialist writer" because
of his central and recurring themes, especially his emphasis on the "truthful life."

33 LYTLE, ANDREW. "A Moveable Feast: The Going To and Fro,"
Sewanee Review, 73 (April–June), 339–43.
Sees the book as "extremely revealing" of the public per-
sonality which was, apparently, there from the start.

34 MANNING, ROBERT. "Hemingway in Cuba," Atlantic, 216 (Aug.),
101–08.
Recollections of visiting Hemingway in Cuba, and the re-
sulting conversations. "He could be fierce in his sensitivity to criticism and competitive in his craft . . .
but he could laugh at himself. The private Hemingway was
an artist. The public Hemingway was an experience."
Reprinted as "Ernest Hemingway" in Atlantic Brief Lives,
edited by Louis Kronenberger, Boston, Little, Brown, 1971.

35 MOORE, L. HUGH, JR. "Mrs. Hirsch and Mrs. Bell in Hemingway's
'The Killers,'" MFS, 11 (Winter), 427–28.
Explains the confusion between the women as a reflection
of the terrible casualness of the hit men as they proceed
to do their job.

36 MORRIS, WILLIAM E. "Hemingway's 'The Short Happy Life of
Francis Macomber,'" Explicator, 24 (Dec.), Item 31.
Traces Hemingway's pattern of reference, seeing "Mrs.
Macomber" as neutral, "Margot" as spiteful, and "the
woman" by the end of the story.

1965

37 PORTZ, JOHN. "Allusion and Structure in Hemingway's 'A
    Natural History of the Dead,'" Tennessee Studies in Litera-
    ture, 10 (1965), 27–41.
        The story, excerpted from Death in the Afternoon, "sug-
    gests that writing fiction was one of Hemingway's methods
    for controlling his painful memories and fears."

38 ROUCH, JOHN S. "Jake Barnes as Narrator," MFS, 11 (Winter),
    361–70.
        Considers the Jake who narrates the story "significantly
    different from the Jake in the novel in that while he has
    lost his romantic belief that there are final answers and
    solutions, he has gained the more stoical assurance that
    he will endure."

*39 SANDER, OSCAR. "Hemingway in Vorarlberg," Vorarlberg, 4 (Oct.),
    6–9.
        Cited in Fitzgerald/Hemingway Annual, 1972.

40 SAN JUAN, E., JR. "Integrity of Composition in the Poems of
    Ernest Hemingway," University Review, 32: 51–58.
        An analysis of separate Hemingway poems.

41 SCHLESINGER, ARTHUR M., JR. A Thousand Days: John F. Kennedy
    in the White House. Boston: Houghton Mifflin, p. 372.
        A message from Hemingway regarding the 1961 inauguration
    is quoted.

42 SCOTT, NATHAN A., JR., ed. Forms of Extremity in the Modern
    Novel. Richmond, Va.: John Knox Press, pp. 35–54.
        "Hemingway and Our 'Essential Worldliness'" by John
    Killinger. Summary of the work and life, stressing Heming-
    way's "basic kinship to the German and French existential-
    ists." Yet Killinger finds Hemingway "incurably romantic
    and primitive—even religious" and his concern with man's
    search for belief as an important contribution to modern
    writing.

43 SKIPP, FRANCIS E. "What Was the Matter with Jacob Barnes?"
    Carrell, 6 (Dec.), 17–22.
        Finds Jake the most creative character in The Sun Also
    Rises, and sees his emasculation as ironic. Suggests that
    Dos Passos was the model for Bill Gorton, another character
    who "can focus his energies and use them creatively."

44 SLABEY, ROBERT M. "The Structure of Hemingway's In Our Time,"
    South Dakota Review, 3 (Autumn), 38–52.

(SLABEY, ROBERT M.)
Finds "the structural arrangement of In Our Time not chronological but ideological," with irony strong "in phrase, situation, and structure."

45   SPILLER, ROBERT E. The Third Dimension, Studies in Literary History. New York: Macmillan, pp. 168-71, 185-86.
Sees Nick Adams as the core of each Hemingway protagonist, and his rite of experience as that of all modern men. Finds that Hemingway's movement from tragedy to tragic irony was important for all contemporary literature.

46   STEGNER, WALLACE, ed. The American Novel: From James Fenimore Cooper to William Faulkner. New York: Basic Books, pp. 192-205.
Chapter 17: "Ernest Hemingway: A Farewell to Arms" by Carlos Baker (essays written for oral presentation over the Voice of America). Contradicts the opinion that A Farewell to Arms was the last "great" Hemingway novel, but does maintain the excellence of this book. Includes biographical correlations, and emphasizes Hemingway's skill in writing, especially in the ending of A Farewell to Arms. Reprinted in Graham, pp. 27-38 (See 1971.A7).

47   TANNER, TONY. The Reign of Wonder: Nativity and Reality in American Literature. Cambridge: Cambridge University Press, pp. 228-57.
"Ernest Hemingway's Unhurried Sensations." Tanner sees Hemingway's strength as his ability to recreate details and moments, a technique not merely stylistic but also reflecting his belief in the senses and the now. He finds Hemingway's reliance on his unhurried sensations strangely like the Transcendentalists' reverence for the actual world.

48   UENO, NAOZO. "An Oriental View of The Old Man and the Sea," East-West Review (Kyoto, Japan), 2 (Spring-Summer), 67-76.
Appreciation for the quiet control and descriptive action.

49   VANDERBILT, KERMIT. "Last Words of Ernest Hemingway," Nation, 201, No. 13 (25 Oct.), 284-85.
Describes the Caedmon record Ernest Hemingway Reading taken from tapes made between 1948 and 1961.

50   WEGELIN, CHRISTOF. "Hemingway and the Decline of International Fiction," Sewanee Review, 73 (April-June), 285-98.
Uses James' fiction to explain Hemingway's, with regard to the international theme. Finds Hemingway's use of the theme very different from James'.

1965

51   WEISS, DANIEL. "The Red Badge of Courage," Psychoanalytic
        Review, 52; Part I (Summer), 32-52; Part II (Fall), 130-54.
        Extended comparison with Hemingway's fiction in this
        psychoanalytical reading.

52   WHITE, WILLIAM. "Hemingway in Korea," Papers of the Biblio-
        graphical Society of America, 59 (April-June), 190-92.
        A history of Hemingway books published in Taiwan (il-
        legally) in English; and a history of Hemingway's books
        available in Korean.

53   WICKES, GEORGE. "Ernest Hemingway Pays His Debts," Shenandoah
        (Winter), pp. 46-54.
        Makes a connection between A Moveable Feast and "Snows,"
        the former being the book that Harry wanted to write be-
        fore he died. Sees A Moveable Feast as a rejection of
        Stein's Autobiography of Alice B. Toklas.

54   WILSON, COLIN. "The Swamp and the Desert: Notes on Powys and
        Hemingway," Eagle and Earwig. London: Baker, pp. 113-127.
        Comparative essay, stressing each author's philosophical
        stance.

55   WILSON, EDMUND. The Bit Between My Teeth: A Literary Chronicle
        of 1950-65. New York: Farrar, Straus & Giroux, pp. 515-25.
        Review of Morley Callaghan's That Summer in Paris, re-
        printed from New Yorker, 39 (23 Feb. 1963). (See 1963.B43.)

1966 A BOOKS

1   HOTCHNER, A. E. Papa Hemingway: A Personal Memoir. New York:
        Random House. Photos.
        An account of Hotchner's friendship with Hemingway the
        last thirteen years of his life. Many quotations from
        Hemingway, as well as many stories told by the author, are
        suspect. It is possible, however, that the account does
        present a realizable picture of Hemingway during the years
        of decline, inaccuracies aside.
        Serialized in the Saturday Evening Post, 239 (12 March
        1966), pp. 32-41, 45-48; (26 March), pp. 36-44, 48, 52,
        77-78, 83; (9 April), pp. 34-47, 50.

2   MONTGOMERY, CONSTANCE CAPPEL. Hemingway in Michigan. New
        York: Fleet. Photos.
        Describing the years 1900 to 1921, when the Hemingway
        family spent their summers in northern Michigan, and Hem-
        ingway's eventual use of this setting and these characters
        in his fiction.

3   SCOTT, NATHAN, JR. Ernest Hemingway, A Critical Essay (pam-
        phlet). Grand Rapids, Mich.: William B. Eerdmans.
            Scott views Hemingway's fiction from the perspective of
        a conjectured philosophy: (1) a sense of the consolatory
        glory of the earth; (2) an awareness of a blackness, nada,
        which contradicts the glory; (3) a dream of the possibility
        of transcendence available, through love. Pp. 19-29 re-
        printed in Wagner, pp. 212-21 (See 1974.A3).

*4 TANIGUCHI, RIKUO. A Study of Hemingway's Works. Tokyo:
        Mikasashobo.
            Cited in Fitzgerald/Hemingway Annual, 1972.

5   YOUNG, PHILIP. Ernest Hemingway: A Reconsideration. Uni-
        versity Park: Pennsylvania State University Press.
            With important additions to the 1952 book, Ernest Heming-
        way (See 1952.A3), this revision adds both a foreword and
        an afterword, some of the material reprinted from Kenyon
        Review, some published for the first time. In retrospect,
        for Young, "Hemingway wrote two very good early novels,
        several very good stories and a few great ones . . . and
        an excellent if quite small book of reminiscence. That's
        all it takes. This is such stuff as immortalities are
        made on."

1966 B   SHORTER WRITINGS

1   ANON. "The Last Days," Time, 87 (15 April), 107. Photo.
            Review of Hotchner's Papa Hemingway as a "rousing good
        book," "an affectionate yet perceptive picture of an old
        friend."

2   ANON. "The Torment of a Master," Newsweek, 67 (11 April), 111.
            Reviews Papa Hemingway as telling "a heartbreaking story"
        of Hemingway's decline.

3   AKMAKJIAN, HIAG. "Hemingway and Haiku," Columbia University
        Forum, 9 (Spring), 45-48.
            Alike in their intensity and power of suggestion, Heming-
        way's prose and haiku poetry share the possibility of
        writer and reader being "in definite and felt relation to
        each other."

4   ALDRIDGE, JOHN W. "A Last Look at the Old Man," in Time to
        Murder and Create: The Contemporary Novel in Crisis. New
        York: David McKay, pp. 185-91.
            Review of The Old Man and the Sea in Scribner Library
        edition. Considers the last twenty years of Hemingway's

1966

(ALDRIDGE, JOHN W.)
life a "progressive decline" and judges harshly To Have and
Have Not, Across the River and Into the Trees, and The Old
Man and the Sea. Reprinted in The Devil in the Fire:
Retrospective Essays on American Literature and Culture,
1951-71, New York, Harper's Magazine Press, 1972, pp. 86-
90 (See 1972.B4).

5   ANDERSON, DAVID D. "Ernest Hemingway, The Voice of an Era,"
Personalist, 47 (April), 234-47.
Sees Hemingway as the real voice of the mid-twentieth
century, not only in his focusing attention on the dilemma,
but also in his voicing his confidence in our choices.

6   BAKER, CARLOS. "Hemingway's Italia," New York Times Book
Review (23 Jan.), p. 2.
A reminiscence of Hemingway's various haunts in Europe,
which Baker had visited the summer of 1965: Venice, the
Montafon Valley in Austria, Luxembourg, Spain. While Hemingway has learned, in his own lifetime, that "chasing
yesterdays is a bum show," Baker points out that wherever
he visited, the people revere Hemingway's memory.

7   BARNES, DANIEL. "Ritual and Parody in 'A Clean, Well-Lighted
Place," Cithara, 5 (May), 15-25.
Sees the story as embodying a Christian message, although
Hemingway works through indirection and even parody. Each
of the waiters is hardly devout, but each recognizes "the
necessity for ritualistic devotion and veneration--and the
courage to endure."

8   BRIDGMAN, RICHARD. "Ernest Hemingway," in The Colloquial Style
in America. New York: Oxford University Press, pp. 195-
230.
By concluding his book with Hemingway's prose, Bridgman
claims that he shaped "the vernacular for general service"
and gave "substance to Gertrude Stein's lessons in abstrac-
tion." Bridgman studies the earliest Hemingway prose as
"experimental," and points to specific changes in dialogue,
ellipses, abstractions, overtones, and diction. Close
attention to many of the short stories.
Reprinted in Wagner, pp. 160-88 (See 1974.A3).

9   BURGESS, ANTHONY. "He Wrote Good," The Spectator, 217
(8 July), 47.
While Burgess has some reservations (that Hemingway
created "a style exactly fitted for the exclusion of the
cerebral"), he concludes that Hemingway "wrote good and
lived good, and both activities were the same."

10   COOPERMAN, STANLEY. "Hemingway's Blue-eyed Boy: Robert
        Jordan and 'Purging Ecstasy,'" Criticism, 8 (Winter), 87-
        96.
            Thinks that Jordan's crusading idealism is only a mani-
        festation of his own psychological need for violence and
        killing as a "purging ecstasy."

11   COWLEY, MALCOLM. The Faulkner-Cowley File, 1944-1962. New
        York: The Viking Press.
            Cowley compares Hemingway and Faulkner in their similar
        habits, love of hunting and the earth, and their relatively
        conservative morality.

12   CROTHERS, GEORGE DUNLAP, ed. An Invitation to Learning. New
        York: Basic Books, pp. 329-36.
            "A Farewell to Arms" by George Dunlap Crothers, Carlos
        Baker and Philip Young.

13   DALEY, ROBERT. The Swords of Spain. New York: Dial Press,
        pp. 84-85. Photos.
            Concerning Hemingway's role in the feud between bull-
        fighters Antonio Ordonez and Luis Miguel Dominguin.

14   DAVIS, ROBERT MURRAY. "Hemingway's 'The Doctor and the
        Doctor's Wife,'" Explicator, 25 (Sept.), Item 1.
            Transfers the judgment expressed in "Fathers and Sons"
        to this story: the doctor is "in a trap that he had
        helped only a little to set."

15   DOS PASSOS, JOHN. The Best Times: An Informal Memoir. New
        York: New American Library.
            Reminiscences of Hemingway in Europe, in the 1920's, and
        in Key West, in the 1930's.

16   DRAKE, R. "The Nada and the Glory," Christian Century, 83
        (14 Dec.), 1539-40.
            Review of Nathan Scott's Ernest Hemingway. Concurs with
        Scott's view of Hemingway as not overtly religious but
        still possessed of a "residual presence." Sees Scott's
        view of Catherine Barkley and Brett Ashley as less sympa-
        thetic; defends them as being, ultimately, morally
        responsible.

17   EBY, CECIL D. "The Real Robert Jordan," American Literature,
        38 (Nov.), 380-86.
            Thinks that the model for Jordan was Robert Merriman, a
        former University of California professor who was the
        highest-ranking American among the volunteers in Spain.
        Reprinted in Grebstein, pp. 43-49 (See 1971.A8).

1966

18   EVANS, ROBERT.   "Hemingway and the Pale Cast of Thought,"
          American Literature, 38 (May), 161-76.
              Evans considers Hemingway's "anti-intellectualism" to be
          "an act of calculated retrenchment, involving a deliberate
          refusal to admit the free play of the higher intellectual
          faculties." Finds Hemingway's world "boring and narrow,"
          "not quite man-sized."
              Reprinted in Waldhorn, pp. 112-126 (See 1973.A7).

19   FERRIS, JOHN.   "Hemingway Is the Star in His Own Tragedy,"
          Life, LX (15 April), 10.
              Sees Hotchner's Papa Hemingway to be "the fall of a
          giant."

20   FRENCH, WARREN.   "A Troubled World," in The Social Novel at the
          End of an Era.   Carbondale: Southern Illinois University
          Press, pp. 87-124.
              Concerned chiefly with For Whom the Bell Tolls, French
          traces Hemingway's attitudes during the 1930's from his
          short stories and various Esquire columns. Other refer-
          ences as well.

21   FRIEDMAN, ALAN.   The Turn of the Novel. New York: Oxford
          University Press, p. 30.
              Sees that Catherine's death in A Farewell to Arms is not
          a resolution but only an expansion of the mood of waste and
          disorder; in The Old Man and the Sea, also, "the openness
          is unrelieved."

22   GALLOWAY, DAVID D.   The Absurd Hero in American Fiction:
          Updike, Styron, Bellow, Salinger. Austin: University of
          Texas Press.
              Notes that Hemingway too was aware of the "absurd," but
          sees that later writers (here, Camus) are more interested
          in the consequences of the absurd vision than in the mani-
          festations of it. Revised edition, 1970.

23   GASTWIRTH, D. E.   "Can Life Have Meaning? A Study of The Sun
          Also Rises," Yale Literary Magazine, 134 (March), 36-41.
              Gastwirth sees The Sun Also Rises as existential, yet
          most critical judgments of the novel approach it from its
          morality--hence a contradiction. For Hemingway, "the
          only value system that has meaning is one that insists
          there are no value systems."

24   GIBSON, WALKER.   Tough, Sweet, and Stuffy. Bloomington:
          Indiana University Press, pp. 28-42.
              "Tough Talk: The Rhetoric of Frederic Henry." Gibson

1966

(GIBSON, WALKER)
> describes Henry as a "tough" talker, comparing the opening
> of A Farewell to Arms with that of Howells' A Modern
> Instance, and comparing diction, modifiers, repetitions,
> imagery, articles, and sentence structure.

25   GINGRICH, ARNOLD. "Scott, Ernest and Whoever," Esquire, 66
     (Dec.), 186-89, 322-25.
> Reminiscences of Hemingway and Fitzgerald from the 1920's
> on. Speaks especially of Hemingway's mistrust of Fitz-
> gerald's own writing. Considers the portrait of Fitzgerald
> in A Moveable Feast generally accurate.
> Reprinted in Esquire, 80 (Oct. 1973), 151-4ff.

26   GLASSNER, WILLIAM A. "A Farewell to Arms," Sewanee Review, 74
     (Spring), 453-69.
> Focuses on Frederic Henry as a noble pagan trying to live
> in a hostile (pagan) world, but in the course of the novel,
> finding a greater understanding and awareness of himself.
> The novel is not merely a story of love and war.

27   GLICKSBERG, CHARLES I. Modern Literature and the Death of God.
     The Hague: Martinus Nijhoff.
> Pp. 13-14: sees Jake Barnes' wish to feel religious as
> symptomatic of many modern writers, that "religious
> feeling" has been lost although it still lives in his
> consciousness. Pp. 44-45: ambivalence toward love as
> substitute for religion, as in A Farewell to Arms. P. 117:
> Hemingway, like so many other novelists, chose art instead
> of religion.

28   GOLDMAN, ALBERT. Review of Papa Hemingway. Vogue, 147 (May),
     146.
> Sees the book as a saddening account of Hemingway's
> inability to recognize his own shortcomings.

29   GOODWIN, K. L. The Influence of Ezra Pound. London: Oxford
     University Press.
> Considers Pound's relationship with Hemingway parallel
> to his earlier involvement with Eliot and Joyce.

30   GORDON, DAVID. "The Son and the Father: Patterns of Response
     to Conflict in Hemingway's Fiction," Literature and Psy-
     chology, 16: 122-38.
> Sees "moral masochism" in the pleasure which Hemingway's
> heroes find in their victimized states. Usually, "the
> hero's essential fear originated in childhood and concerns
> his relationship with his father," as seen in the spectrum
> of Hemingway's novels and stories.

1966

31   HAND, HARRY E. "Transducers and Hemingway's Heroes," <u>English Journal</u>, 55 (Oct.), 870-71.
     The "analogy of Hemingway's world, hero, and code as input, transducer and output does not explain every facet of the Hemingway hero. It does help, however, to explain the method of characterization and a style based on straightforward dialogue and simple description."

32   HARLOW, BENJAMIN C. "Some Archetypal Motifs in <u>The Old Man and the Sea</u>," <u>McNeese Review</u>, 17: 74-79.
     Sees the symbolism and allegory in <u>The Old Man and the Sea</u> to parallel the "death to rebirth archetype."

33   HART, JEFFREY. "The Two Faces of Hemingway," <u>National Review</u>, 18 (28 June), 632, 634.
     Review of <u>Papa Hemingway</u> as a "marvelously entertaining" and "deeply moving" book. Questions Hotchner's treatment of Hemingway's Catholicism and his suicide.

34   HATCH, ROBERT. "Hemingway Gossip," <u>Harper's</u>, 232 (June), 101-02.
     Says that <u>Papa Hemingway</u> adds only "gossip, not insight" to the Hemingway life. Hatch quotes Hemingway's anguish about the impossibility of any writer's "retiring."

35   HATTAM, EDWARD. "Hemingway's 'An Alpine Idyll,'" <u>MFS</u>, 12 (Summer), 261-65.
     If not based on an existing Tyrolean tall tale, the story seems reminiscent of the Alpine custom of macabre humor in connection with the dead.

36   HAYES, CURTIS W. "A Study in Prose Styles: Edward Gibbon and Ernest Hemingway," <u>Texas Studies in Literature and Language</u>, 7 (Winter), 371-86.
     In analyzing Edward Gibbons and Hemingway's prose styles using "a generative/transformational grammar," Hayes finds that Gibbon's style is "grand," "majestic," and "complex," whereas Hemingway's is "simple."
     Reprinted in <u>Statistics and Style</u>, edited by Lubomir Dolezel and Richard W. Baily, New York, American Elsevier, pp. 80-91.

37   HAYS, PETER L. "Hemingway and the Fisher King," <u>University Review</u>, 32 (Spring), 225-28.
     If Hemingway's "God Rest You Merry, Gentlemen" is not based on the fisher king archetype, it is certainly rooted in universals. Suggests that Hemingway knew Weston's <u>From Ritual to Romance</u>.

(HAYS, PETER L.)
Reprinted in The Limping Hero: Grotesques in Literature,
New York, New York University Press, 1971 (See 1971.B64);
and in Benson, pp. 222-27 (See 1975.A3).

38 HEMINGWAY, MARY. "My Husband, Ernest Hemingway," Look, 30
(6 Sept.), 62-68.
First public admission of the suicide, and other biographical details. Photos.
Reprinted in Fellici Oriana's The Egotists: Sixteen Sur-
prising Interviews, Chicago, Regnery/Reilly and Lee, 1968,
pp. 116-30.

39 _____. "Under Water; Down Under," Holiday, 40 (Sept.), 64-
65ff.
Largely travelogue with little social criticism thrown
in; little comment about Hemingway.

40 HICKS, GRANVILLE. "No Compromise with Life, SR, 49 (9 April),
29-30.
Review of Papa Hemingway and Young's Reconsideration.
Admires Young's book, but is skeptical about Hotchner's
anecdotes. "Both Hotchner's book and Young's give us a
better, fairer understanding of Hemingway the man than we
have previously had."

41 HOFFMAN, FREDERICK J. "Hemingway and Fitzgerald" in American
Literary Scholarship: An Annual, 1964, edited by James
Woodress. Durham, N. C.: Duke University Press, pp. 82-88.
Surveys criticism on both authors published during 1964.

42 HOTCHNER, A. E. "Papa Hemingway," The Sunday Times Magazine
(11 Sept.), pp. 8-13, 15-17, 19, 21.
Biographical highlights of Hotchner's relationship with
Hemingway.

43 HOVEY, RICHARD B. "A Farewell to Arms: Hemingway's Liebestod,"
University Review, 33 (Winter), 93-100.
The love affair in the novel is indicative of Hemingway's
"vision of life and a fresh awareness of the strengths and
limitations of his art" (See 1967.B20).

44 _____. "The Old Man and the Sea: A New Hemingway Hero,"
Discourse, 9 (Summer), 283-94.
Sees that Santiago is more broadly representative of the
human race, more likely a character than other of Hemingway's heroes.

1966

45 HOVEY, RICHARD B. "The Sun Also Rises: Hemingway's Inner
    Debate," Forum (Houston), 4 (Summer), 4-10.
        The question is whether or not love exists; sees that
    Brett is as incomplete as Jake, Romero idealized out of
    proportion, and Cohn less damned than Jake would wish.

46 HOWELL, JOHN M. "Hemingway and Fitzgerald in Sound and Fury,"
    Papers on Language and Literature, 2 (Summer), 234-42.
        Faulkner rejected Hemingway's "romantic despair and
    cynicism" and thus Howell thinks that this novel contains
    parodies of The Sun Also Rises and The Great Gatsby.

47 HYMAN, STANLEY EDGAR. Standards: A Chronicle of Books for
    Our Time. New York: Horizon Press.
        Pp. 28-32: "The Best of Hemingway," to be found in The
    Sun Also Rises, a chronicle of defeat and loss, and the
    short stories, "authentic masterpieces, small-scale but
    immortal." Pp. 209-13: "Ernest Hemingway with a Knife,"
    on A Moveable Feast, which he regrets, both for its malice
    and its inept writing.

48 KAPLAN, HAROLD. "Hemingway and the Passive Hero," in The
    Passive Voice: An Approach to Modern Fiction. Athens:
    Ohio University Press, pp. 93-110.
        Sees Hemingway as recording "a favorite myth of our time,"
    that of the wounded hero. But for Hemingway, while experi-
    ence is painful, it also is initiatory--and sometimes re-
    demptive. Kaplan sees the "passive" reaction of the Hem-
    ingway protagonists as similar to that of more contemporary
    absurd heroes and as such, hardly negative.

49 KRAMER, DALE. Chicago Renaissance, The Literary Life in the
    Midwest, 1900-1930. New York: Appleton-Century.
        Pp. 325-26: Hemingway's friendship with Anderson in
    Chicago, 1920-21; pp. 337-38: Hemingway reads manuscript
    of The Torrents of Spring to an unwilling Bernardine Szold
    ("'By God, THIS will show him up!'").

50 LANGFORD, RICHARD E. and WILLIAM E. TAYLOR, eds. The Twenties,
    Poetry and Prose: 20 Critical Essays. Deland, Fla.:
    Everett Edwards Press.
        Pp. 82-86: "Ernest Hemingway and the Rhetoric of
    Escape" by Robert O. Stephens ties Hemingway's language to
    his pervasive theme of escape.
        Pp. 87-91: "Implications of Form in The Sun Also Rises,"
    by William L. Vance. Sees the structure of the novel com-
    bining both naturalistic (episodic) and Aristotelian (cir-
    cular) elements; and thus achieving the mood of "essential

(LANGFORD, RICHARD E. and WILLIAM E. TAYLOR)
fragmenting skepticism" appropriate to Hemingway in the
1920's.
Pp. 92-94: "Hemingway as Moral Thinker: A Look at Two
Novels" by Paul Ramsey, claims that The Sun Also Rises and
For Whom the Bell Tolls exemplify the Hemingway philosophy,
that one adopts the attitudes of stoicism and radical indi-
vidualism in the hope of finding "friendship, dignity, and
tender sexual love."
Pp. 95-98: "Faulkner, Hemingway, and the 1920's" by
William Van O'Connor studies the reciprocal interest between the two men, their admiration and jealousy for each
other.

51   LEWIS, ROBERT W. "Vivienne de Watteville, Hemingway's Com-
        panion on Kilimanjaro," Texas Quarterly, 9 (Winter), 75-85.
        In the manuscript of the story, a quotation from de
     Watteville's 1935 Speak to the Earth (the account of her
     African safari) follows the epigraph, but is then cancelled
     out.
     Reprinted in Howell, pp. 101-09 (See 1969.A9).

52   LEWIS, ROBERT W., JR. and MAX WESTBROOK. "The Texas Manuscript
        of 'The Snows of Kilimanjaro,'" Texas Quarterly, 9 (Winter),
        66-101.
        Three-part study: both authors discuss the nature and
     significance of the manuscript; Lewis then explains the
     influence upon Hemingway of the writings of de Watteville;
     Westbrook then explains how the manuscript suggests a new
     interpretation of the imaginative flight at the end of the
     story.

53   LISCA, PETER. "The Structure of Hemingway's Across the River
        and Into the Trees," MFS, 12 (Summer), 232-50.
        Understanding the fictional strategy makes this novel
     one of Hemingway's best. Lisca stresses that the third-
     person is really first, that the novel is connected through
     imagery, and that Renata as character serves many functions.
     He considers Across the River and Into the Trees a kind of
     modern Divine Comedy.
     Reprinted in Wagner, pp. 288-306 (See 1974.A3).

54   LUPAN, RADU. "The Old Man and the World: Some Final Thoughts
        on Ernest Hemingway," Literary Review, 10 (Winter), 159-65.
        Hemingway's attempts to become a great writer did not win
     him that honor: "his legend established him as such--but
     not his works."

1966

55   MORAVIA, ALBERTO. "The Ghost of Hemingway," Atlas, 11 (June), 337-40.

        Translated in Corriere Della Sera. Creates the ghost of Hemingway through visits to his Cuban home; focuses on the Spanish Civil War years, and on the tension between social activism and aesthetic values in Hemingway.

56   MOSES, W. R. "Victory in Defeat: 'Ad Astra' and A Farewell to Arms," Mississippi Quarterly, 19 (Spring), 85-89.

        Parallels between Faulkner's short story and the Hemingway novel suggest more than the "family resemblance between war stories."

57   MUGGRIDGE, MALCOLM. "Books," Esquire, 65 (June), 34, 36.

        Review of Papa Hemingway. Sees Hotchner's book as "authentic impressions of Hemingway by someone who saw a lot of him and knew him well, in his decline as in his prime." Sees Hotchner as "a somewhat commonplace writer himself."

58   MUSTE, JOHN M. Say That We Saw Spain Die. Seattle: University of Washington Press.

        Many references to Hemingway's involvement, both politically and literarily, in the Spanish Civil War.

59   SHEED, WILFRED. "Hemingway Si, Papa No," Commonweal, 84 (13 May), 221-23.

        Defends Hotchner's "sycophancy" because being friends with Hemingway involved such a posture: "Hemingway expected his friends to be as compliant as his heroines."

60   SHULMAN, ROBERT. "Myth, Mr. Eliot, and the Comic Novel," MFS, 12 (Winter), 395-403.

        Contends that The Waste Land served as "a target and a point of departure for such . . . novels . . . as The Sun Also Rises."

61   STAVROU, CONSTANTINE. "Nada, Religion, and Hemingway," Topic: A Journal of the Liberal Arts, 12 (Fall), 5-20.

        Sees no religious feeling at all in Hemingway's work. Even what he terms "nostalgia," was kept from being turned into belief because of "life's painful and unpleasant realities."

62   STEPHENS, ROSEMARY. "'In Another Country': Three as Symbol," University of Mississippi Studies in English, 7: 77-83.

        Traces Hemingway's use of three as symbol in the story.

63 STEVENS, WALLACE. Letters of Wallace Stevens, edited by Holly
    Stevens. New York: Alfred A. Knopf, pp. 411-12.
        Letter to Henry Church, July 2, 1942: "obviously he
    [Hemingway] is a poet and I should say, offhand, the most
    significant of living poets, so far as the subject of
    EXTRAORDINARY ACTUALITY is concerned."

64 STONE, EDWARD. Voices of Despair: Four Motifs in American
    Literature. Athens: Ohio University Press.
        Many references, since Stone sees Hemingway as creating
    a kind of affirmation in the reticence and actual silences
    of his personae, despite the more apparent despair that
    permeates his work.

65 STRANDBERG, VICTOR H. "A Palm for Pamela: Three Studies in
    the Game of Love," Western Humanities Review, 20 (Winter),
    37-47.
        Traces the theme of the game of love through A Farewell
    to Arms, Kalidasa's Shakuntala, and Shakespeare's Romeo
    and Juliet.

66 STUCKEY, W. J. The Pulitzer Prize Novels: A Critical Backward
    Look. Norman: University of Oklahoma Press.
        Discussion of the prize Hemingway did receive (for The
    Old Man and the Sea) and the one he did not (for For Whom
    the Bell Tolls).

67 SWANN GALLERIES, INC. Hemingway in Depth: A Remarkably Com-
    plete Collection. New York: Swann Galleries, Oct. 6,
    1966, Auction catalogue, pp. 1-17.
        See "Record Prices for Hemingway," Antiquarian Bookman,
    38 (24 Oct. 1966), 1603.

68 SYLVESTER, BICKFORD. "Hemingway's Extended Vision: The Old
    Man and the Sea," PMLA, 81 (March), 130-38.
        Sees that the novel presents "a coherent metaphysical
    scheme--of a philosophical naturalism which, although
    largely mechanistic in principle, embraces the realm of
    human affairs and gives transcendent meaning to the harsh
    inevitabilities Hemingway has always insisted upon re-
    cording."
    Reprinted in Jobes, pp. 80-96 (See 1968.A9).

69 _____. "'They Went Through this Fiction Every Day': Informed
    Illusion in The Old Man and the Sea," MFS, 12 (Winter),
    473-77.
        Sees that in the novel, Hemingway's view of the world

1966

(SYLVESTER, BICKFORD)
has not "gone soft," and uses as evidence the structural
parallel between the opening dialogue and closing, the relationship between Manolin and Santiago.

70 TEBBEL, J. "Papa's Troubled Legacy," <u>SR</u>, 49 (9 April), 30-31,
91-92. Portrait.
Recounting of Mary Hemingway's lawsuit against Hotchner
because <u>Papa Hemingway</u> was so inaccurate, and she saw its
publication as a misuse of Hemingway's friendship. The
court, however, found otherwise.

71 WALCUTT, CHARLES CHILD. "Hemingway's Naked Eyeballs," in
<u>Man's Changing Mask: Modes and Methods of Characterization
in Fiction</u>. Minneapolis: University of Minnesota Press,
pp. 305-14.
Sees that Hemingway's protagonists often serve as "naked
eyeballs," giving the reader seeming uncolored views of
events, allowing the reader therefore to participate fully
in the fictional process. The self dissolves "into pure
will . . . . The Hemingway hero is a lens moving around a
great circle into which he looks."

72 WASSERSTROM, WILLIAM. "Hemingway, the <u>Dial</u>, and Ernest Walsh,"
<u>South Atlantic Quarterly</u>, 65 (Spring), 171-77.
Sees Hemingway's revenge against Walsh (in <u>A Moveable
Feast</u>) characteristic, since "Hemingway bore a lifelong
grudge against anyone to whom he was indebted for cheer or
grief."

73 WEEKS, EDWARD. "Peripatetic Reviewer," <u>Atlantic</u>, 217 (May),
122-124.
Review of <u>Papa Hemingway</u>. Emphasizes Hemingway's
thorough enjoyment of life, no matter what he was doing.

74 WESTBROOK, MAX. <u>The Modern American Novel: Essays in Criti-
cism</u>. New York: Random House.
Defends Hemingway's "vision" as profound because it is
presented symbolically. His use of sport imagery creates
allegory for purposes a more realistic writer might employ
factual political and sociological details.

75 WHITE, WILLIAM. "For Hemingway Buffs," <u>ABC</u>, 16 (May), 27-28.
Brief annotation for 1965 critical articles on Hemingway.

76 _____. "Hemingway as Reporter: An Unknown News Story,"
<u>Journalism Quarterly</u>, 43 (Autumn), 538-42.
The unsigned news story from the Toronto <u>Daily Star</u>,

(WHITE, WILLIAM)
Sept. 25, 1923, reports an interview of survivors of the
Yokohama earthquake.

77 _____. "Hemingway Hunting in Scandanavia," ABC, 16 (Jan.),
22-24.
Recounts his collecting books (translations of Hemingway) in Oslo, Stockholm, and Copenhagen.

78 _____. "Hemingway as Translator: Kiki's Grandmother," English
Language Notes, 4 (Dec.), 128-32.
Because Hemingway was dissatisfied with the translation
of Kiki's Memoirs, he translated Chapter 12 himself, published here.

79 _____. "'The Old Man and the Sea' as a German Textbook," The
Papers of the Bibliographical Society of America, 60
(Jan.-March), 89-90.
White has located an abridged text of the novel which is
used to teach English to German students, and annotated.
There are thirty-five cuts, principally dealing with base-
ball, fishing, etc. They come in the first half of the
novella.

80 WICKES, GEORGE. "Hemingway to His Boswell," New Republic, 154
(23 April), 24-27.
Review of Hotchner's Papa Hemingway, which "reads like
the script of a bad movie about The Decline and Fall of
the Wounded Gladiator." Strangely, Wickes feels it may
also be "an authentic account" of Hemingway's last thirteen
years.

81 YOUNG, PHILIP. "Hemingway and Me: A Rather Long Story,"
Kenyon Review, 28 (Jan.), 15-37.
Recounts the story of Hemingway's objections to his 1952
study, and their subsequent relationship.
Reprinted in Three Bags Full, Essays in American Fiction,
New York, Harcourt, Brace, 1972, pp. 3-29 (See 1972.B114).

82 _____. "On Disremembering Hemingway," Atlantic, 218 (August),
45-49.
Points out the fallacies and borrowings in Papa Hemingway; makes of the pretentious work a moral issue: Mr.
Hotchner "is going to have to live with this book for the
rest of his days, and not just on it."
Reprinted in Three Bags Full, Essays in American Fiction,
New York, Harcourt, Brace, 1972, pp. 55-67 as "I Disremem-
ber Papa" (See 1972.B114).

1967

1967 A BOOKS

1   BAKER, SHERIDAN. Ernest Hemingway: An Introduction and In-
         terpretation. New York: Holt, Rinehart & Winston.
         Sees that, because "we all respond to the romantic dream
         of embattled self," Hemingway will continue to be read,
         despite the limitations of his view and attitude. Chrono-
         logical study of all the fiction. Baker finds that by the
         last decade of his writing, Hemingway's "despair" had
         turned to "existential courage." He thinks that the best
         of the early works--"In Another Country," "Now I Lay Me,"
         and The Sun Also Rises, representative of "the early inner
         cry"--balance the three masterpieces of "undefeat," "Fifty
         Grand," "The Undefeated," and The Old Man and the Sea.

*2   BRUTTINI, ADRIANO. Nick Hemingway. Siena: Libreria Ticci.
         Cited in Fitzgerald/Hemingway Annual, 1972.

*3   EGRI, PETER. Hemingway. Budapest: Gondolat.
         Cited in Fitzgerald/Hemingway Annual, 1972.

4   HANNEMAN, AUDRE. Ernest Hemingway: A Comprehensive Bibliogra-
         phy. Princeton, N. J.: Princeton University Press.
         Including secondary materials as well as primary, this
         bibliography contains all versions and editions of Heming-
         way's books, his appearances in anthologies, his many con-
         tributions to newspapers and periodicals, the translations
         of his work, a selected list of the primary library holdings,
         secondary references in books and articles, and a complete
         index. Supplement published in 1975, same publisher
         (1975.A2).

1967 B SHORTER WRITINGS

1   ANON. "Hero as Celebrity," Time, 89 (19 May), 133-34, 136.
         In reviewing By-Line, finds that Hemingway's best re-
         porting occurred during the Spanish Civil War; later,
         Hemingway "became a parody of himself."

2   BAKER, CARLOS. "The Slopes of Kilimanjaro: A Biographical
         Perspective," Novel: A Forum on Fiction, 1 (Fall), 19-23.
         Adapted for American Heritage, 19 (Aug. 1968), 40-43,
         90-91. Baker thinks that the story combines "true stuff"
         and invention, and mirrors Thoreau's Walden in its atten-
         tion to natural detail and its reminiscent mode.
         Reprinted in Howell, pp. 55-59 (See 1969.A9).

3   BEATTY, JEROME, JR. "Hanging Up on Hemingway," Esquire, 67
         (Feb.), 116.

1967

(BEATTY, JEROME, JR.)
  A long conversation with Hemingway, which Beatty finally
  terminated out of desperation. Quotes Hemingway as saying,
  "My only concern is that my stories are straight and good."

4   BENSON, FREDERICK R. Writers in Arms. New York: New York
      University Press.
        Subtitled "The Literary Impact of the Spanish Civil War,"
      this book includes discussion of Malraux, Orwell, Regler,
      Koestler, and Hemingway (pp. 60-63, 123-29, 292-96, passim).

5   BRADFORD, M. E. "On the Importance of Discovering God:
      Faulkner and Hemingway's The Old Man and the Sea," Missis-
      sippi Quarterly, 20 (Summer), 158-62.
        Because Faulkner rarely commented on other people's
      fiction, his review of The Old Man and the Sea is impor-
      tant. Finds significant his pleasure in some Doctrine of
      Nature.

6   BROPHY, BRIGID, MICHAEL LEVEY, and CHARLES OSBORNE. Fifty
      Works of English and American Literature we could do with-
      out. London: Rapp & Carroll, pp. 149-50: "Ernest Heming-
      way: A Farewell to Arms."

7   BURGESS, ANTHONY. The Novel Now: A Guide to Contemporary
      Fiction. New York: W. W. Norton, pp. 30-31.
        Favors The Sun Also Rises and The Old Man and the Sea
      as the best examples of Hemingway's "action fiction," al-
      though his short stories show "the paring-down process at
      its best." The work holds its magic, however.

8   COOPERMAN, STANLEY. "Death and Cojones: Frederic Henry," in
      World War I and the American Novel. Baltimore: The Johns
      Hopkins Press, pp. 181-90.
        Reprinted from "Death and Cojones: Hemingway's A Farewell
      to Arms," South Atlantic Quarterly, 63 (Winter 1964).
      (See 1964.B8.)

9   COWLEY, MALCOLM. "Papa and the Parricides: An Assessment of
      the Reassessments of Ernest Hemingway," Esquire, 67 (June),
      100-01, 103, 160, 162.
        Defends Hemingway's work as being "so clearly permanent"
      that critical attacks seem meaningless. "American litera-
      ture . . . is vastly richer now than it was when Hemingway
      started writing, but it is not yet so rich that it can af-
      ford to disown and devalue one of its lasting treasures."

1967

10   COWLEY, MALCOLM. "The Twenties in Montparnasse," SR, 50
      (11 March), 51-55, 98-101.
         Describes Paris as the young writers, including Heming-
      way, knew it in the early 1920's.

11   CRANE, R. S. The Idea of the Humanities and Other Essays
      Critical and Historical. Chicago: University of Chicago
      Press.
         Pp. 303-14: "Ernest Hemingway: The Killers." Pp. 316-
      17: comments on "The Short Happy Life of Francis Macomber."

12   DUSSINGER, GLORIA R. "'The Snows of Kilimanjaro': Harry's
      Second Chance," Studies in Short Fiction, 5 (Fall), 54-59.
         Finds that Hemingway developed Harry's value through the
      narrative structure, and then tests that value through the
      death-dream. Sees the story as affirmative.
      Reprinted in Howell, pp. 158-61.

13   FINKELSTEIN, I. "Sovetskaja kritika o Xeminguee," Voprosy
      literatury, 11 (Aug.), 174-90.
         Thanks to I. Kaskin, Hemingway is honored in Russia, al-
      though his pessimism is overrated by some critics.

14   FRENCH, WARREN, ed. The Thirties: Fiction, Poetry, Drama.
      Deland, Fla.: Everett Edwards, Inc., pp. 21-30.
         "Hemingway's Dark and Bloody Capital" by Sheldon N.
      Grebstein. Finds Hemingway's best writing during the
      1930's in the stories. Some parallels with James M. Cain
      are also mentioned.

15   GALLIGAN, EDWARD L. "Hemingway's Staying Power," Massachusetts
      Review, 8 (Summer), 431-39.
         The imitators of Hemingway have "made us forget how radi-
      cal and unconventional a writer he really was." Likes the
      books by Mailer, Bourjaily, and Algren because they are
      not mere criticism, but "deeply personal and metaphorical."

16   HEMINGWAY, MARY. "Hemingway's Spain," SR, 50 (11 March), 48-
      49, 102-04, 107. Photos.
         Stresses Hemingway's sensory pleasures in Spain--the
      smells of olive trees, cured leather, seas, forests, wild-
      flowers; the feel of rocks and suede; the sight of faces,
      blond grain, paintings; the taste of native dishes and
      wines.

17   HICKS, GRANVILLE. "The Novelist as Newspaperman," SR, 50
      (27 May), 23-24.

(HICKS, GRANVILLE)
Reviews <u>By-Line</u> and finds the columns and letters excellent. Hemingway's aim to write as well as possible existed in this material also.

18 HOFFMAN, FREDERICK J. "Hemingway and Fitzgerald" in <u>American Literary Scholarship: An Annual, 1965</u>, edited by James Woodress. Durham, N. C.: Duke University Press, pp. 90-103.
Surveys criticism of both authors published during 1965.

19 HOLLAND, ROBERT B. "Macomber and the Critics," <u>Studies in Short Fiction</u>, 5 (Winter), 171-78.
Although most critics of the story have concluded that Margot killed her husband, they overlook Hemingway's phrase that she "shot at the buffalo." That she is a bitch does not necessarily make her a murderer.
Reprinted in Howell, pp. 137-41 (<u>See</u> 1969.A9).

20 HOVEY, RICHARD B. "<u>A Farewell to Arms</u>: Hemingway's Liebestod II," <u>University Review</u>, 33 (Spring), 163-68.
Sees that Henry's black view of love is due to his limited and narcissistic experience (<u>See</u> 1966.B43).

21 HOWELL, JOHN M. "The Macomber Case," <u>Studies in Short Fiction</u>, 4 (Winter), 171-72.
A parallel to the story recounted in <u>Green Hills of Africa</u> suggests that Hemingway himself was the guilty party in the death of Macomber, through an objectified fantasy.

22 JOSEPHSON, MATTHEW. <u>Infidel in the Temple: A Memoir of the Nineteen-Thirties</u>. New York: Knopf, pp. 405-36.
"Hemingway Goes to Spain" plus other references to Josephson's visit to Key West during 1936-37.

23 KARSH, YOUSUF. <u>Karsh Portfolio</u>. London: Nelson, pp. 81-83. Photo.
The story behind the photos Karsh took of Hemingway in 1957.

24 KAUFFMANN, STANLEY. "Before and After Papa," <u>New Republic</u>, 156, No. 23 (10 June), 18, 35.
Review of <u>By-Line</u> which he finds useful for showing the development of Hemingway's eye and ear, and the sources for his fiction. Splits Hemingway's career at <u>The Sun Also Rises</u> (pre-famous and famous) and prefers the earlier writer.

1967

25 KIRSHNER, SUMNER. "From the Gulf Stream into the Main Stream: Siegfried Lenz and Hemingway," Research Studies (Washington State University), 35 (June), 141-47.
   Sees much of Lenz's early writing as "an attempt to cope with the influence of Hemingway and to develop his own style."

26 KOBLER, JASPER F. "Confused Chronology in The Sun Also Rises," MFS, 13 (Winter), 317-20.
   Decides that the days and dates are "totally confused" and for no purpose: "Hemingway simply did not go back and check his facts."

27 KORN, BARBARA. "Form and Idea in Hemingway's 'Big Two-Hearted River,'" English Journal, 56 (Oct.), 979-81.
   Finds the story particularly relevant to "the young person's struggle to reconcile himself to the world as it is."

28 KRUSE, HORST H. "Ernest Hemingway's 'The End of Something': Its Independence as a Short Story and Its Place in the 'Education of Nick Adams,'" Studies in Short Fiction, 4 (Winter), 152-66.
   Finds that interpreting this story in conjunction with other Hemingway stories distorts it, and the most powerful meaning results from reading it as a separate work. Reprinted in Benson, pp. 210-22 (See 1975.A3).

29 LANDIS, ARTHUR H. The Abraham Lincoln Brigade. New York: Citadel Press.
   Scattered references to Hemingway's participation in the 11th Brigade.

30 LANOUX, ARMAND. "Un homme nommé Hemingway," A la Page, No. 37 (July), pp. 1008-14.
   Hemingway wrote best about men in groups.

31 LOEB, HAROLD. "Hemingway's Bitterness," Connecticut Review, 1, No. 1, 7-24.
   Comments that often in his writing, Hemingway showed his tendency to "denigrate or travesty friends and others who had assisted him."
   Reprinted in Sarason, pp. 111-35 (See 1972.A8).

32 MAGEE, JOHN D. "Hemingway's 'Cat in the Rain,'" Explicator, 26 (Sept.), Item 8.
   The use of natural as opposed to artificial light symbolizes the wife's sterile existence.

33   MALOFF, SAUL. "Farewell to Arms," Newsweek, 69 (5 June), 102.
      Likes the materials in By-Line; thinks Hemingway's best
      writing occurred "where his heart was."

34   MAYNARD, REID. "The Decay Motif in 'The Snows of Kilimanjaro,'"
      Discourse, 10 (Autumn), 436-39.
      Finds the story "a parable of the predicament of the
      artist in a materialistic world," made clear by Hemingway's
      use of gangrene.

35   MEACHAM, HARRY M. The Caged Panther: Ezra Pound at Saint
      Elizabeth's. New York: Twayne.
      Hemingway's part in attempting to have Pound released
      from St. Elizabeth's is described.

36   [METHUEN]. Notes on Hemingway's The Old Man and the Sea.
      London: Methuen.
      Summary comments designed to help students pass tests on
      the novel. Includes questions and answers.

37   MIZENER, ARTHUR. Twelve Great American Novels. New York: The
      New American Library.
      "The Sun Also Rises, 1926" clarifies the notion that
      Jake Barnes, as well as Robert Cohn, was a romantic, but
      contends that Jake's values are superior because they are
      "earned," "actual," and based on experience, not on illu-
      sionary ideals.

38   POLI, BERNARD J. Ford Madox Ford and the Transatlantic Re-
      view. Syracuse, N. Y.: Syracuse University Press.
      Discusses Hemingway's connection with transatlantic re-
      view during the Paris years.

39   REARDON, JOHN. "Hemingway's Esthetic and Ethical Sportsmen,"
      University Review, 34 (Oct.), 13-23.
      Sees Hemingway's interest in sport and its rules as an
      image for his philosophical position: life as contest,
      with honesty, knowledge, and developing skill as paramount,
      a mature attitude instead of an adolescent one.
      Reprinted in Wagner, pp. 131-44 (See 1974.A3).

40   RUBIN, LOUIS D. The Teller in the Tale. Seattle: University
      of Washington Press.
      Attempts to locate the strength of Hemingway's first-
      person narration in The Sun Also Rises; sees that all kinds
      of writing--even landscape--contribute to the drama of the
      novel. Finds in Hemingway's later writing "a marked
      falling-off in fictional intensity."

1967

41 SANDERS, BARRY. "An Unresolvable Hemingway Enigma," <u>ABC</u>, 18,
    No. 1, 8-9.
        Sanders traces the title <u>A Moveable Feast</u> to a number of
    sources: a conversation with A. E. Hotchner, a letter,
    Camus' <u>The Stranger</u>, Howells' <u>A Modern Instance</u>, and a
    comment by Zelda Fitzgerald.

42 SCHNEIDER, DANIEL J. "The Symbolism of <u>The Sun Also Rises</u>,"
    <u>Discourse</u>, 13 (Summer), 334-42.
        At the end of <u>The Sun Also Rises</u>, Jake "moves toward in-
    creased self-control." Sees the novel as an antithesis
    between "undisciplined self-absorption and impurity and
    disciplined self-control and purity," represented by Cohn
    and Romero.

43 SCOVILLE, SAMUEL. "The Weltanschauung of Steinbeck and Heming-
    way: An Analysis of Themes," <u>English Journal</u>, 56 (Jan.),
    60-63.
        Compares the allegorical novels, <u>The Pearl</u> and <u>The Old
    Man and the Sea</u>, in that Santiago and Kino are related to
    the sea. Sees Kino's struggle as pathetic, Santiago's as
    noble.

44 STEINER, GEORGE. <u>Language and Silence</u>. New York: Atheneum,
    pp. 30-31.
        Sees Hemingway's reduction of language to be a parallel
    reduction of subject matter ("Imagine trying to translate
    the consciousness of Raskolnikov into the vocabulary of
    'The Killers'").

45 STEPHENS, ROBERT O. and JAMES ELLIS. "Hemingway, Fitzgerald,
    and the Riddle of 'Henry's Bicycle,'" <u>English Language
    Notes</u>, 5 (Sept.), 46-49.
        The phrase from <u>The Sun Also Rises</u> is identified in a
    letter of Fitzgerald to Maxwell Perkins as an allusion to
    the legend that Henry James was rendered impotent by an
    injury (bicycle riding) which exempted him from service in
    the Civil War.

46 STEPHENS, ROBERT O. "Some Additions to the Hemingway Check-
    List," <u>ABC</u>, 17 (April), 9-10.
        Current bibliography.

47 STONE, EDWARD. "Some Questions about Hemingway's 'The Killers,'"
    <u>Studies in Short Fiction</u>, 5 (Fall), 12-17.
        Questions the abilities of Max and Al to so thoroughly
    understand Summit when they are city dwellers; but sees the
    story as successful, capable of standing alone rather than
    in the company of other Nick Adams stories.

48   TAMKE, ALEXANDER. "Jacob Barnes's 'Biblical Name': Central
     Irony in The Sun Also Rises," English Record, 18 (Dec.),
     2-7.
          Ironic use of the name Jacob, since Jacob of Genesis was
     "the very epitome of patriarchal fertility and biblical
     fullness of promise."

49   TARBOX, RAYMOND. "Blank Hallucinations in the Fiction of Poe
     and Hemingway," American Imago, 24 (Winter), 312-43.
          When certain Poe and Hemingway characters find themselves
     in situations of stress, they turn to sleep and half-sleep
     states (Otto Isakower, "half-sleep" and B. D. Lewin,
     "dream screen").

50   TOOLE, WILLIAM B., III. "Religion, Love and Nature in A Fare-
     well to Arms: The Dark Shape of Irony," CEA Critic, 29
     (May), 10-11.
          Sees that the religious allusions in A Farewell to Arms
     illuminate the philosophical significance of the relation-
     ship between Catherine and Frederic, who feel that they
     live in a world "fundamentally malevolent."

51   TURNBULL, ANDREW. "Perkin's Three Generals," New York Times
     Book Review (16 July), p. 2ff.
          Comparison of the careers of Fitzgerald, Hemingway, and
     Thomas Wolfe with regard to Perkins' role, and to their
     attitudes toward one another.

52   _____. Thomas Wolfe. New York: Charles Scribner's Sons,
     pp. 133-34, 137-38, 192-94.
          On Perkins' relationship with Hemingway, of the three
     authors, Turnbull says that Hemingway "needed" Perkins the
     least.

53   WALZ, LAWRENCE A. "Hemingway's 'The Killers,'" Explicator, 25
     (Jan.), Item 38.
          Sees motif of confused sexuality as part of theme. Main
     thrust of story is that the world is not what it seems.
     Examples of mixed sex: George as Nick's boyfriend (to
     Max); Max and Sam being described as "girlfriends in the
     convent"; George would "make some girl a nice wife"; the
     image of Al with a shotgun hidden under his coat (pregnancy).

54   WEEKS, EDWARD. "'Captain' Hemingway," Atlantic, 220 (July),
     109-10.
          Review of By-Line, with reference to the fact that in
     1944, French partisans gave Hemingway the honorific title
     of "Captain."

1967

55   WERTHEIM, STANLEY. "The Conclusion of Hemingway's The Sun Also
        Rises," Literature and Psychology, 17, No. 1.
           Although Hemingway frequently makes use of extended ob-
        jects as phallic symbols, the policeman's baton in The Sun
        Also Rises is one case where the symbolism achieves "a
        mood of ironic poignancy."

56   WHITE, RAY LEWIS. "Hemingway's Private Explanation of The
        Torrents of Spring," MFS, 13 (Summer), 261-63.
           Works from five letters of Hemingway to Anderson, in
        which he explains his parody of Dark Laughter. Though
        apologetic, Hemingway "refused to conceal his distaste for
        what he considered to be sloppy, sentimental writing and
        borrowed thinking."

57   WHITE, WILLIAM, ed. Introduction to By-Line: Ernest Hemingway.
        New York: Scribner's.
           Discusses Hemingway's use of the journalistic material in
        his fiction, and points to the fact that Hemingway, "no
        matter what he wrote or why he was writing, or for whom,
        was always the creative writer."

58   WHITE, WILLIAM. "Collected Hemingway: A Japanese Translation,"
        The Serif, 4, No. 1 (March), 30-32.
           Notes a Japanese edition (9 vol.) of Hemingway which he
        feels is the most complete Hemingway collection in any
        language.

59   _____. "Hemingway: He Parlayed Journalism into Literary
        Fame," Grossroots Editor, 8, No. 3 (May-June), 12-14, 27.
           Discusses Hemingway's use of journalism in his fiction.

60   _____. "More on Hemingway," ABC, 17, No. 8 (April), 10-11.
           Notation of bibliographic materials.

61   WIEGAND, WILLIAM. "The Non-Fiction Novel," New Mexico Quar-
        terly, 37 (Autumn), 243-57.
           A comparison of Truman Capote's In Cold Blood and Green
        Hills of Africa, to the detriment of the latter. Wiegand
        finds that Hemingway's journalistic techniques are less
        effective than Capote's use of fictional devices.

62   WITTKOWSKI, WOLFGANG. "Gekreuzigt im Ring," Deutsche Viertel-
        jahrsschrift, 41 (May), 258-82.
           Sees that Santiago's suffering and fighting are stylized
        on two models, that of the boxer in the ring and that of
        the crucified person.

63   WYATT, BRYANT N. "Huckleberry Finn and the Art of Ernest Hem-
        ingway," Mark Twain Journal, 13 (Summer), 1-8.
        Finds that many of Hemingway's techniques and interests
        return to Twain, even though his effects were unique and
        his position in literature undeniable.

1968 A BOOKS

1   ARNOLD, LLOYD R. High on the Wild with Hemingway. Caldwell,
        Idaho: The Caxton Printers, Ltd.
        A memoir, complete with photos, of Hemingway in his
        Ketchum, Idaho, days.

2   GURKO, LEO. Ernest Hemingway and the Pursuit of Heroism.
        New York: Crowell.
        Gurko studies the man (in a long biographical chapter),
        each of the major novels, the less important ones col-
        lectively, the non-fiction, and the short stories, uni-
        fying his discussions with the concept of "heroism." For
        Hemingway, the test of heroism is "the crisis situation,
        the breaking point . . . the outer limits of energy and
        tension" and this heroic behavior is "a reaction to the
        moral emptiness of the universe."

3   HOVEY, RICHARD B. Hemingway: The Inward Terrain. Seattle:
        University of Washington Press.
        Basically Freudian in his methodology, Hovey handles
        that device with restraint. One theme convincingly con-
        nects Eros and Thanatos in the major fiction.

4   JOOST, NICHOLAS. Ernest Hemingway and the Little Magazines:
        The Paris Years. Barre, Mass.: Barre Publishers.
        With careful and colorful detail, Joost outlines Heming-
        way's dealings with The Double-Dealer, transatlantic re-
        view, Little Review, This Quarter, transition, Poetry,
        The Dial, and Der Querschnitt.

5   RICHARDS, NORMAN. Ernest Hemingway. Chicago: Children's
        Press.
        Photos, drawings, and bibliography are included in this
        biography intended for children sixth grade and beyond.

6   STEPHENS, ROBERT O. Hemingway's Non-fiction: The Public
        Voice. Chapel Hill: University of North Carolina Press.
        In examining Hemingway's essays and journalism, Stephens
        creates for us the writer's "self-explaining, public
        voice." He analyzes the writing in regard to its ideas,

1968

to its revelation of Hemingway, its connection with the
fiction, and on its own artistic grounds. An appendix
includes a chronological listing of the non-fiction.

7   TAKIGAWA, MOTOO. Hemingwei Saiko: Reconsiderations of Heming-
     way. Tokyo: Nanundo.
        Survey of nearly all Hemingway's fiction with special
     attention to thematic patterns (much emphasis on death and
     violence as Hemingway uses them); Takigawa's concept of
     "unreal images" (personified by Jordan, Renata, and Santi-
     ago) is of some critical interest.

*8   JACOBBI, RUGGERO, ed. Ernest Hemingway: Premio Nobel per la
     letteratro 1964. Milan: Fabbri.
        Cited in Fitzgerald/Hemingway Annual, 1972.

9   JOBES, KATHARINE T., ed. Twentieth Century Interpretations of
     The Old Man and the Sea: A Collection of Critical Essays.
     Englewood Cliffs, N. J.: Prentice-Hall.
        Contents: pp. 1-17: Introduction by the editor.
        pp. 18-26: "The Old Man and the Sea: Vision/Revision"
     by Philip Young, from Ernest Hemingway: A Reconsideration,
     University Park, The Pennsylvania State University Press,
     1966, pp. 123-33, 274-75.
        pp. 27-33: "The Boy and the Lions" by Carlos Baker,
     from Hemingway: The Writer as Artist, Princeton, Prince-
     ton University Press, 1963, pp. 304-11.
        pp. 34-40: "Fakery in The Old Man and the Sea" by
     Robert P. Weeks, from College English, 24 (Dec. 1962),
     188-92.
        pp. 41-55: "New World, Old Myths" by Claire Rosenfield,
     previously unpublished. Sees The Old Man and the Sea as
     an example of the folk tale using "confrontation between
     the hero and a large indigenous animal he both fears and
     admires." Anthropological study of both Faulkner and Hem-
     ingway.
        pp. 56-63: "A Ritual of Transfiguration: The Old Man
     and the Sea" by Arvin R. Wells, from University Review,
     30 (Winter 1963), 95-101.
        pp. 64-71: "The Heroic Impulse in The Old Man and the
     Sea" by Leo Gurko, from English Journal, 44 (Oct. 1955),
     pp. 377-82.
        pp. 72-80: "The Old Man and the Sea: Hemingway's
     Tragic Vision of Man" by Clinton S. Burhans, Jr., from
     American Literature, 31 (Jan. 1960), 446-55.
        pp. 81-96: "Hemingway's Extended Vision: The Old Man
     and the Sea" by Bickford Sylvester, from PMLA, 81 (March
     1966), 130-38.

(JOBES, KATHARINE T.)
pp. 97-102: "The Old Man and the Sea and the American Dream" by Delmore Schwartz, from "The Fiction of Ernest Hemingway: Moral Historian of the American Dream," in Perspectives U. S. A., No. 13 (Autumn 1955), 82-88.
pp. 103-113: "View Points," excerpts as below. P. 103: Frederick I. Carpenter, from "'The American Myth': Paradise (To Be) Regained," PMLA, 74 (Dec. 1959), 606.
pp. 103-06: Earl Rovit from Ernest Hemingway, New York, Twayne, 1963.
pp. 106-08: Malcolm Cowley from "Hemingway's Novel Has the Rich Simplicity of a Classic," New York Herald Tribune Book Review, 29, No. 4 (7 Sept. 1952), 1, 17.
P. 108: Leslie Fiedler from An End to Innocence, Boston, Beacon Press, 1955, p. 194.
pp. 108-09: Nemi D'Agostino from "The Later Hemingway," Sewanee Review, 68 (Summer 1960), 482-93.
pp. 109-10: Robert Gorham Davis from "Hemingway's Tragic Fisherman," New York Times Book Review (7 Sept. 1952), pp. 1, 20.
pp. 110-12: Philip Rahv from "Hemingway in the 1950's" from Image and Idea, New York, New Directions, 1957, pp. 192-95.
p. 112: Philip Toynbee from "Hemingway," Encounter, 17, No. 4 (Oct. 1961), 86-88.
pp. 112-13: "Ernest Hemingway" from Paris Review Interview, No. 18 (Spring 1958), 61-89.
pp. 114-16: Chronology.

1968 B   SHORTER WRITINGS

1   ATKINS, ANSELM. "Ironic Action in 'After the Storm,'" Studies in Short Fiction, 5 (Winter), 189-92.
Illustrates Hemingway's understatement and also his "irony of action." In both the manner of telling and the structure, the ironic stance deepens the events and the emotion. Finds especially effective the dynamic ending which contrasts with the understatement elsewhere. Reprinted in Benson, pp. 227-30.

2   BAKER, CARLOS. "The Slopes of Kilimanjaro," American Heritage, 19 (August), 40-43, 90-91.
Reprinted with revisions from Novel, 1 (Fall 1967), 19-23 (See 1967.B2).

3   BEEBE, MAURICE and JOHN FEASTER. "Criticism of Ernest Hemingway: A Selected Checklist," MFS, 14, No. 3 (Autumn), 337-69.

1968

(BEEBE, MAURICE and JOHN FEASTER)
Parts I and II list general studies and comment on individual works respectively; supersedes the 1955 checklist.

4   BEVIS, R. W., M. A. J. SMITH, JR., and G. BROSE. "Leopard
Tracks in 'The Snows . . .'," <u>American Notes And Queries</u>,
6 (April), 115.
Speculates that Reusch's <u>Mt. Kilimanjaro and Its Ascent</u>,
1927, may have given Hemingway the information about the
dead leopard.

5   BRADBURY, MALCOLM. "Sad Voyage," <u>New Statesman</u>, 75 (22 March),
386-87.
Review of <u>The Fifth Column and the Four Stories of the
Spanish Civil War</u>, <u>By-Line</u>, and Young's <u>Reconsideration</u>.
After Hemingway's "personal style" became a "mythology,"
Hemingway tried to make himself a <u>guru</u> by imitating his
heroes.

6   BRUCCOLI, MATTHEW J. "Ernest Hemingway as Cub Reporter,"
<u>Esquire</u>, 70 (Dec.), 207, 265.
Reprints an unsigned front page story, "Battle of Raid
Squads," from <u>Kansas City Star</u>, Jan. 6, 1918; battle wit-
nessed by Hemingway.

7   BURHANS, CLINTON S., JR. "The Complex Unity of <u>In Our Time</u>,"
<u>MFS</u>, 14 (Autumn), 313-28.
Sees the order and the unity to give a thematic progression to the work, that Hemingway was moving toward a
positive affirmation by the final stories.
Reprinted in Benson, pp. 15-29 (<u>See</u> 1975.A3).

8   CANNELL, KATHLEEN. "Scenes with a Hero," <u>Connecticut Review</u>,
2, No. 1 (Oct.), 5-12.
Reminiscence about Hemingway--not at his chivalric best--
in the early Paris years.
Reprinted in Sarason, pp. 145-50 (<u>See</u> 1972.A8).

9   CECIL, L. MOFFITT. "The Color of <u>A Farewell to Arms</u>," <u>Research
Studies</u> (Washington State University), 36 (June), 168-73.
Sees colors as part of the juxtaposed image pattern;
"the predominant colors are, first, red and black, then
white, and finally gray."

10   COCHRAN, ROBERT W. "Circularity in <u>The Sun Also Rises</u>," <u>MFS</u>,
14 (Autumn), 297-305.
Sees <u>The Sun Also Rises</u> as not cynical, but rather the
voice of a worldly-wisdom which corrects a false, wordy
optimism but is not pessimistic.

11 CURRAN, RONALD T. "The Individual and the Military Institution
       in Hemingway's Novels and Colliers Dispatches," Revue des
       Langues Vivantes, 34: 26-39.
          Sees Hemingway caught in the dilemma of maintaining the
       importance of individualism but also realizing that, in the
       modern age, one might sometimes need to be committed to an
       institution as well.

12 DUSSINGER, GLORIA R. "Hemingway's 'The Snows of Kilimanjaro,'"
       Explicator, 26 (April), Item 67.
          The story contains "no evidence that Helen and Harry are
       married, and much evidence that they are not."

13 EARNEST, ERNEST P. Expatriates and Patriots: American
       Artists, Scholars, and Writers in Europe. Durham, N. C.:
       Duke University Press, pp. 255-60.
          Description of Hemingway's early Paris years. Sees their
       appeal for him, set against the restrictive American so-
       ciety, in his fiction and columns.

14 FARQUHAR, ROBIN H. "Dramatic Structure in the Novels of
       Ernest Hemingway," MFS, 14 (Autumn), 271-82.
          Examination of four novels in terms of the structure of
       tragic drama shows Hemingway to have been conscious of
       such forms.

15 FAULKNER, WILLIAM. Lion in the Garden, Interviews with William
       Faulkner, 1926-62, edited by James B. Meriwether and Michael
       Millgate. New York: Random House.
          Of the many references to Hemingway included, most are
       favorable. Faulkner's opinion is that "what he has done
       is very fine" (p. 107).

16 FIEDLER, LESLIE A. The Return of the Vanishing American. New
       York: Stein and Day, pp. 144-47.
          In this study of the fictional use of the American
       Indian, Fiedler points out that Hemingway wrote a great
       deal about Indians, sometimes quite directly (as the
       Michigan characters in his short stories); sometimes dis-
       guised "as European peasants in For Whom the Bell Tolls."
       His attitudes toward them, however, are often "banal," and
       nearly always "old-fashioned."

17 FREELAND, BAYNE. "Letter to the Editor of Studies in Short
       Fiction," Studies in Short Fiction, 5 (Spring), iii-v.
          Answers many of Stone's objections to "The Killers,"
       pointing out that Summit, Ill., is a Chicago suburb.

1968

18   FRENCH, WARREN and WALTER E. KIDD, eds. American Winners of
      the Nobel Literary Prize. Norman: University of Oklahoma
      Press, pp. 158-92.
         "Ernest Hemingway" by Ken Moritz. Stresses the irony of
      Hemingway's receiving the prize in 1954 because the two
      qualities that earned it for him--"the code and the style"
      --had existed since the 1924 In Our Time; Moritz does see
      the Hemingway hero as affirmative.

19   GANZEL, DEWEY. "Cabestro and Vaquilla: The Symbolic Structure
      of The Sun Also Rises," Sewanee Review, 76 (Winter), 26-48.
         Sees Jake Barnes as cabestro, steer, sexually passive,
      who keeps the bulls from danger; Brett Ashley as vaquilla,
      the mate of the fighting bull, used to train fighters, an
      object of desire and contention among the bulls. Ganzel
      sees both learning restraint, acquiring self-knowledge,
      and becoming able to endure.

20   GIFFORD, WILLIAM. "Ernest Hemingway: The Monsters and the
      Critics," MFS, 14 (Autumn), 255-70.
         Sees Hemingway as neither an "ordinary" novelist or a
      lyric poet, but rather a writer of "heroic narrative."
      His theme is, usually, "the struggle against fate" rather
      than social choices.

21   GILLESPIE, GERALD. "Hemingway and the Happy Few," Orbis
      Litterarum, 23: 287-99.
         Sees that Hemingway is most interested in the manifesta-
      tion of a "life force," whether it be shown by animals,
      fish, or men.

22   GOTXARDE, R. E., Z. M. GIL'DINA, and Z. P. DOROFEENA, eds.
      Problemy lingnistiki i zarubeznoj literatury. Riga:
      Zinatne, pp. 205-22.
         "Hemingway's New Epic Genre in His Spanish Novel" by
      R. E. Gotxarde. Account of the innovation in novel form
      and purpose achieved in For Whom the Bell Tolls.

23   GREEN, JAMES L. "Symbolic Sentences in 'Big Two-Hearted
      River,'" MFS, 14 (Autumn), 307-12.
         Finds the sentence rhythms within this story indicative
      of changes in the hero's psychological state.

*24   GRIFFIN, GERALD R. "Hemingway's Fictive Use of the Negro:
      'the curious quality of incompleteness,'" Hudson Review,
      1: 104-111.
         Cited in Benson, 1975.A3, p. 324.

25 HAGOOD, THOMAS NEAL. "Humor in Hemingway's Toronto Articles," McNeese Review, 19: 48-58.
    Concentrates on Hemingway's use of irony and understatement for comic effects.

26 HEMINGWAY, PATRICK. "My Papa, Papa," Playboy, 15 (Dec.), 197-98.
    Biographical reminiscence.

27 HOFFMAN, FREDERICK J. "Hemingway and Fitzgerald," American Literary Scholarship: An Annual, 1966, edited by James Woodress. Durham, N. C.: Duke University Press, 85-94.
    Surveys criticism of both authors published during 1966.

28 HOTCHNER, A. E. "I Remember 'Papa' Hemingway," Reader's Digest, 93 (Oct.), 148-53.
    Biographical profile, emphasizing Hemingway's urge to participate fully in all experience.

29 IRWIN, RICHARD. "Of War, Wounds, and Silly Machines: An Examination of Hemingway's 'In Another Country,'" The Serif, 5, No. 2 (June), 21-29.
    Considers in what way Hemingway is a naturalist because, even though his world is controlled by factors beyond individual will, it differs from that of authors like Dreiser and Zola. Thinks the difference is a matter of focus, with Hemingway treating the character's emotional response instead of the world's indifference.

30 JOOST, NICHOLAS. "Ernest Hemingway and The Dial," Neophilologus, 52 (April and July), 180-90, 304-13.
    A description of Hemingway's relationship to the poetry magazine which rejected some of his early work.

31 KERMODE, FRANK. "Hemingway's Last Novel," in Continuities. London: Routledge and Kegan Paul, pp. 161, 167.
    Sees A Moveable Feast as a work of fiction, perhaps Hemingway's "best book since the 1920's" because the prose is strong, suggestive with no attitudenizing. The book is about writing, about "heroic apprenticeship."

32 KOSKIMIES, RAFAEL. "Notes on Ernest Hemingway's For Whom the Bell Tolls," Orbis Litterarum, 23: 276-86.
    Focuses on Hemingway's portrait of the communist leader André Massart, Pilar's story of her lover Finito de Palencia, and the love story of Jordan and Maria.

1968

33   LEITER, LOUIS H. "Neutral Projections in Hemingway's 'On the
      Quai at Smyrna,'" Studies in Short Fiction, 5 (Summer),
      384-86.
         Sees the sketch as balanced between factually despairing
      details and the compassion in the acts of the participants
      and the narrator.

34   LIEDLOFF, HELMUT. "Two War Novels: A Critical Comparison,"
      Revue de Littérature Comparée, 42 (Sept.), 390-406.
         Sees that A Farewell to Arms is superior to Remarque's
      Im Westen nichts Neues, although both are fine novels.

35   McALMON, ROBERT and KAY BOYLE. Being Geniuses Together 1920-
      1930. Garden City, New York: Doubleday.
         In this double reminiscence, Hemingway is pictured as
      opportunistic and curt, aware at all times of the people
      and occasion that could provide him with literary
      "possibility."

36   MacLEISH, ARCHIBALD. "Ernest Hemingway," in A Continuing
      Journey. Boston: Houghton Mifflin, pp. 307-12.
      Reprinted from "His Mirror Was Danger," Life, 51 (14 July
      1961), 71-72 (See 1961.B40).

37   MADDEN, CHARLES F., ed. Talks with Authors. Carbondale:
      Southern Illinois University Press, pp. 73-88.
         "Carlos Baker on Ernest Hemingway." Baker makes inter-
      esting points about Hemingway's practices of writing and
      his concepts of characterization, stressing that Hemingway
      would never "expound at length on the motivation."

38   MADDEN, DAVID, ed. Tough Guy Writers of the Thirties. Carbon-
      dale: Southern Illinois University Press.
         Pp. 18-41: "The Tough Hemingway and His Hard-Boiled
      Children" by Sheldon N. Grebstein. Sees Hemingway's mode
      and characters as a transition between formal fiction and
      the tough-guy novels of the 1930's (especially in To Have
      and Have Not and the short stories). Grebstein attributes
      this influence to Hemingway's use of violence, his portrayal
      of cosmic indifference, and characters who are physically
      brave, susceptible to emotion (despite stoic poses), and
      willing to meet death. Stylistically, Hemingway's "tough
      style" depends on short and simple sentences, repetition
      and parallelism, and a purged diction. Pp. 42-50: "Focus
      on To Have and Have Not: To Have Not: Tough Luck" by
      Philip Young. Cites Hemingway's "The Killers" and To Have
      and Have Not as an influence on the "Hard-Boiled School of
      Fiction." Young primarily analyzes the latter's weaknesses--
      in terms of structure and character.

39   MAHONY, PATRICK J.   "Hemingway's 'A Day's Wait,'" <u>Explicator</u>,
        27 (Nov.), Item 18.
            The two-paragraph hunting scene in the story "is a vital
        sub-plot and focus of ironic counterpoint and symbolic
        value."

40   MAINI, DARSHAN SINGH, ed.   <u>Variations on American Literature</u>.
        New Delhi: U. S. Educational Foundation in India.
            Pp. 76-85: "The World and Experience of the Hemingway
        Hero" by S. P. Das.
            Pp. 89-92: "<u>The Old Man and the Sea</u>: A Reading" by
        Jai S. Gahlot.
            Pp. 86-88: "The Style of Ernest Hemingway" by Vishaw M.
        Kapoor.

41   MARIN, DAVE.   "Seven Hours with Papa," <u>Southwest Review</u>, 53
        (Spring), 167-77.
            Basically reminiscence (Marin found Hemingway warm, sympa-
        thetic, ingenuous) with some comments about <u>A Farewell to
        Arms</u> and Hemingway's "rich spoken vernacular."

42   MORRIS, WRIGHT.   <u>The Territory Ahead: Critical Interpretations
        of American Literature</u>. New York: Harcourt, Brace,
        pp. 133-46.
            "The Function of Style." Sees Hemingway's style as a
        trap; the writer could not develop through it. Polished
        as it is, it is ultimately restrictive, to both craft and
        vision.

43   MUNSON, GORHAM.   "A Comedy of Exiles," <u>Literary Review</u>, 12
        (Fall), 41-75.
            Munson discusses <u>The Sun Also Rises</u> as roman à clef, and
        reminisces about <u>Secession</u>, dada, and the younger writers'
        interest in technique.

44   MURRAY, DONALD.   "Hong Kong Letter: Bombs, Books, and Heming-
        way," <u>ABC</u>, 18 (March), 16-21.
            Bibliographic comment.

45   NASH, JAY ROBERT.   "Ernest Hemingway, The Young Years & the
        Chicagoans Who Knew Him," <u>ChicagoLand</u>, 5 (August), 19-25.
            A detailed recollection of Hemingway during the World
        War I period.

46   NOBLE, DAVID W.   <u>The Eternal Adam and the New World Garden</u>:
        <u>The Central Myth in the American Novel Since 1830</u>. New
        York: George Braziller.
            Viewing literature from an historical perspective, Noble
        cites Hemingway (in a chapter titled "The Lost Generation")

1968

(NOBLE, DAVID W.)
as writing from the "sterile senility" of defeated
Puritanism. He feels that Hemingway's hero "is a simple
Deerslayer," robbed of innocence in the face of terror.

47 ORLOVA, RAISA. The Work of Ernest Hemingway. U.S.S.R.:
Novosibirsk.
Close reading of For Whom the Bell Tolls with emphasis
on Hemingway's mixture of "realistic prose" and "elevated
poetry." Orlova then relates For Whom the Bell Tolls to
all of Hemingway's earlier writing, seeing many similari-
ties.
Reprinted in Carl R. Proffer, Soviet Criticism of American
Literature in the Sixties: An Anthology, Ann Arbor, Mich.,
Ardis Publishers, 1972 (See 1972.B79).

*48 ORTIZ, SERGIO. "Your Friend, Ernest Hemingway," Los Angeles
Herald-Examiner California Living (1 Dec.), pp. 8, 10-11.
Cited in Hemingway Notes, II.

49 PATMORE, DEREK, ed. My Friends When Young: The Memoirs of
Brigit Patmore. London: Heinemann.
Recalls Hemingway as an "extremely sensitive man," "the
kindest and most loyal," "ever grateful to Ezra Pound for
his early encouragement."

50 ROSS, FRANK. "The Assailant-Victim in Three War-Protest
Novels," Paunch, No. 32 (August), pp. 46-57.
Compares Dos Passos' Three Soldiers, Mailer's The Naked
and the Dead, and A Farewell to Arms.

51 RYAN, WILLIAM JAMES. "Uses of Irony in To Have and Have Not,"
MFS, 14 (Autumn), 329-36.
Though rated one of Hemingway's poorer novels, To Have
and Have Not utilizes some interesting ironies.

52 ST. JOHN, DONALD. "Hemingway and the Girl Who Could Skate,"
Connecticut Review, 2: 10-19.
Recollections of Dorothy Connable from the winter of
1919-20.

53 _____. "Hemingway and Prudence," Connecticut Review, 5, No. 2
(April), 68-84.
Description of Hemingway's life in Petosky, Michigan;
also tracing the history of Prudence Boulton, the model
for the Indian girl in "Fathers and Sons" and "Ten
Indians."

54   _____. "Indian Camp Camp," <u>Carleton Miscellany</u>, 9 (Winter).
            St. John interviews Hemingway's sister Sunny (Mrs. E. J.
        Miller) at the family's summer home on Walloon Lake, Michi-
        gan.
        Reprinted in <u>Best Magazine Articles: 1968</u>, edited by
        Gerald Walker, New York, Crown Publishers, 1968, pp. 236-48.

55   _____. "Interview with Hemingway's 'Bill Gorton,'" <u>Connecticut</u>
            <u>Review</u>, 1, No. 2, 5-12 and 3, No. 1 (1969), 5-23.
            Conversation with Bill Smith (at 70) in which he dis-
        cusses not only the Paris years for Hemingway but also his
        writing habits, friendships, and locations for the fiction
        set in Michigan.
        Reprinted in Sarason, pp. 155-188 (<u>See</u> 1972.A8).

56   SCHNEIDER, DANIEL J. "Hemingway's <u>A Farewell to Arms</u>: The
            Novel as Pure Poetry," <u>MFS</u>, 14 (Autumn), 283-96.
            Places Hemingway's fiction in the lyric camp rather than
        the epic because incident, character, and style support
        one dominant mood or emotion. Close attention to the use
        of words and phrases in <u>A Farewell to Arms</u>.
        Reprinted in Graham, pp. 66-82 (<u>See</u> 1971.A7); and in
        Wagner, pp. 252-66 (<u>See</u> 1974.A3).

57   SCHORER, MARK. <u>The World We Imagine: Selected Essays</u>. New
            York: Farrar, Straus & Giroux, pp. 299-402.
            "Some Relationships: Gertrude Stein, Sherwood Anderson,
        F. Scott Fitzgerald, and Ernest Hemingway." Surveys the
        relationships (early and continuing) among the four
        writers; Hemingway's separation from Stein and Anderson,
        and later from Fitzgerald; and the disastrous effects of
        his isolation on his later writing and life.

58   SHARMA, D. R. "Ernest Hemingway: His Consciousness of Human
            Predicament," <u>Panjab University Research Bulletin (Arts)</u>,
            72, 14, pp. 1-30.
            Sees Hemingway's focus as the individual pitted against
        heavy odds. For Hemingway, the fundamental reality of
        human experience is infinite suffering. Sees self-
        knowledge through this suffering.

59   SLATTERY, SISTER MARGARET PATRICE. "Hemingway's <u>A Farewell</u>
            <u>to Arms</u>," <u>Explicator</u>, 27 (Oct.), Item 8.
            Locates the pattern of spatial motion in the novel as
        important both thematically and structurally.

60   SMITH, JULIAN. "'A Canary for One': Hemingway in the Waste-
            land," <u>Studies in Short Fiction</u>, 5 (Summer), 355-61.

1968

(SMITH, JULIAN)
Describes the ending of the story as "not so much a sur-
prise ending as a surprise meaning."
Reprinted in Benson, pp. 233-38 (See 1975.A3).

61 STEIN, MEYER L. Under Fire, The Story of American War Cor-
respondents. New York: Julian Messner, pp. 85-86, 142.
Hemingway as "special" reporter in Spanish Civil War and
during World War II.

62 TURNBULL, ANDREW. Thomas Wolfe. New York: Scribner's.
Scattered references to Hemingway in the discussions of
Maxwell Perkins and the contemporary scene.

63 VAN NOSTRAND, A. D. Everyman His Own Poet. New York: McGraw-
Hill, pp. 255-57.
Sees Death in the Afternoon as another piece of writing
which defies categorization.

64 WEEKS, LEWIS E., JR. "Mark Twain and Hemingway: 'A Catastrophe' and 'A Natural History of the Dead,'" Mark Twain
Journal, 14 (Summer), 15-17.
Comparison of the two in the perspective of the handling
of the grotesque.

65 WEINTRAUB, STANLEY. The Last Great Cause: The Intellectuals
and the Spanish Civil War. New York: Weybright and
Talley, pp. 179-220.
"Things Unsimple: 'Hemingstein' at War."

66 WEST, RAY B., JR. The Writer in the Room: Selected Essays.
East Lansing: Michigan State University Press.
Pp. 142-57: "Ernest Hemingway: The Failure of Sensi-
bility," reprinted from Sewanee Review, 53 (Winter 1945)
(See 1945.B12).
Pp. 158-74: "A Farewell to Arms," reprinted from The
Art of Modern Fiction, edited by West and Robert W. Stall-
man, New York, Rinehart, 1949 (See 1949.B20).
Pp. 185-204: "The American Short Story," reprinted from
The Short Story in America: 1900-1950, Chicago, Regnery,
1952 (See 1952.B74).

67 WHITE, WILLIAM. "Addenda to Hanneman: Hemingway's 'The Old
Man and the Sea,'" The Papers of the Bibliographical
Society of America, 62 (Oct.-Dec.), 613-14.
Lists a previously unrecorded abridged edition of The
Old Man and the Sea presently used as a textbook in
Holland.

68 _____. "Books About Hemingway Abroad," ABC (April), p. 23.
   Despite the great quantity of Hemingway materials translated into other languages, the level of criticism written
   in languages other than English is not high.

69 _____. "Ernest Hemingway: The Wild Years and By-Line," Bookman's Weekly and Antiquarian Bookman, 40 (4 Dec.), 1988.

70 _____. "Errors in By-Line: Ernest Hemingway," ABC, 18, No. 10
   (Summer), 24.
   Errata listing for White's book.

71 _____. "Hemingway's Spain," ABC, 19, No. 3 (Nov.), 22.
   Praises recent ABC-TV documentary concerning Hemingway's
   feeling for Spain. Also recommends J. Michener's Iberia,
   pp. 490-502, "Colloquies on Hemingway."

72 _____. "Notes on Hemingway, West, Tolkien and Wise," ABC, 18,
   No. 5-6 (Jan.-Feb.), 30-31.
   Lists recent paperback issues by and on Hemingway.

73 YAKOVLEV, EGOR. "Shazhite: po Kom Zvonil Kolokol" [Say, for
   Whom the Bell Tolled], Zhurnalist (Moscow), 1: 56-61.
   Makes use of conversations with General-Major Kh.
   Mamsurov about the Spanish Civil War.

74 YEVISH, IRVING A. "The Sun Also Exposes: Hemingway and Jake
   Barnes," Midwest Quarterly, 10 (Oct.), 89-97.
   Reads the novel as revealing that Hemingway, through
   Jake, must "remove himself from the society of the lost in
   order that he be reborn into a new society."

75 YOUNG, PHILIP. "Locked in the Vault with Hemingway," New York
   Times Book Review (29 Sept.).
   Speaks of the quantity of manuscript (16,000 pages, of
   which 3000 have never been published), the great care Mary
   Hemingway had given them, and the sometimes great distance
   between early drafts and finished writing.
   Reprinted in Rendezvous, 5, No. 2, pp. 1-5 (See 1970.B131);
   and Three Bags Full, Essays in American Fiction, New York,
   Harcourt, Brace, 1972, pp. 68-75 (See 1972.B114).

76 _____. "Scott Fitzgerald on His Thirtieth Birthday Sends a
   Small Gift to Ernest Hemingway," MFS, 14 (Summer), 229-30.
   A letter of Fitzgerald which parodies the interchapters
   from Hemingway's In Our Time.

77 YU, BEONGCHEON. "The Still Center of Hemingway's World,"
   Phoenix (Korea), 12 (Spring), 15-44.

1968

>   Depicts Hemingway as an artist with a controlling life
>   vision, whose actions and art stem from his stable philoso-
>   phy, of which the sport and contest imagery is a vivid
>   representation.
>   Reprinted in Wagner, pp. 109-31 (See 1974.A3).

1969 A BOOKS

1   BAKER, CARLOS. Ernest Hemingway: A Life Story. New York:
>   Scribner's.
>   The authorized biography, this book includes much new
>   material and excellent documentation. Baker refrains from
>   treating the fiction in much detail, explaining early that
>   this is not a critical biography, but in some ways his men-
>   tion of the stories and novels without adequate commentary
>   is frustrating and incomplete. Many photos.

2   BENSON, JACKSON J. Hemingway: The Writer's Art of Self
>   Defense. Minneapolis: University of Minnesota Press.
>   Focusing on Hemingway's pervasive use of irony, Benson
>   analyzes all the major fiction. Where possible, he also
>   accounts for humor and wit. The "self-defense" of the
>   title lies partly in Hemingway's own surety in his craft,
>   and partly in Benson's feeling that Hemingway's "tough-guy"
>   style was his defense against emotional and linguistic
>   bankruptcy.

3   PETERSON, RICHARD K. Hemingway: Direct and Oblique. The
>   Hague: Mouton.
>   Supplementing his comments on style with close readings
>   of the fiction, Peterson locates patterns of word usage,
>   symbols, and syntax. He concludes with a discussion of
>   the types of Hemingway "phonies" and "heroes."

4   SEWARD, WILLIAM. My Friend Ernest Hemingway. New York:
>   A. S. Barnes and Co.
>   Reminiscence of Seward's friendship with the author,
>   with more attention to Hemingway's writing than most
>   memoirs contain.

*5 SUKOSD, MIHALY. Hemingway vilaga. Budapest: Europa K.
>   Cited in Fitzgerald/Hemingway Annual, 1972.

6   WHITE, WILLIAM. Guide to Ernest Hemingway: An Essay (pam-
>   phlet). Columbus, Ohio: Charles E. Merrill Publishing Co.
>   Biographical and critical highlights of Hemingway's
>   career.

1969

7   WYLDER, DELBERT E. <u>Hemingway's Heroes</u>. Albuquerque, New
        Mexico: University of New Mexico Press.
        A study of the seven novels, including <u>The Torrents of</u>
    <u>Spring</u>, in which Wylder finds a parody of the sentimental
    hero. The anti-hero is created in Jake Barnes, Frederic
    Henry, and Harry Morgan; the mythic hero in Robert Jordan.
    Colonel Cantwell becomes a "tyrant hero" and Santiago,
    "the sinning hero as saint."

8   YOUNG, PHILIP and CHARLES MANN. <u>The Hemingway Manuscripts</u>:
        <u>An Inventory</u>. University Park: Pennsylvania State Uni-
    versity Press.
        An interim listing of all manuscripts and papers, Mrs.
    Hemingway's holdings, containing over 19,500 pages, of
    which more than 3000 pages are unpublished. The items
    number to 332.

9   HOWELL, JOHN M., ed. <u>Hemingway's African Stories: The</u>
        <u>Stories, Their Sources, Their Critics</u>. New York: Charles
    Scribner's Sons.
        Contents: pp. 1-2: Introduction by editor.
        pp. 55-59: "The Slopes of Kilimanjaro" by Carlos Baker,
    reprinted from <u>American Heritage</u>, 19 (Aug. 1968), 40-43,
    90-91.
        pp. 60-62: "Asia Minor" by Charles A. Fenton, reprinted
    from <u>The Apprenticeship of Ernest Hemingway</u>. New York:
    Farrar, Straus & Giroux, 1954, pp. 178-84.
        pp. 93-94: "Hemingway's Riddle of Kilimanjaro: Idea
    and Image" by Robert O. Stephens, reprinted from <u>American</u>
    <u>Literature</u>, 32 (March 1960), 84-87.
        pp. 101-09: "Vivienne de Watteville, Hemingway's Com-
    panion on Kilimanjaro" by Robert W. Lewis, Jr., reprinted
    from <u>Texas Quarterly</u>, 9 (Winter 1966), 75-85.
        pp. 113-15: "Dangerous Game" by Carlos Baker, reprinted
    from <u>Hemingway, The Writer as Artist</u>, Princeton University
    Press, 1963, pp. 186-91.
        pp. 116-18: "The Hero and the Code" by Philip Young,
    reprinted from <u>Ernest Hemingway: A Reconsideration</u>,
    University Park, Pennsylvania State University Press, 1966,
    pp. 69-74.
        pp. 119-128: "The Shorter Happy Life of Mrs. Macomber"
    by Warren Beck, reprinted from <u>MFS</u>, 1 (Nov. 1955), 28-37.
        pp. 129-136: "Ernest Hemingway: The Short Happy Life
    of Francis Macomber" by R. S. Crane, reprinted from <u>The</u>
    <u>Idea of the Humanities and Other Essays Critical and His-</u>
    <u>torical</u>, 2 vols., Chicago, The University of Chicago Press,
    1967, II, pp. 315-26.

1969

(HOWELL, JOHN M.)
    pp. 137-141: "Macomber and the Critics" by Robert B. Holland, reprinted from Studies in Short Fiction, 5 (Winter 1967), 171-78.
    pp. 142-144: "'The Snows of Kilimanjaro': Commentary" by Caroline Gordon and Allen Tate, reprinted from The House of Fiction, New York, Charles Scribner's Sons, 1950, pp. 419-23.
    pp. 145-149: "The Leopard and the Hyena: Symbol and Meaning in 'The Snows of Kilimanjaro,'" by Marion Montgomery, reprinted from University of Kansas City Review, 27 (June 1961), 277-82.
    pp. 150-157: "'The Snows of Kilimanjaro': A Revaluation" by Oliver Evans, reprinted from PMLA, 76 (Dec. 1961), 601-07.
    pp. 158-161: "'The Snows of Kilimanjaro': Harry's Second Chance," by Gloria R. Dussinger, reprinted from Studies in Short Fiction, 5 (Fall 1967), 54-59.

10   McCAFFERY, JOHN K. M., ed. Ernest Hemingway: The Man and His Work. New York: Cooper Square Publishers.
    Re-issued from 1950 edition (See 1950.A1).

11   WHITE, WILLIAM, ed. The Merrill Studies in The Sun Also Rises. Columbus, Ohio: Charles E. Merrill Publishers.
    Contents: pp. iii-iv: Preface by the editor.
    pp. 2-4: "Expatriates" by Conrad Aiken, reprinted from New York Herald Tribune Books (31 Oct. 1926), p. 4.
    pp. 5-8: "Readers and Writers" by Ernest Boyd, reprinted from Independent, 117 (20 Nov. 1926), 594.
    pp. 9-11: "Out of Little, Much" by Cleveland Chase, reprinted from SRL, 3 (11 Dec. 1926), 420-21.
    pp. 12-14: "Warfare in Man and among Men" by Laurence S. Morris, reprinted from New Republic, 48 (22 Dec. 1926), 142-43.
    pp. 15-16: "Fiction [Fiesta]" by Edwin Muir, reprinted from Nation & Athenaeum, 41 (2 July 1927), 450-452.
    pp. 17-19: "Hard-Boiled" by Allen Tate, reprinted from Nation, 123 (15 Dec. 1926), 642, 644.
    pp. 20-21: "Sad Young Man," reprinted from Time, 8 (1 Nov. 1926), 48.
    pp. 22-23: "Fiesta," reprinted from TLS (30 June 1927), p. 454.
    pp. 26-36: "The Way It Was" by Carlos Baker, from Hemingway: The Writer as Artist, Princeton University Press, 1963.
    pp. 37-52: "Jake Barnes and Spring Torrents" by Sheridan Baker, from Ernest Hemingway: An Introduction and Interpretation, New York, Holt, Rinehart & Winston, 1967.

(WHITE, WILLIAM)
pp. 53-57: "The Sun Also Rises" by James T. Farrell, reprinted from New York Times Book Review (1 Aug. 1943), pp. 6, 14.
pp. 58-72: "The Sun Also Rises: An Essay in Applied Principles" by Earl Rovit, reprinted from Ernest Hemingway, New York, Twayne, 1963.
pp. 73-85: "The Death of Love in The Sun Also Rises" by Mark Spilka, reprinted from Twelve Original Essays on Great American Novels, edited by Charles Shapiro, Detroit, Mich., Wayne State University Press, 1958, pp. 238-56.
pp. 86-90: "The Sun Also Rises: A Commentary" by Philip Young, reprinted from Ernest Hemingway, New York, Rinehart, 1952.
pp. 91-106: "Commencing with the Simplest Things" by Malcolm Cowley, reprinted from Three Novels of Ernest Hemingway, New York, Charles Scribner's Sons, 1962, pp. ix-xxviii.

1969 B SHORTER WRITINGS

1   ANON. "Ernest, Good and Bad," Time, 93 (18 April), 102-04. Photos.
Sees the Baker biography as good, and his approach—"a kind of uncompromised sympathy"—excellent for conveying both the charm and the torment.

2   AIKEN, WILLIAM. "Hemingway's 'Ten Indians,'" Explicator, 28 (Dec.), Item 31.
Previous critics identify Prudence Mitchell as the tenth Indian; Aiken feels the reference is to Nick. He is like the other Indians in that he too celebrates in town, is mocked by the Garners, and sleeps off his trip.

3   ANDERSON, SHERWOOD. Sherwood Anderson's Memoirs, A Critical Edition, edited by Ray Lewis White. Chapel Hill, N. C.: University of North Carolina Press.
Reminiscence about the young Hemingway, and Anderson's pride in his achievements.

*4   ANDREWS, LARRY. "'Big Two-Hearted River': The Essential Hemingway," Missouri English Bulletin, 25 (May), 1-7. Cited in Hemingway Notes, II.

5   BAKER, CARLOS. "Ernest Hemingway: Living, Loving, Dying," Atlantic Monthly, 223 (Jan.-Feb.), 45-67, 91-118. Excerpts from Ernest Hemingway: A Life Story (See 1969.A1).

1969

6   BAKER, CARLOS. "Taking the Beard Off Hemingway," <u>Book World</u>
        (<u>Chicago Tribune</u>) (16 March), pp. 1-6.
            Previously unpublished pictures of Hemingway from Baker's
        personal collection. None of these appear in the biography;
        captions by Baker.

7   _____. Review of <u>The Fifth Column and the Four Stories of the</u>
        <u>Spanish Civil War</u>, <u>SR</u>, 52 (20 Sept.), 36-37.
            Demonstrates "Hemingway's skill in developing metaphors
        from the circumstances of his narrative," "one of the hall-
        marks of his genius." Baker sees the play as poor because
        of its "superficial" heroine and poorly resolved dramatic
        conflict.

8   BARNES, CLIVE. "Late Notes on Camp plus Papa Hemingway,"
        <u>Holiday</u>, 45 (June), 8, 10-11.
            Nominates Hemingway as the great American literary figure,
        a reputation enhanced by Baker's biography. Thinks Heming-
        way's greatness lay partly in the fact that he understood
        pain and sorrow, and could re-create it as well.

9   BENSON, JACKSON J. "Literary Allusion and the Private Irony
        of Ernest Hemingway," <u>Pacific Coast Philology</u>, 4 (April),
        24-29.
            Sees that the young Hemingway was influenced--sometimes
        straightforwardly, sometimes ironically--by Laurence Sterne
        and Henry Fielding.

10 BRUCCOLI, MATTHEW J. "'The Light of the World': Stan Ketchel
        as 'My Sweet Christ,'" <u>Fitzgerald/Hemingway Annual</u>,
        pp. 125-30.
            Seeing Michigan middleweight boxer Stan Ketchel as the
        ironic Christ figure, Bruccoli reads the story with Alice
        as the sympathetic center, and the story as another initia-
        tion story, similar to "The Killers."

11 _____. "A Lost Book Review: <u>A Story-Teller's Story</u>," <u>Fitz-</u>
        <u>gerald/Hemingway Annual</u>, pp. 71-75.
            Reprinting of a review of Hemingway of the Anderson book,
        originally appearing in <u>Ex Libris</u>, March, 1925 with a com-
        panion note by Gertrude Stein.

12 CARLIN, STANLEY A. "Anselmo and Santiago: Two Old Men of the
        Sea," <u>ABC</u>, 19: 12-14.
            Comparisons between <u>For Whom the Bell Tolls</u> and <u>The Old</u>
        <u>Man and the Sea</u>.

13 CLARK, C. E. FRAZER, JR. "Hemingway at Auction: A Brief Sur-
        vey," Fitzgerald/Hemingway Annual, pp. 105-24.
        Clark traces the history of Three Stories and Ten Poems
    and in our time to show that prices of Hemingway books re-
    mained stable until the mid-1950's, when an in our time
    inscribed to Sylvia Beach (which had sold for $150 in
    1948), brought $2800. Auction record included.

14 CRANE, JOHN KENNY. "Crossing the Bar Twice: Post-Mortem
        Consciousness in Bierce, Hemingway, and Golding," Studies
        in Short Fiction, 6, No. 4 (Summer), 361-76.
        Views "The Snows of Kilimanjaro" in relation to Bierce's
    "An Occurrence at Owl Creek Bridge" and Golding's Pincher
    Martin, finding Golding's manipulation of post-mortem
    consciousness the most effective.

15 CUNARD, NANCY. These Were the Hours: Memories of My Hours
        Press, Reauville and Paris 1928-1931. Carbondale:
        Southern Illinois Press, pp. 127-28.
        When Ezra Pound was being discussed, Cunard mentions
    that Hemingway "never spoke more charmingly and gently."

16 D'AVANZO, MARIO L. "Hemingway's A Farewell to Arms, Chapter
        XXV," The Explicator, 27 (Jan.), Item 39.
        Sees Count Greffi as the image of what Frederic Henry
    can best hope to be: "old and fulfilled without being
    senile, stoic without despairing, wise without being
    cynical, skeptical without being nihilistic, simpatico
    and charitable without the gift of faith."

17 _____. "The Motif of Corruption in A Farewell to Arms," Lock
        Haven Review, 11: 57-62.
        Speaks of the variety of corruption--moral and physical--
    in evidence among the soldiers, civilians, politicians and
    even a priest in Italy. "This motif of corruption . . .
    helps to explain why Henry, who is a man of essential in-
    tegrity, can be justified in taking flight."

18 EGRI, PETER. "The Relationship Between the Short Story and
        the Novel, Realism and Naturalism in Hemingway's Art.
        Part I: 1923-1929," Hungarian Studies in English, L.
        Kossuth University, Debracen, 4: 105-26.
        Considers Hemingway's use of shifting narrative view-
    point, and other technical changes, as only relatively im-
    portant compared to the thematic changes in what Egri sees
    as Hemingway's changing periods. For example, Egri finds
    that after 1950, Hemingway is influenced by the defeat of
    Fascism, the ideological, political, and emotional chill

1969

(EGRI, PETER)
of a Cold War fraught with the danger of World War III,
and the imminence of death from illness and old age. Sees
The Old Man and the Sea as proof of Hemingway's importance
to world literature.

19   ELLMANN, RICHARD. "The Hemingway Circle," New Statesman
(15 Aug.), pp. 213-14.
In reviewing Baker's biography, Ellmann contends that
Hemingway was "a braggart but not a phony." His early
works "underplay his achievements" but in later writing
his prowess is more insistent. His weakness lies in his
language, "an idiom of proprietorship rather than compre-
hension."

20   FLORA, JOSEPH M. "Hemingway's 'Up in Michigan,'" Studies in
Short Fiction, 6, No. 4 (Summer), 465-66.
Locates the title phrase to be a brutal pun as well as
idiomatic Michigan usage, rather than a phrase from Irving
Berlin's "I Want to Go Back to Michigan."

21   FRENCH, WARREN, ed. The Forties: Fiction, Poetry, Drama.
Deland, Fla.: Everett/Edwards, Inc.
Sees Across the River and Into the Trees not as a war
novel but as a book "really about Hemingway and his
struggle with the critics" (sees The Old Man and the Sea
in somewhat the same perspective). For Whom the Bell Tolls
rises above the biographical identification.

22   GLICKSBERG, CHARLES I. The Ironic Vision in Modern Literature.
The Hague: Martinus Nijhoff.
Sees Hemingway's protagonists as ironic anti-heroes:
"If the idea of the 'nada' of existence in A Farewell to
Arms cannot be considered 'tragic,' it certainly underlines
the absurd plight of the anti-hero, who rebels in vain
against his fate of victimization."

23   GOLDEN, HERBERT H., ed. Studies in Honor of Samuel Montefiore
Waxman. Boston: Boston University Press, pp. 158-76.
"Gironella and Hemingway: Novelists of the Spanish
Civil War" by Robert L. Sheehan. Sees For Whom the Bell
Tolls as the climax of Hemingway's art because it creates
a political reality as well as a personal one.

24   GOLDMAN, ALBERT. "Hemingway: Papa as King Lear," Newsweek,
73 (21 April), 112, 114. Portraits.
Reviews Baker's biography as accurate but sad. Describes
Hemingway's failure as being that "Hemingway lost his

(GOLDMAN, ALBERT)
   capacity to discover new regions, to be surprised by fresh
   revelations, to suspend the irritable impulse toward self-
   assertion."

25   HART, JEFFREY. "Fitzgerald and Hemingway: The Difficult
     Friend," National Review, 21, No. 1 (14 Jan), 29-31.
        Discusses the writers' influence on one another: "Each
     was intensely aware of the other and aware not only of the
     other as a writer but as a mythic presence as well." Sees
     Fitzgerald in "Poor Julian" of Snows, and as the second
     most important character in A Moveable Feast; Hemingway,
     conversely, is Tommy in Tender Is the Night.

26   _____. "Hemingway: Sunlight and Night-Face," National Review,
     21 (22 April), 390-91.
        Review of Baker biography as "prodigious" in its research,
     but faults it for failing to present the fact that Heming-
     way "lived his life on the edge of a trauma."

27   HELLMAN, LILLIAN. An Unfinished Woman--A Memoir. Boston:
     Little, Brown.
        Pp. 67-73: accounts of Fitzgerald's later fear of
     Hemingway; pp. 102-04: in Madrid with the Hemingways
     during a shelling.

28   HICKS, GRANVILLE. "Hemingway: The Complexities That Animated
     the Man," SR, 52 (19 April), 31-33, 43.
        In reviewing the Baker biography, Hicks admires its ob-
     jectivity, Baker's ability to see a clay foot or two on
     the writer who was also "a hero." As Hicks emphasizes,
     whatever else Hemingway was, he was a disciplined and
     effective writer.

29   HILFER, ANTHONY C. The Revolt from the Village: 1915-1930.
     Chapel Hill, N. C.: University of North Carolina Press,
     p. 237.
        Mention of Hemingway's disappointment with Sherwood
     Anderson's novels in the later 1920's.

30   HILL, JOHN S. "To Have and Have Not: Hemingway's Hiatus,"
     Midwest Quarterly, 10 (Summer), 349-56.
        Considers the novel "unbearably dull" because of its
     chaotic structure, lack of theme, and poor character
     treatment.

31   HOAR, VICTOR. Morley Callaghan. Toronto: The Copp Clark
     Publishing Co., p. 15.

1969

(HOAR, VICTOR)
"Inevitably Callaghan's stylistic achievement is going
to be compared to Hemingway's." Hoar finds Callaghan's
prose "the homelier of the two, but that could be its
virtue."

32   HOFFMAN, FREDERICK J.   "Ernest Hemingway" in Fifteen Modern
American Authors, edited by Jackson Bryer. Durham, N. C.:
Duke University Press.
A comprehensive survey of criticism on Hemingway from
1924 to 1967--biographical, bibliographical, and interpre-
tive.
Reprinted with additions by Melvin J. Friedman in Sixteen
Modern American Authors, edited by Jackson Bryer. Durham,
N. C.: Duke University Press, 1974, pp. 367-416.

33   HOFFMAN, MICHAEL J.   "From Cohn to Herzog," Yale Review, 58
(March), 342-58.
Sees Herzog as Hemingway's Robert Cohn "in disguise
slipping in the back door." Contradicts the notion of
"code" in The Sun Also Rises; says the novel shows instead
the failure of the code. Describes Cohn's code as based
on enduring friendship and love, on intellectualism, and
on discussion. Both Cohn and Herzog are "naifs in the
American tradition of the radical innocent," with the dif-
ference that Bellow writes with some humor.

34   HOLLANDER, JOHN.   Review of Fifth Column and the Four Stories
of the Spanish Civil War, Harper's, 239 (Dec.), 146.
Finds the stories "long-winded" in a generally unfavorable
review.

35   HOWE, IRVING.   "The Wounds of All Generations," Harper's, 238
(May), 96-102.
Finds Baker's biography an account of Hemingway's
"prowess with rod and gun" and his travels, but thinks the
art of biography should provide more salient details. Pre-
fers the work of Philip Young and Edmund Wilson; wishes
Baker had spent more space on the best of Hemingway, The
Sun Also Rises, A Farewell to Arms, and the stories.

36   HUGHES, JOHN W.   "Age of the Emotive Man," New Leader, 52
(24 Nov.), 19-20.
Review of The Fifth Column and the Four Stories of the
Spanish Civil War. Sees Hemingway's achievement that he
fused "traditional forms with new and exotic areas of experience," but his limitation is that "he is unable to ex-
tend beyond the personal."

37   JOHNSTON, KENNETH G. "Counterpart: The Reflective Pattern in
         Hemingway's Humor," Kansas Quarterly, 1, No. 3, pp. 51-57.
           Points out that Hemingway used humorous chapters in A
         Farewell to Arms as contrast and subtle repetition of theme
         and effect, as in the barber episode (Chapter XIV), the
         racetrack scene (Chapter XX), and the collapsing umbrella
         episode (Chapter XXXVII).

38   KOPF, JOSEPHINE Z. "Meyer Wolfsheim and Robert Cohn: A Study
         of a Jewish Type and Stereotype," Tradition: A Journal of
         Orthodox Jewish Thought, 10: 93-104.
           For both Hemingway and Fitzgerald, and their culture,
         Jewishness carried the negative qualities of corruption
         and weakness; creating these stereotypes was thus an easy
         way of identifying ignoble characters.

39   LEBOWITZ, ALAN. "Hemingway in our Time," Yale Review, 58
         (Spring), 321-41.
           Finds that Hemingway's limited philosophical viewpoint
         determines his importance now only as a historical phe-
         nomenon: he presents a romantic and escapist answer to
         life's meaninglessness, and never moves beyond this out-
         moded view.

40   [LEVINE, DAVID]. Pens and Needles. Literary Caricatures by
         David Levine. Selected and Introduced by John Updike.
         Boston: Gambit, pp. 16-17.

41   LIGHT, JAMES F. "Between Legend and Man," Nation, 208 (26 May),
         671-74.
           Sees that the Baker biography presents the contrast be-
         tween the legend and the man. Approves Baker's treatment:
         he "recognizes all the giants in these legends, but he
         worships none."

42   LIGHT, MARTIN. "Of Wasteful Deaths: Hemingway's Stories
         About the Spanish War," Western Humanities Review, 23
         (Winter), 29-42.
           Sees these five seldom-studied stories as important
         records of several aspects of Hemingway's Spanish Civil
         War experience.
         Reprinted in Benson, pp. 64-77 (See 1975.A3).

43   LISCA, PETER. "Steinbeck and Hemingway: Suggestions for a
         Comparative Study," Steinbeck Newsletter, 2 (Spring),
         9-17.
           Comparative study of similarities and differences in
         themes, settings, characters, styles, points of view, and
         literary careers.

1969

44　LOEB, HAROLD. "Ernest Hemingway: A Life Story," <u>Southern</u>
　　<u>Review</u>, 5 (Summer), 1214–1225.
　　　　Thinks that the Baker treatment presents Hemingway as
　　"somewhat less pleasant than he actually was." Personal
　　reminiscence.

45　LONG, ROBERT EMMET. "Fitzgerald and Hemingway on Stage,"
　　<u>Fitzgerald/Hemingway Annual</u>, pp. 143–44.
　　　　Reviews the 1968 Trevor Reese play, <u>Before I Wake</u>, the
　　subject of which is "the warring friendship" of the two
　　writers. The two-character play draws heavily on letters
　　by Hemingway and Fitzgerald for its dialogue.

46　McCARTHY, PAUL. "Chapter Beginnings in <u>A Farewell to Arms</u>,"
　　<u>Ball State University Forum</u>, 10 (Spring), 21–30.
　　　　Sees these beginnings as extremely dense, serving to
　　"introduce characters, places and themes" and also clari-
　　fying and enriching irony and symbol "through many cross
　　references, contrasts, and repetitions."

47　McCORMICK, JOHN. "Sound of Hooves: Dedication of Bust,
　　Pamplona," <u>Sports Illustrated</u>, 31, No. 1 (7 July), 60–64,
　　69–71.
　　　　Dedication of bust to Hemingway and naming of street
　　("Paseo de Hemingway") provides vehicle for McCormick's
　　reminiscence about the San Fermin fiesta.

48　McNAMARA, EUGENE. Review of <u>The Fifth Column and the Four</u>
　　<u>Stories of The Spanish Civil War</u>, <u>America</u>, 121 (18 Oct.),
　　333.
　　　　Sees the play as "romantic melodrama," but finds it,
　　like the stories, revealing the Spanish people as "vic-
　　timized," "but rising above their natural limitations."

49　MARSDEN, MALCOLM M. "Hemingway's Symbolic Pattern: The Basis
　　of Tone," <u>Discourse</u>, 12: 16–28.
　　　　Marsden sees Hemingway using three kinds of patterns: in
　　early writing, his symbolism helps him create bitterness;
　　in the central work, his pattern suggests "the acceptance
　　of the inevitable"; and in the third period Hemingway tried
　　to "evoke a tone of awe and wonder."

50　MERIWETHER, JAMES B. "The Text of Ernest Hemingway" in <u>Bib-</u>
　　<u>liography and Textual Criticism: English and American</u>
　　<u>Literature, 1700 to the Present</u>, edited by O. M. Brack,
　　Jr. and Warner Barnes. Chicago: University of Chicago
　　Press, pp. 314–333.
　　　　Reprinted with revisions from <u>Papers of the Bibliographical</u>
　　<u>Society of America</u>, 57, 1963 (<u>See</u> 1963.B32).

1969

51   MOSS, ARTHUR H. "The Many Ways of Hemingway," Connecticut
         Review, 2 (Oct.), 14-16.
             Soon after In Our Time was published, Hemingway--pre-
         viously soft-spoken and diffident--began fitting the Hem-
         ingway legend.

52   _____. "More Ways of Hemingway," Connecticut Review, 3: 43-44.
             An addition to Moss's earlier memoirs.

53   MURPHY, GEORGE D. "Hemingway's The Sun Also Rises," Explicator,
         28 (Nov.), Item 23.
             The novel contains repeated references to water which
         create "a sustained and often ironic symbolism of ritual
         purification and emotional regeneration."

54   NAGLE, J. M. "View of Literature Too Often Neglected,"
         English Journal, 58 (March), 399-407.
             Opts for close textual reading, using the opening of The
         Old Man and the Sea as illustration.

55   NIN, ANAÏS. The Diary of Anaïs Nin, 1939-44, III, edited by
         Gunther Stuhlmann. New York: Harcourt, Brace and World,
         p. 69.
             On the unfavorable reviews of Hemingway's work by the
         Marxist critics.

*56   NOLAND, RICHARD W. "A New Look at Hemingway," Hartford Studies
         in Literature, 1, pp. 140-45.
             Cited in Fitzgerald/Hemingway Annual, 1972.

57   OAG, SHAY. In the Presence of Death: Antonio Ordonez. New
         York: Coward-McCann.
             Reminiscence of Hemingway's role as aficionado and re-
         corder of the art of bullfighting.

58   PAUL, KENNETH. "Vintage Hemingway," Newsweek, 74 (8 Sept.),
         88.
             Review of The Fifth Column and the Four Stories of the
         Spanish Civil War. Sees the play as an "unresolved period
         piece, talky and shallow."

59   PETRARCA, ANTHONY J. "Irony of Situation in Ernest Hemingway's
         'Soldier's Home,'" English Journal, 58, No. 5 (May), 664-67.
             Juxtaposes Krebs' past and present. Sees that the irony
         exists because he enlisted to preserve a way of life that
         he can no longer enjoy; he becomes homeless.

1969

60 PRESCOTT, PETER S. "Hemingway: The Whole Truth and Nothing
        But," Look, 33 (29 April), 6.
        Sees Hemingway as combining "bravado and vulnerability,"
        and there locates his appeal to young readers. Finds the
        biography "tasteful" and "extraordinary," but rather dull,
        dominated by the massive quantity of fact.

61 RAHV, PHILIP. Literature and the Sixth Sense. Boston:
        Houghton Mifflin, pp. 351-57.
        "Hemingway in the 1950's," reprinted from Commentary, 14
        (Oct. 1952). (See 1952.B62.)

62 RANDALL, DAVID A. Dukedom Large Enough. New York: Random
        House, pp. 235-41.
        "Hemingway and the Printed Word." Anecdotes about Hem-
        ingway in the publishing world, that he did not accept
        criticism gracefully.

63 REICHARD, DANIEL P. "None Are to be Found More Clever than
        Ernie," English Journal, 58, No. 5 (May), 668-72.
        Discusses Hemingway's high school experience in
        journalism.

64 RICHARDSON, ROBERT. Literature and Film. Bloomington:
        Indiana University Press.
        Uses the ordinariness of the film To Have and Have Not,
        prepared in part by Faulkner, to show that even the best
        material has not necessarily produced great movies. Also
        sees Hemingway's interest in point of view as contributing
        to that of film-makers'.

65 SALE, ROGER. Review of The Fifth Column and the Four Stories
        of the Spanish Civil War, Hudson Review, 22 (Winter), 709-
        10.
        Sees it as a "collection of scraps," written to make
        money.

66 SAMUELS, CHARLES THOMAS. "The Heresy of Self-Love," New
        Republic, 160 (26 April), 28-32.
        Sees the Baker biography as disappointing since, despite
        all the material at his command, Baker has not done more
        than assemble it.

67 SARASON, BERTRAM D. "Hemingway in Havana: Two Interviews,"
        Connecticut Review, 3 (Oct.), 24-31.
        With Dr. Armondo Chardiet, who considered Hemingway "an
        idealist," "always pursuing something," and with Robert

(SARASON, BERTRAM D.)
>T. E. Schuyler, who described Hemingway as "immensely
friendly and very strong and bear-like . . . not at all
self-conscious about himself or anything."

68 _____. "Lady Brett Ashley and Lady Duff Twysden," <u>Connecticut</u>
<u>Review</u>, 2 (April), 5-13.
>Sarason claims that Brett was modeled on Lady Duff, but
believes that Hemingway purposely made "gross distortions"
in his characterization.
Reprinted in Sarason, pp. 228-40 (<u>See</u> 1972.A8).

*69 SAROYAN, WILLIAM. "In All Earnestness," <u>Time</u>, 2 (May), 6.
Cited in <u>Hemingway Notes, II</u>.

70 SCHROTH, RAYMOND A. "Hemingway's Truth," <u>America</u>, 120, No. 18
(3 May), 534.
>Review of Baker's biography. Finds Hemingway hard to
respect because of the "sick cult of 'manly' violence that
Hemingway at his worst epitomized."

71 SHEPHERD, ALLEN. "Taking Apart 'Mr. and Mrs. Elliot,'"
<u>Markham Review</u>, 2, No. 1 (Sept.), 15-16.
>Comparison of edited version in 1925 <u>In Our Time</u> and
"original" version in 1938 <u>Short Stories</u>. Finds the
edited version an improvement.

72 SIMMONS, MICHAEL K. "A Look into <u>The Glass Mountain</u>," <u>American</u>
<u>Literature</u>, 41 (Nov.), 422-25.
>Discussion of Joseph Warren Beach's novel based on the
Hadley Richardson-Hemingway marriage and divorce.

73 SMITH, JULIAN. "Christ Times Four: Hemingway's Unknown
Spanish Civil War Stories," <u>Arizona Quarterly</u>, 25 (Spring),
5-17.
>These four stories are "worth studying as a major group
of related stories" because they illustrate Hemingway's
"fullest use of the Christian motifs of sacrifice and
communion, though without the promise of rebirth or
redemption."

74 SMITH, ROGER H. "Authors & Editors," <u>Publishers Weekly</u>, 195,
No. 13 (31 March), 15-17.
>Describes Baker's method of assembling Hemingway's
letters, interviewing, and collating all material over
the process of writing the biography.

1969

75   SPENDER, STEPHEN.   Review of The Fifth Column and the Four
          Stories of the Spanish Civil War, New York Review of Books,
          13 (25 Sept.), 3–8.
             Fits Hemingway's writing during the 1930's into an
          apolitical category; says that Hemingway wrote about war
          because that was his obsession.

76   STEINER, GEORGE.   "Across the River and Into the Trees," New
          Yorker, 45 (13 Sept.), 147–50, 155.
             Reviews Baker's biography unfavorably, criticizing it
          for its turgid banalities and failure to give us Hemingway
          as writer.

77   STONE, EDWARD.   A Certain Morbidness, A View of American Litera-
          ture. Carbondale: Southern Illinois University Press,
          pp. 161–63.
             Analysis of Henry's dream sequence in A Farewell to Arms,
          using Freudian terms.

78   STRANDBERG, VICTOR H.   "Eliot's Insomniacs," South Atlantic
          Quarterly," 68 (Winter), 67–73.
             According to Leslie Fiedler, Hemingway's insomniacs were
          "his greatest achievement." This achievement makes Heming-
          way's disdain for Eliot somewhat ironic, since Eliot had
          earlier used similar characters in his poetry.

79   TORCHIANA, DONALD T.   "The Sun Also Rises: A Reconsideration,"
          Fitzgerald/Hemingway Annual, pp. 77–103.
             A rebuttal of the view that The Sun Also Rises depicts a
          lost generation. Torchiana stresses Hemingway's dislike
          of Eliot, his affirmation of the earth, and his central
          role in the novel's relationships and dynamics.

80   UNRUE, JOHN.   "Hemingway and the New Masses," Fitzgerald/Hem-
          ingway Annual, pp. 131–34.
             Surveys Hemingway's varying position during the 1930's
          with the Marxist critics who wrote for New Masses.

81   VANDERBILT, KERMIT.   "The Sun Also Rises: Time Uncertain,"
          Twentieth Century Literature, 15 (Oct.), 153–54.
             Sees that the novel contains several structural errors
          based on "discrepancies both in calendar time and plot
          duration."

82   WALDMEIR, JOSEPH J.   American Novels of the Second World War.
          The Hague: Mouton.
             Sees Henry, like Dos Passos' John Andrews, rejecting
          all responsibility to a war-making society, and ironically
          prefiguring a decade in which affirmation replaced nada.

83 WEATHERBY, W. J. "Hemingway's Manuscripts," The Times Literary
       Supplement (7 Aug.), p. 883.
          Description of the remaining papers and manuscripts.
       See also TLS (14 Aug.), p. 906.

84 WELLS, ELIZABETH. "A Comparative Statistical Analysis of the
       Prose Styles of F. Scott Fitzgerald and Ernest Hemingway,"
       Fitzgerald/Hemingway Annual, pp. 47-67.
          Wells notes that Hemingway "was not a monolithic writer,"
       that his style changed from the short, clipped simple-
       sentence pattern of In Our Time to the much longer and more
       rhythmic expression of For Whom the Bell Tolls, "a pro-
       gression toward more complexity and variety in all matters
       except diction, which remained "the same monosyllabic,
       Anglo-Saxon cast." Many specifics are included in this
       valuable analysis.
          Reprinted in Benson, pp. 129-35, as revised (See 1975.A3).

85 WHITE, WILLIAM. "Frederic or Frederick Henry in A Farewell to
       Arms," ABC, 20, No. 2 (Oct.), 22.
          Notes critics' tendency to misspell names.

86 _____. "Hemingway and Fitzgerald" in American Literary
       Scholarship: An Annual, 1967, edited by James Woodress.
       Durham, N. C.: Duke University Press, pp. 96-112.
          Survey of criticism on both authors published during 1967.

87 WICKES, GEORGE. "Ernest Hemingway in Montparnasse," in
       Americans in Paris, 1909-1939. Garden City, New York:
       Doubleday, pp. 145-87.
          Wickes discusses the important Paris years for Hemingway
       (and Pound, Stein, Fitzgerald, cummings, and Dos Passos),
       tracing his relationships with people and the little maga-
       zines and presses.

88 WYCHERLY, H. ALAN. "Hemingway's 'The Sea Change,'" American
       Notes and Queries, 7 (Jan.), 67-68.
          Sees that the story's theme is lesbianism, and its hero
       is a loser "because he has to face a problem beyond his
       ability to cope with it."

89 YOKELSON, JOSEPH B. "A Dante-Parallel in Hemingway's 'A Way
       You'll Never Be,'" American Literature, 41 (May), 279-80.
          Describes the second lieutenant in the story as Charon.

90 YOUNG, PHILIP. Review of The Fifth Column and the Four Stories
       of the Spanish Civil War, New York Times Book Review
       (21 Sept.), p. 6.

1969

(YOUNG, PHILIP)
Sees Hemingway as the leading character of both the play and the stories; admires the stories, but finds the play a definite failure.

1970 A   BOOKS

*1   CARLUCCI, CARLO. Ernest Hemingway Dieci Anni Dopo. Cenobio, Switzerland: Casa Editrice Cenobio Lugano.
Cited in Fitzgerald/Hemingway Annual, 1972.

2   GELLENS, JAY, ed. Twentieth Century Interpretations of "A Farewell to Arms": A Collection of Critical Essays.
Englewood Cliffs, N. J.: Prentice-Hall.
Contents: pp. 1–14: Introduction by the editor.
pp. 15–27: "The Unadulterated Sensibility" by Ray B. West, Jr., reprinted from Sewanee Review, 55 (Winter 1945), pp. 120–35.
pp. 28–32: "Loser Take Nothing" (editor's title) by Philip Young, from Ernest Hemingway: A Reconsideration, University Park, Pennsylvania State University Press, 1966, pp. 89–95.
pp. 33–40: "Learning to Care" (editor's title) by Earl Rovit, from Ernest Hemingway, New York, Twayne, 1963, pp. 98–106.
pp. 41–53: "The Tough Romance" by Robert W. Lewis, Jr., from Hemingway on Love, Austin, University of Texas Press, 1964, pp. 39–54.
pp. 54–55: "Rain as Disaster" (editor's title) by Malcolm Cowley, from Introduction to the Portable Hemingway, New York, Viking Press, 1944, p. 16. This excerpt and the next two comprise what Gellens has titled "Symposium on Sensibility and/or Symbol in A Farewell to Arms."
pp. 55–56: "The Unreferable Rain" (editor's title) by Louis L. Martz, from "The Saint as Tragic Hero" by Martz in Tragic Themes in Western Literature, edited by Cleanth Brooks, New Haven, Yale University Press, 1955, pp. 153–54.
pp. 56–64: "The Mountain and the Plain" by Carlos Baker from Hemingway: The Writer as Artist, Princeton University Press, 1963, pp. 94–96, 101–08.
pp. 64–71: "Hemingway's Ambiguity: Symbolism and Irony" by E. M. Halliday, reprinted from American Literature, 27 (1956), 57–63.
pp. 72–90: "The 'Dumb Ox' in Love and War" by Wyndham Lewis, from Life and Letters, 10 (April 1932), 33–45.
pp. 91–102: "Ciphers at the Front," (editor's title) by D. S. Savage, reprinted from "The Realist Novel in the Thirties: Ernest Hemingway," Focus, 2 (1946), 7–27.

(GELLENS, JAY)
    pp. 103-05: "The Existential Hero" by John Killinger, from <u>Hemingway and the Dead Gods</u>, Lexington, University of Kentucky Press, 1960, pp. 46-48.
    pp. 105-07: "Small Hips, Not War" (editor's title) by Norman Friedman, from "Criticism and the Novel: Hardy, Hemingway, Crane, Woolf, Conrad," <u>Antioch Review</u>, 17 (1958), 352-55.
    pp. 108-11: "The Secret Wound" (editor's title) by Frederick J. Hoffman, from <u>The Twenties: American Writing in the Postwar Decade</u>, New York, Viking Press, 1955, pp. 67-72.
    pp. 111-12: "Love and Death" by Leslie Fiedler, from <u>Love and Death in the American Novel</u>, New York, Stein & Day, 1966, pp. 317-18.
    pp. 112-14: "Farewell the Separate Peace" by Edgar Johnson, from <u>Sewanee Review</u>, 48 (1940), 289-90.
    pp. 114-15: "The Human Will" (editor's title) by Maxwell Geismar, from <u>Writers in Crisis: The American Novel Between Two Wars</u>, Boston, Houghton Mifflin Co., 1942, pp. 46-47.
    pp. 116-18: Chronology
    pp. 119-20: Notes on contributors
    p. 121: Bibliography.

3   WHITE, WILLIAM, ed. <u>The Merrill Checklist of Ernest Hemingway</u>. Columbus, Ohio: Charles E. Merrill Publishing Co.
    Brief listing of primary and secondary Hemingway materials.

<u>1970 B SHORTER WRITINGS</u>

1   ANON. "Hemingway's Unstill Waters," <u>TLS</u> (16 Oct.), 1193-94.
    Finds <u>Islands in the Stream</u> "the most interesting Hemingway novel to appear since <u>For Whom the Bell Tolls</u>." The chief objection rests with Mrs. Hemingway and the publishers for not clarifying the textual policies used in editing the manuscript.

2   ADAMS, SAM. "The Sun Also Sets," <u>Sports Illustrated</u>, 32 (29 June), 56-60.
    Memoir of Cayetano Ordonez (the Pedro Romero of <u>The Sun Also Rises</u>) in 1955.
    Reprinted in Sarason, pp. 212-221 (<u>See</u> 1972.A8).

3   ALDRIDGE, JOHN W. "Hemingway Between Triumph and Disaster," <u>SR</u>, 53 (16 Oct.), 23-26, 39.
    Finds <u>Islands in the Stream</u> a sad novel because, in

1970

(ALDRIDGE, JOHN W.)
   writing it, Hemingway is ready to die ("he is tired to
   death of life"). According to Aldridge, nothing motivates
   these characters but a vague sense of duty; life has no
   meaning.
   Reprinted as "'Islands in the Stream'" in <u>The Devil in the
   Fire: Retrospective Essays on American Literature and
   Culture, 1951-1971</u>, New York, Harper's Magazine Press,
   1972, pp. 91-100 (<u>See</u> 1972.B4).

4   ANDERSON, PAUL V. "Nick's Story in Hemingway's 'Big Two-
    Hearted River,'" <u>Studies in Short Fiction</u>, 7 (Fall), 564-
    72.
       Sees Nick gradually gaining self-confidence from the
    beginning of the story as he acts, performs tasks, to re-
    habilitate himself; and views the ending as affirmative in
    that Nick knows his own limits.

5   ARLEN, MICHAEL J. <u>Exiles</u>. New York: Farrar, Straus & Giroux,
    pp. 224-26.
       Reminisces about the meeting between Hemingway and the
    author of <u>The Green Hat</u>.

*6 BAKER, CARLOS. "Lieutenant Hemingway, 1918," <u>Famous Writers
    Annual: Book One</u>. Westport, Conn.: Famous Writers School,
    pp. 48-56.
       Cited in <u>Hemingway Notes, II</u>.

7   BARBA, HARRY. "The Three Levels of 'The End of Something,'"
    <u>West Virginia University Philological Papers</u>, 17: 76-80.
       The three levels are the literal or descriptive, the
    dramatic, and the symbolic, the latter keyed to the old
    mill.

*8 BARRY, BILL. "The Key West Days of Ernest Hemingway," <u>Boston
    Sunday Globe</u> (13 Dec.), Magazine Section, pp. 16-23, 25-26.
       Cited in <u>Fitzgerald/Hemingway Annual, 1972</u>.

9   BENNETT, WARREN. "Character, Irony, and Resolution in 'A
    Clean, Well-Lighted Place,'" <u>American Literature</u>, 42
    (March), 70-79.
       Detailed reading of the story in which Bennett contends
    that the young waiter is "reality's dupe and victim" as he
    hurries home.
    Reprinted in Benson, pp. 261-69 (<u>See</u> 1975.A3).

10 BENSON, JACKSON J. "Patterns of Connection and Their Develop-
    ment in Hemingway's <u>In Our Time</u>," <u>Rendezvous</u>, 5 (Winter),
    37-52.

(BENSON, JACKSON J.)
>Traces the history, as known, of each story and vignette, and concludes that Hemingway's juxtaposition was skillful, based on "the act of seeing." Benson cites the influence of Pound and Anderson, but finds nothing affirmative in the collection: it is rather "a prose poem of terror."

11 BERRY, THOMAS ELLIOTT. The Newspaper in the American Novel, 1900-1969. Metuchen, N. J.: The Scarecrow Press, pp. 78-79.
>Points out the relatively slight use Hemingway made of the newspaper world in his fiction. Even Hemingway's "newspapermen, one and all, are drawn almost completely as characters apart from the day to day activity of the working journalist."

12 BISHOP, JIM. "A Letter from Hemingway [to Mark Hellinger]," Syndicated column in various newspapers, as Detroit Free Press (16 Dec.), p. 17.
>Calls the relationship "a case history of male affection and endearment."

13 BRADBURY, MALCOLM. "Broken Stoic," The Manchester Guardian Weekly, North American Edition (24 Oct.), p. 18.
>Reviews Islands in the Stream as a "middle" book, ranking above Across the River and Into the Trees and The Old Man and the Sea; particularly admires Hemingway's characterization of Hudson.

14 BRENNER, GERRY. "Epic Machinery in Hemingway's For Whom the Bell Tolls," MFS, 16, No. 4 (Winter), 491-504.
>Describes such characteristics of the epic as catalogue, extended simile, formal language (by the use of Spanish), single action, noble theme and hero, single-faceted characters, omniscient point of view, and others.

15 BROYARD, ANATOLE. "Papa's Disappointing 'Big One,'" Life, 69 (9 Oct.), 10.
>Finds Islands in the Stream full of rhetoric and often pointless action, but does credit Hemingway with continuing the struggle to endure.

16 BRUCCOLI, MATTHEW J. Review of Islands in the Stream, Fitzgerald/Hemingway Annual, pp. 245-46.
>Considers the novel "good" Hemingway, but not great. He notes that there are "no surprises," "no new techniques or themes. The writing, especially in the conversations, is wordy for Hemingway, but then he did not have the chance to revise and cut."

1970

17   BRUCCOLI, MATTHEW J.   Introduction to <u>Ernest Hemingway, Cub</u>
      <u>Reporter: Kansas City Star Stories</u>. Pittsburgh: Univer-
      sity of Pittsburgh Press.
         Includes Theodore Brumback's "With Hemingway Before <u>A</u>
      <u>Farewell to Arms</u>."

18   M.J.B. [BRUCCOLI, MATTHEW J.] "Francis Macomber and Francis
      Fitzgerald," <u>Fitzgerald/Hemingway Annual</u>, p. 223.
         Appalled as Hemingway was at Fitzgerald's confessional
      essays in <u>Esquire</u>, the fact that he includes mention of
      him in "The Snows of Kilimanjaro," also 1936, seems to
      indicate that his using a hen-pecked "Francis" in the story
      is personally significant.

19   _____. "'Oh, Give Them Irony and Give Them Pity,'" <u>Fitzgerald/</u>
      <u>Hemingway Annual</u>, p. 236.
         <u>Dial</u> editor Gilbert Seldes used the phrase "irony and
      pity" in his favorable review of <u>The Great Gatsby</u>. Because
      Hemingway was never lauded by <u>The Dial</u>, he satirized the
      phrase in <u>The Sun Also Rises</u> and again in <u>A Moveable Feast</u>.

20   BUNNELL, WALTER A. "Who Wrote the Paris Idyll? The Place and
      Function of <u>A Moveable Feast</u> in the Writing of Ernest Hem-
      ingway," <u>Arizona Quarterly</u>, 26 (Winter), 334-46.
         Sees <u>A Moveable Feast</u> as aligned with the body of Heming-
      way's fiction rather than non-fiction. He stresses what
      he considers "inversion" in Hemingway's self-portraits.

21   CHARTERS, JAMES. "Pat and Duff: Some Memories," <u>Connecticut</u>
      <u>Review</u>, 3, No. 2, pp. 24-27.
         Charters reminisces about Pat Guthrie and Duff Twysden;
      the connections between them and Hemingway are tenuous.

22   CLARK, C. E. FRAZER, JR. "The Beginnings of Dealer Interest
      in Hemingway," <u>Fitzgerald/Hemingway Annual</u>, pp. 191-93.
         A history of the earliest sales of Hemingway books; the
      first, March 10, 1930, in New York, of <u>in our time</u> at $160.

23   _____. "This Is the Way It Was on the <u>Chicago</u> and at the
      Front: 1917 War Letters," <u>Fitzgerald/Hemingway Annual</u>,
      pp. 153-69.
         The only connection with Hemingway is that eventually,
      in 1918, he too crossed on the <u>Chicago</u>.

24   COOK, BRUCE. "A Posthumous Hemingway Novel Yields Both Gold
      and Platitude," <u>The National Observer</u>, 9 (5 Oct.), 19.
         Sees <u>Islands in the Stream</u> as a mixture of Hemingway's
      best and weakest.

25   COWLEY, MALCOLM. "A Double Life, Half Told," Atlantic, 226
         (Dec.), 105-06, 108.
              As he reviews Islands in the Stream, Cowley depicts Hem-
         ingway playing a tortured double life to the end--"the
         great man in public" versus the "humble and persistent"
         writer, "too deeply wounded to write even a single sentence
         after standing there [at his worktable] all day."

26   _____. A Many-Windowed House, Collected Essays on American
         Writers and American Writing. Carbondale: Southern
         Illinois University Press.
              P. 34: connects Hemingway with Stephen Crane and
         (p. 212) Hawthorne; p. 146: denies that Hemingway was a
         naturalist; finds that his writing "reveals some moral
         quality, usually stoicism or the courage of a frightened
         man."

27   CROSBY, CARESSE. "The Last Time I Saw Hemingway," Fitzgerald/
         Hemingway Annual, p. 240.
              From a 1970 letter, a memory of drinking champagne with
         Hemingway in the Ritz bar in Paris.

28   DAVENPORT, GUY. "Hemingway as Walter Pater," National Review,
         22 (17 Nov.), 1214-15.
              Sees Hemingway as a tough aesthetician and Islands in the
         Stream a study in the beauty of violence. He objects to
         the publication, however.

29   DAVIES, PHILLIPS G. and ROSEMARY R. "'A Killer Who Would Shoot
         You for the Fun of It': A Possible Source for Hemingway's
         'The Killers,'" Iowa English Yearbook, 15 (Fall), 36-38.
              Sees the story based on a real event, the murder of
         boxer "Bill" Brennan by Joseph Pioli and James Hughes in
         Brennan's cafe, June, 1924.

30   DAVIS, ROBERT MURRAY. "'If You Did Not Go Forward': Process
         and Stasis in A Farewell to Arms," Studies in the Novel,
         2 (Fall), 305-11.
              Finds A Farewell to Arms to be about "process" and to
         study the "realization" of Frederic Henry that comes as a
         result of that process. Discusses rain-snow, mountain-
         plain, and day-night imagery in support.

*31   DE MARR, MARY JEAN. "Hemingway's Narrative Methods," Indiana
         English Journal, 4 (Spring), 31-36.
              Cited in Hemingway Notes, II.

1970

32   DOERNER, JOAN BENNETT. "Hemingway's Scrap Heap Hardly Does
      Him Justice--Another Novel Scrounged," Houston Chronicle
      (4 Oct.), p. 18.
           Finds Islands in the Stream dull, pretentious, hardly
      readable.

33   DOUGHERTY, FATHER L. M. "Father L. M. Dougherty Talks About
      Ernest Hemingway," Rendezvous, 5, No. 2 (Winter), 7-17.
           Reminiscence about Hemingway's Sun Valley days, between
      1940 and 1950.

34   DREW, FRASER. "April 8, 1955 with Hemingway: Unedited Notes
      on a Visit to Finca Vigia," Fitzgerald/Hemingway Annual,
      pp. 108-116.
           Presents Hemingway as a gentle and perceptive person.
      Hemingway denies the importance of a Kansas City Star
      editor and of literary criticism, but confirms that of
      religion. Refers to The Sun Also Rises as "the most moral
      book he had ever written."

35   DURANT, WILL and ARIEL DURANT. "Ernest Hemingway," in Inter-
      pretations of Life: A Survey of Contemporary Literature.
      New York: Simon and Schuster, pp. 28-42.
           In his personal and largely biographical response to
      Hemingway, Durant stresses the complete unity of life and
      writings. He considers For Whom the Bell Tolls the best
      novel, and Hemingway's work "the most influential fiction
      of his time."

36   EARNEST, ERNEST. The Single Vision. New York: New York
      University Press, pp. 144-50.
           Sees the Hemingway hero as autobiographical, with one
      difference--that Hemingway "tried to live up to the legend
      he had created." Finds true excellence in the early work.

37   EPSTEIN, JOSEPH. "The Sun Also Sets: Starring Papa," The
      Washington Post Book World (11 Oct.), pp. 1, 3.
           Finds the "Bimini" section of Islands in the Stream the
      best; predicts that the novel will re-establish Hemingway's
      reputation.

38   ETULAIN, RICHARD. "Ernest Hemingway and His Interpreters of
      the 1960's," Rendezvous, 5, No. 2 (Winter), 53-70.
           A Survey of sixteen full-length studies, biographical
      and critical, published during the decade.

39   FERGUSON, CHARLES A. "Hemingway 'Novel' Has Three Unrelated
      Parts," The New Orleans Times-Picayune (11 Oct.), Sec. 2,
      p. 6.

260

1970

(FERGUSON, CHARLES A.)
  Troubled by the apparent lack of cohesion in Islands in
  the Stream, Ferguson also objects to the space given Honest
  Lil, "one of the most forgettable characters in American
  literature."

40 FLEISSNER, R. F. "The Macomber Case: A Sherlockian Analysis,"
    Baker Street Journal, 20, No. 3 (Sept.), 154-56, 169.
      Seeks to answer whether or not Margot's killing of her
    husband was accidental. Finds no help in the story proper
    so relies on a "source clue," found in Dickens, where Mrs.
    Micawber would "never desert" her husband. Since Mrs.
    Macomber did desert hers, she might also kill him.

41 FOOTE, TIMOTHY. "Papa Watching," Time, 96 (5 Oct.), 90, 92.
      Sees Islands in the Stream as a curio, publishable if at
    all because of the world's interest in Hemingway the person.

42 FRENCH, WARREN, ed. The Fifties: Fiction, Poetry, Drama.
    Deland, Fla.: Everett/Edwards, Inc., pp. 41-50.
      "Hemingway's Craft in The Old Man and the Sea" by Sheldon
    N. Grebstein. Sees the novella as near-drama, dominated by
    patterns of darkness-light-darkness, land-sea-land, inner-
    outer-inner. He notes also the use of rapidly shifting
    point of view, but claims that no technical analysis can do
    justice to the skill of Hemingway's craft.

43 FRIEDMAN, MELVIN J. and JOHN B. VICKERY, eds. The Shaken
    Realist: Essays in Modern Literature. Baton Rouge:
    Louisiana State University Press, pp. 5-20.
      "The Silence of Ernest Hemingway" by Ihab Hassan. Finds
    the early Hemingway work superior (In Our Time he calls
    "the best written by an American in our century") because
    its style mirrors the "pure sound" of almost inexpressible
    anguish. "Hemingway saw life as he saw art: a process of
    laying bare to the bone. Men strip their illusions as they
    must shed their flesh." In that recognition, Hassan finds
    the Hemingway greatness.
    Reprinted in The Dismemberment of Orpheus, New York, Oxford
    University Press, 1971 (See 1971.B61).

44 GERSTENBERGER, DONNA and GEORGE HENDRICK. The American Novel;
    A Checklist of Twentieth Century Criticism on Novels since
    1789. II, Criticism Written 1960-1968. Chicago: The
    Swallow Press, pp. 164-77.
      Hemingway items.

1970

45 GILMER, WALKER. <u>Horace Liveright, Publisher of the Twenties</u>.
    New York: David Lewis, pp. 120–25.
        The history of Hemingway's acceptance by Boni & Liveright
    in 1925, and their later rejection of <u>The Torrents of Spring</u>.

46 GINGRICH, ARNOLD. "Publisher's Page: Notes on <u>Bimini</u>,"
    <u>Esquire</u>, 74 (Oct.), 6, 12.
        Admires the <u>Bimini</u> section which <u>Esquire</u> published, but
    has reservations about the rest of <u>Islands in the Stream</u>.

47 GOLDHURST, WILLIAM. "The Hypenated Ham Sandwich of Ernest
    Hemingway and J. D. Salinger: A Study in Literary Con-
    tinuity," <u>Fitzgerald/Hemingway Annual</u>, pp. 136–150.
        Relates the run-away American boy (Nick Adams, Seymour
    Glass) to Huck Finn.

48 GUENTHER, PAUL F. and NICHOLAS T. JOOST. "Little Magazines
    and the Cosmopolitan Tradition," <u>Papers on Language and
    Literature</u>, 6: 100–110.
        A study of the Berlin magazine <u>Der Querschnitt</u>, to which
    Hemingway contributed poems.

49 GUTKIND, LEE ALLEN. Five-part series in <u>The Greenville News</u>
    on Hemingway in Wyoming.
        "Wyoming People Remember Hemingway with Fondness"
    (28 Sept.), p. 8; "Wyoming Lets a Man Be Honest With Him-
    self" (29 Sept.), p. 8; "While Writing, Hemingway 'Always
    Had a Bottle,'" (30 Sept.), p. 8; "Hemingway Stopped
    Working To Hunt Bear" (1 Oct.), p. 58; "Why Did Hemingway
    Quit Wyoming's Solitude?" (2 Oct.), p. 26.

50 HALL, JEFFREY. "Papa: Portrait of Author Emerges in 'Islands
    in the Stream,'" <u>The Richmond Times-Dispatch</u> (4 Oct.),
    Section F, p. 4.
        Sees the book as Hemingway's most autobiographical,
    "wiser than some in its self-deprecation."

51 HALPER, ALBERT. <u>Goodbye Union Square, A Writer's Memoir of
    the Thirties</u>. Chicago: Quadrangle Books, p. 43.
        Discusses whether <u>A Farewell to Arms</u> was a "slick" novel
    or an "important" one.

52 HANNEMAN, AUDRE. "Hanneman Addenda," <u>Fitzgerald/Hemingway
    Annual</u>, pp. 195–218.
        Includes fifty items omitted from the bibliography, and
    sixty-seven other books on Hemingway.

53   _____. "Hanneman Addenda," Fitzgerald/Hemingway Annual,
      pp. 343-46.
         Listing of work by Hemingway published, in English and
      translation, since 1966.

54   HARDER, KELSIE B. "Hemingway's Religious Parody," New York
      Folklore Quarterly, 26: 76-77.
         Sees the dialogue in "A Clean, Well-Lighted Place" as
      parodying the Paternoster and the Ave Maria, as a means of
      allowing the older waiter's view to dominate.

55   HARTWELL, RONALD. "What Hemingway Learned from Ambrose Bierce,"
      Research Studies, 38: 309-11.
         Sees Bierce's "An Occurrence at Owl Creek Bridge" influ-
      encing the escape scene in A Farewell to Arms.

56   HAYASHI, TETSUMARO. "A Farewell to Arms: The Contest of Ex-
      perience," Kyushu American Literature, 12: 14-19.
         Sees the climactic interchanges among characters ("con-
      tests") as a chief means of illustrating Henry's development.

57   HEALEY, WINIFRED. "When Ernest Hemingway's Mother Came to
      Call," Fitzgerald/Hemingway Annual, pp. 170-72.
         Mrs. Hemingway's sense of humor and good contralto voice
      are emphasized in this reminiscence.

58   HEATON, C. P. "Style in The Old Man and the Sea," Style, 4:
      11-27.
         Noticing particularly rhythmic effects (such as the
      sparing use of punctuation), Heaton concludes that in The
      Old Man and the Sea the prose is "clear, forceful and
      direct."

59   HEMINGWAY, MARY. "Ernest's Homework," Book-of-the-Month Club
      News (Fall), pp. 5, 12.
         Brief reminiscence of Hemingway at home, working; recalls
      special tower room where Hemingway was "too lonely."

60   HOGAN, WILLIAM. "Hemingway's Unfinished Novel," San Francisco
      Examiner and Chronicle (4 Oct.), "This World" Section,
      pp. 34, 40.
         Was disappointed in Islands in the Stream as being too
      autobiographical and generally poorly written.

61   HOWE, IRVING. "Great Man Going Down," Harper's, 241 (Oct.),
      120-25.
         Although seeing some elements in Islands in the Stream

1970

(HOWE, IRVING)
as "pleasing," Howe objects to the undisguised autobiographical elements, to its failure as a whole, and to its publication as a "finished" work.

62   HUBBELL, JAY B. "1922: A Turning Point in American Literary
      History," <u>Texas Studies in Literature and Language</u>, 12:
      481-92.
         Survey of the culture and literature of the mid-twenties
      as repudiating the past as being "Puritan" and "Victorian."
      Claims that Hemingway has achieved a place in American
      letters equal to that of Thoreau, Hawthorne and Whitman.

63   HYNAN, PATRICK. <u>Hemingway</u>. Toronto: Canadian Broadcasting
      Corporation.
         A two-record album of the reminiscences of Hadley Maurer,
      Sylvia Beach, Ezra Pound, Mary Hemingway, Archibald MacLeish,
      Malcolm Cowley, A. E. Hotchner, General Charles T. Lanham,
      Harold Loeb, Morley Callaghan, Ben Finney, Philip Young.
      Toby Bruce, Sir Peter Wykeham, Bill Smith, and Marcelline
      Sanford. The speakers discuss Hemingway's work, attitudes,
      youth, development, friendships, courage and decline, gener-
      osity and truculence, and death.

64   JACKSON, THOMAS J. "The 'Macomber' Typescript," <u>Fitzgerald/
      Hemingway Annual</u>, pp. 219-220.
         Housed at Southern Illinois University at Carbondale,
      the typescript is close to the published story as readers
      know it; although changes were made by <u>Cosmopolitan</u> editors
      for its original publication, Hemingway changed it back
      again before it appeared in a collection. The basic "am-
      biguity" in the story remains.

65   JAIN, S. P. "'Hills Like White Elephants': A Study," <u>Indian
      Journal of American Studies</u>, 1, No. 3, 33-38.
         Sees the female Jig as completely sympathetic, though
      hardly "ignorant."

66   JOHNSTON, KENNETH G. "The Star in Hemingway's <u>The Old Man and
      the Sea</u>," <u>American Literature</u>, 42: 388-91.
         Shows how the star Rigel in the constellation of Orion
      is central thematically and structurally.

67   JONES, EDWARD T. "Hemingway and Cezanne: A Speculative
      Affinity," <u>Unisa English Studies</u>, 8, No. 2, pp. 26-28.
         Finds similarities in method and structure between the
      two artists.

68 JOOST, NICHOLAS. "Ernest Hemingway," Contemporary Literature,
      11, No. 2 (Spring), 293-302.
      Reviews four critical books on Hemingway.

69 KANN, HANS-JOCHIM. "Ernest Hemingway's Knowledge of German,"
      Jahrbuch für Amerikastudien, 15: 221-32.
      Comments on Hemingway's vocabulary and reading ability;
      notes that his German characters were sympathetic.

70 KEATS, JOHN. The Life and Times of Dorothy Parker: You Might
      as Well Live. New York: Simon and Schuster.
      Recounts several years of friendship in the mid-20's.

71 KIMBALL, W. J. "Hemingway and the Code," Ventures, 6: 18-23.
      A summary of the "code" which is accurate in The Sun Also
      Rises and A Farewell to Arms, but less valuable in later
      novels.

72 KIRSCH, ROBERT. "'Islands in the Stream" a Worthy Addition to
      the Hemingway Canon," Los Angeles Times Calendar (18 Oct.),
      p. 46.
      Positive review.

73 KOBLER, J. F. "Hemingway's 'The Sea Change': A Sympathetic
      View of Homosexuality," Arizona Quarterly, 26: 318-24.
      Kobler admits Hemingway's disapproval of homosexuality,
      but with an apparent compassion.

74 KRAUS, W. KEITH. "Ernest Hemingway's 'Hills Like White Ele-
      phants': A Note on a 'Reasonable Source,'" English Record,
      21, No. 2, pp. 23-26.
      Thinks the story might be based on a Robert Cohn-Frances
      Clyne situation, and finds the word reasonably a key as
      used in both The Sun Also Rises and this story.

75 KRUSE, HORST H. "Hemingway's 'Cat in the Rain' and Joyce's
      Ulysses," Literatur in Wissenschaft und Unterricht [Kiel],
      III, pp. 28-30.
      Suggests that the man in the rubber cape parallels
      Joyce's guest in a raincoat, identified as Death; thus
      presaging the death of the marriage in the Hemingway story.

76 LANZINGER, KALUS, ed. Americana-Austriaca: Beitrage zur
      Amerikakunde. Vienna: W. Braumuller, II, pp. 3-14.
      "Hemingway's 'Moment of Truth'" by John R. Dunbar. Con-
      siders Death in the Afternoon more significant than the
      novels because the importance to Hemingway of "the moment"
      is more readily apparent.

1970

77 LEHMAN-HAUPT, CHRISTOPHER. "The Case of the Missing Annota-
    tions," New York Times (30 Sept.), p. 45.
        Sees Islands in the Stream a failure because Hemingway
    "had not yet found any universal meaning in the still-
    private experience it records." Considers the book a crude
    draft.

78 LEWIS, CLIFFORD. "The Short Happy Life of Francis Scott
    Macomber," Etudes Anglaises, 23, No. 3 (July-Sept.), 256-61.
        Sees Fitzgerald as a possible source for the protagonist;
    suggests viewing the Macomber story as a reflection of Fitz-
    gerald and "The Snows of Kilimanjaro" as a reflection of
    Hemingway.

79 LEWIS, ROBERT W., JR. "Hemingway's Concept of Sport and
    'Soldier's Home,'" Rendezvous, 5, No. 2 (Winter), 19-27.
        Centers on the dichotomy between an orderly "sport" and
    chaotic life: sport provides for Hemingway the semblance
    of meaning.
    Reprinted in Benson, pp. 170-80 (See 1975.A3).

80 LEWIS, ROBERT W., JR. and MAX WESTBROOK. "'The Snows of Kili-
    manjaro' Collated and Annotated," Texas Quarterly, 13,
    No. 2, pp. 67-143.
        Using the typescript with holograph revisions, the
    Esquire text (1936), a 1949 Esquire reprint, the text in
    the 1938 The Fifth Column and the First Forty-Nine Stories
    (as well as the 1939 English edition), Lewis and Westbrook
    give readers the version that they feel is "closest to the
    author's intention."

81 LINEBARGER, J. M. "Eggs as Huevos in The Sun Also Rises,"
    Fitzgerald/Hemingway Annual, pp. 237-39.
        Eggs represent cojones, Linebarger claims, because of
    the places in the novel when Hemingway emphasizes them.
    Romero, significantly, never eats eggs.

82 LONG, ROBERT EMMET. Review of Islands in the Stream, Common-
    weal, 92 (23 Oct.), 99-100.
        Even though the Hemingway style remains masterful, Long
    finds the novel poorly structured, with hackneyed themes.

83 LONGMIRE, SAMUEL E. "Hemingway's Praise of Dick Sisler in The
    Old Man and the Sea," American Literature, 42: 96-98.
        Son of the famous George Sisler, Dick was a two-day
    national hero in Cuban baseball, winter, 1945-46. He hit
    a ball out of Tropical Stadium one day, and had three home
    runs in one game.

84   MACAULEY, ROBIE. "100-Proof Old Ernest, Most of It Anyway,"
      New York Times Book Review (4 Oct.), pp. 1, 51.
         Finds Islands in the Stream "a complete, well-rounded
      novel" revealing the very best Hemingway. He considers it
      better than any novel by current American writers.

85   McCLELLAND, DAVID M. "Hemingway's Colonel Appropriately Quotes
      Jackson," Fitzgerald/Hemingway Annual, p. 234.
         Finds Cantwell's thought of Stonewall Jackson's last
      words appropriate: Jackson had taught at Virginia Military
      Institute and, as a graduate from V.M.I., Cantwell would be
      familiar with the earlier hero.

86   McLENDON, JAMES. "Ernest Hemingway: The Key West Years,"
      Jacksonville Times-Union and Journal (11, 18, 25 Oct. and
      1 Nov.), pp. 4, 6-8; 6-8, 70; 4-6, 8; and 10-11.
         Reminiscence.

87   MADDEN, DAVID, ed. American Dreams, American Nightmares.
      Carbondale: Southern Illinois University Press.
         Pp. 19-24: "The Dream of the New" by Leslie Fiedler.
      Considers The Torrents of Spring as the "liveliest of all
      his books," in contrast to the "solemn and dull late novels."
         Pp. 45-57: "The Shifting Illusion: Dream and Fact" by
      Maxwell Geismar. Sees Hemingway's peak of greatness in the
      "dark stories of the thirties"; regrets that so little of
      his work had to do with the United States, and that he
      failed to reach "maturity."
         Pp. 58-75: "The Compulsive Design" by Irving Malin.
      Sees many of Hemingway's characters, like those of Faulkner,
      doomed by their need to create "designs," to control their
      environment. Even Nick Adams fails, in that he does not
      ever confront the swamp.

88   MAI, ROBERT P. "Ernest Hemingway and Men Without Women,"
      Fitzgerald/Hemingway Annual, pp. 173-86.
         Traces the patterns of female domination in Hemingway's
      life and the resulting bitterness, followed by the need to
      test and prove oneself as seen in The Old Man and the Sea.

89   MANN, CHARLES W., JR. "Once Again the Familiar Hemingway Is
      With Us," Library Journal, 95 (1 Sept.), 2827.
         Islands in the Stream is a "big, impressive, haunting
      book."

90   MARTINE, JAMES J. "A Little Light on Hemingway's 'The Light
      of the World,'" Studies in Short Fiction, 7 (Summer), 465-
      67.

1970

(MARTINE, JAMES J.)
Cites parallels between this story and Maupassant's "La
maison tellier" in its "ironic use of religious imagery,"
for central scenes of "maudlin sentimentality," and for the
general point of never believing what any woman says.
Reprinted in Benson, pp. 196–203 (See 1975.A3).

91 MILFORD, NANCY. Zelda: A Biography. New York: Harper and
Row.
Many references, among them, pp. 113–17: mutual admiration between Fitzgerald and Hemingway; 122: Zelda's
jealousy of that friendship.

92 MILLER, EVELYN E. "A Trilogy of Irony," English Journal, 59,
No. 1 (Jan.), 59–62.
Discusses the way irony pushes the adolescent reader into
certain insights; uses Hemingway's "Old Man at the Bridge"
to show "irony of situation."

93 MILLER, WAYNE CHARLES. An Armed America: Its Face in Fiction.
New York: New York University Press, pp. 93–130: "World
War I and the Novel of Cultural Protest." Compares Hemingway's fiction with that of Ambrose Bierce and Herman Mel-
ville and finds that all Hemingway's fiction is war fiction
in some respect.

94 MONTGOMERY, MARION. "Emotion Recollected in Tranquility:
Wordsworth's Legacy to Eliot, Joyce, and Hemingway,"
Southern Review, 6: 710–21.
Sees a similarity in attitudes but also in artistic
methods (the use of the commonplace, the objective correl-
ative); views A Moveable Feast as another "Tintern Abbey."

95 NORDELL, RODERICK. "The Sea as Mirror: Hemingway's View of
Himself," The Christian Science Monitor (8 Oct.), p. 13.
Thinks Islands in the Stream is excessively autobiographical; does admire Hemingway's sense of duty in the face of
pain.

96 OLDSEY, BERNARD. "The Novel in the Drawer," The Nation, 211
(19 Oct.), 376, 378.
Describes Islands in the Stream as bad autobiography,
without adequate structure or focus; would have preferred
it be termed a "work-in-progress."

97 PAIGE, WHITNEY. "Hemingway's Michigan," Travel & Camera, 33
(July–Aug.), 32–37.

1970

(PAIGE, WHITNEY)
Quotations from Hemingway's stories and the Baker biography are matched with pictures of Michigan countryside and photos of Hemingway's childhood.

98   PAVESE, CESARE. American Literature: Essays and Opinions, translated by Edwin Fussell. Berkeley: University of California Press: pp. 107, 184.
Refers to the "adolescent and unfeeling naughtinesses of Hemingway" but also sees him as one of the American writers who sought the "whole man," a deeper realism.

99   PORTERFIELD, WALTON D. "In a Big Novel, Ernest Hemingway Returns 'In All His Magnificence,'" The Milwaukee Journal (4 Oct.), Part 5, p. 4.
Too long, Islands in the Stream has both power and a mature philosophy.

100 RICKS, CHRISTOPHER. "At Sea with Ernest Hemingway," New York Review of Books, 15 (8 Oct.), 17–19.
Sees Islands in the Stream as suicidal, representative of Hemingway's mood and the condition of his art.

101 RODGERS, PAUL C., JR. "Levels of Irony in Hemingway's 'The Gambler, the Nun, and the Radio,'" Studies in Short Fiction, 7 (Summer), 439–49.
A structural analysis, Rodger's essay depicts this story as considerably bleaker than "A Clean, Well-Lighted Place." He emphasizes the ironic stance of the narrator.

102 ROGERS, JEAN M. and GORDON STEIN. "Bibliographical Notes on Hemingway's Men Without Women," PBSA, 64, pp. 210–13.
Identifies the first printing of the 1927 edition by weight and folio marking.

103 ROSS, ISHBELL. The Expatriates. New York: Thomas Y. Crowell Co., pp. 255–66.
"Hemingway and Fitzgerald," biography and reminiscence of the Paris years.

104 RUBIN, LOUIS D., JR. "New Hemingway Novel Poses Questions," The Washington Sunday Star (4 Oct.), p. E-1.
Would rather this had been published as "working manuscript" instead of finished product.

105 ST. JOHN, DONALD. "Leicester Hemingway: Chief of State," Connecticut Review, 3, No. 2, pp. 5–19.
Cites correspondence and discussions with Hemingway's brother.

1970

106   SARASON, BERTRAM D. "Pauline Hemingway: In Tranquility,"
      Fitzgerald/Hemingway Annual, pp. 127-35.
          Recording of his visit with Hemingway's second wife in
      Key West.

107   SEARS, DONALD A. and MARGARET BOURLAND. "Journalism Makes the
      Style," Journalism Quarterly, 47 (Autumn), 504-09.
          The authors apply quantitative analysis to the works of
      eight authors, four of whom had journalistic experience.
      See certain characteristics in those four samples.

108   SINGER, KURT. "Senor Hemingway's House Near Havana," Book
      World (31 May), p. 8.
          Descriptive essay.

109   SKIPP, FRANCIS E. "Nick Adams: Prince of Abyssinia," Carrell,
      11, Nos. 1-2 (June-Dec.), 20-26.
          Compares Hemingway's writings and Johnson's Rasselas and
      finds similarities in the human experiences recorded, the
      empirical epistemology used, and their belief in a sub-
      jective reference for moral judgment. For both, experience
      precedes formulation of philosophy. Both employ tutor
      figures.

110   SLATOFF, WALTER J. With Respect To Readers, Dimensions of
      Literary Response. Ithaca: Cornell University Press.
          Scattered references, wondering whether readers can under-
      stand what prompts authors to create posturing heroes, as
      Hemingway did in Across the River and Into the Trees and,
      to a lesser extent, in The Sun Also Rises.

111   SMITH, JULIAN. "Hemingway and the Thing Left Out," Journal of
      Modern Literature, 1, No. 2, pp. 169-82.
          Dealing with three stories--"In Another Country," "Now I
      Lay Me," and "God Rest You Merry, Gentlemen"--in which some
      relatively important factual information has been suppressed.
      Like the iceberg principle, Hemingway's omission is also an
      evocative technique.
          Reprinted in Benson, pp. 135-47 (See 1975.A3); and Wagner,
      pp. 188-200 (See 1974.A3).

112   _____. "More Products of the Hemingway Industry," Studies in
      Short Fiction, 7: 638-46.
          Smith reviews five studies of Hemingway's work.

113   SMITH, WILLIAM B. "A Wedding Up in Michigan," Fitzgerald/
      Hemingway Annual, pp. 124-26.
          Reminiscence of the Sept. 3, 1921, wedding, with photos.

114   SOLOTAROFF, THEODORE. The Red Hot Vacuum. New York: Atheneum.
      Sees Hemingway as representative of a kind of angst as
      well as technical control no longer basic to the fiction
      of the sixties.

115   SRIVASTEVA, RAMESH. "Hemingway's 'Cat in the Rain': An Inter-
      pretation," Literary Criterion, 9, No. 2 (Summer), 79-84.
      Interprets it as a story of alienation and the fertility-
      wish of the wife, with rain as symbol.

116   STAFFORD, WILLIAM T. "Hemingway/Faulkner: Marlin and Catfish?"
      Southern Review, 6: 1191-1200.
      Sees that the two authors had different ambitions in
      their writing; admires them both.

117   STEINER, PAUL. "Intimately Yours—but Don't Quote Me,"
      Escapade (March), p. 36.
      Includes a letter from Hemingway dated Sept. 7, 1949.

118   STEWART, LAWRENCE D. "Hemingway and the Autobiographies of
      Alice B. Toklas," Fitzgerald/Hemingway Annual, pp. 117-23.
      Finds Hemingway's censure of Stein to rest mostly with
      Alice, whom—Stewart concludes—Hemingway detested at least
      partly because of her alleged comments in The Autobiography
      of Alice B. Toklas.

119   TANAKA, KEISUKE. "The Bipolar Construction in the Works of
      Ernest Hemingway," Kyusha American Literature, 12: 32-44.
      Working from several titles of Hemingway's novels, Tanaka
      finds the idea of contrast central in much of the fiction—
      life and death, innocence and experience—as well as con-
      trasts in time, place, and social classes.

120   THOMANECK, JURGENS K. A. "Hemingway's Riddle of Kilimanjaro
      Once More," Studies in Short Fiction, 7 (Spring), 326-27.
      Shows that Hemingway may have found the symbol of the
      leopard at 5000 meters from A. E. Johann's Gross ist Afrika
      (Berlin, 1939), p. 316.

121   THOMAS, PETER. "A Lost Leader: Hemingway's 'The Light of the
      World,'" Humanities Association Bulletin, Canada, 21 (Fall),
      14-19.
      Stresses that Hemingway intended to place this first in
      Winner Take Nothing; relates the story to a biblical source.

122   UPDIKE, JOHN. "Papa's Sad Testament," New Statesman, 80 (16
      Oct.), 489.
      Sees that Islands in the Stream lacks any pattern; laments
      the absence of editorial controls.

1970

123 VAIDYANATHAN, T. G. "Did Margot Kill Francis Macomber?"
Indian Journal of American Studies, 1, No. 3, pp. 1-13.
Comments on the "motivational ambiguity" of the story;
concludes that the ambiguity remains because of the
shifting narrative point of view.

124 VON ENDE, FREDERICK. "The Corrida Pattern in For Whom the Bell
Tolls," Re: Arts and Letters, 3 (Sept.), 63-70.
Relates the structure of the novel to the actual parts
of the corrida de toros. By giving Jordan and his band
this further symbolic significance, Hemingway ennobles
their endeavors.

125 VORPAHL, BEN M. "Ernest Hemingway and Owen Wister: Finding
the Lost Generation," LC, 36: 126-37.
Using correspondence between the two, Vorpahl concludes
that Wister gave Hemingway encouragement, admiration for
Kipling, and a love for the Rockies.

126 WAIN, JOHN. "No Surprises," The London Observer Review
(11 Oct.), p. 33.
Finds in Islands in the Stream a solid, if somewhat uninventive, accomplishment, of middle rank among the novels.

127 WHITE, WILLIAM. "Hemingway and Fitzgerald" in American Literary
Scholarship: An Annual, 1968, edited by J. Albert Robbins.
Durham, N. C.: Duke University Press, pp. 107-17.
Survey of criticism on both authors published during 1968.

128 WOLFE, THOMAS. The Notebooks of Thomas Wolfe, edited by
Richard S. Kennedy and Paschal Reeves. Chapel Hill, N. C.:
University of North Carolina Press.
From 1929 on, Wolfe consistently praised Hemingway as
being a true "modern," though he was sometimes envious of
Hemingway's established reputation.

129 WOLFF, GEOFFREY. "Out of the Desk," Newsweek, 76 (12 Oct.),
118-20.
"A very bad novel with a few bright moments," Islands in
the Stream should be considered a curiosity.

130 WYLDER, DELBERT E. "Hemingway's Satiric Vision--The High
School Years," Rendezvous, 5, No. 2 (Winter), 29-35.
Finds in even Hemingway's high school writing an in-
cisive vision, "an attempt to see things as they really
are."

131   YARDLEY, JONATHAN. "How Papa Grew," New Republic, 163 (10 Oct.),
          25-26, 30.
             Finds that Islands in the Stream has only flickers of the
          Hemingway greatness; is a failure because Hemingway became
          too much absorbed in his own legend.

132   YOUNG, PHILIP and CHARLES W. MANN, JR. "Fitzgerald's Sun Also
          Rises: Notes and Comments," Fitzgerald/Hemingway Annual,
          pp. 1-9.
             Letter from Fitzgerald concerning The Sun Also Rises
          leads the authors to conjecture on his role in the final
          cutting of the novel (the omitted sections are also
          described).

1971 A BOOKS

1   FARRINGTON, S. KIP, JR. Fishing with Hemingway and Glassel.
          New York: David McKay Co.
             Farrington makes clear in this reminiscence that, con-
          trary to some legend, Hemingway was an expert fisherman,
          and knew a great deal about fishing and waters.

2   LONGYEAR, CHRISTOPHER RUDSTON. Linguistically Determined
          Categories of Meaning--A Comparative Analysis of Meaning
          in "The Snows of Kilimanjaro." The Hague: Mouton.
             A linguistic comparison of the Hemingway story in English
          and in the 1950 German translation by Annemarie Horschitz-
          Horst, in order to determine the effects on readers of
          types of meaning inherent in the author's language choices.

3   NAHAL, CHAMAN. The Narrative Pattern in Ernest Hemingway's
          Fiction. Rutherford, N. J.: Fairleigh Dickinson University
          Press.
             Nahal sees Hemingway's fiction as moving in a passive-
          active-passive shape (or a "systolic" and "diastolic"
          pattern). The reader follows the forward motion; then
          rests; then continues, so that his interest is maintained
          throughout.

4   O'CONNOR, RICHARD. Ernest Hemingway. New York: McGraw-Hill,
          American Writers Series.
             Juvenile biography.

5   WATKINS, FLOYD C. The Flesh and the Word: Eliot, Hemingway,
          Faulkner. Nashville, Tenn.: Vanderbilt University Press.
             Seeing the early work of all three writers as their best,
          Watkins attributes this excellence to the concrete, spare

1971

(WATKINS, FLOYD C.)
method. The absence of rhetoric, of abstract thinking in
their art, he attributes to their reaction to the times
(World War I and its aftermath). With the exception of
The Old Man and the Sea, he finds the later writing of each
marred by indirect philosophizing and cumbersome phrasing,
the turn away from the original clarity and precision.

6   WATTS, EMILY STIPES. Ernest Hemingway and the Arts. Urbana,
Ill.: University of Illinois Press.
A thorough study of Hemingway's interest in, and--perhaps--
use of, painting, sculpture, and architecture. Cezanne,
Goya, and many other painters; Surrealism and Dadaism--
Watts shows them all represented in Hemingway's fiction.

7   GRAHAM, JOHN, ed. Merrill Studies in "A Farewell to Arms."
Columbus, Ohio: Charles E. Merrill Company.
Contents: pp. iii-iv, Preface by the editor.
pp. 3-8: "A Review of A Farewell to Arms" by Malcolm
Cowley, reprinted from New York Herald Tribune Books
(6 Oct. 1929), pp. 1, 16.
pp. 9-13: "'Nothing Ever Happens to the Brave'" by T. S.
Matthews, reprinted from New Republic, 60 (9 Oct. 1929),
pp. 208-10.
pp. 14-19: "A Review of A Farewell to Arms" by Henry
Seidel Canby, reprinted from SRL, 6 (12 Oct. 1929), 231-32.
pp. 20-22: "A Review of A Farewell to Arms" by Clifton
P. Fadiman, reprinted from Nation, 129 (30 Oct. 1929),
497-98.
pp. 23-24: "A Review of A Farewell to Arms" by B. E.
Todd, reprinted from The Spectator, 143 (16 Nov. 1929),
727.
pp. 27-38: "Ernest Hemingway: A Farewell to Arms" by
Carlos Baker, reprinted from Chapter 17 of The American
Novel from Cooper to Faulkner, New York, Basic Books, 1965,
pp. 192-205.
pp. 39-45: "The Religion of Death in A Farewell to Arms"
by James F. Light, reprinted from MFS, 7 (Summer 1961),
169-73.
pp. 46-54: "Ernest Hemingway: Joy Through Strength" by
Otto Friedrich, reprinted from The American Scholar, 26
(Autumn 1957), 519-24.
pp. 55-65: "The Stopped Worlds of Ernest Hemingway" by
Charles Vandersee, unpublished. Comparison of Henry
Fleming with Frederic Henry, seeing the latter as the
center of A Farewell to Arms and his initiation into life--
and death--as the central conflict.

1971

(GRAHAM, JOHN)
    pp. 66-82: "Hemingway's A Farewell to Arms: The Novel
as Pure Poetry" by Daniel J. Schneider, reprinted from MFS,
14 (Autumn 1968), 283-96.
    pp. 83-87: "Language as a Moral Code in A Farewell to
Arms" by Blanche Gelfant, reprinted from MFS, 9 (Summer
1963), pp. 173-76.
    pp. 88-95: "Ernest Hemingway: The Meaning of Style"
by John Graham, reprinted from MFS, 6 (1960-61), pp. 298-313.

8   GREBSTEIN, SHELDON N. Merrill Studies in "For Whom the Bell
   Tolls." Columbus, Ohio: Charles E. Merrill Publishers.
    Contents: iii-v: Preface by the editor.
    pp. 2-5: "The Soul of Spain" by Howard Mumford Jones,
reprinted from SRL, 23 (26 Oct. 1940), 5, 19.
    pp. 6-15: "Review of For Whom the Bell Tolls" by Alvah
C. Bessie, reprinted from New Masses, 37 (5 Nov. 1940),
25-29. "A Postscript" added in 1970 only intensifies
Bessie's earlier objections to the novel.
    pp. 16-17: "Books of the Week" by J. N. Vaughan, re-
printed from Commonweal, 33 (13 Dec. 1940), 210.
    pp. 18-20: "Thou Tellest Me, Comrade" by Gilbert
Highet, reprinted from Nation, 152 (1 March 1941), 242.
    pp. 21-23: "Mr. Hemingway's New Novel" by Graham Greene,
reprinted from The Spectator, 166 (7 March 1941), 258.
    pp. 24-29: "Current Literature" by V. S. Pritchett, re-
printed from The New Statesman and Nation, 21 (15 March
1941), pp. 275-76.
    pp. 32-42: "Ernest Hemingway's Spanish Civil War Ex-
perience" by David Sanders, reprinted from American Quarterly, 12 (Summer 1960), 133-43.
    pp. 43-49: "The Real Robert Jordan" by Cecil D. Eby,
reprinted from American Literature, 38 (Nov. 1966), 380-86.
    pp. 50-55: "'For Whom the Bell Tolls': The Origin of
General Golz" by Jerzy R. Krzyzanowski, reprinted from
Polish Review, 7 (1962), 69-74.
    pp. 56-70: "From The Social Novel at the End of an Era"
by Warren French, reprinted from the book, Carbondale,
Southern Illinois University Press, 1966, pp. 87-91 and
109-24.
    pp. 71-79: "Mechanized Doom: Ernest Hemingway and the
Spanish Civil War" by Allen Guttmann, reprinted from The
Massachusetts Review, 1 (May 1960), 541-47, 557-61.
    pp. 80-90: "Not Spain but Hemingway" by Arturo Barea,
reprinted from Horizon, 3 (May 1941), 350-61, translated
by Ilsa Barea.
    pp. 91-93: "The English of Hemingway's Spaniards" by
John J. Allen, reprinted from South Atlantic Bulletin, 28
(Nov. 1961), 6-7.

1971

(GREBSTEIN, SHELDON N.)
    pp. 94-101: "The Martyrdom of Robert Jordan" by William
T. Moynihan, reprinted from College English, 21 (Dec. 1959),
127-32.
    pp. 102-06: "The Power of the Tacit in Crane and Heming-
way" by Robert P. Weeks, reprinted from MFS, 8 (Winter
1962), 415-18.
    pp. 107-112: "Hemingway's Tyrannous Plot" by Thornton H.
Parsons, reprinted from University of Kansas City Review,
27 (Summer 1961), 261-66.
    pp. 113-122: "From Ernest Hemingway" by Earl Rovit, re-
printed from the book, New York, Twayne, 1963, pp. 136-46.

1971 B SHORTER WRITINGS

1   ANON. "Review," Virginia Quarterly Review, 47 (Winter),
       p. viii.
       Thinks Islands in the Stream is a reasonably successful
novel with its themes being logical continuations of the
rest of Hemingway's writing.

2   ALDERMAN, TAYLOR; KENNETH ROSEN; and WILLIAM WHITE. "Current
       Bibliography," Hemingway Notes, 1 (Fall), 10-13.
       Lists books and essays from the past five years.

3   ALEXANDER, ARCHIBALD S. "Collecting Hemingway," Fitzgerald/
       Hemingway Annual, pp. 298-301.
       Besides describing his own experience, Alexander includes
a letter from Fitzgerald praising The Torrents of Spring
as "about the best comic book ever written by an American."

4   ANDERSON, WILLIAM R. "Islands in the Stream--the Initial Re-
       ception," Hemingway/Fitzgerald Annual, pp. 326-32.
       Anderson summarizes thirty reviews: thirteen, "basically
favorable"; nine, "favorable"; eight, "ambivalent or
neutral." Checklist of reviews included.

*5   ANO, FUMIO. "Hemingway and Politics," Bulletin of the College
       of General Education of Tohoku University (Sendai, Japan),
       12, No. 2, pp. 105-20.
       Cited in Hemingway Notes, II.

*6   BAKER, CARLOS. "Hemingway and Princeton," Princeton History,
       1: 39-49.
       Cited in Fitzgerald/Hemingway Annual, 1972.

7   BARTLET, NORMAN. "Hemingway: The Hero as Self," Quadrant,
       15, No. 3 (May-June), 13-20.

(BARTLET, NORMAN)
Discusses the deflating of the Hemingway myth; sees
Thomas Hudson as autobiographical, and finds his inability
to understand other kinds of people one of Hemingway's
major weaknesses.

*8   BASS, EBEN.   "Hemingway at Roncesvalles," New England Modern
Language Association Newsletter, 2 (Feb.), 1-7.
Cited in Journal of Modern Literature, 1971, p. 819.

9   BASSETT, CHARLES W.   "Katahdin, Wachusett, and Kilimanjaro:
The Symbolic Mountains of Thoreau and Hemingway," Thoreau
Journal Quarterly, 3, No. 2, pp. 1-10.
Finds the writers alike in seeking a "vision of oneness"
in their "symbolic ascent of mountains."

10   BEJA, MORRIS.   Epiphany in the Modern Novel.   Seattle: University of Washington Press.
Relates the modernist fictional tactic--used by Hemingway
and other writers--of capturing the "exact feel of a moment
in time and space" to Joyce's epiphanic methods.   Uses the
In Our Time vignettes and stories as examples.

11   BERTHOFF, WARNER.   Fictions and Events: Essays in Criticism
and Literary History.   New York: E. P. Dutton.
Speaks of Hemingway's "unbalancing effort after honesty
and immediacy of feeling," but does include In Our Time
as a major work in American literature.

12   BLANTON, SAM.   "To Know the Big Fish," Water Sport, 5 (Aug.),
23-25.
Account of Hemingway's fishing trips in 1932 and 1933
with Joe Russell (seventy-one marlin all told) and his
purchase of the Pilar in 1934.   Says Russell was one model
for Morgan in To Have and Have Not.   Concludes that Hemingway wrote "perhaps better about fishing, boats, the sea
and a man's love for the outdoors than anyone before or
since."

13   BLUEFARB, SAMUEL.   "The Search for the Absolute in Hemingway's
'A Clean, Well-Lighted Place' and 'The Snows of Kilimanjaro,'" Bulletin of the Rocky Mountain MLA, 25:   3-9.
Both stories contain a sense of a complete void and,
whereas the waiter has nothing tangible, Harry at least
maintains the idealization of his writing.

14   BOCAZ, SERGIO H.   "El Ingenioso Hidalgo Don Quijote de La
Mancha and The Old Man and the Sea: A Study of the Symbolic
Essence of Man in Cervantes and Hemingway," Bulletin of the

1971

(BOCAZ, SERGIO H.)
Rocky Mountain Modern Language Association, 25: 49-54.
   Stresses parallels between Don Quixote and Santiago in
their knowledge and acceptance of truth, their moral stance,
and their ability to act. They each maintain rapport with
nature.

15   BORGES, JORGE LUIS. An Introduction to American Literature.
      With Esther Zemborain de Torres. Lexington: The University
      Press of Kentucky, pp. 50-51.
         Sketch of Hemingway's life, with emphasis on his Michigan
      surroundings, his life as sportsman and "craftsman, a
      scrupulous artisan."

16   BRADBURY, MALCOLM and DAVID PALMER, eds. The American Novel
      and the Nineteen Twenties, Stratford-Upon-Avon Studies 19.
      London: Edward Arnold.
         Many references to Hemingway; see especially pp. 11-35:
      "Style of Life, Style of Art and the American Novelist in
      the Nineteen Twenties" by Malcolm Bradbury; pp. 59-83:
      "Social Criticism in the American Novel in the Nineteen
      Twenties" by Henry Dan Piper; pp. 151-63: "Ernest Heming-
      way's Genteel Bullfight" by Brom Weber; and pp. 233-62:
      "The Hostile Environment and the Survival Artist: A Note
      on the Twenties" by Eric Mottram.

17   BRUCCOLI, MATTHEW J., ed. Ernest Hemingway's Apprenticeship:
      Oak Park, 1916-1917. Washington, D. C.: NCR Microcard
      Editions.
         Foreword by Russell J. Fuoy giving biographical informa-
      tion about Hemingway.

18   BUTWIN, DAVID. "Turning the Keys," SR, 54 (27 Feb.), 38-40.
         Description of the house in Key West where Hemingway and
      Pauline lived during the 1930's, and an interview with
      Hemingway's friend Toby Bruce.

19   CADY, EDWIN H. The Light of Common Day: Realism in American
      Fiction. Bloomington: Indiana University Press, pp. 204-
      06.
         Sees the importance of Hemingway (and Eliot, Faulkner,
      and O'Neill) as being not the realization of darkness but
      the fact that their writing came to offer something more,
      "not innocence but, beyond innocence, responsibility" (as
      in For Whom the Bell Tolls and The Old Man and the Sea).

20   CAPRA, FRANK. The Name Above the Title. New York: Macmillan,
      p. 138.

(CAPRA, FRANK)
"Despite his lean, bare prose, Hemingway was a gee-whizzer . . . . He lived, wrote and died in a fireworks display."

21 CAVE, RAY. "Introduction to An African Journal," Sports Illustrated, 35 (20 Dec.), 40-41.
Preview of sections of the journal to be published later.

22 CHURCHILL, ALLEN. The Literary Decade. Englewood Cliffs, N. J.: Prentice-Hall.
Pp. 236-46: account of Hemingway's relationships with both Liveright and Scribner's; p. 170: Mencken's judgment of Hemingway as "a bad boy who's probably afraid of the dark."

23 CLARK, C. E. FRAZER, JR. "'Buying Commission Would Cut Out Waste': A Newly Discovered Hemingway Contribution to the Toronto Daily Star," Fitzgerald/Hemingway Annual, pp. 209-11.

24 _____. "The Crosby Copy of In Our Time," Fitzgerald/Hemingway Annual, pp. 236-38.
Notes that the Crosbys thought In Our Time "the best of all." Includes annotated Contents page and Hemingway's inscription.

25 _____. "'La Vie est beau avec Papa,'" Fitzgerald/Hemingway Annual, pp. 189-93.
Describes Hemingway's annotation and inscription to Gerald and Sara Murphy in Today Is Friday, 1926.

26 CODY, MORRILL. "The Sun Also Rises Revisited," Connecticut Review, 4, No. 2 (April), 5-8.
Reminiscences of Hemingway and the prototypes for his characters in The Sun Also Rises.
Reprinted in Sarason, pp. 265-70 (See 1972.A8).

27 COINDREAU, MAURICE. "William Faulkner and Ernest Hemingway," in The Time of William Faulkner. Columbia, S. C.: University of South Carolina, pp. 72-74.
Sees Hemingway as less important than Faulkner, but "not a negligible author" and deserving of the Nobel prize.

*28 COR, LAURENCE W. "Hemingway, Montherlant, and 'Animal Tragedy,'" in Proceedings: Pacific Northwest Conference on Foreign Languages, edited by Walter C. Kraft. Oregon State University, pp. 202-07.
Cited in PMLA bibliography.

1971

29 COWLEY, MALCOLM. "A Letter from Malcolm Cowley," Fitzgerald/
      Hemingway Annual, pp. 317-18.
        Brief history of his Portable Hemingway and Faulkner, in
      which he suggests using Jungian terms rather than Freudian
      to describe Hemingway.

30 COYNE, JOHN R. "Isn't It Pretty To Think So?", The Alterna-
      tive, 4 (May), 16-17.
        Review of Islands in the Stream. Praises the novel for
      its sustained dialogue, three-part structure unified by
      Hudson, action, and humor (sees Hemingway as poking fun
      at the exaggerated self-image he created).

31 CRANE, JOHN. "Rare or Seldom-Seen Dust Jackets of American
      First Editions: VI," Serif, 8, No. 3, pp. 29-31.
        Among others, Crane describes three Hemingway items.

32 CRUTTWELL, PATRICK. "Fiction Chronicle," Hudson Review, 24
      (Spring), 180.
        Sees Hemingway as "a minor romantic poet" in terms of
      modern American fiction.

33 DAVISON, RICHARD A. "Carelessness and the Cincinnati Reds in
      The Old Man and the Sea," Notes on Contemporary Literature,
      1, No. 1, pp. 11-13.
        Sees Hemingway's placing the Reds in the American League
      teams as an error.

34 DAVISON, RICHARD ALLAN. "Hemingway's A Farewell to Arms,"
      Explicator, 29, Item 46.
        Connects "Western Wind," the gentle rain (as Christ
      symbol), and Catherine as serving as ironic religious
      symbols, with even the romantic love as no substitute for
      a religion.

35 DITSKY, JOHN. "Hemingway, Plato, and The Hidden God," Southern
      Humanities Review, 5 (Summer), 145-47.
        Approaches For Whom the Bell Tolls through Donne's "De-
      votions, 17," and finds that Hemingway has used Donne's
      concepts of sensuality and spirituality rather than the
      strictly Christian concepts Brooks identifies in The
      Hidden God.

36 DONALDSON, SCOTT. "Hemingway's Morality of Compensation,"
      American Literature, 43, No. 3 (Nov.), 399-420.
        Studies Hemingway's use of monetary and financial imagery,
      his translation of concepts of "value" in all his writing
      into fiscal terms.

37 DOXEY, WILLIAM S. "The Significance of Seney, Michigan, in
      Hemingway's 'Big Two-Hearted River,'" Hemingway Notes, 1
      (Fall), 5-6.
        Because Hemingway uses Seney in both a poem and a story,
      Doxey feels it is an important image for the loss of youth,
      as well as destruction.

38 DREW, FRASER. "Recollections of a Hemingway Collector," Fitz-
      gerald/Hemingway Annual, pp. 294-97.
        Anecdotes about Hemingway's generosity, both in signing
      and giving books.

39 EWELL, NATHANIEL M., III. "Dialogue in Hemingway's 'A Clean,
      Well-Lighted Place,'" Fitzgerald/Hemingway Annual, pp. 305-
      06.
        Ewell claims that two slugs of type must have been mis-
      placed, rather than one.

40 FARRINGTON, KIP. "Remembering Great Men and Great Fish:
      Excerpt from Fishing with Hemingway and Glassell," Field &
      Stream, 75 (April), 54-55.

41 FICKEN, CARL. "Point of View in the Nick Adams Stories,"
      Fitzgerald/Hemingway Annual, pp. 212-35.
        Finds Hemingway using a more objective point of view in
      the early stories, more complex in the later: "Hemingway
      matched his narrative perspective with his hero's mental
      state."
        Reprinted in Benson, pp. 93-121 (See 1975.A3).

42 FITZ, REGINALD. "The Meaning of Impotence in Hemingway and
      Eliot," Connecticut Review, 4 (April), 16-22.
        Connects both writers' use of sexual wounding to the
      depersonalization of this century, pointing out that Hem-
      ingway, unlike Eliot, could not move beyond the self-
      destruction of his early work.

43 FRAZIER, GEORGE. "Hemingway: July 2, 1961," The Boston Globe
      (2 July), p. 36.
        Commemorates the tenth anniversary of Hemingway's death
      by listing all the books written about him.

44 FUJIMOTO, YUKIO. "The Relationship Between Santiago and Mano-
      lin," SALCS, 7: 26-33.
        Finds the love between the two to be an important part
      of the story's impact; Manolin acts as "interpreter" of
      Santiago's character and experience.

1971

45 GAILLARD, THEODORE L., JR. "The Critical Menagerie in 'The
    Short Happy Life of Francis Macomber,'" English Journal,
    60 (Jan.), 31-35.
        Tries to reach students by finding that Hemingway uses
    animals as a standard against which to measure human be-
    havior. Lists all animal imagery.

46 GANZEL, DEWEY. "A Farewell to Arms: The Danger of Imagina-
    tion," Sewanee Review, 79, No. 4 (Autumn), 576-97.
        Not a love or war story, A Farewell to Arms presents one
    of Hemingway's enduring concerns, "a man, often of military
    or para-military status, who is forced to recognize the
    inevitability of death . . . trying to secure something of
    value from its onslaught." Sees the novel as affirmative.

47 GERVASI, FRANK. "The Liberation of Gertrude Stein," SR, 54
    (21 Aug.), 13-14, 57.
        Quotes Stein on Hemingway as disappointing. She speaks
    in 1944 of her private high hopes for his abilities, and
    her gradual disillusionment: "Success, success, success
    . . . . That was what drove him, not a search for truth."

48 GINGRICH, ARNOLD. Nothing But People: The Early Days at
    Esquire, A Personal History 1928-1958. New York: Crown.
        Pp. 84-90: personal friendship with Hemingway and his
    various writings; p. 246: Hemingway's enthusiasm for Ezra
    Pound. Other references.

49 GLEAVES, EDWIN S. "Hemingway and Baroja: Studies in Spiritual
    Anarchism," Revista de Estudios Hispánicos, 5: 363-75.
        Finds Baroja's choice of "spiritual anarchism" influential
    in Hemingway's pre-For Whom the Bell Tolls career.

50 GLICKSBERG, CHARLES. "The Hemingway Cult of Love," in The
    Sexual Revolution in Modern American Literature. The
    Hague: Martinus Nijhoff, pp. 82-95.
        Sees Hemingway as a leading proponent of the new sexual
    ethic of this century, whose characters manage--though
    promiscuous--to work out their own moral code. Glicksberg
    sees "the sexual revolution" as predictable, stemming for
    the most part from "the metaphysics of despair."

51 GOODMAN, PAUL. "The Sweet Style of Ernest Hemingway," New York
    Review of Books, 17, No. 11 (30 Dec.), 27-28.
        Uses modified linguistic analysis to approach the Heming-
    way style, and concludes that the style--like his charac-
    ters--is "passive." Despite Hemingway's reliance on active
    verbs, the events his characters initiate do not actualize

(GOODMAN, PAUL)
    them, yet neither do they doom them (as would the events
    in a naturalist's writing). Goodman finds Hemingway's work
    lasting not because of his quasi-existential view, but be-
    cause "he is sweetly devoted to writing well . . . .
    writing is his 'existential act.'"
    Reprinted in his Speaking and Language: Defense of Poetry,
    New York, Random House, 1972 and Wagner, pp. 153-160 (See
    1974.A3).

52 GORDON, DAVID J. "Some Recent Novels: Connoisseurs of Chaos,"
        Yale Review, 60: 428-37.
        Sees Islands in the Stream as concerned with "survival,"
    but finds the book "saturated in vanity and self-pity."

53 GREINER, DONALD J. "The Education of Robert Jordan: Death
        with Dignity," Hemingway Notes, 1 (Fall), 14-20.
        Sees For Whom the Bell Tolls as a study in death with
    dignity: Hemingway was not obsessed with death but was
    here using various kinds to reinforce his theme, that "each
    man's death is a private act because only he knows all of
    the particular circumstances."

54 _____. "Emerson, Thoreau, and Hemingway: Some Suggestions
        About Literary Heritage," Fitzgerald/Hemingway Annual,
        pp. 247-61.
        Sees Hemingway as a latter-day Transcendentalist, and
    the Paris influence as secondary. "The point is that Hem-
    ingway's despair or cynicism does not negate his idealism."

55 GRENBERG, BRUCE L. "The Design of Heroism in The Sun Also
        Rises," Fitzgerald/Hemingway Annual, pp. 274-89.
        Sees Jake as the essential Hemingway hero: Jake seeks
    fulfillment within himself; he learns that knowledge is a
    "continuous process"; and in Book III comes to accept his
    life.

56 GROSECLOSE, BARBARA S. "Hemingway's 'The Revolutionist': An
        Aid to Interpretation," MFS, 17, No. 4 (Winter), 565-69.
        Discussion of the short story in relation to the trecento
    and quattrocento painters, especially Andrea Mantegna and
    his painting The Dead Christ. Sees Hemingway's references
    to painters as a further means of contrasting the young
    revolutionary and the old narrator.

57 GROSS, THEODORE. The Heroic Ideal in American Literature.
        New York: The Free Press.
        Sees Hemingway rejecting even "the concept of heroism."

1971

(GROSS, THEODORE)
In "Ernest Hemingway, The Renunciation of America," Gross points out that Hemingway's influence has been far greater than technical or literary; it has been in his attitude of "absolute denial." From In Our Time, with its "unrelieved despair that seems unnatural in so young a man," to The Old Man and the Sea with its themes of renunciation, Hemingway has used the obsessive work ethic, the mistrust of abstractions, the salvation of love in all his work. So absolute has been his influence, Gross contends, that more contemporary writers "can think affirmatively largely because Hemingway expressed renunciation with so impressive a finality."

58   GUTKIND, LEE ALAN. "The Young Man and the Mountains," Tropic, 4 (April), 12-16.
On Hemingway's decade in the Wyoming mountains.

59   HAMBURGER, ERIC. "Pound, Ford and 'Prose': the Making of a Modern Poet," Journal of American Studies, 5, No. 3 (Dec.), 281-92.
Important comments on the blurring of distinction between poetry and prose from the beginning of the 1900's on.

60   HANDY, WILLIAM J. Modern Fiction: A Formalist Approach. Carbondale: Southern Illinois University Press.
Handy's emphasis is on applying the "new critical" approach to longer fiction, using the premise that the image in poetry equals the scene in fiction. Doing so adds positive dimensions to The Old Man and the Sea.

61   HASSAN, IHAB. "Hemingway: Valor Against the Void," in The Dismemberment of Orpheus. New York: Oxford University Press, pp. 80-109.
Reprinted, enlarged, from 1970.B43.

62   HAUCK, RICHARD BOYD. A Cheerful Nihilism: Confidence and "The Absurd" in American Humorous Fiction. Bloomington: Indiana University Press, p. 241.
Finds Hemingway less adept than Faulkner and Twain; sees The Old Man and the Sea as a "parable of absurd confidence."

63   HAUGER, B. A. "First Person Perspective in Four Hemingway Stories," Rendezvous, 6, No. 1, pp. 29-38.
Claims that Hemingway uses this point of view to emphasize theme instead of to explain character; he illustrates his thesis using "Fifty Grand," "My Old Man," "Now I Lay Me," and "An Alpine Idyll."

64   HAYS, PETER L. "'Soldier's Home' and Ford Madox Ford," Heming-
         way Notes, 1 (Fall), 21-22.
            Sees this story as similar to descriptions from Ford's
         Some Do Not and Joyce's Dubliners and Portrait of the
         Artist.

64a   HESS, J., ed. "Jack Hemingway Remembers His Father," National
         Wildlife, 9, No. 2 (Feb.-March), 12-15.
            Discusses the "conservation habit" Hemingway passed on
         to his sons (distributing fish to the poor, founding Inter-
         national Big Game Fishing Association) with the result that
         two of his sons are in conservation work.

65   HIRSCH, FOSTER. Review of Islands in the Stream, Mediterranean
         Review (Spring), pp. 27-29.
            Sees the novel as almost self-parody, with Hemingway
         narrowing in "obsessionally" on his concepts of "heroic
         masculinity."

66   HOTCHNER, A. E. "The Guns of Hemingway," True, 52 (Sept.),
         49, 51-52, 54.
            Reminisces about Hemingway's love for hunting, especially
         game birds, and his adeptness at teaching Hotchner. In-
         cludes a description of Hemingway's guns and several hunting
         experiences.

67   HOWARD, MICHAEL S. Jonathan Cape, Publisher/ Herbert Jonathan
         Cape, G. Wren Howard. London: Jonathan Cape.
            Recounts Cape's interest in Hemingway (In Our Time and
         Fiesta) and their "firm friendship," lasting until Cape's
         death in 1960.

68   HOWELL, JOHN M. "Hemingway's Riddle and Kilimanjaro Reusch,"
         Studies in Short Fiction, 8: 469-70.
            Includes a letter from Richard Reusch, who did find a
         leopard at the peak of the mountain.

69   HURWITZ, HAROLD M. "Hemingway's Tutor, Ezra Pound," MFS, 17,
         No. 4 (Winter), 469-82.
            Comprehensive tracing of the Pound/Hemingway relation-
         ship in Paris from 1922 through 1925, with accurate identi-
         fication of many of Hemingway's prose techniques with
         Pound's poetic ones.
         Reprinted in Wagner, pp. 8-21 (See 1974.A3).

70   JAIN, S. P. "Some Hemingway Stories: Perspectives and Re-
         sponses," Literary Half-Yearly, 12, No. 1, pp. 53-64.
            Compares "The Battler," "A Way You'll Never Be," and "A
         Natural History of the Dead" thematically.

1971

71   JOHNSTON, KENNETH G. "The Great Awakening: Nick Adams and the
     Silkworms in 'Now I Lay Me,'" Hemingway Notes, 1 (Fall),
     7-10.
         Thinks Hemingway used the silkworm and its life cycle
     as an analogy to Nick's psychological state.

72   _____. "Hemingway and Mantegna: The Bitter Nail Holes,"
     Journal of Narrative Technique, 1 (May), 86-94.
         Notes there are six direct references to this artist in
     Hemingway's work; locates them, and considers them bitter
     reminders of human suffering and sacrifice.

73   KASHKEEN, IVAN. "Letters of Ernest Hemingway to Soviet Writers,"
     Fitzgerald/Hemingway Annual, pp. 197-208.
         Three long letters reprinted from Soviet Literature (Nov.
     1962) include Hemingway's comments on Russia, writing, and
     Communism.

74   KAUFMANN, DONALD L. "The Long Happy Life of Norman Mailer,"
     MFS, 17 (Autumn), 347-59.
         Sees Mailer and Hemingway as "kind of Siamese twins" in
     their attitudes toward the "eno-primitive," the status of
     females, and their "narcissism." While Hemingway's lan-
     guage is marked by his own "one man style," Mailer's is
     one of "versatility."

75   KENNER, HUGH. The Pound Era. Berkeley: University of Cali-
     fornia Press.
         Many references to Hemingway during the Paris years in
     this study of the great influence of Pound (and Henry
     James) on the innovation in modern letters.

76   KOVACS, JOZSEF. "Ernest Hemingway, Máté Zalka and Spain. To
     the Symbolic Meaning of The Old Man and the Sea," Acta
     Litteraria Academiae Scientiarum Hungaricae, 13: 315-24.
         Suggests viewing The Old Man and the Sea as the fourth
     part of a tetralogy (first three parts are the three
     sections of Islands in the Stream). Thinks Hemingway's
     understanding of the Spanish Civil War was crucial to his
     development, just as it was to the Hungarian Zalka.

77   KRONENBERGER, LOUIS, ed. Atlantic Brief Lives. Boston:
     Little, Brown.
         "Ernest Hemingway" by Robert Manning, reprinted partly
     from Atlantic, 216 (Aug. 1965), 101-08 (See 1965.B34).

78 KRUSE, HORST. "Ernest Hemingways Kunst der Allegorie: Zeit-
genössische, liter-arische und biblische Anspielungen in
'God Rest You Merry, Gentlemen,'" Jahrbuch für Amerika-
studien, 16: 128–50.
Sees the story as an attack upon organized religion and
puritanism; studies the subtle allusions to the carol, the
Bible, Shakespeare's Merchant of Venice, and Twain's The
Mysterious Stranger.

79 KUEHL, JOHN and JACKSON R. BRYER, eds. Dear Scott/Dear Max,
The Fitzgerald-Perkins Correspondence. New York: Scribners.
Many references, showing Perkins' continual concern for
both Fitzgerald and Hemingway.

80 LATHAM, AARON. Crazy Sundays: F. Scott Fitzgerald in Hollywood. New York: Viking Press.
Presents Hemingway as a rough boor, who consistently in-
terfered with Fitzgerald's friends and work.

81 LIVINGSTON, HOWARD. "Religious Intrusion in Hemingway's 'The
Killers,'" English Record, 21, No. 3 (Feb.), 42–44.
Finds the fact that Hemingway mentions Al's Judaism and
Max's Catholicism his way of stressing the sterility of
religion.

82 LODGE, DAVID. "Hemingway's Clean, Well-Lighted, Puzzling
Place," EIC, 21 (Jan.), 33–56.
A detailed examination of the text, particularly its
dialogue, emphasizing Hemingway's skill with repetition
"to generate a kind of verbal intensity similar to lyric
poetry."
Reprinted in The Novelist at the Crossroads and Other
Essays on Fiction and Criticism, Ithaca, Cornell University
Press, 1971, pp. 184–202.

83 LUTWACK, LEONARD. Heroic Fiction: The Epic Tradition and
American Novels of the Twentieth Century. Carbondale:
Southern Illinois University Press.
Sees that For Whom the Bell Tolls reflects a positive
philosophy of hope.

84 McCORMICK, JOHN. The Middle Distance, A Comparative History
of American Imaginative Literature: 1919–1932. New York:
Free Press.
Includes much material about Hemingway's earlier writing
and a good discussion of his central place in the 1920's
literary scene. "With the exception of T. S. Eliot and
William Faulkner, no recent American writer's place in
literary history is more secure than Ernest Hemingway's."

1971

85 McILVAINE, ROBERT M. "A Literary Source for the Caesarian
        Section in A Farewell to Arms," American Literature, 43
        (Nov.), 444-47.
            Finds a "partial model" for Catherine's death in that of
        Angela Witla in Dreiser's The "Genius."

86 MANNEN, ETHEL. Young in the Twenties: A Chapter of Auto-
        biography. London: Hutchinson.
            Reminiscence of the reception of A Farewell to Arms, but
        recalls her own dislike of Hemingway's "staccato style of
        writing" and the "quality of male sexual aggressiveness."

87 MARTINE, JAMES J. "Hemingway's 'Fifty Grand': The Other
        Fight(s)," Journal of Modern Literature, 2 (Sept.), 123-27.
            Refutes other sources and claims the 1922 Light-heavy-
        weight championship of the world, between Battling Siki and
        Georges Carpentier, where a frame-up became a double cross.
        Probably a composite of several fights.
        Reprinted in Benson, pp. 198-203 (See 1975.A3).

88 MATTHEWS, HERBERT L. A World in Revolution: A Newspaperman's
        Memoir. New York: Charles Scribner's Sons.
            Covering the Spanish Civil War with Hemingway.

89 MAY, CHARLES. "Is Hemingway's 'Well-Lighted Place' Really
        Clean Now?" Studies in Short Fiction, 8 (Spring), 326-30.
            Argues against the 1964 Hagopian reading; sees the change
        in the old waiter as an important dynamic in the story.

90 MAYNARD, REID. "Leitmotif and Irony in Hemingway's 'Hills Like
        White Elephants,'" University Review, 37: 273-75.
            Sees the repetition of the word two as ironic leitmotif.

91 MIZENER, ARTHUR. The Saddest Story: A Biography of Ford
        Madox Ford. New York: World, pp. 338-44.
            Recounts Hemingway's playing editor of the summer trans-
        atlantic review while Ford was in the States. Other
        references.

92 MONRO, DICK. "Letter from the Publisher," Sports Illustrated,
        35 (6 Dec.), 11.
            Announces publication of Hemingway's "African Journal"
        beginning Dec. 20; reprints a facsimile page of the
        manuscript.

93 MONTEIRO, GEORGE. "'Between Grief and Nothing': Hemingway
        and Faulkner," Hemingway Notes, 1 (Spring), 13-14.
            Summarizes several possible "borrowings" from Hemingway

(MONTEIRO, GEORGE)
in Faulkner's Wild Palms, and points out that Jordan's final
realization in For Whom the Bell Tolls parallels that of
Harry Wilbourne after Charlotte's death.

94   _____. "Hemingway: Contribution Toward a Definitive Bibliography," PBSA, 65: 411-14.
Adds several foreign items to the Hemingway bibliography.

95   _____. "Not Hemingway But Spain," Fitzgerald/Hemingway Annual,
pp. 309-11.
Recent Spanish translations of "A Clean, Well-Lighted
Place" omit the final 334 words, including the two prayers.

96   MOSHER, HAROLD F. "The Two Styles of Hemingway's The Sun Also
Rises," Fitzgerald/Hemingway Annual, pp. 262-73.
Mosher finds that Hemingway uses "staccato" (simple and
complex) sentences in passages describing depression,
failure, animosity; and "rhythmical" sentences (more complicated compound structures) for the affirmative passages.
Because staccato style pervades the ending, Mosher sees it
as depressing.

97   MURRAY, DONALD. "Hemingway's Waste Land: The Controlling Water
Symbolism of The Sun Also Rises," Hemingway Notes, 1
(Spring), 20-26.
Sees Hemingway's pervasive use of water in The Sun Also
Rises as the most direct result of Eliot's poem.

98   MYERS, MARSHALL. "A Tagemic Analysis of Hemingway's 'A Very
Short Story,'" in From Soundstream to Discourse: Papers
from the 1971 Mid-America Linguistics Conference. Columbia:
University of Missouri Press.
Interesting compilation of technical data.

99   NEWMAN, M. W. "The Earliest Ernest: 'A Born Genius' at Oak
Park High School," Chicago Daily News (31 July-1 Aug.),
Panorama Section, pp. 4-5.
Biographical reminiscence.

100   NIN, ANAÏS. The Diary of Anaïs Nin, 4, 1944-47, edited by
Gunther Stuhlmann. New York: Harcourt, Brace, Jovanovich,
p. 66.
Finds Hemingway's work representative of the "literalness"
America suffers from.

1971

101   PECKHAM, MORSE. "Ernest Hemingway: Sexual Themes in His
Writing," Sexual Behavior, 1, No. 4 (July 1971), 62–70.
Sees that Hemingway uses sexual intercourse to break
through the one-ness that traps all modern men.

102   PERELMAN, S. J. "The Machismo Mystique, or some views on the
various aspects of masculinity, as demonstrated by Ernest
Hemingway, Mike Todd, F. Scott Fitzgerald, and a sensuous
shrimp from Providence, Rhode Island," McCall's, 98 (Feb.),
88–89, 168–69.
Burlesque anecdote of a Hemingway variation on prize-
fighting.

*103   PERKINS, MICHAEL. "The Impotence of Being Ernest," Screw
(31 May), p. 13.
Cited in Fitzgerald/Hemingway Annual, 1972.

104   PRIGOZY, RUTH. "A Matter of Measurement; the Tangled Relationship Between Fitzgerald and Hemingway," Commonweal, 95
(29 Oct.), 103–06, 108–09.
Sees Hemingway's animosity toward Fitzgerald to be a
reflection of his paranoia. By 1929, Hemingway was trying
to break off the strong friendship of 1925–26, and his
attacks on Fitzgerald continued to the end. Prigozy sees
the problem as the effect of each man's public personality.
Reprinted in Discussion, 95 (17 Dec.), 267 ff.

105   SCHMIDT, DOLORES BARRACANO. "The Great American Bitch,"
College English, 32 (May), 900–05.
Study of character types, caricatures, and character
motivations of Hemingway's female characters.

106   SCHORER, MARK. "John Dos Passos: A Stranded American,"
Atlantic (March), pp. 93–96.
Compares Hemingway with Dos Passos in their physical
stature and their attitudes; comments that Islands in the
Stream is a parody of Hemingway's best writing; and claims
for even Hemingway's death, a championship.

*107   SHARMA, D. R. "Moral Frontiers of Ernest Hemingway," Panjab
University Research Bulletin, 2 (Aug.), 49–59.
Cited in Hemingway Notes, III.

*108   SMITH, GODFREY, ed. 1,000 Makers of The Twentieth Century.
London: David & Charles; Newton Abbot, n.p.
"Ernest Hemingway" by George MacBeth.

109   SMITH, JULIAN. "Eyeless in Wyoming, Blind in Venice: Heming-
        way's Last Stories," Connecticut Review, 4 (April), 9-15.
        Considers Hemingway's 1957 stories "the true capstone"
        to his career, with Blindy in "A Man of the World" a sort
        of Christ figure.

110   STARRETT, VINCENT. "Where's Papa? Ernest Hemingway: A Re-
        membrance and Reevaluation," Chicago Tribune Sunday Maga-
        zine (18 July), pp. 26, 28, 30, 32, 39.
        Describes the forces that shaped Hemingway; judges his
        posthumous works, and concludes that he was a unique genius.

111   STEWART, DONALD OGDEN. "Recollections of Fitzgerald and Hem-
        ingway," Fitzgerald/Hemingway Annual, pp. 177-88.
        Of The Sun Also Rises, Stewart concludes that it was
        "nothing but a report on what happened. There's no crea-
        tion, no imagination. This is journalism." Excerpts from
        an autobiography-in-progress, includes several interesting
        tales, from 1919 through the Paris years.

112   STONE, EDWARD. "Hemingway's Mr. Frazer: From Revolution to
        Radio," Journal of Modern Literature, 1 (March), 375-88.
        Compares two versions of the story (Scribner's Magazine,
        May, 1933, and Winner Take Nothing, Oct., 1933) and finds
        Hemingway's changes very significant, especially the ad-
        dition of the last paragraph.

113   SYLVESTER, BICKFORD. "Hemingway's Unpublished Remarks on War
        and Warriors," in War and Society in North America, edited
        by J. L. Granatstein and R. D. Cuff. Toronto: T. Nelson
        and Sons, pp. 135-52.
        Stresses that in Hemingway's letters to Charles T.
        Lanham, he opts for idealistic disregard for individual
        survival.

114   THEROUX, PAUL. "Lord of the Ring: Hemingway's 'Last Novel,'"
        Encounter, 36 (Feb.), 62-66.
        Sees Islands in the Stream as an autobiographical "suicide
        note," best left unpublished. "Self-slaughter" is seen as
        the only logical end for Hemingway's "destroying hero."

*115 THOMSEN, CHRISTIAN E. "Liebe und Tod in Hemingway's Across
        the River and Into the Trees," Neuren Sprachen, 20 (Dec.),
        665-74.
        Cited in Hemingway Notes, II.

1971

116 TOMKINS, CALVIN. Living Well Is the Best Revenge. New York: Viking.
In this biography of Gerald and Sara Murphy, Tomkins describes Hemingway as one part of the 1920 Paris scene, always a competitive one.

117 WALZ, LAWRENCE A. "'The Snows of Kilimanjaro': A New Reading," Fitzgerald/Hemingway Annual, pp. 239-45.
Walz traces the three contrasts of the story: Harry's past vs. his present; Harry vs. Helen; and Harry's present vs. his future. He concludes that Harry finds fulfillment because he remains undefeated.

118 WARNER, FRED. "Hemingway's Death: Ten Years Later," Hemingway Notes, 1 (Spring), 16-19.
Speculations on the artistic temperament, with special attention to The Fifth Column.

119 WEBER, RONALD. "A Pilgrim Reports from Hemingway's Michigan (Have They Really Forgotten?)," Detroit (Detroit Free Press Magazine), 22 (Aug.), 19-22.
On people and scenes in Hemingway's Michigan, the Petosky-Traverse City area.

120 WHITE, WILLIAM. "Hemingway and Fitzgerald," in American Literary Scholarship: An Annual, 1969, edited by J. Albert Robbins. Durham, N. C.: Duke University Press, pp. 122-36.
Survey of criticism on both authors published during 1969.

121 _____. "Hemingway on Postage Stamps," Hemingway Notes, 1 (Fall), 3-4.
Describes stamps honoring Hemingway in Czechoslovakia, the Republic of New Atlantis, and Cuba.

122 _____. "Supplement to Hanneman: Articles, 1966-1970," Hemingway Notes, 1 (Spring), 3-12.
Lists books and essays from 1964 to 1970.

123 WILCOX, EARL. "Jake and Bob and Huck and Tom: Hemingway's Use of Huck Finn," Fitzgerald/Hemingway Annual, pp. 322-24.
Another statement of dichotomies, that Cohn is the romantic and Jake the realist in The Sun Also Rises. Wilcox compares Hemingway's early treatments of Cohn and Barnes with Twain's presentations of Tom and Huck.

124 WILSON, EDMUND. "An Effort at Self-Revelation," New Yorker, 46 (2 Jan.), 59-62.
Includes a plot summary of Islands in the Stream but has

1972

(WILSON, EDMUND)
little patience with Hemingway's wordiness and organization. Wilson does admire a developing tension between
Hudson and his environment; he also praises the descriptions of nature, and predicts that the novel is an important one.
Reprinted in The Devils and Canon Barham, New York, Farrar,
Straus, and Giroux, 1973.

125 YALOM, I. D. and M. "Ernest Hemingway: A Psychiatric View,"
Archives of General Psychiatry, 24: 485-94.
Attempts to presuppose the reasons for Hemingway's suicide
by presenting the major psychological conflicts in both his
life style and fiction.

1972 A BOOKS

1 BAKER, CARLOS. Hemingway, The Writer as Artist. Princeton:
Princeton University Press.
Fourth edition includes nearly 25% new material. The
two opening biographical chapters have been revised, and
separate chapters on A Moveable Feast and Islands in the
Stream added. A biographical approach to the latter books
provides much new information. True to his earlier symbolic interest, Baker reads the military order given to
Thomas Hudson in Islands in the Stream as the author's
moral injunction as well: "Continue searching carefully
westward."

2 BAKKER, J. Ernest Hemingway: The Artist as Man of Action.
Assen: Van Gorcum & Comp. N. V.
Bakker sees Hemingway's active life as a complement to
his search for perfection in his craft. His interest
lies in the Nick Adams stories and the early novels,
finding To Have and Have Not, Across the River and Into
the Trees, and The Old Man and the Sea disappointing. The
book fails to consider other criticism written since the
mid-60's.

3 GRIEG, HARALD. Out Fishing with Hemingway (pamphlet). Translated by Charles Kegel. Pocatello: Idaho State University
Press.
Grieg stresses Hemingway's importance as "the writer, the
incomparable master of style, the reviving force of American literature, and the model for countless foreign
writers."

1972

4   KLIMO, VERNON (JAKE) and WILL OURSLER. Hemingway and Jake:
    An Extraordinary Friendship. Garden City, New York:
    Doubleday.
        An attempt to humanize Hemingway, not always successful.
    Some interesting references to other writers.

5   McLENDON, JAMES. Papa: Hemingway in Key West. Miami, Fla.:
    E. A. Seeman.
        McLendon covers the years 1928 to 1940, describing Heming-
    way's life and writings. Also includes a bibliography.

6   SUTHERLAND, FRASER. The Style of Innocence: A Study of Heming-
    way and Callaghan. Toronto: Clarke, Irwin & Co.
        Discusses each writer's fiction and life, and then cor-
    relates their careers. Sutherland finds similarities in
    characters ("broken men," "initiates," "boon comrades,"
    "victimized women"), aesthetic ideals, and influences.

7   WALDHORN, ARTHUR. A Reader's Guide to Ernest Hemingway.
    New York: Farrar, Straus, & Giroux, Inc.
        A useful study of Hemingway's life, style, and themes,
    the book includes readings of all the major fiction,
    separate chapters on the Nick Adams stories and on Heming-
    way as poet, dramatist, journalist and satirist. It also
    includes an annotated bibliography, a list of films made
    from Hemingway's fiction, and other materials. Chapter I
    reprinted in Waldhorn, pp. 1-17.

8   SARASON, BERTRAM D. Hemingway and The Sun Set. Washington,
    D. C.: Microcard Editions.
        Contents: pp. vii-xii: Preface by the editor.
        pp. 3-110: "Hemingway and The Sun Set" by the editor.
    Much description of The Sun Also Rises as roman à clef.
        pp. 111-135: "Hemingway's Bitterness" by Harold Loeb,
    reprinted from Connecticut Review, 1 (1967), 7-24.
        pp. 136-144: "With Duff at Ascain" by Harold Loeb, re-
    printed from The Way It Was, New York, S. G. Phillips,
    1959.
        pp. 145-150: "Scenes with a Hero" by Kathleen Cannell,
    reprinted from Connecticut Review, 2, No. 1 (1968), 5-12.
        pp. 150-188: "Interview with Hemingway's 'Bill Gorton,'"
    by Donald St. John, reprinted from Connecticut Review, 1
    (1968), 5-12 and 3 (1969), 5-23.
        pp. 189-206: "Interview with Donald Ogden Stewart" by
    Donald St. John, reprinted from Stewart's "Recollections
    of Fitzgerald and Hemingway" in Fitzgerald/Hemingway Annual,
    1971, pp. 177-88.

(SARASON, BERTRAM D.)

    pp. 207-211: "'Montoya' Remembers The Sun Also Rises," by Leah Rice Koontz, unpublished interview with Juanito Quintana.

    pp. 212-221: "The Sun Also Sets" by Sam Adams, reprinted from Sports Illustrated (29 June 1970).

    pp. 225-27: "On the Characters in The Sun Also Rises" by Robert McAlmon (letter to Norman Holmes Pearson).

    pp. 228-240: "Lady Brett Ashley and Lady Duff Twysden" by Bertram D. Sarason, reprinted from Connecticut Review, 2 (1969), 5-13.

    pp. 241-246: "Pat and Duff, Some Memories" by James Charters, reprinted from Connecticut Review, 3 (1970), 24-27.

    pp. 247-255: "Fitzgerald's The Sun Also Rises: Notes and Comment" by Philip Young and Charles W. Mann, reprinted from Fitzgerald/Hemingway Annual, 1970, pp. 1-9.

    pp. 256-259: "Letter to Ernest Hemingway by F. Scott Fitzgerald," reprinted from Fitzgerald/Hemingway Annual, 1970, pp. 10-13.

    pp. 260-270: "Two Essays on Ford Madox Ford" by Kathleen Cannell, reprinted from (1) The Christian Science Monitor (23 Dec. 1965) and (2) Providence Sunday Journal (20 Sept. 1964).

    pp. 271-274: "Duke Zizi" by James Charters, unpublished.

    pp. 275-279: "Cavalier and Cowboy: Goodbye to all that, Mr. Ford Braddocks Ford" by Bernard Poli, unpublished.

1972 B   SHORTER WRITINGS

1   ABRAHAMS, WILLIAM. "Hemingway: The Posthumous Achievement," Atlantic, 229 (June), 98-101.
    Finds The Nick Adams Stories an unfortunate example of the editor taking extreme liberties with materials. Even so, Abrahams admires the stories, taken singly, without fitting them into a "shadowy fictional autobiographical novel."

2   ALDERMAN, TAYLOR; KENNETH ROSEN; and WILLIAM WHITE. "Current Bibliography," Hemingway Notes, 2, No. 1 (Spring), 9-13.
    Items from 1969 to 1972.

3   _____. "Current Bibliography," Hemingway Notes, 2, No. 2 (Fall), 7-12.
    Current items.

4   ALDRIDGE, JOHN W. The Devil in the Fire: Retrospective Essays on American Literature and Culture, 1951-1971. New York:

1972

(ALDRIDGE, JOHN W.)
Harper's Magazine Press.
Views Hemingway's fiction as finding a value in the loss of stability and of belief, and his first two novels (his best) as presenting a "moral network" of code, style, and theme. Laments the inhospitability of the American culture to its artists, and thinks part of Hemingway's personal unhappiness came from that cultural impasse. Reprints three earlier essays on Hemingway, "Homage to Hemingway," "A Last Look at the Old Man," and "'Islands in the Stream.'"

5 ALINEI, TAMARA. "The Corrida and For Whom the Bell Tolls," Neophilologus, 56, No. 4 (Oct.), 487-92.
Sees that Hemingway uses the bullfight structure to present Spain's struggle for independence, especially in the scenes with Pablo.

6 ALLEN, MICHAEL J. B. "The Unspanish War in For Whom the Bell Tolls," Contemporary Literature, 13, No. 2 (Spring), 204-12.
Sees Hemingway taking the expected physical violence of the war a step beyond, to "metaphysical violence," important in that it tests the characters involved so that they can define "living well" and "dying well."

7 ANDERSEN, DAVID M. "Basque Wine, Arkansas Chawin' Tobacco: Landscape and Ritual in Ernest Hemingway and Mark Twain," Mark Twain Journal, 16, No. 1, pp. 3-7.
Compares the two wine-sharing scenes in The Sun Also Rises with the "tobacco chawin'" scene from Huckleberry Finn.

8 BARRETT, WILLIAM. "Winner Take Nothing" in Time of Need: Forms of Imagination in the Twentieth Century. New York: Harper and Row, pp. 64-95.
Sees Hemingway's concern with style--in all his actions and his writing--as a moral act. His perfect blending of "balance, rhythm and simplicity" compensates for his narrow range of insight and uninventive plots. His greatest merit is that the fiction does propose moral judgment, that apocalypse gives way to meaning.

9 BLUEFARB, SAM. The Escape Motif in the American Novel: Mark Twain to Richard Wright. Columbus, Ohio: Ohio University Press.
Considers A Farewell to Arms in his progression.

10 BRIAN, DENNIS, ed. "The Importance of Knowing Ernest," Esquire, 77 (Feb.), 98-101, 164-66, 168-70.

(BRIAN, DENNIS)
Interviews Lillian Ross, A. E. Hotchner, Malcolm Cowley, Truman Capote, Carlos Baker, George Plimpton, William Seward, and John and Mary Hemingway. Discussion concerns both Hemingway the man and the Ross profile of him; the former comments reveal the writer's complex and sometimes contradictory nature, and his confidence in his own work.

11   BRUCCOLI, MATTHEW and JENNIFER McCABE ATKINSON, eds. As Ever, Scott Fitz--. Philadelphia: Lippincott.
Many references, showing that Fitzgerald took an active part in helping Hemingway secure agents, publishers, and good contracts.

12   [BRUCCOLI, MATTHEW J. and C. E. F. CLARK, JR.]. F. Scott Fitzgerald and Ernest Hemingway in Paris. Bloomfield Hills, Michigan and Columbia: Bruccoli-Clark.
Catalogue of An Exhibition at the Bibliothèque Benjamin Franklin, in Conjunction with A Conference at the Institute de Études Américaines 23-24 June. Paris, France.

13   BURNAM, TOM. "The Other Ernest Hemingway," Neuphilologische Mitteilungen, 73, No. 1 (1972), 29-36.
Surveys Hemingway's intellectual side.

14   BUTCHER, FANNY. Many Lives--One Love. New York: Harper and Row, pp. 427-38.
Sees Hemingway as a serious and dedicated writer to whom all other concerns were secondary.

15   CARSON, DAVID L. "Symbolism in A Farewell to Arms," ES, 53: 518-22.
By centering on the first chapter of A Farewell to Arms, Carson defines the pervasive symbols that operate throughout the novel. Such pattern of associative symbols allows Hemingway to avoid the "sandhill" school of naturalism.

16   CASS, COLIN S. "The Love Story in For Whom the Bell Tolls," Fitzgerald/Hemingway Annual, pp. 225-35.
Case sees the love story as successful, "an adequate counter-balance to war." Jordan becomes a complete hero because of both kinds of activity.

17   CHATTERTON, WAYNE. "Textbook Uses of Hemingway and Faulkner," College Composition and Communication, 23, No. 3 (Oct.), 292-96.
Consideration of use of model sentences in composition texts; faults the texts on grounds that Hemingway and

1972

(CHATTERTON, WAYNE)
Faulkner do not commonly follow rules. A more distinctive style is more wayward, less a practical model.

18   [CHURCH, RALPH]. "Sherwood Comes to Town," Fitzgerald/Hemingway Annual, pp. 149-56.
One chapter from a manuscript found in a California bookshop, a description of the 1926-27 winter in Paris, with mention of Anderson's reaction to Hemingway's The Torrents of Spring.

19   CLARK, C. E. FRAZER, JR. "Hemingway in Advance," Fitzgerald/Hemingway Annual, pp. 195-206.
Description of Hemingway's books which were available in advance of formal publication, and the differences between them and the later versions.

20   _____. "Kiki and Her 'Sympatique Montparnasseur,'" Fitzgerald/Hemingway Annual, pp. 269-71.
Describes the way Hemingway came to write an introduction for the American edition of Kiki's Memoirs.

21   CRUNDEN, ROBERT M. From Self To Society, 1919-1941. Englewood Cliffs, N. J.: Prentice-Hall.
Views Hemingway's motivation as "religion, its loss, and the need for a replacement." "A nihilist by faith, a writer by vocation: the combination meant that Hemingway sublimated all his religious energies into his art."

22   DAVIDSON, ARNOLD E. "The Ambivalent End of Francis Macomber's Short, Happy Life," Hemingway Notes, 2, No. 1 (Spring), 14-16.
Sees Margot's confusion of aiming at buffalo-husband as "the perfect objective correlative for her own mixed feelings."

23   DELANEY, PAUL. "Robert Jordan's 'Real Absinthe' in For Whom the Bell Tolls," Fitzgerald/Hemingway Annual, pp. 317-20.
Delaney views Jordan's fondness for absinthe as a character-marking trait; he more generally considers Hemingway's use of drink in the novel.

24   DOWDY, ANDREW. "Hemingway & Surrealism: A Note on the Twenties," Hemingway Notes, 2, No. 1 (Spring), 3-6.
Sees The Torrents of Spring as an outgrowth of French Surrealism as well as a parody, and places it in the company of Doctor Transit, Doodab, The Eater of Darkness and other novels.

25 EDELSON, MARK. "A Note on 'One Reader Writes,'" Fitzgerald/
    Hemingway Annual, pp. 329-31.
        "This page of fiction is Hemingway's 'Portrait of a
    Lady,'" his use of her letter and her interior monologue
    a deft if ironic portrait.

26 FLANNER, JANET. "If Either of Us Ever Killed Ourself, the
    Other Was Not To Grieve," Life, 73 (28 July), 17.
        Excerpt from Paris Was Yesterday. Flanner's last
    meeting with Hemingway, August 1944, when they agreed
    that suicide could be a "permissible act of liberation
    from whatever humiliating bondage on earth could no
    longer be borne with self-respect."

27 ____. Paris Was Yesterday, 1925-1939, edited by Irving
    Drutman. New York: Viking Press.
        Recollections of Hemingway during the Paris years, The
    Sun Also Rises, friendship with Pound and Stein.

28 FORD, HUGH, ed. The Left Bank Revisited: Selections from the
    Paris Tribune, 1917-1934. University Park: Pennsylvania
    State University Press.
        Includes many comments on Hemingway, especially Eugene
    Jolas' "Open Letter to Ernest Hemingway," a 1923 review of
    Stein, Ford's praise for the Contact publications, and
    other items of interest.

29 GENT, GEORGE. "Hemingway's Letters Tell of Fitzgerald," New
    York Times (25 Oct.), p. 38.
        Discusses Hemingway's letters to Arthur Mizener from
    1949 to 1951.

30 GINGRICH, ARNOLD. "Publisher's Page," Esquire, 77 (Feb.), 6.
        Comments on Brian's composite interviews about Hemingway,
    and noted that Hemingway would get a good laugh at the
    interviewees squabbling among themselves.

31 GORDON, GERALD T. "Hemingway's Wilson-Harris: The Search for
    Values in The Sun Also Rises," Fitzgerald/Hemingway Annual,
    pp. 237-44.
        Sees Wilson-Harris as a complement to Jake and Bill;
    believes this character is based on Eric Dorman-Smith,
    Hemingway's Irish friend from Milan, 1918.

32 GREBSTEIN, SHELDON N. "The Structure of Hemingway's Short
    Stories," Fitzgerald/Hemingway Annual, pp. 173-93.
    Reprinted in Hemingway's Craft, Carbondale, Southern
    Illinois University Press, 1973.
        (See 1973.A3.)

1972

33 GRECO, ANNE. "Margot Macomber: 'Bitch Goddess' Exonerated,"
    Fitzgerald/Hemingway Annual, pp. 273-80.
        Sees the woman's verbal attacks as her attempt "to force
    her husband into recognizing his disgrace so that he might
    work out some means of atonement." Thinks Wilson's in-
    ability to understand Margot is critical to the story.

34 GRIMES, CARROLL. "Hemingway: 'Old Newsman Writes,'" Fitz-
    gerald/Hemingway Annual, pp. 215-23.
        Close reading of a Hemingway letter for Esquire, Dec. of
    1934, shows "his ability to handle such disparate topics
    as war, literature, and journalism" as well as playing
    columnist.

35 GUNN, GILES B. "Hemingway's Testament of Human Solidarity: A
    Literary and Theological Critique of For Whom the Bell
    Tolls," Christian Scholar's Review, 2 (Winter), 99-111.
        Sees the novel as Hemingway's most mature philosophical
    statement.

36 HAMALIAN, LEO. "Hemingway as Hunger Artist," Literary Review,
    16 (Fall), 5-13.
        The motif of "gustatory images" and scenes in much of
    Hemingway's writing (here, eleven of the stories) convinces
    Hamalian that "appetite was for Hemingway something more
    than itself . . . . the act of appeasing the appetite is a
    way of knowing the self."

37 HAMILTON, JOHN BOWEN. "Hemingway and the Christian Paradox,"
    Renascence, 24: 141-54.
        Sees the fish as the "organic, symbolic center" of The
    Old Man and the Sea; and Santiago as the privileged man
    who "almost unknowing discovered in a great fish the great
    paradox of suffering and grace."

38 HANNEMAN, AUDRE. "Hemingway in Portuguese: More Hanneman
    Addenda," Hemingway Notes, 2, No. 1 (Spring), 17-19.
        Listing of items in Portuguese.

39 "Hemingway Checklist," Fitzgerald/Hemingway Annual, pp. 347-67.
        Supplementary listing of secondary items from the mid-
    sixties to the present.

40 HEMINGWAY, GRACE HALL. "Two Grace Hall Hemingway Letters,"
    Fitzgerald/Hemingway Annual, pp. 301-02.
        Speaks of her son's generosity and kindness to her, and
    offers to sell copies of the Tabula with his "prophecy,"

41 HEMINGWAY, MARY. "An American Appreciation: Ernest's Idaho
    and Mine," World, 7 (Dec.), 34-37.
       Biographical comments, but nothing related to Hemingway
    as writer.

42 HEMINGWAY, PATRICK. "Son Also Rises," Newsweek, 80 (16 Oct.),
    48, 51.
       Patrick teaching wild life conservation in Tanzania's
    Serengeti National Park, in the shadow of Mt. Kilimanjaro.
    Comments that none of Hemingway's three sons is a writer.

43 HIGGINS, GEORGE V. "Rooting in Papa's Closet to Discover . . .
    14 Pages?!" National Observer, 11 (29 April), 21.
       Finds The Nick Adams Stories interesting but objects to
    issuing a collection with so little new material.

44 HOFFA, WILLIAM. "Ezra Pound and George Antheil: Vorticist
    Music and the Cantos," American Literature, 44, No. 2
    (March), 52-73.
       Some involvement of Hemingway in Pound's various con-
    certs and other musical interests.

45 HOWELL, JOHN M. and CHARLES A. LAWLER. "From Abercrombie &
    Fitch to the First Forty-Nine Stories: The Text of Ernest
    Hemingway's 'Francis Macomber,'" Proof, 2: 213-81.
       Tracing versions of the story, and notes on typescripts,
    the editors suggest that the ambiguity of Margot's shooting
    at the buffalo may parallel that of Wilson's using the car.
    The "manner of the accident" is central in these changes.

46 HUBBELL, JAY B. Who Are the Major American Writers? Durham,
    N. C.: Duke University Press.
       Many references; Hubbell affirms the primacy of Hemingway
    in modern letters.

47 INGERSOLL, R. STURGIS. Recollections of a Philadelphian at
    Eighty. Philadelphia: National Publishing Co., pp. 80-86;
       Recalls a brief friendship in Sun Valley when Hemingway
    was writing For Whom the Bell Tolls, 1939.

48 JOHNSTON, KENNETH G. "Journeys Into the Interior: Hemingway,
    Thoreau and Mungo Park," Forum (Houston), 10, No. 2,
    pp. 27-31.
       Comparison of both Thoreau's and Hemingway's allusive
    use of Mungo Park, African explorer. For Thoreau, Park
    was searching through introspection for the divine; for
    Hemingway, Park's faith marked him as naive.

1972

49 KAWIN, BRUCE. <u>Telling It Again and Again: Repetition in
      Literature and Film</u>. Ithaca: Cornell University Press.
         Views <u>The Sun Also Rises</u> as "a constructively repetitive
      novel about destructive repetition," and Hemingway's nearly
      emotionless characterization as a "neutralization" and
      "falsification" of reality.

50 KOBLER, J. F. "Francis Macomber as Four-Letter Man," <u>Fitz-
      gerald/Hemingway Annual</u>, pp. 295-96.
         De-codes Wilson's comment that Macomber was a "four-
      letter" man, to <u>shit</u>.

51 KROLL, ERNEST. "A Note on Victor Llona," <u>Fitzgerald/Hemingway
      Annual</u>, pp. 157-58.
         Description of the Peruvian who translated many modern
      American novelists into French during the 1920's, and his
      unfinished book of reminiscences, <u>I Knew Them in Paris</u>.

52 LANDSBERG, MELVIN. <u>Dos Passos' Path to U.S.A.</u> Boulder: The
      Colorado Associated University Press.
         P. 107: Hemingway is listed as among Dos Passos' closest
      friends; pp. 182-83: his defense of Hemingway as craftsman;
      his plea that writers need not be politically oriented;
      many other references.

53 LARSON, E. Review of <u>The Nick Adams Stories</u>, <u>Carleton Miscel-
      lany</u>, 12 (Spring), 76-81.
         Suggests a more accurate arrangement of the stories and
      laments the greediness of the publishers.

54 LAURENCE, FRANK M. "Hollywood Publicity and Hemingway's Popu-
      lar Reputation," <u>JPC</u>, 6 (Summer), 20-31.
         Sees Hollywood's publicity as responsible in part for
      making Hemingway a culture hero at every level of American
      society.

55 LEVY, ALAN. "Ezra Pound's Voice of Silence," <u>New York Times
      Magazine</u> (9 Jan.), pp. 14-15, 59-68.
         In one of Pound's rare comments toward the end of his
      life, he praised Hemingway's writing.

56 LINEBARGER, J. M. "Symbolic Hats in <u>The Sun Also Rises</u>,"
      <u>Fitzgerald/Hemingway Annual</u>, pp. 323-24.
         Brett's hat is considered a symbol, and Hemingway's
      mention of it traced through the novel.

57 LINGEMAN, RICHARD R. "More Posthumos [sic] Hemingway," <u>New
      York Times</u> (25 April), p. 41.

(LINGEMAN, RICHARD R.)
   Sees that The Nick Adams Stories does not create any new
impressions; fails to find them a unity. Commends Hemingway's editorial judgment for cutting much of the writing
which is replaced in this collection.

58   LLONA, VICTOR. "The Sun Also Rose for Ernest Hemingway,"
        Fitzgerald/Hemingway Annual, pp. 159-71.
        Clear account of Hemingway's fascination with the craft
     of writing, in the Paris years.

59   LONGSTREET, STEPHEN. We All Went To Paris: 1776-1971. New
        York: Macmillan, pp. 307-14.
        Hemingway in Paris.

60   MacDONALD, SCOTT. "Implications of Narrative Perspective in
        Hemingway's 'The Undefeated,'" Journal of Narrative Tech-
        nique, 2: 1-15.
        Sees Zurito, not Manuel, as true hero--a man aware, un-
     defeated, in every sense.

61   McHANEY, THOMAS L. "Anderson, Hemingway, and Faulkner's The
        Wild Palms," PMLA, 87 (May), 465-74.
        Survey of allusions to Hemingway and Anderson in this
     novel. On the basis of his reading, McHaney finds that
     Faulkner is closer to Anderson in his view of life and
     fiction than he is to Hemingway.

62   McNALLEY, JAMES. "A Hemingway Mention of Gentlemen," Fitz-
        gerald/Hemingway Annual, pp. 333-34.
        Relates the word to the praise of Fitzgerald, and more
     directly to literary critics.

63   McSWEENEY, KERRY. "The First Hemingway Hero," Dalhousie Re-
        view, 52 (Summer), 309-14.
        Review of The Nick Adams Stories. Sees the collection
     as a new way of looking at Nick, but regrets the arrange-
     ment of the stories.

64   MAGNY, CLAUDE-EDMONDE. The Age of the American Novel, The
        Film Aesthetic of Fiction Between the Two Wars. Translated
        by Eleanor Hochman. New York: Frederick Ungar Publishing
        Co. Originally published in 1948, pp. 144-60.
        "Hemingway, or the Exaltation of the Moment." Speaks of
     the influence of Hemingway on French writers. Sees Jordan
     as Hemingway's most fully realized hero because he is no
     longer "adolescent." Only in For Whom the Bell Tolls does
     Hemingway's style work to its best effect, making use of a
     Bergsonian concept of time.

1972

65 MANN, CHARLES W., JR. Review of "African Journal" in Sports
    Illustrated, Fitzgerald/Hemingway Annual, pp. 395-96.
        Laudatory review of the series; Mann suggests book publi-
    cation.

66 _____. "Young Hemingway: A Panel," Fitzgerald/Hemingway
    Annual, pp. 113-44.
        Conversation among Frederick Spiegel, William Horne,
    Lewis Clarahan, Raymond George, and Mrs. Sue (Lowrey)
    Kesler, chaired by Mann: Hemingway appears as a busy, in-
    quisitive, kindly young man, loyal to friends and family,
    with no interest in girls or drinking. Includes the tran-
    script of his excellent grades at Oak Park High School.

67 MARTIN, JUDITH. "The Importance of Being Ernest," The Washing-
    ton Post (30 Oct.), pp. B1, B2.
        Surveys eight Hemingway letters to Arthur Mizener between
    1949 and 1951.

68 MONTEIRO, GEORGE. "Hemingway and Spain: A Response to Wood-
    ward," Hemingway Notes, 2, No. 2 (Fall), 16-17.
        Continues the argument with Robert Woodward in Hemingway
    Notes, 2, No. 1.

69 _____. "Hemingway's Christmas Carol," Fitzgerald/Hemingway
    Annual, pp. 207-13.
        Sees a three-part focus in "God Rest You Merry, Gentle-
    men": that of the boy, the surgeons' conflicts, and the
    narrator's story. Objects to Hemingway's frequent Christian
    references as misleading.

70 MOTTRAM, ERIC. "Living Mythically: The Thirties," Journal of
    American Studies, 6: 267-87.
        Places Hemingway in brief association with New Masses;
    draws parallels between Hemingway's stoicism and that of
    Spencer Tracy in his 25 movies; also F. D. Roosevelt's
    attitudes.

71 MURRAY, EDWARD. The Cinematic Imagination: Writers and Motion
    Pictures. New York: Frederick Ungar Publishing Co.,
    pp. 218-43.
        "Ernest Hemingway--Cinematic Structure in Fiction and
    Problems in Adaptation." Discusses the films made from
    Hemingway's fiction and concludes that Hemingway's work,
    like that of Joyce, was not readily adaptable for film.
    Sees that in the 1930's, however, Hemingway's fiction made
    more use of the devices of screen-writing (To Have and Have
    Not, For Whom the Bell Tolls, "Snows," and "The Capital of

(MURRAY, EDWARD)
the World"), shifting point of view, dissolving from objective to subjective, and utilizing what Murray calls "a
filmic imagination."

72 PAULY, THOMAS H. and THOMAS DWYER. "Passing the Buck in The
Sun Also Rises," Hemingway Notes, 2, No. 2 (Fall), 3-6.
A criticism of Jake's "pocketbook philosophy," pointing
out that few experiences give Jake happiness, regardless
of their "cost."

73 PIERCE, J. F. "The Car as Symbol in Hemingway's 'The Short
Happy Life of Francis Macomber,'" South Central Bulletin,
32 (Winter), 230-32.
Sees that the relative positions of the three characters
within the car parallel their dominance-submission roles in
the story.

74 PINSKER, SANFORD. "Rubbing Against the American Grain: Writing
After Hemingway," Quadrant, 17, No. 6 (Nov.-Dec.), 48-54.
Views literature of the 1950's and 1960's as repudiating
Hemingway's machos ethic. Sees in writers such as Bellow a
movement away from action toward cultural meditation, and
black humor, as well as reportage.

75 PRESCOTT, PETER S. "Big Two-Hearted Writer," Newsweek, 79
(17 April), 100, 104.
Review of The Nick Adams Stories. Quotes D. H. Lawrence's
opinion that the early Hemingway stories might be read as
"a fragmentary novel," but objects to the sequence of the
stories here.

76 _____. "Hemingway: The Last Wheeze," in Soundings, Encounters
with Contemporary Books. New York: Coward, McCann &
Geoghegan, pp. 74-76.
Likes some parts of Islands in the Stream but generally
finds the prevalent Hemingway philosophy, like Hudson,
tired and lonely.

77 PRICE, REYNOLDS. Things Themselves: Essays and Scenes. New
York: Atheneum, pp. 176-213.
"For Ernest Hemingway." A grudging reminiscence turns
into a thankful one ("For being a strong force in both my
own early awareness of a need to write and my early sense
of how to write. Maybe the strongest.") with the publication of Islands in the Stream. Price sees "Bimini" as
Hemingway's "finest sustained fiction." Comments on the
Hemingway prose rhythm, themes ("saintliness," "goodness,"
the "quest for virtue"), and style.

1972

78   PRIZEL, YURI. "Hemingway in Soviet Literary Criticism,"
     American Literature, 44 (Nov.), 445-456.
         This survey of Russian critical opinion from 1955 to
     1970 shows that these critics see Hemingway as a realist,
     but are increasingly prone to emphasize his aesthetics in-
     stead of politics. Prizel thinks Hemingway is popular in
     the Soviet Union because of his "powerful, fast-moving
     prose," his treatments of love, and his anti-fascism.

79   PROFFER, CARL R., ed. and trans. Soviet Criticism of American
     Literature in the Sixties: An Anthology. Ann Arbor:
     Ardis Publishers.
         Pp. 116-148: "For Whom the Bell Tolls" by Raisa Orlova
     (See 1968.B47); pp. 181-89: "What Is Hemingway's Style?"
     by Ivan Kashkin.

80   REYNOLDS, BRAD. "Afternoon with Mary Hemingway," America, 126
     (25 March), 319-20.
         At Ketchum, Mary recalls Hemingway's love of hunting and
     natural beauty.

81   REYNOLDS, MICHAEL S. "Two Hemingway Sources for In Our Time,"
     Studies in Short Fiction, 9, No. 1 (Winter), 81-86.
         Finds sources for Chapters 6 and 9.

82   ROBINSON, FORREST D. "Frederic Henry: The Hemingway Hero as
     Story Teller," CEA Critic, 34, No. 4 (Fall), 13-16.
         Sees Henry as an active force in A Farewell to Arms be-
     cause he is re-enacting the events he tells.

83   ROSS, MORTON L. "Bill Gorton, the Preacher in The Sun Also
     Rises," MFS, 18, No. 4 (Winter), 517-27.
         Attempt to define The Sun Also Rises's morality by
     viewing Gorton as conveyor of the moral code. Unlike most
     of the characters in the novel, Gorton speaks in maxims.

84   ROVIT, EARL. Review of The Nick Adams Stories, Hemingway Notes,
     2, No. 2 (Fall), 18-19.
         Finds the new collection "disappointingly bland," and
     thinks these stories are stronger in small doses. Nick as
     character does not develop.

85   SAMSELL, R. L. "Paris Days with Ralph Church," Fitzgerald/
     Hemingway Annual, pp. 145-47.
         Biographical note about this friend of Hemingway's,
     Anderson's, and Stein's.

86 SCHNEIDER, PIERRE. "Paris: Many Moods of Montherland," <u>New York Times</u> (24 Oct.), p. 34.
    In this obituary of Montherland, Schneider makes the comparisons with Hemingway: both were wounded in World War I, both tried their hands at bullfighting, both committed suicide, both "pedastalled the self and extolled the quest of pleasure."

87 SCHULBERG, BUD. <u>The Four Seasons of Success</u>. New York: Doubleday & Co.
    Uses Hemingway as a prime example of what he calls "Number One-ism," the cultural push for success; and quotes Fitzgerald's comments on <u>For Whom the Bell Tolls</u> (praise but the reservation that Hemingway's "mind doesn't grow").

88 SEIB, KENNETH. "<u>Trout Fishing in America</u>: Brautigan's Funky Fishing Yarn," <u>Criticism</u>, 18, No. 2, pp. 63-71.
    Sees Brautigan's prose as a hip collage that includes elements of Hemingway.

89 SHEPHERD, ALLEN. "Hudson's Cats in Hemingway's <u>Islands in the Stream</u>," <u>Notes on Contemporary Literature</u>, 2 (Sept.), 3-6.
    Three of Hudson's eleven cats are used to relate to people in his reminiscence: his first wife; a fighter; and himself.

90 _____. "The Lion in the Grass (Alas?): A Note on 'The Short Happy Life of Francis Macomber,'" <u>Fitzgerald/Hemingway Annual</u>, pp. 297-99.
    Sees Hemingway's sudden shift into the mind of the lion as an important tactic, contrasting the brute courage with Macomber's cowardice at that point.

91 _____. "'Other Things,' Unanswerable Questions: Hemingway's <u>Islands in the Stream</u>," <u>Antigonish Review</u>, 9 (Spring), 37-39.
    Sees central question of book: what went wrong with Hudson's life and what is there left? Decides the problem lies with the "other things" of his life, interfering with his real work.

92 SKOW, JOHN. "A Moveable Feast," <u>Time</u>, 99 (1 May), 81-82.
    Sees <u>The Nick Adams Stories</u> as fine examples of Hemingway's compression resulting in magnificent "tension."

93 SLAVUTYCH, YAR. "Ernest Hemingway in Ukranian Literature," in <u>Proceedings of the Comparative Literature Symposium</u>, 5. Modern American Fiction: Insights and Foreign Lights. Edited by Wolodymyr T. Zyla and Wendell M. Aycock. Texas

1972

(SLAVUTYCH, YAR)
Technical University, Jan. 27-28, pp. 67-76.
Discusses popularity of Hemingway in Ukranian translations (now available: three novels, one play, twenty short
stories).

94 STEINBERG, LEE. "The Subjective Idealist, 'Quest for True
Man' in Hemingway's For Whom the Bell Tolls," Literature
and Ideology, 13, pp. 51-58.
Sees Jordan as involved in a quest; events in the novel
provide a series of testing encounters. Objects to Hemingway's closing the novel with all attention on Jordan, un-
dermining both the title and the progression of the work.

95 STEPHENS, ROBERT O. Review of Ernest Hemingway's Apprenticeship, Resources for American Literary Study, 2 (Spring),
115-16.
Sees its publication as protection against more biographical fallacies about Hemingway.

96 _____. "Language Magic and Reality in For Whom the Bell Tolls,"
Criticism, 14 (Fall), 151-64.
Sees the urgency of Hemingway's characters to communicate
expressed through their interest in "language magic"--with
the tendency to presume necessary connections between words
and things or actions and to assume control over events and
feelings by the power of words. Jordan stands at the center
of this attempt.
Reprinted in Wagner, pp. 266-79 (See 1975.A3).

97 SUGG, RICHARD P. "Hemingway, Money and The Sun Also Rises,"
Fitzgerald/Hemingway Annual, pp. 257-67.
Sees Hemingway's use of money as indicative of characters'
moral attitudes; they value getting "their money's worth."
Sugg also comments on "A Clean, Well-Lighted Place," "Fifty
Grand," and the African stories.

98 SUTHERLAND, FRASER. "Hemingway and Callaghan, Friends and
Writers," Canadian Literature, 53 (Summer), 8-17.
Describes the friendship running from 1923 to 1929.

99 TWITCHELL, JAMES. "The Swamp in Hemingway's 'Big Two-Hearted
River,'" Studies in Short Fiction, 9 (Summer), 275-76.
Suggests that the swamp may be imaginary, symbolic of
Nick's mental state during the story.

1972

100   VANDERVEIDE, MARJORIE. "Afternoon with Mary Hemingway,"
       Writers Digest, 52 (June), 28-30, 43.
            Describes her position as sole executor of Hemingway's
       literary estate.

101   VANISTARTT, QUESTIN. "Hemingway and The Sun Set," Connecticut
       Review, 5, No. 2 (April), 16-17.
            Recollections about his own stay in Paris in the later
       1920's and his reactions give him support for Sarason's
       identifications.

102   VOPAT, CAROLE GOTTLIEB. "The End of The Sun Also Rises: A
       New Beginning," Fitzgerald/Hemingway Annual, pp. 245-55.
            Discusses the changes in Barnes' personality through the
       novel, with a focus on the last of Book III. Vopat sees
       Barnes as having changed profoundly, recognizing people's
       needs and relationships.

103   WAGNER, LINDA W. "The Sun Also Rises: One Debt to Imagism,"
       Journal of Narrative Technique, 2, No. 2 (May), 88-98.
            A comparison between Hemingway's prose techniques and
       Pound's 1913 Imagist dicta. Wagner sees the novel as "a
       masterpiece of suggestion," a positive depiction of the
       primary characters.

104   _____. "The Marinating of For Whom the Bell Tolls," Journal
       of Modern Literature, 2, No. 4 (Nov.), 533-46.
            Studies Hemingway's news dispatches, the five stories,
       and The Fifth Column, locating elements in each which
       later coalesced into For Whom the Bell Tolls. She justi-
       fies each thematic strain in the novel as being representa-
       tive of Hemingway's growing interest in the war from 1936
       on.
       Reprinted in Wagner, pp. 200-212 (See 1975.A3).

105   WEEKS, ROBERT P. "Cleaning Up Hemingway," Fitzgerald/Hemingway
       Annual, pp. 311-13.
            Weeks lists two typographical errors which have existed
       through many printings of "My Old Man" and "Fifty Grand."

106   WHITE, WILLIAM. "Bill Gorton/Grundy in The Sun Also Rises,"
       Hemingway Notes, 2, No. 2 (Fall), 13-15.
            In the first two printings of the novel, Bill Gorton
       appears as Bill Grundy; some translations perpetuate the
       confusion.

107   _____. "Hemingway," National Observer, 11 (24 June), 12.
            Letter to the editor about Hemingway's suicide.

1972

108 WHITE, WILLIAM. "Hemingway and Fitzgerald," American Literary
       Scholarship: An Annual, 1970, edited by J. Albert Robbins.
       Durham, N. C.: Duke University Press, pp. 132-48.
         Survey of criticism on both authors published during 1970.

109 WHITMAN, ALDEN. "Hemingway's Letters Reproach Critics," New
       York Times (9 March), p. 36.
         Comments about ten Hemingway letters to Charles Poore.

110 WINSTON, ALEXANDER. "If He Hadn't Been a Genius He Would Have
       Been a Cad," American Society of Legion of Honor Magazine,
       43: 25-40.
         Describes the young Hemingway.

111 WOODWARD, ROBERT. "Robert Jordan's Wedding/Funeral Sermon,"
       Hemingway Notes, 2, No. 1 (Spring), 7-8.
         Suggests a parallel between Jordan's leave-taking of
       Maria and the Bible (John 14:2-6 and Ruth 1:16); expands
       Monteiro's note of influence between For Whom the Bell
       Tolls and The Wild Palms.

112 YOUNG, PHILIP. "'Big World Out There': The Nick Adams
       Stories," Novel, 6: 5-19.
         Young discusses analyses of each of the stories with
       background material about the collection.
         Reprinted in Benson, pp. 29-45 (See 1975.A3).

113 _____. Preface to The Nick Adams Stories. New York: Scrib-
       ner's.
         All extant Nick Adams stories, including eight unpublished
       sketches or stories, arranged chronologically, consistent
       with Young's feeling that Nick is an important continuing
       character in the Hemingway canon.

114 _____. Three Bags Full, Essays in American Fiction. New York:
       Harcourt, Brace.
         Pp. 3-29: "Hemingway and Me: A Rather Long Story,"
       reprinted from Kenyon Review, 28 (Jan. 1966). (See
       1966.B81.)
         Pp. 30-54: "The End of Compendium Reviewing," reprinted
       from Kenyon Review, 26 (Autumn 1964). (See 1964.B58.)
         Pp. 55-67: "I Disremember Papa," reprinted from Atlantic,
       218 (Aug. 1966). (See 1966.B82.)
         Pp. 68-75: "Locked in the Vault with Hemingway," re-
       printed from New York Times Book Review (29 Sept. 1968).
       (See 1968.B76.)

1973

115 ZIOLKOWSKI, THEODORE. <u>Fictional Transfigurations of Jesus</u>.
     Princeton, N. J.: Princeton University Press.
          Although Ziolkowski does not consider Hemingway's
     writing in this book, he does point out, of Santiago, that
     "no character who lies down or dies with his arms out-
     stretched . . . is safe from the critical cross."

<u>1973 A BOOKS</u>

1 BROER, LAWRENCE R. <u>Hemingway's Spanish Tragedy</u>. University,
     Alabama: The University of Alabama Press.
          Broer claims that Hemingway was at home in Spain, and he
     explores the Spanish culture to determine its appeal. He
     further believes that the later Hemingway heroes differ
     from the early ones at least partly because Hemingway in-
     creasingly identified with the Spanish fatalistic world
     view.

2 BRUCCOLI, MATTHEW J. and C. E. FRAZER CLARK, JR., compilers.
     <u>Hemingway at Auction, 1930-1973</u>. Introduction by Charles
     W. Mann. Detroit: Gale Research Co.
          A reference guide which also includes excerpts from the
     many Hemingway letters which were originally quoted from
     in auction catalogues.

3 GREBSTEIN, SHELDON NORMAN. <u>Hemingway's Craft</u>. Carbondale:
     Southern Illinois University Press.
          Grebstein attempts to find terms for elements of Heming-
     way's craft, stressing the motifs of journey and inward-
     outward-inward movement of many stories and novels; the
     use of dialogue, sentence rhythm, paragraphing, and imagery.
     The book concludes with a chapter on Hemingway's humor,
     which Grebstein finds to be satiric and purposefully
     vitriolic. Includes summaries of manuscript variations
     for <u>A Farewell to Arms</u> and <u>For Whom the Bell Tolls</u>.

4 KVAM, WAYNE E. <u>Hemingway in Germany: The Fiction, the Legend,
     and the Critics</u>. Athens: Ohio University Press.
          Analysis of Hemingway's reputation in Germany especially
     since World War II. Separate chapters on each of the
     major novels, the stories, and Hemingway's style in general.
     An epilogue continues the study through 1971. Kvam stresses
     that German readers respond to Hemingway as "a fellow suf-
     ferer" and "a model for living." The "darker books (<u>Across
     the River and Into the Trees</u> and <u>The Old Man and the Sea</u>)"
     are the most popular.

1973

5   PEARSALL, ROBERT BRAINARD. The Life and Writings of Ernest
     Hemingway. Amsterdam, Holland: Dodopi NV.
         A general reading of Hemingway's work, from the perspec-
     tive that craft was consistently important to him. Pearsall
     also identifies Hemingway as extremely American; his empha-
     sis here is needed. Not without errors, the book also con-
     tains unfounded statements of judgment, as that the plot of
     A Farewell to Arms is "creaky" or that Santiago is "an il-
     literate lumpen."

6   SHAW, SAMUEL. Ernest Hemingway. New York: Frederick Ungar
     Publishing Co.
         A quick survey of Hemingway's work and career, largely
     sympathetic with the writer's position in the modern world.
     Includes brief chronology and briefer bibliography.

7   WALDHORN, ARTHUR, ed. Ernest Hemingway: A Collection of
     Criticism. New York: McGraw-Hill.
         Contents: pp. 1-17: "Artist and Adventurer: A Bio-
     graphical Sketch" by the editor, reprinted from his A
     Reader's Guide to Ernest Hemingway, New York, Farrar,
     Straus, & Giroux, 1972, Chapter I.
         pp. 18-34: "Ernest Hemingway: The Meaning of Style" by
     John Graham, reprinted from MFS, 6 (Winter 1960), 298-313.
         pp. 35-55: "Hemingway's Ambiguity: Symbolism and Irony"
     by E. M. Halliday, reprinted from American Literature, 28
     (March 1956), 1-22.
         pp. 56-82: "The Snows of Ernest Hemingway" by Bern
     Oldsey, reprinted from Wisconsin Studies in Contemporary
     Literature, 4 (Spring-Summer, 1963), 172-98.
         pp. 83-91: "Hemingway Achieves the Fifth Dimension" by
     Frederick I. Carpenter, reprinted from PMLA, 69 (Sept.
     1954), 611-18.
         pp. 92-111: "Ernest Hemingway, Literary Critic" by
     Daniel Fuchs, reprinted from American Literature, 36 (Jan.
     1965), 431-51.
         pp. 112-126: "Hemingway and the Pale Cast of Thought"
     by Robert Evans, reprinted from American Literature, 38
     (May 1966), 161-76.
         pp. 127-140: "The World and an American Myth" by Philip
     Young, reprinted from Ernest Hemingway: A Reconsideration,
     University Park, Pennsylvania State University Press, 1966.
         pp. 141-150: Selected Bibliography.

1973 B SHORTER WRITINGS

1   ANON. "Discussion at the Paris Conference," Fitzgerald/Heming-
     way Annual, pp. 77-81.

(ANON.)
Harold Loeb denies chasing Hemingway with a gun; Cody describes Hemingway's facility with French as "sufficient"; discussion of Hemingway's letter to Jed Kiley protesting the latter's book.

2 AGENT, DAN. "The Hair on Hemingway's Chest," Lost Generation Journal, 1 (May), 12–15.
Questions Hemingway's ultra-masculine stances, both in his life and fiction.

3 ALDERMAN, TAYLOR. Review of The Nick Adams Stories, The Alternative, 6 (March), 24–25.
Calls the previously unpublished stories and fragments "an odd lot, decidedly inferior" to things that were published. Contends that Hemingway did not think of the Nick Adams stories as a unit.

4 ALDERMAN, TAYLOR; KENNETH ROSEN; and WILLIAM WHITE. "Hemingway: A Current Bibliography," Hemingway Notes, 3, No. 1 (Spring), 11–13.
Listing of recent items.

5 _____. "Hemingway: A Current Bibliography," Hemingway Notes, 3, No. 2 (Fall), 12–16.
Listing of recent items.

6 ALDRIDGE, JOHN W. "Afterthoughts on the 20's," Commentary, 56 (Nov.), 37–41.
Rejects Cowley's view of the period, and sees that Hemingway wrote, for the rest of his life, "out of a fading memory of emotional and intellectual premises" created during that decade.

6a ALLEN, MARY. "Hail To Arms: A View of For Whom the Bell Tolls," Fitzgerald/Hemingway Annual, pp. 285–93.
Faulting the novel because Pilar and Maria have no children and "do little to preserve life," Allen sees Jordan as a kind of "anti-Christ." She objects to what she calls "the increasingly murderous path" of Hemingway's tests of courage for his protagonists.

7 APPEL, BENJAMIN. "Miss America and the Look-Back Boys," Literary Review, 17, No. 1 (Fall), 5–34.
Finds Maria in For Whom the Bell Tolls "that dream girl on loan from Hollywood."

1973

8   ARNER, ROBERT D. "Hemingway's 'Miracle' Play: "Today is
        Friday" and the York Play of the Crucifixion," <u>Markham
        Review</u>, 4, No. 1 (Oct.), 8-11.
            Suggests the medieval York play (<u>Christi Crucifixio</u>) as
        possible source for the Hemingway play; also views the
        play as part of Hemingway's preoccupation with the ritual
        of noble dying.

9   ASSELINEAU, ROGER. "Hemingway in Paris," <u>Fitzgerald/Hemingway
        Annual</u>, pp. 11-32.
            Recounts Hemingway's years in Paris, 1921-28, summarizing
        his work habits, friendships, artistic education, and the
        city's atmosphere. Claims that Hemingway "loved Paris be-
        cause he loved life and love"; loved Spain "because he was
        fascinated by death."

10 BEEKMAN, E. M. "Raymond Chandler and an American Genre," <u>Massa-
        chusetts Review</u>, 14, No. 1 (Winter), 149-73.
            Compares Chandler's heroes with Hemingway's, seeing the
        latter's as "passive." Finds that their novels share the
        tone of "melancholy and brooding."

11 BIDLE, KENNETH E. "<u>Across the River and Into the Trees</u>: Rite
        De Passage à Mort," <u>Fitzgerald/Hemingway Annual</u>, pp. 259-70.
            Sees Hemingway's pervasive use of ritual, and characters
        involved in ritualistic action, as one of the strongest of
        his fictional motifs. Reads <u>Across the River and Into the
        Trees</u> as an effective novel containing a series of such
        rites--"baptism, confirmation, holy orders, sacred dining,
        matrimony, penance, extreme unction, and blood sacrifice."
        His theory makes much of Cantwell's behavior explicable.

12 BOGAN, LOUISE. <u>What the Woman Lived, Selected Letters of
        Louise Bogan, 1920-1970</u>, edited by Ruth Limmer. New York:
        Harcourt, Brace.
            In 1926, Bogan "discovered a wonderful man--Ernest Hem-
        ingway--who really can write simple declarative sentences."
        Other references.

13 BRADBURY, MALCOLM. <u>Possibilities: Essays on the State of the
        Novel</u>. New York: Oxford University Press.
            Finds Hemingway, with Stein, responsible for "a fresh
        infusion of post-adjectival, post-causal style."

14 BRASHER, JIM. "Hemingway's Florida," <u>Lost Generation Journal</u>,
        1 (Fall), pp. 4-8. Illustrations. Descriptive essay.

314

15 M.J.B. [BRUCCOLI, MATTHEW J.] "Ways of Seeing Hemingway,"
    Fitzgerald/Hemingway Annual, pp. 197-207.
        Discussion of Ross's Profile and Hemingway's reactions
    to it, with reproductions of corrections by both Mary and
    Hemingway. Hemingway had suggested only minor revisions.

16 BRYER, JACKSON R. "Fitzgerald and Hemingway," American Literary
    Scholarship: An Annual, 1971, edited by J. Albert Robbins.
    Durham, N. C.: Duke University Press, pp. 120-48.
        Survey of criticism on both authors published during 1971.

17 CLARK, C. E. FRAZER, JR. "Recent Hemingway at Auction," Fitz-
    gerald/Hemingway Annual, pp. 295-97.
        Records prices up to $1900 for a single Hemingway letter.

18 CODY, MORRILL. "Remarks by Morrill Cody," Fitzgerald/Hemingway
    Annual, pp. 39-42.
        Reminiscence about Hemingway's borrowing some of the
    notes for This Must Be the Place, with Jimmy Charters, and
    never returning them.

19 COWLEY, MALCOLM. "Hemingway: the Image and the Shadow,"
    Horizon, 15 (Winter), 112-17.
        Stresses Hemingway's desire to excel in whatever he did;
    amazing physical energy; required comparatively little
    sleep. Personal charisma was unavoidable, and Cowley
    thinks the legend should be studied. Early fears returned
    after Hemingway's triumphal tour of Spain in the summer of
    1959; then his will, courage, and mind collapsed. (Cowley
    insists that Hemingway's influence on Faulkner is "greater
    than has been widely recognized.")

20 _____. A Second Flowering, Words and Days of the Lost Genera-
    tion. New York: Viking Press.
        Discusses Hemingway as a member of the World War I liter-
    ary generation, with both biographical and critical emphasis.
    Praises In Our Time and The Sun Also Rises, and also de-
    scribes the last writing (unpublished as well as published)
    and the last years. Pp. 48-73: "Hemingway in Paris" and
    pp. 216-32: "Hemingway the Old Lion."

21 _____. "What Books Survive from the 1930's?" Journal of Ameri-
    can Studies, 7: 293-300.
        Finds that even seemingly apolitical novels reflect the
    spirit and concerns of the 1930's; considers For Whom the
    Bell Tolls one of the most representative of the books
    during the decade.

315

1973

22   DAVIDSON, ARNOLD E.   "The Dantean Perspective in Hemingway's
      A Farewell to Arms," Journal of Narrative Technique, 3:
      121-30.
          Stresses that the complex narrative methods parallel
      those of Dante's Inferno: in each, the protagonist speaks
      to both describe and judge his earlier experiences. There-
      fore, the reader can see him as he was and as he was
      changed; and can also see the way his experience colors
      his narration.

23   DAVIDSON, CATHY N.   "Laughter Without Comedy in For Whom the
      Bell Tolls," Hemingway Notes, 3, No. 2, pp. 6-9.
          Studies several kinds of laughter used in For Whom the
      Bell Tolls--all relatively humorless--and the ironic effect
      they have.

24   DAVIS, ROBERT MURRAY.   "Irony and Pity Once More," Fitzgerald/
      Hemingway Annual, pp. 307-08.
          Traces the The Sun Also Rises phrase to the title Irony
      and Pity: A Book of Tales by Paul Eldridge, published in
      1926.

25   DAVIS, ROBERT M.   "The Nick Adams Stories; A Review Essay,"
      Southern Humanities Review, 7, No. 2 (Spring), 215-19.
          Questions the ordering of the stories and Young's
      assumptions throughout.

26   DOS PASSOS, JOHN.   The Fourteenth Chronicle, Letters and
      Diaries of John Dos Passos, edited by Townsend Ludington.
      Boston: Gambit.
          Many references to Hemingway.

27   DOWDY, ANDREW.   Movies Are Better Than Ever: Wide-Screen
      Memories of the Fifties. New York: William Morrow.
          Concludes of the movies made from Hemingway's works,
      "The wrong people bought the books and then destroyed
      them." Peter Viertel's adaptation of The Old Man and the
      Sea amounted to "reading Hemingway to pictures."

28   DUGGAN, MARGARET M.   "Hemingway Checklist," Fitzgerald/Heming-
      way Annual, pp. 357-62.
          Items dating from 1961 to 1972.

29   ELIAS, ROBERT H.   "Entangling Alliances with None": An Essay
      on the Individual in the American Twenties. New York:
      Norton.
          Sees Hemingway as creating heroes whose accomplishments
      are "unaided," more often than not in reaction to the pre-
      vailing social code.

30   ENGEL, MONROE, ed. <u>Uses of Literature</u>. Cambridge: Harvard
         English Studies, 4: 187-204.
         "No Farewell to Arms" by Alan Lebowitz. Thinks Heming-
      way's "conscious" intention to write of love as a positive
      alternative to war fails, in that the disastrous outcome of
      his love for Catherine shows his fear of domesticity and
      his real need for violence.

*31   <u>Ernest Hemingway</u>. McGraw-Hill Films.
         Unseen.

32   FARRELL, JAMES T. "Ernest Hemingway," <u>Fitzgerald/Hemingway</u>
         <u>Annual</u>, pp. 215-225.
         Previously unpublished comments on Hemingway's writing
      since <u>The Sun Also Rises</u>, in which he argues that Hemingway
      did not "grow," that his short stories are valuable, but
      that most of his writing is "sensationalistic" (connected
      with that of Stephen Crane and the psychology of the 1890's).

33   FLORA, JOSEPH M. "Biblical Allusion in <u>The Old Man and the</u>
         <u>Sea</u>," <u>Studies in Short Fiction</u>, 10 (Spring), 143-47.
         Suggests that Santiago's desire to go "far out" has an
      affinity with <u>Luke</u> 5:4-11, and sees this correspondence as
      an important link with Christian thought.

34   _____. "Jacob Barnes' Name: The Other Side of the Ledger,"
         <u>English Record</u>, 24 (Fall), 14-15.
         Traces origin of segments of hero's name.

35   FOX, STEPHEN D. "Hemingway's 'The Doctor and the Doctor's
         Wife,'" <u>Arizona Quarterly</u>, 29, No. 1 (Spring), 19-25.
         Sees the story as a portrait of civilized half-truths,
      of the "webs of planted perspective and concealed motive."
      An important part of Nick's cycle.

36   FRANK, WALDO. <u>Memoirs of Waldo Frank</u>, edited by Alan Trachten-
         berg. Amherst: University of Massachusetts Press.
         Compares Frank with Hemingway, and finds the former to
      be more of a man in his moral commitment.

37   GADO, FRANK, ed. <u>First Person, Conversations on Writers &</u>
         <u>Writing</u>. Schenectady, New York: Union College Press.
         Glenway Westcott, p. 5, discusses Hemingway as experi-
      mentor; John Dos Passos, pp. 44-46, comments on Hemingway
      as a stylist and person.

38   GILLIAM, FLORENCE. "Remarks by Florence Gilliam," <u>Fitzgerald/</u>
         <u>Hemingway Annual</u>, pp. 43-48.
         Stresses the eclectic and international scene in Paris
      during the 1920's.

1973

39 GINSBERG, ALLEN. "Ginsberg" (interview), Cottonwood Review
     (Winter), pp. 45-52.
         Sees Hemingway as a "very, very great technician . . . .
     in his prose of his last years he is much underestimated."

40 HAIG, STIRLING. "Hemingway and Stendhal," PMLA, 88 (Oct.),
     1192-93.
         Replies to Stephens' PMLA essay in March of 1973.

41 HASSAN, IHAB. Contemporary American Literature, 1945-1972,
     An Introduction. New York: Frederick Ungar Publishers.
         P. 31: compares Hemingway and Norman Mailer and Brauti-
     gan; p. 63: Hemingway as important short story writer,
     creator of a new form.

42 HIPKISS, ROBERT A. "Ernest Hemingway's The Things That I Know,"
     Twentieth Century Literature, 19 (Oct.), 275-82.
         Sees Across the River and Into the Trees as highly
     affirmative.

43 HOLDER, ROBERT C. "Count Mippipopolous and Greffi," Hemingway
     Notes, 3, No. 2, pp. 3-6.
         Considers these two characters representative of the
     ethic Hemingway's younger protagonists develop; each has
     come to terms with the unfriendly world through adopting
     "a severely limited set of values."

44 HOWELL, JOHN M. "Hemingway's 'Metaphysics' in Four Stories of
     the Thirties: A Look at the Manuscripts," ICarbS, 1,
     No. 1, pp. 40-51.
         Howell analyzes four stories preceding For Whom the Bell
     Tolls--including "After the Storm" and "Short Happy Life"--
     to show that Hemingway was even then approaching the theme
     of "spiritual union" so apparent in the novel.

45 JOHNSON, ROBERT O. "Hemingway's 'How Do You Like It Now,
     Gentlemen?': A Possible Source," American Literature, 45,
     No. 1 (March), 114-117.
         Suggests that source of the question may be the third
     act of The Rehearsal, 1671, by George Villiers, Second
     Duke of Buckingham. Line is delivered by a character
     named Bayes, a hack writer, obsessed with his reputation.

46 KAZIN, ALFRED. Bright Book of Life: American Novelists and
     Storytellers from Hemingway to Mailer. Boston: Atlantic-
     Little, Brown, pp. 3-20.
         "A Dream of Order": sees Hemingway as the embodiment of
     the belief that "experience can look entirely to literature

(KAZIN, ALFRED)
for its ideal," and--eventually--faults him for his complete reliance on craft. Sees that Hemingway's obsession
with the act of writing--remarkable as it was, and remarkable as some of its results were--does not continue into
the contemporary period. Kazin feels the more influential
writers have become Faulkner and Nathanael West.

47 KILLINGER, JOHN. The Fragile Presence, Transcendence in Modern
Literature. Philadelphia: Fortress Press.
P. 25: sees that Hemingway occupies "an era of transi-
tion between one tacitly acknowledged world-view and
another." P. 66: A Farewell to Arms gave us a serious
hero; later novels such as Catch-22 feature an "absurdly
comic figure."

48 KLISE, THOMAS S. Hemingway. Peoria, Illinois: Thomas B.
Klise, n.d.
Narration on record, with a reading script, of Heming-
way's life. Listed in Hemingway Notes, IV.

49 KNOLL, ROBERT E. "Ezra Pound at St. Elizabeth's," Prairie
Schooner, 47, No. 1 (Spring), 1-13.
Quotes Pound as saying "'What Hemingway did nobody could
improve on. Nobody could touch him in what he was doing.'"
Hemingway had come to Pound immediately, seeking help.

50 LASATER, ALICE E. "The Breakdown in Communication in the
Twentieth-Century Novel," Southern Quarterly, 12, No. 1
(Oct.), 1-14.
Sees The Sun Also Rises as example of the failure of
communication, of modern people's alienation from each
other.

51 LEHAN, RICHARD. A Dangerous Crossing: French Literary Existentialism and the Modern American Novel. Carbondale: Southern
Illinois University Press, pp. 35-79.
"French and American Existentialism: Dos Passos, Hemingway, Faulkner." Study of the influence of Hemingway and
other American writers on Sartre and Camus, finding
stylistic correspondences as well as thematic ones.
Points out that the Americans created the character of the
"innocent," person who manages to live in his absurd yet
demanding world.

52 LeVOT, ANDRE. "Fitzgerald in Paris," Fitzgerald/Hemingway
Annual, pp. 49-76.
Contrasts Fitzgerald's life in Paris with that of Heming-
way, who "shared for a while the life of the poor." Also

1973

(LeVOT, ANDRE)
 uses the tortoise and the hare analogy to describe Fitzgerald's feeling that he was a tortoise compared to
 Hemingway.

53 LOEB, HAROLD. "Remarks by Harold Loeb," <u>Fitzgerald/Hemingway</u>
 <u>Annual</u>, pp. 33-38.
  Discusses meeting Hemingway, getting Liveright to publish
 <u>In Our Time</u>, and Pamplona.

54 LONGSTREET, STEPHEN. Review of Klimo and Sarason, <u>Fitzgerald/</u>
 <u>Hemingway Annual</u>, pp. 319-26.
  Reminisces about Paris during the 1920's.

55 MacDONALD, SCOTT. "The Confusing Dialogue in Hemingway's 'A
 Clean, Well-Lighted Place,'" <u>Studies in American Fiction</u>,
 1: 93-101.
  Summary of the various confusions already in print.

56 MEADOR, JOHN M., JR. "Addendum to Hanneman: Hemingway's <u>The</u>
 <u>Old Man and the Sea</u>," <u>PBSA</u>, 47: 454-57.
  A correction to Hanneman's description of <u>The Old Man</u>
 <u>and the Sea</u>.

57 MONTEIRO, GEORGE. "Hemingway, O. Henry, and the Surprise
 Ending," <u>Prairie Schooner</u>, 47, No. 4 (Winter), 296-302.
  Sees Hemingway's short story as employing "his own brand
 of the surprise ending," usually using unexpected irony.
 Hemingway writes to "dismiss" O. Henry in 1934, yet the
 two stories most like his appear within two years, "Snows"
 and "Short Happy Life."

58 _____. "Hemingway's Pleiade Ballplayers," <u>Fitzgerald/Hemingway</u>
 <u>Annual</u>, pp. 299-301.
  Discusses errors already made by translators in identi-
 fying some of the baseball players appearing in Hemingway's
 major works.

59 _____. "The Limits of Professionalism: A Sociological Approach
 to Faulkner, Fitzgerald and Hemingway," <u>Criticism</u>, 15:
 145-55.
  Using sociologist Talcott Parson's work about medical
 practices, Monteiro seeks answers for Hemingway's seeming
 fascination with the image of the world as hospital, using
 "Indian Camp."

60 MOSS, HOWARD. "The Poet's Story," <u>Prose</u>, 7 (Fall), 189-208.
  Sees Hemingway as a poet who more obviously changed

1973

(MOSS, HOWARD)
tactics in his prose. "The interest in words stays steady
but the language is stripped down. . . . The metaphor
ceases to be central, though the motif may take its place."
Reprinted as introduction to his collection of the same
title, New York, Macmillan, 1973, pp. ix-xx.

61   NAGEL, JAMES. "The Narrative Method of 'The Short Happy Life
of Francis Macomber,'" Research Studies, 41: 18-27.
Corrects what he views as the erroneous description of
"simple" point of view in the story. Locates five narrative perspectives, and finds that a close study of method
shows not only Macomber's growth but Wilson's hypocrisy,
and the fact that Margot's shooting was accidental.

62   NAKHDJARANI, ERIK. "Of Strength and Vulnerability: An Interview with Philip Young," Dialogue (University of Pittsburgh
at Bradford, Pa.), 1, No. 4 (Jan.), 5-22.
Young points out that 20 years ago few readers acknowledged
the importance of Nick Adams, that the so-called "violence"
in Hemingway's fiction is suitable to his subjects, and
that the Hemingway world was very different, and much less
neurotic, than the Kafka world. Young places The Sun Also
Rises and most of A Farewell to Arms on the same level of
excellence as the short stories, and considers Hemingway
on a par with Thoreau as the best prose stylist ("poet")
in American letters.

63   NILSEN, DON L. F., ed. Meaning: A Common Ground of Linguistics
and Literature. Cedar Falls, Iowa, pp. 179-87.
"Role Structures in Content Analysis: A Case Grammar
Approach to Literature" by Walter A. Cook. Using deep
structure analysis, Cook uses The Old Man and the Sea as
a model.

64   NORTON, CHARLES A. "The Alcoholic Content of A Farewell to
Arms," Fitzgerald/Hemingway Annual, pp. 309-14.
Considers the kind of drink, and the manner of its con-
sumption, significant to characterization in The Sun Also
Rises and A Farewell to Arms.

65   O'BRIEN, JOHN. "I Am Sure I Saw Ernest Hemingway . . . "
Fitzgerald/Hemingway Annual, pp. 303-05.
Recalls seeing Hemingway in 1927, and the impact The Sun
Also Rises had on young writers in 1929.

66   PEARSON, JANET LYNNE. "Hemingway's Women," Lost Generation
Journal, 1 (May), 16-19.
Discussion of the prototypes of Hemingway's heroines.

1973

67   PEDEN, WILLIAM. "The American Short Story During the Twenties,"
     Studies in Short Fiction, 10, No. 4 (Fall), 367-73.
         Sees the explosive proportion in quantity and quality
     stemming from World War I, a resistance against tradition,
     as illustrated in Hemingway's fiction.

68   PEICH, MICHAEL. "Hemingway and Kiki's Memoirs," Fitzgerald/
     Hemingway Annual, pp. 315-16.
         Various issues of the book, and the appearance of Heming-
     way's introduction to it.

69   PHILLIPS, STEVEN R. "Hemingway and the Bullfighter: The
     Archetypes of Tragedy," Arizona Quarterly, 29, 1 (Spring),
     37-56.
         Sees that the essential configuration of man and animal
     locked in mortal struggle underlies much of Hemingway's
     fiction. Bullfight parallels Dionysus.

70   POWNALL, DAVID E. Articles on Twentieth Century Literature:
     An Annotated Bibliography, 1954 to 1970. III. New York:
     Kraus-Thomson Publishers, pp. 1476-1553.
         Hemingway items.

71   PRESLEY, JOHN W. "'Hawks Never Share': Women and Tragedy in
     Hemingway," Hemingway Notes, 3, No. 1, pp. 3-10.
         Sees Hemingway's women as "subtle threats," bent on
     depleting the psychic and sexual reserves of the male.
     Sees the sketchiness of Hemingway's women as not necessarily
     a weakness; many of his men are also mere outlines.

72   RAEBURN, JOHN. "Death in the Afternoon and the Legendary Hem-
     ingway," Fitzgerald/Hemingway Annual, pp. 243-57.
         Finds that the "legendary Hemingway" was created by the
     "dynamic relationship between his self-advertisement in
     his non-fiction and the mass media's exploitation of his
     public personality," mostly in the 1930's.

73   RILEY, CAROLYN, ed. Contemporary Literary Criticism: Excerpts
     from Criticism of the Works of Today's Novelists, Poets,
     Playwrights, and Other Creative Writers. Detroit, Michigan:
     Gale Research, Vol. I, pp. 141-44.
         Hemingway items.

74   ROBINSON, CHARLES E. "James T. Farrell's Critical Estimate of
     Hemingway," Fitzgerald/Hemingway Annual, pp. 209-14.
         Describes Farrell's writing about Hemingway in 1936, 1961,
     1963, and 1964; information about the Farrell-Hemingway
     friendship.

75 RUBENSTEIN, JILL. "A Degree of Alchemy: A Moveable Feast as
     Literary Autobiography," Fitzgerald/Hemingway Annual, pp.
     231-42.
          Sees Hemingway's use of fictional techniques (figurative
     language, symbolism, point of view) as valuable in sustain-
     ing his memoirs as excellent reading.

76 RUBIN, LOUIS D., JR., ed. The Comic Imagination in American
     Literature. New Brunswick, N. J.: Rutgers University
     Press.
          William Harmon in "'Anti-Fiction' in American Humor"
     places Hemingway squarely at the center of the anti-novel
     tradition, noting that his heroes aim not for plot symmetry
     but "sincerity," even if such a pose leads to literary in-
     competence. Allen Guttman in "Jewish Humor" points out
     Norman Mailer's debt to Hemingway.

77 RUHM, HERBERT. "Hemingway in Schruns," Commonweal, 99
     (28 Dec.), 344-45.
          Visits the Hotel Taube where Hemingway stayed in 1925-26.

*78 SALZMAN, JACK. "Prelude to Madness: A Look at 'Soldier's
     Home' and 'For Esme: With Love and Squalor,'" Rikkyo
     Review, 33: 103-12.
          Cited in Journal of Modern Literature, Bibliography, 1972.

79 SCHNEIDERMAN, LEO. "Hemingway: A Psychological Study,"
     Connecticut Review, 6, No. 2 (April), 34-49.
          Describes the conscious and unconscious preoccupations
     of Hemingway's fiction as revealing a loss of faith combined
     with a persistent will to believe, manifested stylistically
     in the sensual and concrete, which serve as replacements
     for the eternal.

80 SHARROCK, ROGER. "Singles and Couples: Hemingway's A Farewell
     to Arms and Updike's Couples," Ariel, 4, No. 4, pp. 21-43.
          Sees both novels as providing variations on the common
     theme of isolation from society through love. Tarbox too
     is threatened by war and violence.

81 SOKOLOFF, ALICE HUNT. Hadley, The First Mrs. Hemingway. New
     York: Dodd, Mead & Co.
          Includes many excerpts from Hadley's letters to Hemingway
     (his to her were lost) and the pervasive view of Hemingway
     as aggressive, exhuberant, eager to learn and experience.
     Many photos from the early 1920's.

1973

82   STEPHENS, ROBERT O. "Hemingway and Stendhal: The Matrix of
          A Farewell to Arms," PMLA, 88, No. 2 (March), 271-80.
          Links A Farewell to Arms to The Charterhouse of Parma:
          retreat from Caporetto analogous to retreat from Waterloo.
          Lists eight other points in common. Thematically, both
          books chronicle the development of a man of earned beliefs.

83   STEWART, DONALD OGDEN. "An Interview," Fitzgerald/Hemingway
          Annual, pp. 83-89.
          Discusses Hemingway's charm, his competitive spirit, and
          the camaraderie of the Murphys, Fitzgeralds, Hemingway,
          and others in the mid-1920's.

84   STUBBS, JOHN. "Love and Role Playing in A Farewell to Arms,"
          Fitzgerald/Hemingway Annual, pp. 271-84.
          Sees Henry and Catherine as characters who play stereo-
          typical roles, roles which Hemingway himself finds inade-
          quate to meet life. The "weakness" of the characters is,
          then, intentional, and not a flaw in Hemingway's artistry.

85   TRAVER, ROBERT. "Hemingway's Big Two-Hearted Secret," Sports
          Afield (July), pp. 46-47, 82-84.
          Description of several of the Michigan locations Heming-
          way used in his fiction.

86   VICKERY, JOHN B. The Literary Impact of The Golden Bough.
          Princeton: Princeton University Press, p. 107.
          Sees Hemingway's importance as stressing the concrete in
          art.

87   VOSS, ANDREW. "The Discovery of a Style: Ernest Hemingway,"
          in The American Short Story, A Critical Survey. Norman:
          University of Oklahoma Press, pp. 220-41.
          Voss credits Hemingway with being "a major force in
          shaping the form and characters of the modern short story."
          Summarizes many stories and The Old Man and the Sea.

88   WAGNER, LINDA W. "The Poem of Santiago and Manolin," MFS, 19,
          No. 4 (Winter), 517-30.
          Stylistic study of The Old Man and the Sea, in which im-
          portance of detail, structure, and prose rhythms are of
          special importance; includes Islands in the Stream. Wagner
          sees the love between Santiago and Manolin as central.

89   WHITE, WILLIAM. "Ernest Hemingway and Gene Tunney," Hemingway
          Notes, 3, No. 2, p. 10.
          Account of a Hemingway-Tunney bout in which the latter
          was forced to throw a punch that almost knocked Hemingway
          out.

90   _____. "Hemingway Items: What Are the Limits?" <u>ABC</u>, 23 (May-
        June), 18-20.
            Questions what rightfully belongs to a Hemingway
        collection.

91   _____. "Two More Hanneman Addenda," <u>Hemingway Notes</u>, 3, pp. 14-
        15.
            Additions to the bibliography.

92   WILSON, DOUGLAS. "Ernest Hemingway, <u>The Nick Adams Stories</u>,"
        <u>Western Humanities Review</u>, 27 (Summer), 295-99.
            Disagrees with the chronology and intent of Young's
        order.

93   WINTERS, YVOR. <u>Yvor Winters: Uncollected Essays and Reviews</u>.
        Chicago: The Sparrow Press.
            Pp. 225-70 (<u>See</u> 1929.B41); pp. 96-99 (<u>See</u> 1930.B18).

94   WITHERINGTON, PAUL. "To Be or Not to Be: Paradox and Fun in
        Hemingway's 'A Way You'll Never Be,'" <u>Style</u>, 6, pp. 56-63.
            Sees Nick's search for balance illustrated in his language
        throughout the story. The very "irresolution" of the piece
        shows his stasis as a positive stance.

95   WOOD, CARL. "<u>In Our Time</u>: Hemingway's Fragmentary Novel,"
        <u>Neuphilologische Mittenlungen</u>, 74, No. 4, pp. 716-26.
            Sees the collection as a unified whole, both structurally
        and thematically.

96   WYRICK, JEAN. "Fantasy as Symbol: Another Look at Hemingway's
        Catherine," <u>Massachusetts Studies in English: A Graduate
        Student Journal</u>, 4, No. 2 (Fall), 42-46.
            Sees Catherine as successful, used in <u>A Farewell to Arms</u>
        as "a symbol of the uncomplicated, peaceful life of love."

1974 A   BOOKS

1   CASTILLO-PUCHE, JOSÉ LUIS. <u>Hemingway in Spain</u>, translated by
        Helen R. Lane. Garden City, New York: Doubleday. Photos.
            Memories of Hemingway in Spain from 1953 to 1960,
        written with warmth and sympathy. Castillo-Puche attributes
        much of Hemingway's personal malaise to his dissatisfaction
        with his writing of <u>The Dangerous Summer</u>.
            Reprinted from the Spanish edition (<u>Hemingway: Entre la
        Vida y la Muerte</u>) published by Ediciones Distino, 1968.

1974

2   BENSON, JACKSON J. and RICHARD ASTRO, eds. Hemingway In Our
      Time. Cornvallis: Oregon State University Press.
      A collection of previously unpublished essays, all
      evaluating or discussing some aspect of Hemingway's cur-
      rent position in American letters.
      Contents: pp. 1-12: Introduction by Jackson J. Benson,
      stressing the currents in criticism. Concludes by placing
      Hemingway in a line of descent from Henry James rather
      than Twain because his writing "is so richly endowed with
      interconnected ideas and evolving techniques that from any
      point of departure, one is led on and on endlessly to
      further study."
      pp. 13-23: "Posthumous Hemingway, and Nicholas Adams"
      by Philip Young. Sees the post-humously published books
      as valuable, with A Moveable Feast "a minor masterpiece"
      and The Nick Adams Stories providing much new insight into
      "the most important single character in Hemingway."
      pp. 25-38: "Sketches of the Author's Life in Paris in
      the Twenties" by George Wickes. Uses A Moveable Feast as
      a means of seeing Hemingway voicing his moral outrage over
      deviant sexuality, his Protestant ethic, and his belief
      that he was a self-made man--fictionalized autobiography,
      Wickes concludes.
      pp. 39-51: "Hemingway's Islands and Streams: Minor
      Tactics for Heavy Pressure" by Joseph De Falco. In re-
      viewing the reception of Islands in the Stream, De Falco
      finds "a widespread tendency to read Hemingway's fiction
      as autobiography and to judge his work by standards alien
      to fiction." He sees this book as another in Hemingway's
      pattern of affirmative themes, with the Gulf Stream re-
      placing the bullring. Man's salvation is in brotherhood.
      pp. 53-65: "Internal Treachery in the Last Published
      Short Stories of Ernest Hemingway" by Delbert E. Wylder.
      Sees Hemingway's "Two Tales of Darkness" as his clearest
      statement on internal treachery, and man's need for love,
      told in near-parable form.
      pp. 67-86: "To Have and Have Not as Classical Tragedy:
      Reconsidering Hemingway's Neglected Novel" by Gerry Brenner.
      Discussion of the tragic hero, murder and revenge, the uni-
      ties, and structure in relation to this often maligned
      novel.
      pp. 87-97: "Hemingway and Fitzgerald" by Peter L. Hays.
      An analysis of Hemingway's indebtedness to Fitzgerald in
      The Sun Also Rises, and a comparison of that novel with
      The Great Gatsby. Hays finds the two novels similar in
      many ways, chiefly in that both involve "frustrated patterns
      of initiation," sports used as moral metaphors, and narra-
      tors who are also protagonists.

(BENSON, JACKSON J. and RICHARD ASTRO)
  pp. 99-111: "A Moveable Feast and Remembrance of Things Past: Two Quests for Lost Time" by Faith G. Norris. Comparison of Proust and Hemingway in their use of nostalgia to create novels of manners.
  pp. 113-143: "Hemingway's Sense of Place" by Robert W. Lewis. By focusing on Hemingway's settings and minor characters, Lewis concludes that the sense of place was crucial to Hemingway: that characters can be identified by their reactions to terrain.
  pp. 145-157: "A Sometimes Great Notion: Ernest Hemingway's Roman Catholicism" by John Clark Pratt. Uses Hemingway's word "technical" to describe the author's personal faith, "conditional Catholicism," and summarizes his belief system as being one sympathetic to the "code" of Catholicism, at least so long as that code reinforced his own personal ethics.
  pp. 159-173: "Rectitude in Hemingway's Fiction: How Rite Makes Right" by John Griffith. Sees Hemingway's concern with "doing things right" as more closely aligned with ritual than with systematic morality. Since ritual is also "valid spiritual achievement," approaching Hemingway only as a moralist can be both misleading and limiting.
  pp. 175-189: "Hemingway and the Modern Metaphysical Tradition" by Michael Friedberg. Sees Hemingway's new prose style as "the language of the new metaphysical ideology of twentieth century fiction," the surface style mirroring an "orderly objective reality" with an underlying current reflecting the complex chaos of subjective reality.
  pp. 191-212: "Hemingway Among the Moderns" by Richard Lehan. Lehan finds Hemingway a contemporary writer because, in all his writing, he "questioned the very meaning of civilization," usually by contrasting an elemental culture with a sophisticated. In his descriptions of "the vital relationship between man and nature" (Santiago), Hemingway is at his best; and in his description of man's "urge to stay in touch with first things," he is at his most modern--but perhaps, Lehan concludes, not modern enough. Hemingway's joys are too mindless; he cannot do battle with the abstractions of contemporary life. His heroes live, but as anachronisms.

3 WAGNER, LINDA WELSHIMER, ed. Ernest Hemingway: Five Decades of Criticism. East Lansing: Michigan State University Press.
  Contents: pp. 1-7: Introduction by the editor.
  pp. 8-21: "Hemingway's Tutor, Ezra Pound" by Harold M. Hurwitz, reprinted from MFS, 17, No. 4 (Winter, 1971-72), 469-82.

1974

(WAGNER, LINDA WELSHIMER)
    pp. 21-38: "An Interview with Ernest Hemingway" by
George Plimpton, reprinted from The Paris Review, 18
(Spring, 1958), 60-89.
    pp. 39-56: "Ernest Hemingway, Literary Critic" by
Daniel Fuchs, reprinted from American Literature, 36 (Jan.
1965), 431-51.
    pp. 57-74: "Hemingway, the Corrida, and Spain" by
Keneth Kinnamon, reprinted from Texas Studies in Literature
and Language, 1 (Spring, 1959), 44-61.
    pp. 75-102: "Ernest Hemingway" by Robert Penn Warren,
reprinted from Selected Essays, New York, Random House,
1951, pp. 80-118.
    pp. 103-09: "The Other Hemingway" by Alan Holder, re-
printed from Twentieth Century Literature, 1963, pp. 153-57.
    pp. 109-131: "The Still Center of Hemingway's World"
by Beongcheon Yu, reprinted from Phoenix (Korea), 12
(Spring, 1968), 15-44.
    pp. 131-44: "Hemingway's Esthetic and Ethical Sports-
men" by John Reardon, reprinted from University Review, 34
(Oct., 1967), 13-23.
    pp. 144-152: "Confiteor Hominem: Ernest Hemingway's
Religion of Man" by Joseph Waldmeir, reprinted from
PMASAL, 42 (1956), 277-81.
    pp. 153-60: "The Sweet Style of Ernest Hemingway" by
Paul Goodman, reprinted from New York Review of Books, 17,
No. 11 (30 Dec. 1971), 27-28.
    pp. 160-88: "Ernest Hemingway" by Richard Bridgman,
from The Colloquial Style in America, New York, Oxford
University Press, 1966, pp. 195-230.
    pp. 188-200: "Hemingway and the Thing Left Out" by
Julian Smith, reprinted from Journal of Modern Literature,
1 (Second issue, 1970-71), 169-82.
    pp. 200-212: "The Marinating of For Whom the Bell Tolls"
by Linda W. Wagner, reprinted from Journal of Modern Literature, 2 (Nov., 1972), 533-46.
    pp. 212-221: "Ernest Hemingway, A Critical Essay" by
Nathan Scott, Jr., reprinted from his pamphlet of the same
title, Grand Rapids, Michigan, William B. Eerdmans, 1966,
pp. 19-29.
    pp. 222-23: "Mr. Hemingway's Dry-Points" by Edmund Wil-
son, reprinted from The Dial, 77 (Oct. 1924), 340-41.
    pp. 224-40: "The Shock of Vision: An Imagist Reading
of In Our Time" by Richard Hasbany. Unpublished. Reads
In Our Time as Imagist poetry with much attention to juxtaposition and phrasing; surveys the relationships in the
1920's between Hemingway and Pound, Eliot, and poetic
aesthetics.

(WAGNER, LINDA WELSHIMER)
    pp. 241-51: "Sunrise Out of the Waste Land" by Richard
P. Adams, reprinted from Tulane Studies in English, 9
(1959), 119-131.
    pp. 252-66: "Hemingway's A Farewell to Arms: The Novel
as Pure Poetry" by Daniel J. Schneider, reprinted from MFS,
14 (Autumn 1968), 283-96.
    pp. 266-79: "Language Magic and Reality in For Whom the
Bell Tolls" by Robert O. Stephens, reprinted from Criticism,
14 (Fall 1972), 151-64.
    pp. 279-87: "Hemingway Achieves the Fifth Dimension" by
Frederick I. Carpenter, reprinted from American Literature
and the Dream, New York, The Philosophical Library, 1955.
    pp. 288-306: "The Structure of Hemingway's Across the
River and Into the Trees" by Peter Lisca, reprinted from
MFS, 12 (Summer 1966), 232-50.
    pp. 306-19: "The Boy and the Lions" by Carlos Baker,
reprinted from Hemingway: The Writer as Artist, Princeton University Press, 1972, pp. 304-11.

1974 B   SHORTER WRITINGS

1   BENERT, ANNETTE. "Survival Through Irony: Hemingway's 'A
        Clean, Well-Lighted Place,'" Studies in Short Fiction, 11,
        No. 2 (Spring), 181-88.
        Sees as important the ways Hemingway achieves the serenity
    of the story: light and cleanliness imagery and the complex
    character of the older waiter; "a totally affirmative
    story."

2   BLOTNER, JOSEPH. Faulkner, A Biography. New York: Random
        House, 2 volumes.
        Many references to Hemingway.

3   BOLLING, DOUGLAS. "Toward Islands in the Stream," South
        Dakota Review, 12, No. 1 (Spring), 5-13.
        Sees the novel's force in Hudson's alienation from life
    and self; always ironically aware of life's futility.

4   BRYER, JACKSON R. "Fitzgerald and Hemingway" in American
        Literary Scholarship: An Annual, 1972, edited by J.
        Albert Robbins. Durham, N. C.: Duke University Press,
        pp. 131-54.
        Survey of criticism on both authors published during 1972.

5   CANADAY, NICHOLAS, JR. "The Motif of the Inner Ring in Heming-
        way's Fiction," CEA Critic, 36, No. 2 (Jan.), 18-21.
        Varying degrees of intimacy within characters' relation-
    ships form "the inner ring."

1974

6   FERBER, STEVE. "The Hunts of Papa Hemingway," Argosy, 280,
        No. 5 (Nov.), 70–71, 80.
            Description of Hemingway's 1934 African safari, his
        rivalry with friend Charles Thompson, and his philosophy
        of hunting.

7   FISHER, DEBORAH. "Genuine Heroines Hemingway Style," Lost
        Generation Journal, 2, No. 2 (Spring–Summer), 35–36.
            Defends Hemingway's characterizations of women as being
        subtle and believable, at least partly because each is
        identified with natural metaphors. Pilar, in fact, reaches
        "the status of a Hemingway hero."

8   FURNAS, JOSEPH CHAMBERLAIN. Great Times, An Informal Social
        History of the U. S. 1914–1929. New York: G. P. Putnam's
        Sons.
            Pp. 67–68: Hemingway as expatriate.
            p. 91: criticism of Hemingway's "ear" for the American
        idiom.
            pp. 244–45: on Hemingway's war fiction.
            p. 265: calls John Reed the "Hemingway" of his genera-
        tion.

9   GILENSON, BORIS. "Hemingway in the Soviet Union," Hemingway
        Notes, 4, No. 1 (Spring), 17–19.
            Discusses the popularity of Hemingway's work in Russia,
        and the role of Ivan Kashkin. Russian readers see Heming-
        way not as an existentialist but as a "life-asserting"
        humanist.

10   GINSBERG, ALLEN. Allen Verbatim, edited by Gordon Ball. New
        York: McGraw-Hill, p. 151.
            Ginsberg recalls that most writers in the 1940's "were
        influenced a lot by Hemingway" rather than looking for
        their own individual prose rhythms.

11   GLICKSBERG, CHARLES I. "Experimental Fiction: Innovation
        Versus Form," Centennial Review, 18, No. 2 (Spring),
        127–50.
            Locates Hemingway in the tradition of the "lyrical
        novel."

12   HICKS, GRANVILLE. Granville Hicks in the New Masses, edited
        by Jack Alan Robbins. Port Washington, N. Y.: Kennikat
        Press.
            Pp. 114–16 (See 1935.B14); pp. 117–19 (See 1937.B30).

13 HOHENBERG, JOHN. The Pulitzer Prizes. New York: Columbia
    University Press.
        Pp. 144-45: controversy over For Whom the Bell Tolls
    which the board declined because of its "romantic sensa-
    tionalism" and "mannered and eccentric" style; pp. 203-04:
    prize awarded to The Old Man and the Sea.

14 JOHNSTON, KENNETH. "Hemingway's 'Wine of Wyoming': Disappoint-
    ment in America," WAL, 9 (Nov.), 159-76.
        Reflection of Hemingway's disillusion with promise in
    his own country.

15 KENNEY, WILLIAM. "Hunger and the American Dream in To Have and
    Have Not, CEA Critic, 36, No. 2 (Jan.), 26-28.
        Imagery of eating and hunger create Hemingway's patterns
    in this novel, his study of the collapse of the American
    dream.

16 KLOTMAN, PHYLLIS R. "The Sun Also Rises on Nueva Andalucia,"
    CEA Critic, 36, No. 2 (Jan.), 31-33.
        Anachronistic, Klotman finds Hemingway's long treatise on
    the death of horses in the bull ring.

17 KOBLER, J. F. "Let's Run Catherine Barkley up the Flag Pole
    and See Who Salutes," CEA Critic, 36, No. 2 (Jan.), 4-10.
        Catherine fails as a character--and perhaps such failure
    was Hemingway's intention--because she is a complete
    romantic.

18 KOSTELANETZ, RICHARD. The End of Intelligent Writing. New
    York: Sheed and Ward.
        P. 45: Dwight Macdonald's criticism of Hemingway;
    p. 245: the importance of consistent support from
    publishers.

19 LeROY, GAYLORD and URSULA BEITZ. "The Marxist Approach to
    Modernism," Journal of Modern Literature, 3, No. 5 (July),
    1158-74.
        Comments that Marxist writers found Hemingway's techniques
    inappropriate to their socialist reality, as in For Whom
    the Bell Tolls.

20 LUCID, R. F. "Three Public Performances: Fitzgerald, Heming-
    way, Mailer," American Scholar, 43 (Summer), 447-66.
        Sees all three as at least partly created by the American
    public, because their work gives off "an element of personal
    presence." Sees Hemingway's strongest trait his sense of
    "knowing." Hemingway did not seek such publicity, unlike
    the other two writers.

1974

21   MacDONALD, SCOTT. "Hemingway's 'The Snows of Kilimanjaro':
     Three Critical Problems," Studies in Short Fiction, 11,
     No. 1 (Winter), 67-74.
         Discusses Hemingway's use of italics, the epigraph, and
     Harry's imagined flight to the mountain in this survey of
     existing criticism.

22   MELLOW, JAMES R. Charmed Circle, Gertrude Stein & Company.
     New York: Praeger Publishers.
         Many references, including Hemingway's early years in
     Paris, the friendship, and his later criticism of Stein
     and her writing.

23   MONTEIRO, GEORGE. "The Education of Ernest Hemingway," Journal
     of American Studies, 8, No. 1 (April), 91-99.
         Correlates much of Hemingway's In Our Time with the 1918
     The Education of Henry Adams. Discusses names, point of
     view, structure, and particularly world view. Extends the
     comparison to Hemingway's later writing as well.

24   _____. "The Reds, the White Sox, and The Old Man and the Sea,"
     Notes on Contemporary Literature, 4, No. 3 (May), 7-9.
         Sees Santiago's misplacement of the Reds as a joke rather
     than an error on Hemingway's part.

25   MOORE, DENNIS. "Hemingway's Michigan, Michigan's Hemingway,"
     Detroit (Detroit Free Press magazine) (24 Nov.), pp. 14-15,
     17-18, 20-21.
         Good coverage of the years Hemingway spent around Petosky
     and the Walloon Lake area; includes interviews with friends
     and "Sunny" Miller. Moore is surprised not more attention
     has been paid to Hemingway in the Michigan area.

26   NIN, ANAÏS. The Diary of Anaïs Nin, 5, 1947-55. New York:
     Harcourt, Brace, Jovanovich, p. 217.
         Criticizes Max Geismar for his negative comments on Hem-
     ingway.

27   OLDSEY, BERNARD. "Of Hemingway's Arms and the Man," College
     Literature, 1, No. 3 (Fall), 174-89.
         Discussion of A Farewell to Arms in terms of title,
     biography, and the relation between this book and the
     canon. Oldsey sees the novel at least partly as the story
     of Henry's initiation to brute fact, enhanced through Hem-
     ingway's recurring use of parody.

28   RAEBURN, JOHN. "Ernest Hemingway: The Public Writer as Popu-
     lar Culture," JPC, 8, No. 1 (Summer), 91-98.

(RAEBURN, JOHN)
    Classifies Hemingway as a "celebrity," a writer whose life may have been of more interest than his writing. His books also sold. Raeburn terms Hemingway "the Theodore Roosevelt" of American literature.

29   ROBINSON, ELEANOR. "Gertrude Stein, Cubist Teacher," <u>Lost Generation Journal</u>, 2, No. 1 (Winter), 12-15.
    Sees Hemingway as being much influenced by Stein's "way of seeing," especially in "Hills Like White Elephants."

30   RODMAN, SELDEN. "Ernest Hemingway," in <u>Tongues of Fallen Angels</u>. Norfolk, Conn.: New Directions, pp. 51-61.
    A 1951 interview published for the first time. Hemingway comments on the Gulf Stream as being "his Yoknapatawpha County" and sends Rodman excerpts from "Ernst von Hemingstein's Journal," farcical literary gossip.

31   ROGERS, ROY. "Hemingway and the Tragic Curve," <u>Hemingway Notes</u>, 4, No. 1 (Spring), 12-16.
    Relates Hemingway's concept of meaningless and usually unwarranted death to the spatial and geographic "curves" imaged in his fiction; sees the same imagery in Mailer's <u>The Naked and the Dead</u>.

32   ROTHER, JAMES. "Modernism and the Nonsense Style," <u>Contemporary Literature</u>, 15, No. 2 (Spring), 187-202.
    Sees Hemingway's style as the writing closest to actual sensation; quotes Stevens' calling Hemingway the poet "OF EXTRAORDINARY ACTUALITY."

33   RUBIN, LOUIS D., JR. "Don Quixote and Selected Progeny: Or, the Journey-Man as Outsider," <u>Southern Review</u>, 10, No. 1 (Jan.), 31-58.
    Discusses Hemingway's use of Cervantean aesthetic in his themes of endurance in a world set against his achievement. Hemingway's code, like Cervantes', is private.

34   SCHROETER, JAMES. "Hemingway via Joyce," <u>Southern Review</u>, 10, No. 1 (Jan.), 95-114.
    Says the importance of <u>Green Hills of Africa</u> has escaped us because the book must be read in the way we read Joyce; <u>Green Hills of Africa</u> is the "key" for <u>The Old Man and the Sea</u>. "Pursuit" is a central word, and in Hemingway's comparing his education as writer with his education as sportsman, Schroeter locates the importance of <u>Green Hills of Africa</u>.

1974

35   SCRIBNER, CHARLES, JR., ed. The Enduring Hemingway, An Anthology of a Lifetime in Literature. New York: Charles Scribner's Sons. Introduction, pp. ix–xxix.
        Stresses Hemingway's readability, and his emphasis on enduring.

36   SHELTON, FRANK W. "The Family in Hemingway's Nick Adams Stories," Studies in Short Fiction, 11 (Summer), 303–05.
        Sees that Hemingway avoids presenting the ideal family all at once; each story shows only partial relationships. Earliest stories show a rejection of family and marriage, but later ones speak of a need for that stability.

37   SMOLLER, SANFORD J. Adrift Among Geniuses: Robert McAlmon, Writer and Publisher of the Twenties. University Park: Pennsylvania State University Press.
        Pp. 89–99: at Rapallo with McAlmon and the "tentative" friendship; 1923, Hemingway's "analysis" of McAlmon.
        pp. 144–47: fishing at Burguete after Pamplona.
        pp. 222–27: Hemingway's influence to get Scribner's to publish McAlmon.
        pp. 243–44: Hemingway as "arch-enemy" of McAlmon.

38   SOMERS, PAUL, JR. "Anderson's Twisted Apples and Hemingway's Crips," Midamerica I, edited by David D. Anderson. East Lansing, Michigan, pp. 82–97.
        Studies the results of various initiation experiences in both writers' stories and novels, and finds Hemingway's outlooks similar to those of Anderson.

39   _____. "The Mark of Sherwood Anderson on Hemingway: A Look at the Texts," South Atlantic Quarterly, 73 (Autumn), 487–503.
        Compares Anderson's "I Want to Know Why" with Hemingway's "My Old Man."

40   SPENDER, STEPHEN. Love-Hate Relations. New York: Random House.
        Pp. 17–23: Hemingway's "empathy" with place reflected in his style.
        pp. 24–25: uses Nick Adams as an example of the "self-realizing" aim in American literature.
        pp. 262–69: about The Sun Also Rises.
        Error on p. 272: Spender notes For Whom the Bell Tolls as title instead of The Sun Also Rises.

41   STEGNER, WALLACE. The Uneasy Chair, A Biography of Bernard De Voto. New York: Doubleday and Co., p. 372.
        Stegner compares De Voto with Hemingway in their "ritual" use of both alcohol and Catholicism." Other references.

42   SULLIVAN, JEREMIAH. "Conflict in the Modern American Novel,"
         Ball State University Forum, 15, No. 2 (Spring), 28-35.
            Sees the conflict between impulse and code behavior in
         Hemingway's novels dating back to that in James' and
         Twain's, rather than following Dreiser or Sherwood Ander-
         son. With Hemingway and the "genteel" writers, it is
         "conscience over impulse."

43   TRAVER, ROBERT. Trout Magic. New York: Crown Publishers.
            Includes some literary detection concerning Hemingway's
         story "Big Two-Hearted River."

44   WAGNER, LINDA W. "A Note on Hemingway as Poet," Midamerica I,
         edited by David D. Anderson, pp. 58-63.
            Sees the poems as evidence of Hemingway's being influenced
         by Pound and the Imagists, but finds them much inferior to
         his prose because of his practice of using the easiest
         poetic devices and of using poetry, often, for vituperation.

45   WHITE, WILLIAM. "Hemingway: A Current Bibliography," Heming-
         way Notes, 4, No. 1 (Spring), 20-24.
            Recent items.

46   WILLIAMS, WILLIAM CARLOS. The Embodiment of Knowledge. Nor-
         folk, Conn.: New Directions, p. 18.
            Sees Hemingway as following Stein's influence, most im-
         portantly, in her use of words as words.

47   YOUNG, PHILIP. "Hemingway's Manuscripts: The Vault Recon-
         sidered," Studies in American Fiction, 2, No. 1 (Spring),
         3-12.
            Young points out that Hemingway was not a good judge of
         his own early-stage writing; that he worked almost entirely
         without agent or editor; and that his customary practice
         was to revise very little.

1975 A BOOKS

1   MILLER, MADELAINE HEMINGWAY. Ernie. New York: Crown.
            In this account of the Hemingway family and its most
         famous member, "Sunny," the younger sister, gives what
         appears to be the most sympathetic picture of her older
         brother. Many new anecdotes and over 130 photos are
         included.

2   HANNEMAN, AUDRE. Supplement to Ernest Hemingway, A Compre-
         hensive Bibliography. Princeton, N. J.: Princeton Uni-
         versity Press.
            Extensive additions to the original listing, through
         1973.

1975

3   WAGNER, LINDA W. Hemingway and Faulkner: Inventors/Masters.
     Metuchen, N. J.: The Scarecrow Press.
     A discussion of both writers from the perspective of
     their parallel apprenticeships during the innovative early
     1900's through the 1920's. The chronological discussion
     includes all the major novels, many short stories, and
     poems by both authors.

4   BENSON, JACKSON J., ed. The Short Stories of Ernest Hemingway:
     Critical Essays. Durham, N. C.: Duke University Press.
     Comprehensive essay collection complete with overview
     essay and bibliography. Contents:
     pp. xi-xv: Introduction by the editor.
     pp. 2-14: "Hemingway and Faulkner: Two Masters of the
     Modern Short Story" by Ray B. West, Jr., reprinted from
     The Short Story in America: 1900-1950, Chicago: Henry
     Regnery Co., 1952.
     pp. 15-29: "The Complex Unity of In Our Time" by Clinton
     S. Burhans, Jr., reprinted from MFS, 14 (Autumn 1968),
     313-28.
     pp. 29-45: "'Big World Out There': The Nick Adams
     Stories" by Philip Young, reprinted from Novel, 6 (Fall
     1972), 5-19.
     pp. 45-53: "Two African Stories" by Carlos Baker, from
     Hemingway: The Writer as Artist, Princeton, Princeton
     University Press, 1972, pp. 186-96.
     pp. 53-63: "No Money for the Kingbird: Hemingway's
     Prizefight Stories" by Charles A. Fenton, from American
     Quarterly, 4 (Winter, 1952), 339-50.
     pp. 64-77: "Of Wasteful Deaths: Hemingway's Stories
     about the Spanish War" by Martin Light, reprinted from
     The Western Humanities Review, 23, No. 1 (Winter 1969),
     29-42.
     pp. 80-84: "The Revision of 'Chapter III' from In Our
     Time" by Charles A. Fenton, reprinted from The Apprentice-
     ship of Ernest Hemingway: The Early Years, New York,
     Viking Press, 1958, pp. 229-36.
     pp. 85-92: "A Clean, Well-Lighted Place" by Frank
     O'Connor, reprinted from The Lonely Voice: A Study of the
     Short Story, Cleveland, World, 1963, pp. 156-69.
     pp. 93-121: "Point of View in the Nick Adams Stories"
     by Carl Ficken, reprinted from Fitzgerald/Hemingway Annual,
     1971, pp. 212-35.
     pp. 121-29: "A Lesson from Hemingway ('The Undefeated')"
     by Francis Christensen, reprinted from Notes Toward a New
     Rhetoric, New York, Harper and Row, 1967, pp. 24-37.
     pp. 129-35: "A Statistical Analysis of the Prose Style
     of Ernest Hemingway: 'Big Two-Hearted River'" by Elizabeth

(BENSON, JACKSON J.)

J. Wells, reprinted with revisions from "A Comparative Analysis of the Prose Styles of F. Scott Fitzgerald and Ernest Hemingway," Fitzgerald/Hemingway Annual, 1969, pp. 47-67.

pp. 135-47: "Hemingway and the Thing Left Out" by Julian Smith, reprinted from Journal of Modern Literature, 1 (1970-71), 169-72.

pp. 150-59: "Hemingway's Two-Hearted River" by Sheridan Baker, reprinted from Michigan Alumnus Quarterly Review, 65 (Winter 1959), 142-49.

pp. 159-67: "Initiation ('Indian Camp' and 'The Doctor and the Doctor's Wife')" by Joseph DeFalco, reprinted from The Hero in Hemingway's Short Stories, Pittsburgh, University of Pittsburgh Press, 1963, pp. 25-39.

pp. 167-70: "Of Human Dignity: 'In Another Country'" by Earl Rovit, reprinted from Ernest Hemingway, New York, Twayne, 1963, pp. 60-65.

pp. 170-80: "Hemingway's Concept of Sport and 'Soldier's Home'" by Robert W. Lewis, Jr., reprinted from Rendezvous, 5 (Winter 1970), 19-27.

pp. 180-87: "Hemingway's 'Now I Lay Me': A Psychological Interpretation" by Richard B. Hovey, reprinted from Literature and Psychology, 15, Spring, 1965, pp. 70-78.

pp. 187-96: "The Killers" by Cleanth Brooks and Robert Penn Warren, reprinted from Understanding Fiction, New York, Appleton-Century-Crofts, 1959, pp. 303-12.

pp. 196-98: "A Little Light on Hemingway's 'The Light of the World'" by James J. Martine, reprinted from Studies in Short Fiction, 7 (Summer 1970), 465-67.

pp. 198-203: "Hemingway's 'Fifty Grand': The Other Fight(s)" by James J. Martine, reprinted from Journal of Modern Literature, 2 (Sept., 1971), 123-27.

pp. 203-10: "Hemingway's 'The Gambler, the Nun, and the Radio': A Reading and a Problem" by Marion Montgomery, reprinted from Forum, 3 (Winter 1962), 36-40.

pp. 210-22: "Ernest Hemingway's 'The End of Something': Its Independence as a Short Story and its Place in the 'Education of Nick Adams'" by Horst H. Kruse, reprinted from Studies in Short Fiction, 4 (Winter 1967), 152-56.

pp. 222-227: "Hemingway and the Fisher King ('God Rest You Merry, Gentlemen')" by Peter L. Hays, reprinted from University Review, 32 (1965-66), 225-28.

pp. 227-30: "Ironic Action in 'After the Storm'" by Anselm Atkins, reprinted from Studies in Short Fiction, 5 (1967-68), 189-92.

pp. 230-32: "Symmetry in 'Cat in the Rain'" by John V. Hagopian, reprinted from College English, 24 (Dec. 1962), 220-22.

1975

(BENSON, JACKSON J.)
pp. 233-38: "'A Canary for One': Hemingway in the Wasteland" by Julian Smith, reprinted from Studies in Short Fiction, 5 (1967-68), 355-61.
pp. 239-50: "The Short Happy Life of Macomber" by Virgil Hutton, reprinted from University Review, 30 (June 1964), 253-63.
pp. 251-61: "The Dark Snows of Kilimanjaro" by Gennaro Santangelo, unpublished. Sees the story as an embarrassment of riches, whose "major unresolved issue centers on Harry's salvation or non-salvation" with the plane ride seen as either a reward, for true repentence, or a dream. Finds the story indicative of Hemingway's own continuing fascination with the life of the artist.
pp. 261-69: "Character, Irony, and Resolution in 'A Clean, Well-Lighted Place'" by Warren Bennett, reprinted from American Literature, 42 (March, 1970), 70-79.
pp. 272-310: "Ernest Hemingway as a Short Story Writer" by the editor. Benson discusses the seminal influences on Hemingway's concept and style of short story writing, his practice in various stories, and his own incalculable influence on subsequent short fiction.
pp. 311-75: Comprehensive Checklist of Hemingway Short Fiction Criticism, Explication, and Commentary.

1975 B   SHORTER WRITINGS

1   BASKETT, SAM. "Toward 'A Fifth Dimension' in The Old Man and the Sea," Centennial Review, 19, No. 4 (Fall), 269-286.
Close reading of imagery and symbolic detail in the novella; Baskett finds Hemingway's accomplishment unusually rewarding from all points of view.

2   BORDINAT, PHILIP. "Anatomy of Fear in Tolstoy and Hemingway," Lost Generation Journal, 3, No. 2 (Spring-Summer), 15-17.
Working from Hemingway's admiration for War and Peace, Bordinat traces the similarities between the two author's treatments of fear, particularly as caught in In Our Time.

3   BROER, LAWRENCE. "'Soldier's Home,'" Lost Generation Journal, 3, No. 2 (Spring-Summer), 11, 32.
A note on Krebs' grave psychic wounds as well as physical ones.

4   BRYER, JACKSON R. "Fitzgerald and Hemingway" in American Literary Scholarship: An Annual, 1973, edited by James Woodress. Durham, N. C.: Duke University Press, pp. 150-78.
Survey of criticism published on both authors during 1973.

338

5   BURHANS, CLINTON S., JR. "Hemingway and Vonnegut: Diminishing Vision in a Dying Age," <u>MFS</u>, 21, No. 2 (Summer), 173-92.
Draws comparisons between Vonnegut and Hemingway as being "middle-Western Americans taken by events in their youth into the wider world. Both undergo in a world war a profoundly traumatic experience which becomes the center of their thought and art. Both reflect the new sense of reality . . . . and are centrally concerned with the problems of illusion and truth . . . . And both stress love and human relationships as meaningful answers to the human condition."

6   DeFALCO, JOSEPH. "Hemingway, Sport, and the Larger Metaphor," <u>Lost Generation Journal</u>, 3, No. 2 (Spring-Summer), 18-20.
Defends Hemingway's use of sport as a "proper construct" for fiction, and surveys his use of it in all his fiction and non-fiction. By using all the varieties of sport known, "Hemingway created a fiction that seems to speak in a metaphorical language all its own."

7   GINSBERG, ELAINE. "The Female Initiation Theme in American Fiction," <u>Studies in American Fiction</u>, 3, No. 1 (Spring), 27-37.
Passing reference to Hemingway as a writer who used men rather than women in his initiation stories, and placed them in settings thoroughly masculine.

8   HAYMAN, DAVID. "An Interview with Alain Robbe-Grillet," <u>Contemporary Literature</u>, 16, No. 3 (Summer), 273-85.
Comments that he feels closer to Faulkner, Dos Passos, and Hemingway than to his own contemporaries.

9   HELFAND, MICHAEL. "A Champ Can't Retire Like Anyone Else," <u>Lost Generation Journal</u>, 3, No. 2 (Spring-Summer), 9-10, 35.
Using <u>Death in the Afternoon</u> and the Nick Adams stories, Helfand stresses that Hemingway saw art as another contest, similar in many ways to sports, with "control and competition" important to both.

10   KENNER, HUGH. "Small Ritual Truths," in <u>A Homemade World, The American Modernist Writers</u>. New York: Alfred A. Knopf, pp. 119-57.
Kenner traces Hemingway's understated, concrete style to Stein's impact on American literary language. He describes the 1920's as the "decade of writing," and Hemingway as a disciple of the mystique of craft, his greatest accomplishment "the hidden Hemingway story," "not reducible to notions out of a handbook."

1975

11 LEWIS, ROBERT W. "Hemingway Ludens," <u>Lost Generation Journal</u>,
        3, No. 2 (Spring-Summer), 7-8, 30.
        A defense of criticism that treats Hemingway's pervasive
    use of sport seriously, and a comparison between Thoreau's
    view of the hunt and Hemingway's.

12 MESSENGER, CHRISTIAN. "Hemingway and the School Athletic
        Hero," <u>Lost Generation Journal</u>, 3, No. 2 (Spring-Summer),
        21-23.
        Sees that Hemingway created a different use of sport as
    metaphor in his fiction because he avoided using "the two
    major strains of modern American sporting heroes--the folk
    or popular sporting hero and the boys' school sports hero."

13 MORRIS, WRIGHT. <u>About Fiction, Reverent Reflections on the</u>
        <u>Nature of Fiction with Irreverent Observations on Writers,</u>
        <u>Readers, & Other Abuses</u>. New York: Harper & Row.
        Much of Morris' text concerns Hemingway, whether as
    Stein's pupil, innovator and craftsman supreme, reporter,
    or seer. Comments on <u>In Our Time</u>, pp. 157-58. <u>See also</u>
    pp. 14, 16, 19, 21-22, 29-31, 55-57, 81, 83, 93, 116-17,
    129, 131, 157-58, 163.

14 ONG, WALTER J., S.J. "The Writer's Audience is Always a
        Fiction," <u>PMLA</u>, 90, No. 1 (Jan.), 9-21.
        Ong uses passages from <u>A Farewell to Arms</u> to illustrate
    that many of Hemingway's distinctive stylistic effects
    accrue not so much from sentence patterns as from Heming-
    way's tactic of "fictionalizing the reader." Ong points
    out that here--and often--"the reader is being cast in the
    role of a close companion of the author." Hemingway
    avoided description, for example, because the reader would
    need none; he too was there. This convention, which Ong
    describes as "the you-and-me relationship, marked by
    tight-lipped empathy based on shared experience," may be
    one of Hemingway's most distinctive traits.

15 SANDERS, DAVE. "Piggott Pandemonium, Hemingway Wasn't a Hit
        in this Town," <u>Lost Generation Journal</u>, 3, No. 2 (Spring-
        Summer), 3-6. Photos.
        A description of the unconventional Hemingway at odds
    with the rural Western town.

16 SCHONHORN, MANUEL. "<u>The Sun Also Rises</u>: I. The Jacob
        Allusion; II. Parody as Meaning," <u>Ball State University</u>
        <u>Forum</u>, 16, No. 2 (Spring), 49-55.
        Sees Hemingway's use of the name Jacob as affirmative,
    relevant to <u>The Sun Also Rises</u> in that "in his manhood he

340

(SCHONHORN, MANUEL)
strove with God." Jake Barnes, too, has matured and is
in control of his fate. Schonhorn also views the Jake-
Brett relationship parodying that between Francis Clyne
and Robert Cohn.

17 SIKJA, GREGORY. "A Portrait of Hemingway as Angler-Artist,"
Lost Generation Journal, 3, No. 2 (Spring-Summer), 12-13.
Traces the development of Hemingway's mature style
through the various columns on fishing written from 1920
on.

18 SIMPSON, LOUIS. Three on the Tower, The Lives and Works of
Ezra Pound, T. S. Eliot, and William Carlos Williams.
New York: William Morrow and Co.
P. 28: sees that Hemingway's stories were "written in
a manner of which the Imagists approved," and sees the
far-reaching influence of his prose to also have furthered
poetic techniques. Pp. 274-75: Williams' recounting the
story of Hemingway's analysis of an animal's carcass.

19 UMPHLETT, WILEY LEE. The Sporting Myth and the American Experience. Lewisburg, Pa.: Bucknell University Press.
Many references to Hemingway's use of the sporting experience as a basic myth, used to suggest wider moral
meanings. Pp. 69-86: "Santiago: The Meaning of Value
in Defeat," sees that The Old Man and the Sea embodies a
number of separate sporting rituals.

20 WAGNER, LINDA W. "Juxtaposition in Hemingway's In Our Time,"
Studies in Short Fiction, XII (Summer), 243-52.
Arrangement of vignettes and stories suggests thematic
relationships.

21 WARREN, ROBERT PENN. "Bearers of Bad Tidings: Writers and
the American Dream," New York Review of Books, 22, No. 4
(20 March), 12-19.
Sees Hemingway as the "end product" of Transcendentalism,
the first American writer to create "the total outcast,
the man who has resigned from society," and by so doing,
to need to create "the stoic ethic of the lonely hero."
Warren sees Hemingway's attitude as self-destructive because it "flattered the maimed self," and tended to separate the self further from its society.

22 WILLIAMS, GURNEY. "Programming Papa," Science Digest, 77
(June), 56-57.

1975

(WILLIAMS, GURNEY)
   Using computer analysis, Darrell Mansell finds that
excerpts from The Old Man and the Sea are closer in
sentence length to Hemingway's writing done in the mid-
30's than to that done in the 1940's or 1950's. The
hypothesis is that The Old Man and the Sea was written
during the mid-1930's.

Index

Emerson, O. B., 1960.B31
Engel, Monroe, 1973.B30
Engstrom, Alfred, 1950.B22
Epstein, Joseph, 1970.B37
Erskine, John, 1933.B9
Etulain, Richard, 1970.B38
Evans, Oliver, 1958.B7; 1961.B17;
    1962.B17; 1969.A9
Evans, Robert, 1966.B18; 1973.A7
Ewell, Nathanial, 1971.B39

Fadiman, Clifton, 1929.B18;
    1933.B10-11; 1935.B8;
    1937.B26; 1938.B18;
    1940.B18; 1941.B38;
    1942.B6; 1957.B19;
    1971.A7
Fagan, Edward, 1957.B9
Fagin, Bryllion, 1938.B19
Falk, Robert, 1955.B16
Farewell to Arms, A, 1929.B1-6,
    B8,B10-11,B14-24,B26-27,
    B32,B34-40,B42; 1930.B5,
    B7,B12; 1931.B7; 1932.B12,
    B14; 1934.B7; 1935.B13;
    1936.B4; 1937.B34-35;
    1944.B1; 1947.B2,B17;
    1949.B8,B11,B20; 1950.B30;
    1951.B3; 1955.B31; 1957.B6,
    B22; 1958.B9; 1959.B38-39;
    1960.B16; 1961.B23,B31,
    B35,B40,B47; 1962.A5,B20,
    B32,B36,B56; 1963.B11;
    1964.B43,B56; 1967.B20,
    B50; 1968.B9,B34,B50,B56,
    B59; 1969.B16-17, B46;
    1970.A2, B30,B56; 1971.A7,
    B34,B46,B85; 1972.B15,
    B82-83; 1973.B22,B80,B82,
    B84; 1974.A3, B26; A Fare-
    well to Arms as play:
    1930.B3,B6,B8,B19
Farquhar, Robin, 1968.B14
Farrell, James T., 1943.B3;
    1945.B6; 1946.B5; 1962.A5;
    1969.A11; 1973.B32
Farrington, Chisie, 1951.B9
Farrington, S. Kip, Jr., 1949.B5;
    1971.A1, B40

Faulkner, William, 1950.B4;
    1952.B31; 1965.B14;
    1968.B15
Feaster, John, 1968.B3
Fenimore, Edward, 1943.B4
Fenton, Charles, 1952.B32-33;
    1954.A1, B31-32; 1957.B10;
    1969.A9; 1975.A3
Ferber, Steve, 1974.B6
Ferguson, Charles, 1927.B11;
    1970.B30
Ferguson, Otis, 1937.B27;
    1941.B17
Fergusson, Francis, 1930.B6;
    1931.B4
Ferris, John, 1966.B19
Ficken, Carl, 1971.B4; 1975.A3
Fiedelson, Charles, Jr., 1959.B17
Fiedler, Leslie, 1955.B17;
    1958.B8; 1959.B18;
    1962.A6, B18; 1963.B16;
    1964.B15; 1968.A9, B16;
    1970.A2, B87
Fiesta. See Sun Also Rises, The
Fifth Column, The, 1937.B7-8;
    1938.B21; 1939.B13;
    1940.B3-4,B7,B11,B19-20,
    B25,B28,B39-40,B42;
    1954.B35
Finkelstein, I., 1967.B13
Finkelstein, Sidney, 1961.B18
First 49, The, 1938.B9,B13,B16-18,
    B20-21,B31; 1939.B1-2,B8,
    B13; 1954.B35
Fisher, Deborah, 1974.B7
Fisher, Paul, 1940.B19
Fitz, Reginald, 1971.B42
Fitzgerald, F. Scott, 1926.B16;
    1945.B7; 1963.B16; 1972.A8
Flanagan, John, 1955.B18
Flanner, Janet, 1965.B15; 1972.B27
Fleissner, R. F., 1970.B40
Fleming, Peter, 1936.B8
Floor, Richard, 1962.B19
Flora, Joseph, 1969.B20;
    1973.B33-34
Flower, Desmond, 1941.B18
Foote, Timothy, 1970.B41
For Whom the Bell Tolls,
    1940.B2-3,B5-6,B10,B13-15,
    B17,B22-23,B26,B29,B31-34,

Gilmer, Walker, 1970.B45
Gingrich, Arnold, 1965.B19;
    1966.B25; 1970.B46;
    1971.B48; 1972.B30
Ginsberg, Allen, 1973.B39;
    1974.B10
Ginsberg, Elaine, 1975.B7
Glassner, William, 1961.B23;
    1966.B26
Gleaves, Edwin, 1971.B49
Glicksberg, Charles, 1966.B27;
    1969.B22; 1971.B50;
    1974.B11
Golden, Harry, 1961.B24
Golden, Herbert, 1969.B23
Goldhurst, William, 1963.B18;
    1970.B47
Goldman, Albert, 1966.B28;
    1969.B24
Goldstone, Adrian, 1956.B30
Goodheart, Eugene, 1956.B11
Goodman, Paul, 1971.B51;
    1974.A3
Goodwin, K. L., 1966.B29
Gordon, Caroline, 1949.B7;
    1957.B13; 1969.A9
Gordon, David, 1966.B30;
    1971.B52
Gordon, Gerald, 1972.B31
Gorman, Herbert, 1926.B17;
    1942.B8
Gould, Gerald, 1926.B18;
    1929.B19
Gould, Jack, 1954.B36
Goxtarde, R. E., 1968.B22
Graham, John, 1960.B6; 1962.A5;
    1971.A7; 1973.A7
Grant, Douglas, 1965.B20
Graves, Robert, 1944.B8
Gray, James, 1946.B6; 1963.B19
Grebstein, Sheldon, 1958.B12;
    1961.B25; 1967.B14;
    1968.B38; 1970.B42;
    1971.A8; 1972.B32;
    1973.A3
Greco, Anne, 1972.B33
Green, James, 1968.B23
Green Hills of Africa, 1934.B19;
    1935.B1-2,B5,B14,B17-18,
    B24-26; 1936.B1-2,B7-9,
    B12; 1951.B5; 1967.B61

Greene, Graham, 1941.B22;
    1971.A8
Gregory, Horace, 1933.B14
Greiner, Donald, 1971.B53-54
Grenberg, Bruce, 1971.B55
Grieg, Harald, 1972.A3
Griffin, Gerald, 1968.B24
Griffith, John, 1974.A2
Grigson, Geoffrey, 1963.B20
Grimes, Carroll, 1972.B34
Groseclose, Barbara, 1971.B56
Gross, Theodore, 1971.B57
Groth, John, 1946.B7; 1956.B13
Guenther, Paul, 1970.B48
Guérard, Albert, 1964.B17
Guérard, Maclin, 1964.B17
Guffey, Don Carlos, 1958.B13
Gunn, Giles, 1972.B35
Gurko, Leo, 1947.B9; 1952.B37;
    1953.B29; 1955.B19;
    1968.A2,A9
Gutkind, Lee, 1970.B49; 1971.B58
Guttmann, Allen, 1960.B7; 1962.A5;
    1971.A8
Gwynn, Frederick, 1959.B22

Hackett, Francis, 1949.B8
Hagood, Thomas, 1968.B25
Hagopian, John V., 1959.B23;
    1962.B21; 1964.B18;
    1975.A3
Haig, Stirling, 1973.B40
Haight, Anne Lyon, 1935.B11
Hale, Nancy, 1962.B22
Hall, Jeffrey, 1970.B50
Hall, Mordaunt, 1932.B14
Halliday, E. M., 1949.B8-9;
    1952.B38; 1953.B30;
    1956.B12; 1959.B17;
    1962.A5-6; 1963.B31;
    1970.A2; 1973.A7
Halper, Albert, 1970.B51
Halverson, John, 1964.B19
Hamalian, Leo, 1972.B36
Hamburger, Eric, 1971.B59
Hamill, Peter, 1961.A1
Hamilton, John, 1972.B37
Hammond, Percy, 1930.B8
Hand, Harry, 1966.B31
Handy, John, 1964.B20

Leighton, Lawrence, 1932.B17
Leiter, Louis, 1968.B33
Lerner, Max, 1943.B6; 1944.B10;
 1945.B8
Le Roy, Gaylord, 1974.B19
Levey, Michael, 1967.B6
Levi, Carlo, 1961.B34
Levin, Harry, 1950.B20; 1951.B14;
 1957.B20; 1959.B5; 1961.A4;
 1962.A6; 1964.B17
Levine, David, 1969.B40
Le Vot, André, 1973.B52
Levy, Alan, 1972.B55
Levy, Alfred, 1959.B32
Lewis, Clifford, 1970.B79
Lewis, R. W. B., 1953.B35;
 1955.B24
Lewis, Robert, 1965.A2;
 1966.B51-52; 1969.A9;
 1970.A2, B79-80; 1974.A2;
 1975.A3, B11
Lewis, Sinclair, 1936.B11-12
 1937.B33
Lewis, Wyndham, 1934.B13;
 1950.B34; 1963.B29;
 1964.B30; 1970.A2
Lewisohn, Ludwig, 1932.B18
Lid, Richard, 1962.B31
Liedloff, Helmut, 1968.B34
Light, James, 1961.B35; 1962.A5;
 1969.B41; 1971.A7
Light, Martin, 1965.B6; 1969.B42;
 1975.A3
Linebarger, J. M., 1970.B81;
 1972.B56
Lingeman, Richard, 1972.B57
Linnemann, William, 1963.B30
Linscott, Roger, 1946.B8
Lisca, Peter, 1966.B53; 1969.B43;
 1974.A3
Littell, Robert, 1927.B16;
 1941.B26
Litz, A. Walton, 1945.B12;
 1963.B31
Livingston, Howard, 1971.B81
Llona, Victor, 1972.B58
Lodge, David, 1971.B82
Loeb, Harold, 1959.B33; 1961.B36;
 1967.B31; 1969.B44;
 1972.A8; 1973.B53
Loggins, Vernon, 1937.B34

Long, Robert, 1969.B45; 1970.B82
Longmire, Samuel, 1970.B83
Longstreet, Stephen, 1972.B59;
 1973.B54
Longyear, Christopher, 1971.B2
Loveman, Amy, 1934.B3
Lovett, Robert, 1932.B19
Lowrey, Burling, 1930.B9;
 1960.B14
Luccock, Halford E., 1934.B14
Lucid, R. F., 1974.B20
Ludovici, Laurence, 1958.B14
Ludwig, Richard, 1959.B34
Lupan, Radu, 1966.B54
Lutwack, Leonard, 1971.B83
Lydenberg, John, 1961.B37
Lyons, Leonard, 1950.B35;
 1952.B48; 1954.B41
Lytle, Andrew, 1965.B33

McAleer, John, 1962.B32
McAlmon, Robert, 1938.B22;
 1962.B33; 1968.B35;
 1972.A8
Macauley, Robie, 1970.B84
McCaffery, John, 1950.A1;
 1969.A10
McCarthy, Paul, 1969.B46
McClelland, David, 1970.B83
McClennen, Joshua, 1953.B36
McCole, C. John, 1937.B35
McCormick, John, 1953.B37;
 1957.B22; 1969.B47;
 1971.B84
McCullers, Carson, 1959.B35
MacDonald, Dwight, 1941.B28;
 1960.B15; 1962.B34
McDonald, Edward, 1936.B10
MacDonald, Scott, 1972.B60;
 1973.B55; 1974.B21
McHaney, Thomas, 1972.B61
Machlin, Milt, 1961.A2
McHugh, Vincent, 1942.B12
McIlvaine, Robert, 1971.B85
McIntyre, O. O., 1929.B25;
 1936.B13
Mackall, Leonard, 1932.B20
McKay, Claude, 1937.B36

Moore, Geoffrey, 1963.B33
Moore, Harry T., 1958.B15
Moore, L. Hugh, Jr., 1965.B35
Mora, Constancia de la, 1939.B10
Moraes, Frank, 1961.B42
Moravia, Alberto, 1966.B55
Moritz, Ken, 1968.B18
Morris, Lawrence, 1926.B22-23;
    1969.A11
Morris, Lloyd, 1949.B14
Morris, William, 1959.B37;
    1965.B36
Morris, Wright, 1958.B16;
    1961.B43; 1963.B34;
    1968.B42; 1975.B13
Morrow, Elise, 1951.B17
Moseley, Edwin, 1962.B39
Moses, W. R., 1959.B38; 1966.B53
Mosher, Harold, 1971.B96
Moss, Arthur, 1969.B51-52
Moss, Howard, 1973.B60
Moss, Sidney, 1964.B34
Motola, Gabriel, 1964.B37
Mottram, Eric, 1971.B16; 1972.B70
Moveable Feast, A, 1964.B16,B22,
    B28,B38; 1965.B29,B33,B53;
    1966.B25,B47,B72;
    1967.B41; 1970.B20;
    1973.B75; 1974.A2
Moylan, Thomas, 1955.B27
Moynihan, William, 1959.B39;
    1971.A8
Mudrick, Marvin, 1952.B51;
    1964.B38; 1969.A11
Muggridge, Malcolm, 1966.B57
Muir, Edwin, 1927.B17; 1937.B41;
    1952.B51; 1969.A11
Muller, Herbert, 1937.B42
Munson, Gorham, 1968.B43
Murphy, George, 1969.B53
Murray, Donald, 1968.B44;
    1971.B97
Murray, Edward, 1972.B71
Mustanoja, Tauno, 1960.B5
Muste, John, 1966.B58
Myers, Marshall, 1971.B98

Nagel, James, 1973.B61
Nagle, J. M., 1969.B54
Nahal, Chaman, 1971.A3

Nakhdjarani, Erick, 1973.B62
Nash, Jay Robert, 1968.B45
Nathan, George Jean, 1934.B15;
    1940.B29
Nilsen, Don, 1973.B63
Nin, Anais, 1969.B55; 1971.B100;
    1974.B26
Noble, David, 1968.B46
Noland, Richard, 1969.B56
Nordell, Roderick, 1970.B95
Norman, Charles, 1961.B44
Norris, Faith, 1974.A2
North, Joseph, 1958.B17; 1964.B39
Norton, Charles, 1973.B64
Norton, Dan, 1944.B11
Nyren, Dorothy, 1961.B45

Oag, Shay, 1969.B57
O'Brien, Edward, 1926.B24;
    1931.B9
O'Brien, John, 1973.B65
O'Connor, Frank, 1963.B35;
    1975.A3
O'Connor, Richard, 1971.A4
O'Connor, William Van, 1945.B12;
    1948.B5; 1956.B20;
    1959.A1; 1962.B41-42;
    1964.B40; 1966.B50
O'Faolin, Sean, 1956.B21;
    1961.B46; 1962.A6
O'Hara, John, 1950.B38; 1954.B44;
    1956.B13
Oldfield, Barney, 1956.B22
Old Man and the Sea, The,
    1952.B1-9,B11,B15-16,
    B19-25,B27,B29-31,B35-36,
    B40-42,B44-47,B51,B56-59,
    B62,B67,B69-71,B73;
    1953.B2-6,B12,B17,B22-23,
    B25,B28,B35; 1954.B49;
    1955.B17,B19; 1956.B23,
    B28-29; 1957.B9,B24;
    1958.B3; 1959.B6,B10;
    1960.B3,B8,B21,B23,B27;
    1961.B61; 1962.A5, B11,
    B39,B52,B57; 1963.B23,
    B26-27,B41-42; 1964.B19,
    B41; 1966.B21,B32,B68-69;
    1967.B5,B36,B43; 1968.A9;
    1969.B12,B54; 1970.B58,B66,
    B83; 1971.B14,B33,B44,B62,
    B76; 1973.B88; 1975.B22

Raeburn, John, 1973.B72; 1974.B28
Rahv, Philip, 1937.B45; 1941.B36;
    1946.B11; 1950.B44;
    1952.B62; 1957.B24;
    1964.B43; 1968.A9;
    1969.B61
Ramsey, Paul, 1966.B50
Randall, David, 1962.B43;
    1969.B62
Rao, K. S., 1960.B20
Rascoe, Burton, 1924.B6; 1925.B6;
    1926.B25; 1927.B19;
    1929.B33-34; 1931.B10;
    1932.B23; 1934.B17;
    1940.B32; 1947.B14
Ray, Man, 1963.B39
Reardon, John, 1967.B39; 1974.A3
Reed, Henry, 1950.B46
Redlich, Rosemarie, 1952.B68
Redman, Ben Ray, 1929.B35;
    1930.B15; 1932.B24;
    1950.B45; 1953.B39
Regler, Gustav, 1959.B40
Reichard, Daniel, 1969.B63
Reid, John, 1937.B46
Reid, Marjorie, 1924.B7
Reid, Stephen, 1963.B40
Reinert, Otto, 1959.B41
Reynolds, Michael, 1972.B81
Richards, Norman, 1968.A5
Richardson, H. Edward, 1958.B19
Richardson, Robert, 1969.B64
Ricks, Christopher, 1970.B100
Riddell, John, 1928.B7; 1937.B28
Rideout, Walter, 1956.B25;
    1961.B49
Riley, Carolyn, 1973.B73
Rink, Paul, 1962.A3
Robbins, J. Albert, 1973.B16
Robbins, Jack, 1935.B14; 1937.B30
Robert, MacLean, 1957.B25
Robinson, Charles, 1973.B74
Robinson, Donald, 1952.B63
Robinson, Eleanor, 1974.B29
Robinson, Forrest, 1972.B82
Robinson, James, 1961.B49
Rodgers, Paul, 1970.B101
Rodman, Selden, 1952.B62;
    1974.B30
Rodrigues, Eusebio, 1962.B44
Rogers, Jean, 1970.B102

Rogers, Roy, 1974.B31
Rolfe, Edwin, 1939.B11
Romaine, Paul, 1931.B12
Root, E. Merrill, 1937.B47
Rosen, Kenneth, 1971.B2;
    1973.B4-5; 1974.A3
Rosene, M. R., 1934.B18
Rosenfeld, Isaac, 1951.B22;
    1962.B45
Rosenfeld, Paul, 1925.B7;
    1928.B8
Rosenfield, Claire, 1964.B17;
    1968.A9
Ross, Danforth, 1961.B50
Ross, Frank, 1968.B50
Ross, Ishbell, 1970.B103
Ross, Lillian, 1949.B15;
    1950.B47; 1962.A6;
    1964.B44
Ross, Mary, 1929.B36
Ross, Morton, 1972.B83
Rother, James, 1974.B32
Rothman, N. L., 1928.B9
Rouch, John, 1965.B38
Rovere, Richard, 1950.B48
Rovit, Earl, 1963.A3; 1968.A9;
    1969.A11; 1970.A2;
    1971.A8; 1972.B84
Ruark, Robert, 1953.B40; 1957.B30
Rubenstein, Annette, 1960.B21
Rubenstein, Jill, 1973.B75
Rubin, Louis, 1967.B40; 1970.B104;
    1973.B76; 1974.B33
Rugoff, Milton, 1950.B49;
    1952.B65
Ruhm, Herbert, 1973.B77
Russell, H. K., 1955.B31
Ryan, William, 1968.B51

Saint John, Donald, 1968.B52-55;
    1970.B105; 1972.A8
Saint John, Robert, 1953.B41
Salzman, Jack, 1973.B78
Sampson, Edward, 1952.B66
Samsell, R. L., 1972.B85
Samuels, Charles, 1969.B66
Samuels, Lee, 1951.B23
Samuelson, Arnold, 1935.B20
Sander, Oscar, 1965.B39
Sanders, Barry, 1967.B41

Von Ende, Frederick, 1970.B124
Vopat, Carole, 1972.B102
Vorpahl, Ben, 1970.B125
Voss, Andrew, 1973.B87

Wagenknecht, Edward, 1952.B72;
    1954.B49
Waggoner, Hyatt, 1955.B39
Wagner, Geoffrey, 1964.B51
Wagner, Linda, W., 1972.B103-04;
    1973.B88; 1974.A3, B44;
    1975.A3, B20
Wagner, Vern, 1957.B32
Wain, John, 1970.B126
Walcutt, Charles C., 1949.B19;
    1955.B28; 1966.B71
Walden Bookshop, 1930.B16
Waldhorn, Arthur, 1972.A7;
    1973.A7
Waldmeir, Joseph, 1956.B29;
    1962.A5,A6; 1969.B82;
    1974.A3
Walker, Warren, 1961.B62
Wallenstein, Marcel, 1950.B56
Walpole, Hugh, 1927.B21; 1929.B40
Walsh, Ernest, 1925.B8
Walter, Erich, 1941.B39
Walz, Laurence, 1967.B53;
    1971.B117
Ward, Alfred, 1930.B17; 1932.B26
Ward, J. A., 1959.B42
Warner, Fred, 1971.B118
Warren, Robert Penn, 1937.B52;
    1942.B4; 1947.B18;
    1951.B31; 1952.B10;
    1958.B24; 1959.B8;
    1962.A6, B56; 1974.A3;
    1975.A3, B21
Warshow, Robert, 1950.B57
Wasserstrom, William, 1966.B72
Waterman, Arthur, 1961.B63
Watkins, Floyd, 1971.A5
Watts, Emily Stipes, 1971.A6
Watts, Richard, 1940.B41
Waugh, Evelyn, 1950.B58-59
Weatherhead, A. K., 1964.B52
Weatherly, W. J., 1969.B83
Weber, Brom, 1971.B16
Weber, Ronald, 1971.B119
Webster, Harvey, 1964.B53

Weeks, Edward, 1935.B25;
    1937.B50; 1950.B60;
    1952.B73; 1966.B73;
    1967.B54
Weeks, Robert, 1957.B33-35;
    1962.A6, B57-58; 1972.B105
Wegelin, Christof, 1965.B50
Weintraub, Stanley, 1968.B65
Weiss, Daniel, 1965.B51
Welland, D. S. R., 1965.A3
Wells, Arvin, 1963.B41; 1968.A9
Wells, Elizabeth, 1969.B84;
    1975.A3
Wertheim, Stanley, 1967.B55
West, Paul, 1963.B42
West, Ray B., 1944.B12; 1945.B12;
    1948.B5; 1949.B20;
    1951.B27-28; 1952.B74;
    1953.B48; 1962.A5,A6;
    1963.B31; 1968.B66;
    1970.A2; 1975.A3
Westbrook, Max, 1964.B54;
    1966.B52,B74; 1970.B80
Wheeler, John, 1961.B64
Whicher, George, 1951.B21;
    1953.B49
Whit, Joseph, 1951.B28
White, E. B., 1950.B61; 1954.B50;
    1960.B15
White, Ray Lewis, 1967.B56
White, William, 1946.B2;
    1952.B75; 1956.B30;
    1961.B65-66; 1962.B59-60;
    1964.B55; 1965.B52;
    1966.B75-79; 1967.B57-60;
    1968.B67-72; 1969.A6,A11;
    B85-87; 1970.A3, B127;
    1971.B2,B120-122;
    1972.B2-3,B107-08;
    1973.B4-5,B89-91; 1974.B45
Whitfield, E., 1953.B50
Whitman, Alden, 1972.B109
Wickes, George, 1965.B53;
    1966.B80; 1969.B87;
    1974.A2
Wiegand, William, 1967.B61
Wilcox, Earl, 1971.B123
Wilder, Thornton, 1938.B12
Williams, Gurney, 1975.B22
Williams, Stanley, 1955.B40
Williams, Tennessee, 1950.B62